The Basi

GLOBAL POLITICS

Raluca Viman-Miller, co-editor

Dlynn Armstrong Williams, co-editor

Contributors:

Craig Greathouse

Jake Greear

Cristian Harris

Scott Meachum

Jonathan Miner

Nathan Price

Samuel Rohrer

Jennifer Schiff

Seyed Hamid Serri

Laurel Wei

Dwight Wilson

UNG

UNIVERSITY of
NORTH GEORGIA™
UNIVERSITY PRESS

Blue Ridge | Cumming | Dahlonega | Gainesville | Oconee

Published by:
University of North Georgia Press
Dahlonega, Georgia

Printing Support by:
Lightning Source Inc.
La Vergne, Tennessee

Book design by Corey Parson.

ISBN: 978-1-940771-84-7

Printed in the United States of America
For more information, please visit: http://ung.edu/university-press
Or e-mail: ungpress@ung.edu

Contents

Part IV: Globalization and its Impact

Part I

Basics of Global Politics

Basic Concepts, Actors, and Influences

1

Raluca Viman-Miller

Abstract

This chapter aims to introduce the main principles, themes, theories, and terms commonly used in the study of international relations. It intends to explain and familiarize students at an introductory level to the study of international relations, with definitions and concepts that form the base of this subject. Using real-life examples, this chapter explains the basic theoretical tenets of the theories of international relations and prepares readers for the chapters that follow.

Learning Objectives

- Understand the collective action problem as a core theme in international relations and how different approaches resolve these issues
- Learn definitions and terms commonly used in international relations
- Understand the importance of the state in the international system and which other actors matter
- Absorb a brief introduction to the principles of the main international relations theories

International Relations as a Field of Study

Modern-day politics increasingly revolves around influences that exceed national borders. It is almost impossible to define our existence nowadays without considering the influence of actors at the global level. As individuals, states, and international institutions become more and more entangled, some would argue that these entanglements benefit all. Others would argue that these changes benefit mostly the rich, while the poor continue to be exploited without gaining any advantages from this new system. Who are the new leaders of the international order? Have we seen the "end of history," or is the universalization of the Western liberal democracy "the only game in town?" How do we explain the rise of new actors, such as China and India, and where do we place non-state actors, such as terrorists? How do the new European arrangements (EU, OSCE) and the military might of Russia matter in today's relations among global actors, and how do these actors, in turn, influence traditional nation-states?

The world is changing—we have no doubts about that—and the direction of these changes is clearly towards a tighter network of actors. All these changes are led by the development of technology and by a reshuffling of coalitions and alliances that have brought on a new economic order which, in turn, creates new losers and winners. These new power arrangements in today's relations among international actors are often debated under the more general term of globalization. Hence, **globalization** is often referred to as a network of societies, actors, and events that, while taking place on the other side of the world, have an impact on their area as well as areas across the globe. Globalization has supporters as well as critics. Kofi Annan, former United Nations Secretary General (1997–2006), says that "arguing against globalization is like arguing against the law of gravity" (*The Globalist*, 2001). Meanwhile, former United States (U.S.) president Jimmy Carter famously states, "I think that globalization, as defined by rich people like us, is a very nice thing, because you're talking about the Internet, about cell phones, about computers. This doesn't affect two-thirds of the people in the world who are living on less than $2 a day. They are never touched positively by globalization" (*The Globalist*, 2002).

In order to argue for or against today's new international system and start defining the terms that characterize it, we should seek to understand how it influences us at various levels in everyday life and how we perceive the changes that are all around us. For citizens of the global community system, it is pretty easy to travel to far and distant places—to seek out their generational roots and search for their ancestors or simply visit a new country. Let's take Ireland, for example. We can take a flight there as soon as next weekend, from any airport near us, and we can visit these magnificent places with great certainty that we will return under normal circumstances. We can exchange our home currency for local currency in order to pay for lodging, transportation, gifts, or food.

This did not used to be the norm. During the mid-nineteenth century, Ireland lost more citizens to emigration to the U.S. than to famine, disease, and poverty combined. The Irish tradition called for an "American wake" in light of this trend. Those who decided to emigrate were treated by their immediate family, friends, and community as people who were never to be seen again, similar to those who died. These relations and friends would gather together and reminisce about the life of the soon-to-be departed, just as they did for those whom they were going to bury the next day. This American wake occurred because the chances for the emigrants' return were very low—assuming, of course, that the emigrant even made it to the American shore. The passage took months and was very expensive; families borrowed money they did not have, often taking loans with excessively high interest rates. The boats bound for the American shores were called "coffin ships," as they were overloaded and over-insured, meaning they became more valuable if they sunk than if they arrived safely to shore. Even if the boats arrived, emigrant death rates from the passage were very high because of poor conditions on board, including contagious diseases spread through compact quarters.

Today's means of transportation and ease of access to advanced technology and fast transit between cultures allow us to connect with and learn about each other, without leaving our neighborhood. We all know how easily we can access international cuisine; Mexican or Jamaican food is a short drive away, while our store shelves are often stocked with food items that originated continents away. On the other hand, this globalized system is blamed for diluting local cultures and traditions. Young individuals, more open to change and novelty, often give up their local customs, traditions, and ways of living, dressing, and behaving within their communities in favor of generic garments, fast food eating, and foreign music—all usually of Western origin. These departures from traditions create a feeling of betrayal, especially among the older or more conservative members of their communities. Globalization is often blamed for all these "evils"—including the departure from traditions. We often find the most anti-globalization feelings among cultures and isolated communities who have lost part of their culture, and they are some of the most vulnerable individuals to extremists' recruiting goals.

Easily available travel can also be used by individuals with malevolent intentions who are coming to the Western world in order to cause harm and attack the values that citizens of the Western world hold dear. Technology is also available to those who intend to use it to destroy the world order: where the winners are viewed as usurpers of the losers, who are thought of as the non-Western cultures, the less educated, the non-Christian, and the impoverished countries of the **Global South**. Travel and technology are just two examples of how globalization and advancement of human relations have both a positive and negative impact.

States make decisions that have an impact on themselves as well as other actors at international levels based on their abilities or natural resources. For instance, the U.S. will trade with other states based on U.S. domestic interests. Russia will honor an embargo (or limited economic relations or reduced trade) with another country if it agrees with the reasons why these measures were put in place. Partnerships for economic benefits or security are decided upon based on the history of the relations between states, based on their particular interests or their economic strengths. At the end of World War II, France and Germany decided that an economic union between the two of them would be beneficial and strengthen the relationship between these two former enemies. That was the beginning of the now well-known European Union. The stronger the state, the higher the chances are that they can negotiate such partnerships from a superior position.

Lesser developed states are the main manufacturing sites for a great deal of goods that are consumed in the Western world. Take a look at your shoes, t-shirts, or backpacks. Chances are high that they are not manufactured in the U.S. These economic relationships, resulting from this new global arrangement, benefit all involved parties because the manufacturing partner gets to employ its citizens while the purchasing partner can use a cheaper labor market. Anti-globalization supporters argue that this relationship is skewed in favor of the richer states that shamelessly exploit the cheaper labor markets without consideration for basic labor or human rights. Pro-globalization activists argue that by simply offering these less developed countries the opportunity to employ an otherwise high number of jobless citizens, these economic relations are beneficial to all those involved.

The same actors, individuals, or states must make decisions on issues that pertain to all of us, regardless of the level of development or strength. These decisions must consider the global impact. The environment, terrorism, and the refugee crisis are viewed as such **global issues**. These are issues that result from our interdependence and affect the global community, and their outcome is based on a global, communal decision-making process. For example, an economic crisis started in the U.S in 2008 and it influenced the entire economic global system, giving way to the European economic crisis and influencing manufacturing plants on the Asian continent. Similarly, the freedom of movement and ideas throughout the international community was one of the factors that brought on a change of structure and government in the Middle East, known as the Arab Spring. While these revolutions aimed to replace the antiquated, anti-democratic governments of the region with the support of international partners—many of which had their own agendas—the Arab Spring gave way to civil wars and ethnic conflicts and resulted in the refugee crisis, which became a new global issue in and of itself.

The question of which state should lead the others in determining global solutions has always been present throughout history. While leadership is costly and rarely rewarding, without a world government in place, strong states frequently step forward to take on this role.

How do we resolve any of the biggest dilemmas we face? How can we get something for as little as possible while avoiding investing our resources to the benefit of others who are looking to catch a free ride? Considering these matters logically and rationally, we all desire to resolve global issues; nevertheless, we face a problem regarding collective interests. Goldstein and Pevehouse (2020) debate the core principles in today's international relations, arguing that "international relations revolves around one key problem: How can a group—such as two or more countries—serve its collective interests when doing so requires its members to forego their individual interests" (p. 4). This dilemma is often referred to as the **collective goods problem**, or commonly referred to as "free riding," "the tragedy of the commons," "burden sharing," and "the prisoner dilemma." What these terms express is the inability to rely on a global police force that can enforce whatever agreements were established at the international level. Hence, lacking a higher authority (or a world government), we must rely on different methods to resolve global issues. Goldstein and Pevehouse survey the preexisting research in this area and in a variety of social sciences and derive three important and distinctive principles: dominance, reciprocity, and identity.

Dominance solves the collective goods problem by ensuring there is a hierarchy and a more powerful actor imposing rules in the system on the weaker actor; in other words, the stronger dominates the weaker. The top of the hierarchy will be reached using not just military power but also a variety of methods and solutions. An international relation system based on the dominance principle is stable because there is a strong actor that can make the defector pay if they run away from common responsibilities. The downside is that some actors might feel frustrated and bullied. The second principle proposed is **reciprocity**. It argues that states will choose to cooperate and not act treacherously because they need to ensure future cooperation of the other states in the system. According to this principle, there is no need for a world government or a world police force because states will cooperate with each other due to their need for each other. The downside is the possibility of slipping into a downward spiral caused by a misperception or an "eye for an eye" situation. The third principle is **identity,** and it relies on the larger feeling of belonging to a community. It does not rely on self-interest; rather, it relies on kinship and selflessness, and actors are willing to invest and sacrifice their own resources for another actor simply because they all belong to the same community. The downside to this principle is the fact that certain actors might feel isolated and excluded.

These principles explain and define relations among states and provide the foundations for the theoretical approaches in international relations. They have different explanatory powers at different points in the evolution of the international system. This does not mean that one of these proposed approaches is better or worse than any other.

International Relations and Global Politics
Global Actors

There are a few terms that we use when we refer to the contemporary **international system**. A common working definition by Pevehouse and Goldstein (2020) defines it as a "set of relationships among the world's states, structured according to certain rules and patterns of interaction" (p. 11). They argue that some rules are implicit while others are explicit, and it defines who is a member of the system, what rights and responsibilities are available, and what type of actions and responses occur normally among states. Within the international system, we refer to **global politics** as the political processes and interactions that take place among actors seeking to gain power, while **international relations** is a more general term which we use to simply define interactions among countries and other international actors. The study of international relations relies on two other important subfields:

1. the study of **international security**, generally defined as the study of making and breaking war and peace, and
2. **international political economy**, defined as the economic interactions taking place among actors in regard to trade and finance among nations.

International relations cannot be studied without involving knowledge from other academic areas, such as economics, sociology, and history, among others. It is difficult to map relations among states without debating the context in which they were formed in the past, how they are formed in the present, and what is likely to happen in the future. We must also map the political evolutions at the international level by including more than just states, which are the traditional actors. It is important to include organizations, such as **multinational corporations** (MNC) (defined as for-profit businesses that function across national borders, often with headquarters in one country and with production, distribution, marketing, and functioning in other countries), aid organizations that function outside of the borders of one specific state, and terrorist organizations that transcend the jurisdiction of one government, etc. All entities that function outside the borders of one state matter because they have connections to governments and other organizations of the same type.

Nongovernmental organizations (NGO) are grassroots movements formed by concerned individuals and have, as their base, a collective action that is not performed on behalf of a specific government but is, instead, concerned with a specific issue, such as freedom, human rights, the environment, or animal rights. They are usually nonprofit. The term **nonstate actors** is often used interchangeably with NGOs, yet NGOs are a subcategory of nonstate actors (together with for-profit MNCs, terrorist organizations, and organized crime syndicates) and are important players in international relations. Nonstate actors are different from the state because a **government** is a group of individuals who are the leaders of a community in a given territory. They organize themselves in institutions which are tasked to create laws based on customs, traditions, and research and to apply public policies. They exercise executive, legislative, and judicial power as set by the laws of the community. There are many types of governments, but the most commonly known are democracy, republic, monarchy, aristocracy, and dictatorship, to name a few.

A government is in charge of a territory and people and has exclusive rights over the use of force. It has control over a territory as defined by international agreements and recognized by international treaties and is thereby considered a country/state with pre-established borders. A government often overlaps a nation—leading to the notion of a nation-state—and enjoys sovereignty over both people and territory. These notions need additional clarifications, as they are vital in understanding how international relations develop and why states are considered to be the main actors.

A **nation** is a stable community of people, formed on the basis of a common language, territory, history, ethnicity, or psychological make-up manifested in a common culture, with common political goals. A nation can include more than one ethnic group. Guibernau (1996) has defined the nation as "a human group conscious of forming a community, sharing a common culture, attached to a clearly demarcated territory, having a common past and a common project for the future and claiming the right to rule itself" (p. 47). B. Anderson (1991) defines the nation as an "imagined community;" he depicts it as a socially constructed community, imagined by the people who perceive themselves as part of that group. Some nations govern territories, while others do not enjoy this privilege. There are nations without states, and sometimes these nations live as minorities in other sovereign states. At other times, these nations are scattered among more than one state. A few examples of **stateless nations** are the Kurds in Southwest Asia, the Romany of Central and Eastern Europe, and the Native American nations of the United States. These nations often desire sovereign territory and lead international and domestic policies that are met by political opposition and adversity. Oftentimes, these stateless groups—such as the Rohingya people from Myanmar, described by the United Nations as the most persecuted minority in the world today—are victims of domestic policies that deny them basic human rights and access to basic human needs, such as the right to obtain citizenship and, in consequence, basic citizenship rights.

A **state** is defined as a territory organized under one government. It is a term used by international law to define an entity that has population, borders, a government, and sovereignty recognized by other states in the international arrangement. The concept of state or country has been used in the study of international relations since the end of the Thirty Years' War that culminated with the

Peace of Westphalia in 1648. This theory marks the transition to viewing states as the primary actors in the international system. States are seen as having supreme and sovereign power over their territories. For Weber (1965), the state is a human community that (successfully) claims the monopoly of the legitimate use of physical force within a given territory (Politics as a Vocation), while Tilly characterizes them as coercion-wielding organizations (Coercion, Capital, and European States). States, not nations, are the standard actors in international politics, simply because states enjoy the special attribute of sovereignty. A standard definition of the concept of **sovereignty** describes it as a state's ability to legislate without legal limitation in the international system, based on laws and policy that the state created for itself without outside interference. A sovereign state has sole control over its territory and its leaders have political authority. Of note is the fact that this definition of sovereignty does not describe any other characteristics of the state other than its ability to be independent and recognized as such in the international system. This means that "bad" states as well as "good" states enjoy sovereignty. If a nation overlaps the state, we define that entity as a **nation-state**. We have states that have one nation (Albania, Poland, Greece, Japan, China). We have states that have more than one nation (the UK comprises England, Scotland, Wales, and Northern Ireland; the Netherlands comprises the Netherlands, Aruba, Curaçao, and St. Maarten; Belgium comprises the Flemings in the north and the French-speaking and German-speaking population in the south). We also have nations that are divided into two different states (Korea, divided into North Korea and South Korea; the German state as divided during the Cold War between the Federal Republic and the Democratic Republic; Moldova, the former Soviet state that was part of Romania until the end of the Second World War).

Global Issues

A global issue is a problem that affects all of us as a global community at the international and domestic level. It is a large issue that exceeds the ability of one actor to resolve it on their own. It often can only be addressed if it is recognized as a global level problem, with state actors—as well as non-state actors—supported by international organizations connecting in order to address this problem. Global issues directly result from the process of globalization; hence, all international actors are inextricably linked. The United Nations (2019) considers itself "the world's only truly universal global organization, the United Nations has become the foremost forum to address issues that transcend national boundaries that cannot be resolved by any one country acting alone." It takes the lead and prides itself at defining and seeking out solutions to these global issues. The United Nations finds that the most urgent global issues are the following:

- Africa
- ageing
- AIDS
- atomic energy
- children
- climate change
- decolonization
- democracy
- ending poverty
- food
- gender equality
- health
- human rights
- international law and justice
- migrations
- oceans and the law of the sea
- peace and security
- population
- refugees
- sustainable development
- water
- youth

These are some of the major categories of problems that the world is facing and that are the responsibility of the global community to fix. We will examine some of these issues, with the understanding that an in depth understanding of any such issue in its entirety and as it presents itself to us today is beyond the scope of this textbook introduction. The ultimate goal is to learn to apply the theories of international relations to issues that have global complexity in order to exemplify how active political decision-making processes develop.

Theories of Global Politics: Realism and Liberalism

Anyone trying to make sense of current international actions in the hopes of discerning patterns of collaboration among actors in order to predict a possible outcome will have a very hard time because no set rules of engagement or clear hierarchy of interests exist. International relations questions are often answered by resorting to **theories** in order to respond logically to major events. According to Lamy, Baylis, Smith, and Owens (2013), a good definition of "theory" for use in political science is

> a proposed explanation of an event or behavior of an actor in the real world. Definitions range from an "unproven assumption" to a "working hypothesis that proposes an explanation for an action or behavior." In international relations, we have intuitive theories, empirical theories, and normative theories (p. 70).

These theories can give answers and explain events, such as why the Iranian government seized a British-flagged tanker in the Strait of Hormuz in July 2019. Patterns identified through theoretical analysis can explain the beginning and evolution of the civil war in Syria as well as the regional uprising known as the Arab Spring. We can explain why some countries join international treaties while others withdraw from them, and we can explain how economic policies are decided at a national level but have and international impact. All these questions and more can only have rational and logical answers if we rely on the patterns that are provided to us by theories. We cannot avoid theory because of its organizing and shaping role. Still, facts come first and theory follows, and we consider the application of theory as a choice. In other words, any outcome can be explained by the application of our choice among possible and equally viable theories. For example, we can measure distance using the imperial measurements (such as inches and miles) or the metric system (centimeters and kilometers). While both measurement systems measure distance from point A to point B, they do so via different approaches.

We all have major theoretical inclinations; we just do not call it theory. Instead, we often interpret events through the filter given to us by the agents of socialization that have formed us. Some of us are prone to violence and see war as a necessity; others consider war a failure on the politicians' part. Some of us are more considerate towards the planet and try to minimizing our carbon footprint; others consider those ideas fruitless and unrewarding.

The central theories of global politics are realism and liberalism, each of which rivals the other and uses basic tenets. These foundational theories were countered by the critical approaches of Marxism, constructivism, feminist theories, and utopianism. These theories will be discussed in detail in Chapters 3, 4, and 5, where we will look at their details and how they function.

The scientific and systematic study of international relations at the beginning of the twentieth century was influenced by the fact that the world had just been involved in World War I, a global conflagration that brought death and destruction to all involved. The American president Woodrow Wilson, in consequence, adopted the new concept of political **idealism,** which argued for a war-free world and which emphasized the way things *ought* to be. Idealism is the forefather of political liberalism, which will be better defined later. Idealism holds that actors at the international level desire peace and prosperity. It is based on a normative assumption of how the world ought to be rather than on how the world currently is as well as the belief that the world can be governed by the rule of law. It was put into practice by states and individuals who formed organizations for the sole purpose of avoiding war. Unfortunately, political idealism does not account for the role played by the desire for power, and it relies exclusively on the assumption that all actors desire peace and prosperity. Idealism was opposed by **realism**, which claims to view things less idealistically and much more realistically and looks at the international system as *it is* rather than as it *ought to be*. While strains of idealism remain present in the international system, realism became the dominant theory due to failures of the League of Nations and the Second World War that followed.

Realism has three basic principles:

1. States are the most important actors in international relations;
2. The main responsibility of leaders is to obtain, secure, and increase power regardless of costs; and
3. The international system is anarchic in nature as no higher authority rules over the sovereign state.

The world described by realist assumptions is not a peaceful and calm system. The actors and individuals are selfish, and they project their selfishness onto the system, leading to inevitable wars which are meant to secure a hierarchy that will hold true for as long as the power balance remains as established upon the war's cessation. Realism seems to be more relevant in contemporary global politics as we witness self-interests that are often pursued without any regard for weaker entities or for the basic concepts of peace and common prosperity. Realism and its tenets argue that this theory is timeless and unchanging and its principles work at any historical moment; the same principles apply during Thucydides and Machiavelli or Reagan and Trump and Bin Laden.

There are three types of realism. **Classical realism** is an endless power struggle due to human's selfish nature with little to zero concern for law or justice. In **neorealism** (also known as **structural realism**), the anarchical structure of the international system, not human nature, determines the selfish approach. States act as they do in order to secure their always-threatened position of power, and the most secure distribution of power is bipolarity. **Neoclassical realism** is a criticism that deems structural realism to be incomplete because it eliminates the individual level analysis and the unit level interests.

The main rival theory of realism is **liberalism**, which argues that everyone wants peace and prosperity, that human nature is good not evil (a carry-over from idealism), that states are not the only actors, that people can enjoy prosperity in a world that is organized by and follows the rule of law, justice, and moral principles, and that actors hold valuable mutually-beneficial goals. According to this theory, states and other actors are rational thinkers that use their rationality for minimizing war and coexisting peacefully— all while fulfilling these interests in peace. Liberal values defend individualism, tolerance, freedom, and constitutionalism in stark contrast to realism's conservativism, which places a higher value on order and authority and is willing to sacrifice personal liberties in the interest of the larger community. Liberalism sees individuals as states in the international system. Liberalism and is based on change and progress since things are continuously evolving.

Consequently, no paradigm can be consistently applied to situations at different times because the actors, their desires, powers, rationality, and position changes. For liberalism, the main actors are not just the states but also non-state actors and groups in general. Their central concern is welfare and security, not realism's *relative* power, and they behave by following principles of cooperation, not self-help. Power is based on issue-specific, case-by-case situations and is mainly **soft power**. The relations among states is based on interests that are coordinated and in collaboration with others, they believe in absolute power. The ideal state of their world is a balanced, just, and equitable system managed by a higher authority, not the anarchic world assumed by realism.

Just like realism, liberalism has its own revised versions that developed over time. Theoreticians, authors, and researchers advanced the liberal theoretical agenda by explaining away some of the weaknesses underlined by realist tenets. Conceding neorealist assumptions as correct, **neoliberals** hold that in the realist's anarchic international structure, the state is the most important actor, and because everyone is using a rational approach, the outcome is still peace and the avoidance of war because war is costly and irrational. In other words, states at all times will prefer cooperation over war, as cooperation is the least costly way to obtain gains, and actors with common interests will try to maximize absolute gains. Neoliberal institutionalists believe that international institutions are both the mediators and the means for obtaining cooperation.

To summarize these two rival theories, realism holds that the international system is anarchic; states seek to maximize power—tangible and intangible—using any means possible, and they struggle for dominance and positions in a hierarchical system. Realism is pessimistic: the future is bleak and based on perpetual competition. These tenets are contradicted by liberalism which considers long-term international cooperation to be possible and which will lead to beneficial gains while avoiding costly wars.

Theories of Global Politics: Critical Approaches

Realism and liberalism are considered mainstream theories, while critical approaches are considered theories that advocate a different approach to international relations and that criticize these traditional views. Neither realism nor liberalism has complete explanatory power; both suffer from some shortcomings. Marxism, feminist theory, and constructivism offer tools necessary to understand trends in international relations and cover some explanatory gaps left open by the traditional theories. These approaches differ from realism and liberalism by not being based on fixed assumptions about states needing to accumulate power (realism) or states seeking only peace, prosperity, and cooperation (liberalism). Marxism looks at the international system from the perspective of a worker, feminist theories look at international relations from the perspectives of women, and constructivism "constructs" a reality based on ideas and values that dictate outcomes.

In the past two decades, the dominance of the two mainstream theories has changed dramatically. They were challenged by the passionate debate between the supporters of realist versus liberal tenets, a debate that exposed weaknesses for both these theories and that made room for a new class of approaches based on the traditional critical interpretation of **Marxist theory**, which argued that the international system is dominated by capitalist views. This theory argues that the capitalist dominant economic system usurps the rights of the workers, and the ideal international system is stateless and classless. Marxism believes that the social, economic and political world should be analyzed as one; it also believes that economic development is the engine behind the most important relations between the proletariat (the working class), the means of production and owners of the means of production, that is, the economic base. The Marxist perspective in international relations is related to ideas of inequity and the way millions of people do not benefit from the global economic development and how, despite more efficient means of production, the rich get richer but the poor do not and instead remain the producing class.

A couple more important and better-known post-Marxist interpretations of the global international system are the **world system theory** (Wallerstein, 1979) and the dependency theory (O'Donnell, Cardoso). Wallerstein's theory divides the world into three distinctive labor units: a core, a semi-periphery, and a periphery. An oversimplified version of this theory explains that the relationship between these three is itself simple: The core is where we have the more skilled workers and a higher standard of living, followed by the semi-periphery where there is a mixture of skilled labor and a prime material exploitation zone, while the periphery is where raw materials originate and the least skilled labor is located.

This system is dynamic, and countries can become semi-periphery by either gaining or losing ground in the international system.

The **dependency theory** preexists the world-system theory, which it holds as an assumption. It argues that underdevelopment is conditioned by external forces, and these countries cannot escape their positions because their development is conditioned by the interests of the much richer countries. Basically, the underdeveloped countries are dependent on the richer countries, with no chances to break that circle.

Feminist theory is an approach that places gender as a focal point in understanding international relations; it looks at how gender both affects international relations and is affected by it. There are a few variants of feminism in international relations, with the first being **liberal feminism**, which advocates equal rights between genders as well as policies meant to promote a more nondiscriminatory approach to politics and more equitable access to power. Another approach is socialist or Marxist feminism which blames the capitalist inequalities and the patriarchal, male dominated system for the unequal role of women in our society. There are many other approaches, including standpoint feminism, postmodern feminism, or postcolonial feminism. They all deal in differences between gender and sex and the role of gender in international relations, and vice versa.

The **constructivist** approach proposes a greater emphasis on the power of ideas and promotes the belief that the international system is socially constructed. Constructivism does not reject the main claims introduced by such traditional theories as neorealism and neoliberalism, but it shows that even those tenets result from a socially-constructed understanding of the international system. Wendt (1992) argues that the stubborn commitment to "crude" forms of materialism is flawed and that even constructions such as "power politics" are socially constructed and do not exist as such in nature; hence, they suffer from human influence. We interact and create rules of engagement, we create a certain construction that can be the agent that serves our interests, we influence these constructions, and we allow them to become a pattern or institutionalized. Basically, international relations are a construction that can and will be modified following our interests, history, character, traditions, and morals. This structure, in turn, will influence our consciousness and identities, and this interaction will reproduce, modify, or eliminate the original structure.

Research Approaches
The Historical Approach

Lamy, Baylis, Smith, and Owens (2013) and Goldstein and Pevehouse (2017) find that there are three main types of research approaches used most often in the study of international relations. They argue that the historical approach, levels of analysis, and the constructivist approach (together with the theories) can offer explanations about decisions and events in global politics. The **historical approach** is arguably the first pertinent and oldest method of research in international politics. It started with the study of the history of relations among states and the reasons why they reached certain decisions, such as war, peace, alliances, and the status quo. The same research method is applied to international relations, and it involves the research of relations among states; it describes them, and it seeks to understand the past and the present in order to have the power to predict the future in a scientific way. If history repeats itself, then we should be wise enough to look at history and see what we would like to repeat and what we would prefer to avoid. Still, the historical approach does not have complete explanatory power; it cannot debate the present based on the analysis of the past and be completely accurate. It relies on the depiction of events and situations as understood by others or as information is available—oftentimes limited—and it must often extrapolate without considering other important variables. Consequently, the historical approach is a useful and complimentary approach to the study of international relations yet often incomplete.

The Social Scientific Approach

As previously mentioned, the scientific approach employs the use of variables and theories. Our curiosity about the relations among different actors at the international level can be answered by looking at the relationship between variables, which we define when we decide the scope of our study. Our curiosity about a specific outcome is called a **research question**, and the potential answer that we would like to prove—as correct or incorrect—is called a **hypothesis**. A hypothesis seeks to explain international relations behavior and offer a prediction for a certain outcome if the same conditions are met in the future, that is, predictability. These hypotheses are tested using variables. There are both independent variables, coded X, and dependent variables, coded Y. The **independent variable** is a stable, controlled variable established by the researcher and used to test the effects of the **dependent variable** upon it. The dependent variables are being tested and measured against the independent variable. The two variables may be associated by cause and effect. If the independent variable changes, then the dependent variable is affected. At times, the hypothesis cannot be answered using this simple model, so it must involve another type of variable called an **intervening variable**, because it is positioned between the independent variable and the dependent variable. For instance, the following hypothesis, "The older the democracy, the more consolidated," contains the independent variable X (age of democracy) and the dependent Y (consolidation). Or "the higher the military expense, the more secure the state," with the independent variable X being money ("the military expense") and the dependent variable Y being the security of the state. We can use an intervening variable to help us establish a more accurate answer for the hypothesis by saying, "the higher the military expense during peaceful times, the more secure the country." Here, we have the same independent and dependent variables with an intervening variable ("during peaceful times") (see Fig 1.1). For the first example, we can use the intervening variable "economic development" and we can formulate it again by using all three types of variables.

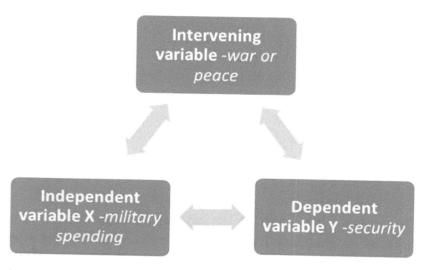

Figure 1.1: Independent, dependent, and intervening variables in the scientific method

Levels of Analysis

Now that we have discussed theories and become familiar with the scientific method, we can consider how we link theories to the scientific approach. Theories are the scientific approach. Their qualities include the following: they have a pattern; they simplify the reality so we can make scientific sense of it; they give us the potential relation between the variable through the causal mechanism; they are logical; they establish sufficient conditions for changes in the dependent variable; and they have assumptions, such as causes and consequences. We know what realism says and we know what the liberal tenets are; hence, we can create a scientific model using one or the other. (Admittedly, this is an oversimplification.) We choose one theory over another because one is more logical and more consistent and offers more explanations than do the other four for our hypothesis.

Singer (1961) proposes a systematic approach to the study of independent variables based on levels of analysis. Based on his proposition, various scales have been created, but most of them contain at least these levels: individual, domestic, and systemic. For the purpose of better understanding the relations among various actors and their role in the formation of international politics, this discussion will consider a four-scale levels of analysis: individual, or human dimension; domestic; interstate; and global.

The **individual level of analysis** seeks to explain outcomes by taking into consideration the human element. What do we see, what do we choose, how do we act as individuals and how do these individual level choices affect the outcome? Great leaders like George Washington, Mahatma Gandhi, and Nelson Mandela and their decision-making process matters just as much as leaders like Joseph Stalin, Adolph Hitler, and Osama bin Laden who display deviant behaviors. We matter as individuals when we vote because we determine the outcome in elections, and these elections designate our next leadership, which in turn determines our behavior at the domestic level.

The **domestic level of analysis** (or state level) seeks to explain outcomes by taking into consideration the state actions as a whole in the international system. The state acts at the international level represented by action groups: its political institutions, like congress, parliament, or the presidency; political organizations, like political parties; and many other actors. It is important to understand the difference between the individual level of analysis (which includes the figurehead, like a president, dictator, or queen, and their *individual* actions at the international level) and the domestic level of analysis (which comprises the president's office or the queen's official position). If a president is an individual and the office of the president is an institution, then the first is to be considered the individual level of analysis while the second is the domestic level of analysis. Democracies, dictatorships, kingdoms, unitary states, or federations all can have different behavior in the international system, behavior being represented by domestic level agents. They can and will act differently, based on domestic interests, policies, and historical realities.

The **interstate level of analysis** (or systemic or international level) seeks to explain outcomes based on the influence of the system on the independent variable. It looks at the interaction between and among states, where states are unitary actors. Examples include one state goes to war against another state, or two states sign a trading agreement or extradition agreement wherein the states act as one actor dealing with another actor. Some authors sometimes include the interstate level as the last classification. For our purposes, we will include one more.

The **global level of analysis** seeks to explain outcomes based on global tendencies, global level interactions, interests, and threats that exceed the more limited interstate level interactions. Issues such as terrorism or the environment are global level issues, and they positively or adversely affect all of us regardless of how much we contribute to the cause because the issue and its effect eventually reach all of us. Similarly, issues such as terrorism might at one specific point in time affect us directly or indirectly, but eventually, we all suffer directly from consequences due to the changes in our security policies. States will change or create new alliances; parliaments will enact new laws. At the individual level, we might miss a flight because we need to take off our shoes and belts at airports that are indifferent to our nationality.

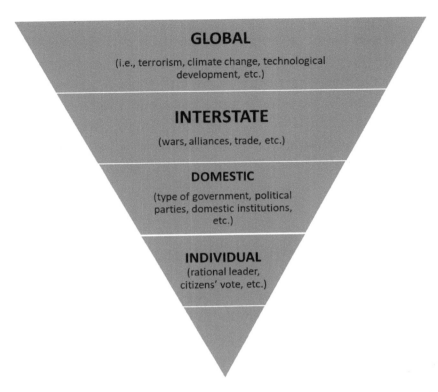

Figure 1.2: Levels of analysis

Figure 1.2 depicts the levels of analysis and shows that even one individual can have a major impact on international relations outcomes and can determine changes. It is not necessary to expect that only state-level decisions should have such significant effects. This approach of using levels of analysis shows how important it is to account for a multitude of actors and consider their power to influence outcomes.

International relations outcomes are not necessarily explained by only one of these levels of analysis. One, two, three, or all four levels of analysis may compete for our understanding of the outcome. For instance, using yet another overly-simplified example, if Hitler would not have been insane, and if he had not gained the trust of the people who voted him into power (individual levels of analysis), and if he had not changed the political system and the institutional arrangement (domestic level of analysis), and if World War I had not ended with problematic peace arrangements (interstate level), and if we had not experienced an idealist tendency (global level), then, perhaps, we would have never had World War II, or at least, parts of World War II would have been different. There is no one level of analysis that offers a better explanation when compared to another; they are just another useful tool in our study of international relations.

Conclusion

This chapter aims to introduce students of international relations to the basic concepts and principles of this discipline. It defines international relations as a field of study, and it seeks to underline the way we use theory in real life. It discusses global actors, their link to global issues, and briefly describes the main theoretical approaches. It also shows the main research approaches that help us answer questions about the international system and the way it works.

It must be underlined that this chapter means to set the stage and serve as an introduction for what will be discussed in later chapters with more in-depth studies of how we "do" international relations today in a globalized era. Globalization is a phenomenon brought to us by the evolution of technology and the fast pace of economic development in a world that increasingly found many benefits from trading abroad and competing outside domestic borders. Although it might have originated in economic and technological development, globalization is now the key word that defines the way we look at international relations. It means that we have more open borders and a greater understanding of each other; that we are gaining knowledge of places and people that were inaccessible to us not long ago. But it also means that, besides the "winners" of the globalization system—those who benefit tremendously from being able to influence others—there are also losers of globalization, and these categories fairly or unfairly deplore the new arrangements. Arguably, globalization destroyed the very fiber of the classic international system based on nation-state and sovereign borders. Castells (2005) argues that the very construction of nation-state—the core of international relations study and the main actor—is threatened by the newly-developed globalization tendencies. States, as we have defined them traditionally, cannot resolve their own issues in the international system; hence, they suffer from a crisis of efficiency. The leaders of the states are often far removed from their base, and this triggers a crisis of legitimacy, as leaders are often ignorant of the real desires of their constituencies. Castells also identifies a crisis of equity, which has its source in the easily-identifiable inequality among states at the international level. If that is the case—and the main traditional actor of international relations is under attack—then we have no means of "walking it back," so we must adjust to the new conditions of the international system.

Not everyone appreciates this globalized system. Not everyone can take advantage of it, while others are clearly at a disadvantage and hence have developed fear and hatred of it. Regardless of our views, we cannot give back the internet, fast travel, or exchanging cotton for T-shirts in a matter of days. All levels of analysis tell us that this globalized system is here to stay and that we must readjust our views about the world in order to accommodate a new analytical outcome. We must be ready to accept, for example, that we live in a world where wars are increasingly carried out less on the ground and more often in cyberspace.

References

Annan, K. (2001). "Kofi Annan on Global Futures." *The Globalist.* Retrieved June 7, 2019, from https://www.theglobalist.com/ kofi-annan-on-global-futures/

Anderse, B. (1991). *Imagined communities: Reflections on the origin and spread of nationalism.* London: Verso.

Cardoso, F. H., & Faletto, E. (1979). "Dependency and development in Latin America." University of California Press.

Carter, J. (2002). "Jimmy Carter: A Noble Man." *The Globalist.* Retrieved June 7, 2019, https://www.theglobalist.com/jimmy-carter-a-noble-man/

Castells, M. (2005). Global governance and global politics. *Political Science and Politics, 38*(1), 9–16.

Goldstein, J. S., & Pevehouse, J. C. (2020). *International relations* (12th ed.). New York: Pearson Longman.

Guibernau, M. M. (1996). *Nationalisms: The nation-state and nationalism in the twentieth century.* Cambridge Polity Press.

Lamy, S. L., Baylis, J., Smith S., Owens, P. (2013). *Introduction to global politics.* Oxford University Press.

Marx, K., & Engels, F. (1998). *The Communist manifesto.* Introduction by E. Hobsbawm (London: Verso).

O'Donnell. G. (1973). *Modernization and bureaucratic authoritarianism.* University of California.

Singer, J. D. (1961). The level-of-analysis problem in international relations. *World Politics, 14*(1), 77–92.

Tilly, C. (2015). *Coercion, capital, and European states, AD 990–1992.* Cambridge, MA: Blackwell.

United Nations. "Global Issues Overview." Retrieved July 1, 2019, from https://www.un.org/en/sections/issues-depth/global-issues-overview/

Wallerstein, I. (1979). *The capitalist world-economy.* Cambridge: Cambridge University Press.

Weber, M. (1965). *Politics as a vocation.* Philadelphia: Fortress Press.

Weidenbaum, M. (2003). Weighing the pros and cons of globalization. *Woodrow Wilson International Center for Scholars.* Retrieved June 29, 2020, from https://www.wilsoncenter.org/sites/default/files/media/documents/publication/Weidenbaum.pdf

Wendt, A. (1992, Spring). Anarchy is what states make of it: The social construction of power politics. *International Organization, 46*(2), 391–425.

The Rise of Modern Politics

2

Raluca Viman-Miller

Abstract

The study of international relations cannot be done without profound knowledge of the historical events that made the states do the things they have done. We cannot arrive in the present without traveling through the past. Hence, we must understand the role of the two World Wars in the contemporary international relations, as well as the importance of the Cold War or advent of terrorism in the creation of contemporary relations among international actors. This chapter summarizes historical events that are significant to the study of international relations, from the Peace of Westphalia to the September 11 terrorist attack on the United States.

Learning Objectives

- Understand the significance of the end of the Thirty Years' War and the Peace of Westphalia as a marker for the beginning of the modern international system
- Have basic knowledge of the revolutionary wars at the end of the eighteenth century, the two World Wars, colonialism, and the Cold War
- Understand the transformation brought about by the historical change in the approach to war since the terrorist attacks on September 11 and how it challenged the international order

We cannot study the evolution of our contemporary international system without understanding our past. History helps us understand our evolution and how the society, politics, and world of today came to be. The past causes the present, and the present causes the future. Hence, George Santayana's observation that those who cannot learn from history are doomed to repeat it fits very well with this idea because all theories aiming to explain reality must have a basis in history—including the calculated behavior and rational approach of the realists and liberals to the obviously historically-based theories of constructivism (see Chapter 1). Whatever happens today is not taking place independent of the past. It is not an isolated phenomenon but, on the contrary, is rooted deeply in previous behavior between two or more actors. We cannot understand the Arab Spring or the conflict between Israel and the Palestinians or the issues in Syria without looking at the history of that region. We will not be able to comprehend why the global threat of terrorism has become such a game changer in international politics in the past decades if we do not understand the frustrations brought on by imperialism and neo-imperialism in relations among rich and poor countries and how globalization has been influencing that. We must understand the reasons for war if we want to be ready to either wage or stop them. We must understand how nationalism works and how it can be turned into a weapon and how faulty international agreements or peace treaties bring on new wars. History is too large for a complete discussion in any single chapter, but this chapter shall take the opportunity to underline the main historical events that led to the contemporary international system.

It is important to understand that globalization and the international system as we know it today is not the overnight creation of a person or a group of people; rather, it is the result of the natural evolution of time. We had elements of what today we call globalization prior to the existence of this term. For instance, we had the Roman Empire that conquered territories on three continents and spread its culture, language, and technology to those newly conquered territories. Yet, the Roman Empire triggered the disappearance of some cultures and the formation of new ones. For example, the Roman Empire conquered the Gauls and ruled present day-France for 500 years, creating a French culture and language. In other words, the Gaulish culture is gone; that population has disappeared, and the language now is different. And these changes occurred through the process of conquest that itself lead to the creation of a new culture and a new language. The Romans were technologically more advanced compared to most cultures they conquered. They built roads, aqueducts, bridges, and dams; they used baths and managed the evacuation of human waste. While some cultures easily accepted Roman rule, others such as the Gauls were conquered, and they were forcefully ruled by the Roman Empire. Force and military strength determined the outcome for the country we now call France. Similarly, a trade route known as the Silk Road stretched from the East to the West and connected China, India, Persia, Egypt, Europe, and Africa, among others. This trade route helped to exchange not only goods but also ideas, cultures, and views as well as the spread of new religious beliefs. These two examples show globalization long before the term came into use. We had actors and interactions; we had power struggles and exchanges; we had much of what we look at today and call international relations. Yet some things were missing, things that we can now identify and trace in the development of the truly globalized international system of today. This chapter will briefly describe the evolution of this system by considering the transformative power of the Westphalian Peace Treaty, the revolutionary wars, the two World Wars, the Cold War, and the post-Cold War conflicts.

The Thirty Years' War and the Peace of Westphalia

Scholars consider the end of the **Thirty Years' War** (1618–1648) as the beginning of modern international relations. This war is also viewed as the last of the European wars fought in the name of religious principles. It ended with the **Peace of Westphalia** in 1648, an agreement that heralded the beginning of new international relations principles. This peace agreement established a couple of very important principles upon which the new international system is founded: (1) the principle of **sovereignty** and (2) the **political rights of monarchs**. Initially a religious war between the Protestant and Catholic factions of the Holy Roman Empire, the Thirty Years' War became one of the most destructive conflicts in the history of the European continent. Wilson (2010) writes than an estimated eight million people died in this conflict. It began when the new Holy Roman emperor, Ferdinand II, in order to achieve his desire of imposing Catholicism as a state religion, mandated that his Protestant subjects adhere to Catholic principles. Soon, the religious component was replaced as the source for conflict by the historical rivalry between the French and the Habsburgs, and the war became a means for establishing the dominant power in the European continent's political affairs. Over the course of 1648, the warring factions agreed to establish a peace process, the Peace of Westphalia, that historians believe ultimately

laid the groundwork for the formation of the modern **nation-state**, establishing fixed boundaries for the countries involved in the fighting and effectively decreeing that residents of a state were subject to the laws of that state and not to those of any other institution, secular or religious (*Thirty Years War*, 2018).

The peace treaty recognized the state's control of and exclusive rights over its territories, a principle that is known in today's modern international relations as sovereignty. In the peace agreements, it was stipulated that the German states, members of the Holy Roman Empire numbering more than 300, should have the right to conduct their own international affairs—hence, recognizing their individual right to self-determination—and the same equal rights and the same privileges, with no differences among themselves. This principle established that sovereignty accorded each state the right to self-determination, a right to which all states were equally entitled, along with the right to conduct their own affairs in the international system, free of any other states' interference.

Since the evolution of the international system towards globalization, some argue that this very backbone of international relations has suffered severe modifications and that lately, the international system has experienced an erosion of the very principle of sovereignty that created relations among states as we know them today. The end of the Thirty Years' War coincided with the **Protestant Reformation.** The Protestant Reformation was a process of rejecting the old Catholic principles on the basis that they had become corrupt and unethical—a development that further weakened papal authority, the ultimate European power that, until then, determined the political arrangements of Europe. While the Protestant Reformation decreased the papal authority in the spiritual realm, the papacy lost most of its political authority following the Peace of Westphalia by allowing "each German prince to designate whether [their] state would be Catholic or Lutheran according to the principles of *cuius region, eius religio* (whose region, his religion)" (Farr, 2005, p. 156).

Kissinger (2015) writes that the Peace of Westphalia also marked the beginning of a novel process: a **diplomatic congress** that established principles of peaceful coexistence and the means of preventing war between states through a **balance of power**, described as a process of equivalence and equilibrium between competing powers. Lamy, Baylis, Smith and Owens (2013) argue that after the

Peace of Westphalia, the international system indeed was marked by these modifications of the main principles of relations among states—a fact proven by the lack of not only religious wars but also any wars in general—as well as by the balance of power arrangements that dominated the politics of the time. Eighteenth and nineteenth century European politics were marked by the determination of the states to preserve their freedom and to mutually recognize each other's rights to independent existence and, above all, by a reliance on the balance of power. The states increasingly relied on diplomacy and international law, elements established by the states themselves. Lamy, et al., quote Knutsen (1997) who writes that the Peace of Westphalia caused a new understanding of international law, where states moved from seeing international law not as divinely inspired but as a set of customs, conventions, and rules of conduct created by the states and their leaders.

Revolutionary Wars and Balance of Power

For two centuries, the international system developed following the principles established by the Peace of Westphalia. The next important historical developments in the evolution of international relations are the revolutionary wars that occurred at the end of the eighteen century. The three revolutions of that era that changed the face of the international system and the way relations among states were created are the American Revolutionary War, the French Revolution, and, according to Lamy, et al (2013), the Haitian Revolution. All these events had at least one thing in common: they fought for independence and **self-determination**. These revolutions sought to free people from the tyranny of monarchies and grant themselves the right to determine their own outcome, to become states and rule themselves as independent sovereign entities in the international system. They mark the beginning of the end for the greatest European monarchies and imperial systems, a transformation still in the process of completion.

The **American Revolutionary War** (1775–1783), also called the American War of Independence, established the independence of the thirteen British colonies and the founding of the United States of America (U.S.). The American colonies fought for self-determination; they desired and won a sovereign, independent state recognized as such by the other actors in the international system. They declared independence in 1776, stopped paying taxes, and no longer recognized British leadership. The British sent troops to fight a war with the Americans, who found support from France, Spain, and the Netherlands. Simms (2008) argues that the British Empire lost an important war that, in effect, marked the end of the first British Empire. The war also realized an important consequence of people creating an identity coupled with some control: after this achievement, others' call for independence will not be delayed. Simms argues that the events that took place in the American colonies cannot be divorced from the European political developments, and what is traditionally called the creation of the American Republic can instead be dubbed the partition of Britain. The British empire was losing its grasp on its overseas territory. Due to the success of the American Revolution, Britain's hold on its colonies became increasingly precarious.

The first **French Revolution** (1789–1799) is part of the same trend. It abolished the monarchy and established a republic. It was also fought under principles that changed the nature of the international system forever. Although marked by turmoil and the demise of the republic under Napoleon, the French Revolution signaled the end of the absolute monarchies in Europe and the beginning of the call for liberal democracies. Lisevey (2001, p. 19) said that "the Revolution created and elaborated . . . the ideal of democracy, which forms the creative tension with the notion of sovereignty that informs the functioning of modern democratic liberal states. This was the truly original contribution of the Revolution to modern political culture."

The **Haitian Revolution** (1791–1804) was based on the same principles of self-determination. It not only sought independence from the French but also joined with a successful slave revolt, resulting in an independent state. It is important to underline that this particular revolution proved that the old European belief system regarding slavery—that slaves are incapable of maintaining their freedom—was wrong. It began the anti-slavery movements in the Americas and British Empire, according to Greggus (2009). The revolution ended in 1804 with the French National Assembly granting freedom to Haiti and its people, thus making Haiti the first nation of freed slaves.

The beginning of the nineteenth century in Europe found Napoleon at the helm of a French monarchy that was defeated by a coalition of European powers in 1815. Significantly, 1815 marked the beginning of a change to what was established in Westphalia, that is, diplomacy, sovereignty, and international law for all through all. The European great powers formed the **Congress of Vienna** (1814–1815), a series of high-level meetings meant to reorganize the European political boundaries after the Napoleonic Wars, reestablish the old monarchies, and redistribute power among themselves to enable a balance of powers and keep peace. It is important to note the use of a collective agreement that resulted in treaties regarding issues of common interest. The congress was, on the continental level, the first instance ever of the main powers joining to formulate treaties and agreements. These treaties maintained the balance of power in Europe up until 1914 (the beginning of World War I) despite the growing interest in establishing new national identities, which had a drastic impact on the map of Europe.

The **Concert of Europe** was an informal European institution that established power relations among the great states. It sought to balance power in Europe by maintaining the status quo, preventing another potential dictator like Napoleon from acceding to power, and upholding the agreements from the Congress of Vienna. This informal agreement among the most powerful players in Europe, including Austria, Britain, France, Prussia, and Russia, intended to preserve the power arrangements, the conservative monarchies and their values, and to control revolutionary forces. Indeed, it managed to do just that all the way to the beginning of the twentieth century, until World War I. By using what we call today in theory **collective security** and balance of power, the great European powers managed to maintain relative peace for almost a century. These concepts will be discussed in more details in Chapters 3 and 4. Another example of power balancing is the **Congress of Berlin** (1878) where representatives of Russia, Great Britain, France, Austro-Hungary, Italy, Germany, the Ottoman Empire, and the four small nations of Greece, Serbia, Romania, and Montenegro sought to avoid war by establishing new borders for these nations—with Serbia, Romania, and Montenegro being declared independent principalities—as well as new occupied territories for the European empires. The great European powers avoided war by agreeing on a new European map and by drawing new territories for the participants in the conference. Their interests were not limited to the European continent. The **Berlin Conference** (1884–1885) formally restructured the great European powers' control over the colonized territories of Africa, partitioning colonial territories in Africa in such way as to avoid conflict among themselves.

Despite their best efforts to maintain a balance of power— in which no one state could predominate over the affairs of the continent—and avoid a war between competing factions, the great European powers eventually lost their equilibrium and headed toward the first global conflagration: World War I. New actors with new ambitions, such as the U.S., emerged on the global scene. The older European empires lost and gained the power accrued since the Congress of Vienna, and, as realist theory will claim, there arose a great need for reorganizing the hierarchy of power on the old continent and on the global scene.

The Two World Wars

As technology advances, so does the success of high yield killings. The first half of the twentieth century experienced two world wars, global-level conflicts meant to rearrange the balance of power in the world. Nothing of comparable scale has happened since then, and these wars should continue to influence our decision-making process, as the atrocities that took place in the name of victory were unprecedented. **World War I** (1914–1918) turned Germany, Austria-Hungary, and the Ottoman Empire against Great Britain, the U.S., France, Russia, Italy, and Japan. These were the main combatant powers, but many smaller nations were also involved with great losses as a result. This global conflagration saw battles carried out on the following continents and locations: Europe, Africa, the Middle East, the Pacific Islands, the Indian Ocean, and the North and South Atlantic Ocean. New military technology resulted in unprecedented carnage, with more than 9 million soldiers killed (some sources say up to 11 million were killed) (*World War I*, 2009).

Besides soldiers and military personnel, civilians suffered casualties from lethal military weapons but also from such war-related ordeals as famine and disease. An estimated 40 million people died as a result of World War I (*First World War (1914-18)*, n.d.).

Historians argue that the real causes of World War I were far from straightforward, comprising instead a mixture of reasons. These included (but were not limited to) **imperialism,** with Africa and Asia as continents fostering new colonial expansion ambitions and being sources of raw materials, thus creating tensions among countries exploiting these areas; **militarism,** with an arms race between Germany (with the largest military buildup), Great Britain, and Russia and a visible growth in influence from military leadership that made war more plausible; **nationalism,** with the dying European empires being continually under siege from nations they were occupying and the desire for an independent nation-state pitting these nations against the political order of the time; followed by the immediate cause, which was the assassination of Archduke Franz Ferdinand.

It is believed that the countries involved in the war did not foresee the level of death and destruction it caused. Indeed, they were actually looking forward to squaring out their differences in what they believed was going to be a short and fast war meant to realign the power houses of the time (Van Evera, 1984). A far different outcome was determined by the evolution of military technologies such as the machine gun, military aircraft, the zeppelin, chemical weapons, the submarine, and the tank, and battle strategies such as **trench warfare**, an elaborate system of fortifications and ditches. Ultimately, in 1918, the German government agreed that it was defeated and accepted an armistice.

What followed was a peace agreement known as the **Treaty of Versailles** (1919), which formally ended the hostilities and established the conditions for the defeated. The victorious Allies imposed a very harsh treatment of war reparations on the Germans (Central Powers) and imputed them—with no afterthought—the reasons for and expenses of World War I. This peace agreement and the harsh conditions it imposed is considered a main reason why a Second World War erupted at the beginning of the twentieth century. A very important figure of that time who marked the future relations among states was the American President, Woodrow Wilson. He articulated his famous **Fourteen Points**, stipulating principles of self-determination, diplomacy, and openness, coupled with the need to establish an international organization formed by the nation-states. It was meant to guarantee territorial integrity and independence—principles that overlap political idealism, the predecessor of liberalism. Wilson was basically establishing the principles of what soon came to be called the **League of Nations**.

This organization is the forerunner of today's United Nations and was the first permanent, collective international security organization, created mainly to prevent war and to avoid a second World War by giving a voice to all members. The League failed because the U.S. chose not to become a member. President Wilson's poor relations with Congress prevented his convincing them of the necessity for membership as well as Great Britain and France's failing to set aside their national interests and accept the principle of collective security.

As already mentioned, the faulty peace treaties from the end of World War I were, arguably, the main reasons for World War II, yet they are not the only ones. The Great Depression of the 1930s and, most importantly, the economic factors following the end of World War I—such as the enormous losses suffered by the European nations on both sides as well as the huge amount of war reparations imposed on Germany—all contributed to what ensued in the relations among states prior to the middle of the twentieth century. The vacuum of power created by the Russian revolution, American isolationism, and decreasing British power allowed Germany and Japan to start an aggressive policy of territorial expansion. In Asia, Japan-occupied Taiwan, Korea, and Manchuria and invaded China, actions which define the strained Chinese-Japanese relations continuing today. Meanwhile in Europe, after electing Adolph Hitler to power, Nazi Germany started a policy of territorial expansion at the expense of its neighbors, pursuing *Lebensraum*, or "living space," a concept which was a critical component of Hitler's expansionist and racial policies. Nazi Germany under Hitler was rearmed and demonstrated increasing aggression against its smaller neighboring states, taking advantage of the weak international response to other extremist governments like Italy's and Spain's, coupled with the extremely difficult domestic living conditions triggered by the Great Depression and the peace accords of World War I. The 1938 **Munich Agreement,** a pitiful attempt of Britain and France to appease Hitler's Germany, allowed Hitler to claim Sudetenland in Czechoslovakia as German territory. Hitler contended that because the area was ethnically German, it should be part of Germany. **Appeasement** is a military strategy that aims to give a state rights over small territorial claims in hopes of quenching its thirst for larger territories, but this strategy proved unsuccessful with Hitler's Germany, and, within a month, he invaded the rest of Czechoslovakia and Poland (1939). Germany thus began its **blitzkrieg**, or "lightning war":

> Blitzkrieg is a military tactic designed to create disorganization among enemy forces through the use of mobile forces and locally concentrated firepower. Its successful execution results in short military campaigns, which preserves human lives and limits the expenditure of artillery. German forces tried out the blitzkrieg in Poland in 1939 before successfully employing the tactic with invasions of Belgium, the Netherlands and France in 1940 (*Blitzkrieg*, n.d.).

This situation caused France and Britain to join the war; Germany was able to meet them with strong resistance (Rich, 1973) because Hitler signed a nonaggression pact with Russia known as **Molotov-Ribbentrop.** By 1941, Hitler betrayed Russia, too, and invaded its western territories. This situation brought the Soviet Union into the war, thereby taking the burden of the Eastern Front and forcing the Germans to split their forces. While the official figure of soldiers and civilian casualties for the USSR numbers around 20 million—by far the largest for any participating country (*Costs of the War*, n.d.)—revisionist historians place the casualties as high as over 40 million dead (*A Message to Putin From 42 Million Dead*, 2017). After 1942, German ethnic cleansing policies triggered the **Holocaust**:

The word "Holocaust," from the Greek words "holos" (whole) and "kaustos" (burned), was historically used to describe a sacrificial offering burned on an altar. Since 1945, the word has taken on a new and horrible meaning: the mass murder of some 6 million European Jews (as well as millions of others, including Romany people, the intellectually disabled, dissidents and homosexuals) by the German Nazi regime during the Second World War (*The Holocaust*, 2009).

The U.S. joined the war effort in 1942 after the December 7, 1941, attack on Pearl Harbor by Japan, an ally of Germany. American involvement was crucial for the outcome of World War II. America's firepower and manpower tilted the war in favor of the Allies, and, by 1944, its role became decisive when British-American forces pushed the Germans from the west while the Russians were pushing the Germans from the east on June 6, or D-Day. The final defeat of Germany came on May 1945, before the war in the Pacific ended and the atomic bomb completed for attack. Intending to shorten the war and force Japan to surrender, the U.S. dropped the first atomic bomb on Hiroshima on August 6, 1945, and the second on Nagasaki on August 9, 1945. It was the first and the (so far) last use of the atomic, nuclear type of weapons of mass destruction in human history.

The end of World War II elevated the U.S. and Soviet Union to the new status of superpowers. A **superpower** is a state in an era when the world is divided politically into these states and their satellites. The two former allies had parted ways not on the friendliest terms and turned their respective ambitions to the newly decolonized territories—but for ideological reasons rather than for economic exploitation. They, then headed straight into a new war, this time a cold war.

The Cold War

Even before World War II was officially over and peace agreements completed, the two former allies, the U.S. and the Soviet Union, stood at opposing ends of the ideological political spectrum. Their subsequent determination to impose capitalist democracies (U.S.) and communism (Soviet Union) on the international system pitted them against each other for the next four-and-a half decades. The **Cold War** (1946–1991)[1] embodied the nature of the international system during this post-World War II period with Washington, D.C., and Moscow at the opposite ends of the ideological spectrum. Characterized by political rivalry, it was a struggle for the hearts and minds of both the peoples and the governments of the world, a dangerous arms race, proxy wars, and economic competition. This war was termed "cold" because the two superpowers never actually engaged in open conflict. Instead, they battled each other by using their influence and their respective military, economic, and political support to attract as many allies or control as many puppet governments as possible. Both sides realized that, given their advanced military technology—especially nuclear weapons—an open war could mean the end of the Earth and human civilization. The international system during the Cold War was characterized by **bipolarity**—which meant that the two superpowers controlled and dominated the other states. During the Cold War, the states of the world were divided and referred to as "First World" states (those allied with the U.S.), "Second World" states (those allied and controlled by the USSR), and "non-aligned" states, or "Third World" states, often comprising developing countries not allied with First or Second world states.

At the end of World War II, when the defeat of Germany was imminent, it became obvious that the Soviet forces had no intention of leaving occupied Central Eastern Europe, and, in Yalta in 1945,

1 The dates of the beginning and the end of the Cold War may differ depending on what event is considered the most important. For instance, literature uses 1945, the end of World War II, or 1946, the year of George Kennan's Long Telegram, or 1947, the introduction of the Truman Doctrine. The same polemic can be found with the dates for the end of the Cold War. Sources will refer to 1989 at the time of the popular uprising in Central Eastern Europe, the successful revolutions against communism, or the Soviet Union's formal collapse in 1991. Neither one of these dates is correct or incorrect; they must be analyzed and understood in context.

U.S.-Soviet-British representatives split the European continent into areas of influence. Figure 2.1 depicts the secret agreement between Winston Churchill and Joseph Stalin regarding Romania, Greece, Yugoslavia, Hungary, and Bulgaria; President Franklin D. Roosevelt was consulted and gave his acceptance. They agreed that the Soviet Union should have a 90% influence in Romania, with the UK having 10%; and 75% in Bulgaria, with the UK having 25%. In Greece, the UK would maintain a 90% influence, with the USSR having 10%, while Hungary and Yugoslavia were split halfway at 50% each.

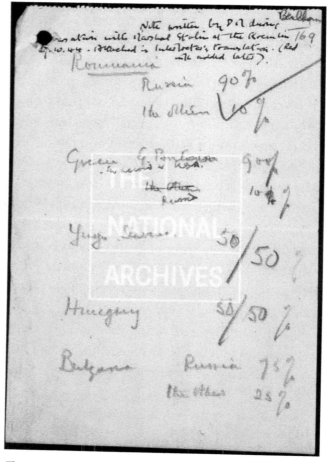

Figure 2.1. The secret agreement between Churchill and Stalin that split Central Eastern Europe into areas of influence (UK National Archives, n.d.).

This was the beginning of the bipolar international political structure that characterized the relations among states up to the end of the Cold War. It was defined by this clear rivalry between the Soviet Union and the U.S. based on their ideological differences and their fight to control as many other states in the system as possible. The start of the Cold War reflected the growing level of mistrust between the two former allies. The Soviet ambition to control European continental affairs was obvious, but so was the American decision not to revert to a policy of isolationism and instead remain involved in promoting their democratic and capitalist ideals, all while defending the interests of their Western democratic allies and rebuilding a European continent based on the U.S.'s views of the world. In 1947, these ambitions led the Truman administration to explain American support of the Mediterranean states of Greece and Turkey through (the now famous) **containment policy**,[2] which was part of the Truman Doctrine. The **Truman Doctrine** is a foreign policy detailed by President Harry Truman before the U.S. Congress in March 1947 calling for the defense and support of free people who were resisting subjugation or outside pressure in order for America to contain and resist Soviet expansion (Wittner, 1980). This policy was reinforced by the economic recovery program known as the **Marshall Plan,** a set of economic and financial aid extended to all European countries, including the USSR. The USSR refused to participate and countered with its own reconstruction programs.

From the political perspective, the U.S. had the Truman Doctrine and containment; from an economic perspective, it had the Marshall Plan; and from a military security perspective, it had the **North Atlantic Treaty Organization (NATO)**. Established in April 1949 by twelve West European allies, the U.S. and Canada, NATO is a collective security military alliance committed to the defense of its members against any external attack. Clearly, one of its

---

2   Containment policy will be used in the coming decades by the United States to push back against attempted Soviet influence. All foreign policy, ideological, economic, military or political decisions meant to oppose Russian influence during the Cold War was placed under the containment policy goal.

main purposes was defense against a potential Soviet invasion. The key article that continues to maintain NATO's viability even today is Article 5, which defines the very essence of collective security, a sort of a musketeer clause of "one for all and all for one." The Soviet responded quickly in 1955 by creating the **Warsaw Pact**, a military alliance comprising the USSR and seven other communist countries meant to serve mutual defense goals and render military aid to its members. It died a natural death at the end of the Cold War and was formally dissolved in 1991.

Despite the fact that relations between the two superpowers improved slightly after the death of Stalin in 1953—resulting in a few high-level meetings between the heads of state—the Soviets could not continue this trend, and, in 1956, they sent troops to invade and crush a popular uprising in Hungary. A similar suppression occurred in 1968 in Czechoslovakia. The U.S., in turn, failed in its attempt to invade Cuba in 1961 in an operation named the Bay of Pigs,[3] and the hostilities between the U.S. and Cuba culminated in the **Cuban Missile Crisis** of 1962. This was the closest we ever came to a nuclear war and World War III. The 13-day standoff between the Soviets and the Americans occurred when the USSR attempted to place nuclear ballistic missiles in Cuba, 90 miles off the shore of the U.S. The Soviets viewed this as a tit for tat measure because the U.S. had already placed nuclear capabilities in Europe in Italy and Turkey, and the Cuban government couldn't have been too much against this new development, considering that the U.S. attempted the Bay of Pigs a few months earlier. An American U2 surveillance plane observed these nuclear capabilities, thus leading to the closest near-miss nuclear event in the history of the world. John F. Kennedy and Nikita Khrushchev stood virtually alone against their closest counselors—who generally argued for using first strike capabilities—by deciding the diplomatic route would likely give humankind a chance. Fursenko and Naftali (1997, p. 263) write that

---

3   Cuba was communist since Fidel Castro and its revolutionary forces won power in 1959.

Khrushchev had famously ended one of his letters by saying that "Now we and you should not pull on the ends of the rope in which you have tied the knot of war, because the more the two of us pull, the tighter the knot will be tied."

The crisis escalated, despite negotiations between the two heads of state and governments, with an American naval blockade meant to prevent Soviet nuclear warheads from reaching Cuba. Ultimately, an agreement was reached, and the two governments stood down once the U.S. committed to never again attempting to interfere in the internal affairs of Cuba and to eliminating their nuclear capability in Turkey and Italy, while the Soviets committed on their part to not again attempting to create a nuclear capable installation in Cuba. As a result, the two superpowers engaged in more cooperation, signing the Limited Test Ban Treaty of 1963, which basically prohibited atmospheric nuclear testing.

This thawing moment did not herald the end of the Cold War. The world powers continued to battle in other parts of the globe. They became involved in dividing and conquering new governments in the Third World countries. Through **proxy wars,** wars in which the U.S. and USSR supported and sustained, advised, and armed different factions usually involved in civil war, the two superpowers continued their attempts to lead the world. The clashing respective interests of the Soviets and the U.S. were clearly visible in the Korean War (1950–1953), the Vietnam War (1955–1975), and the Soviet invasion of Afghanistan (1979), just to name a few instances.

Initially, both superpowers had comparable technology and access to new armament; both were more than capable of obliterating the other with no potential for recovery. By the 1980s, it was clear that Soviet power was overstated and that American technological advancement, backed by a strong economy, far exceeded Russian capabilities. In the end, Mikhail Gorbachev, the last leader of the Soviet Union, through his perestroika and glasnost policies brought the Cold War to an end. **Perestroika** is a series of economic and political reforms initiated in the 1980s meant to restart a bankrupt economic system and a problematic political system. **Glasnost,** meaning "transparency," encompasses a series of political reforms meant to reform the dying Communist Party of the Soviet Union. These two reform policies are widely credited with not only ending the Cold War but also causing the dissolution of the Soviet Union in 1991. Scholars argue that Gorbachev's initiating these reforms essentially admitted to the Soviets' being in trouble and signaled what soon followed: the breakdown of the Soviet Union's control over the Central East European communist camp, followed by revolutions and reforms that overthrew all communist systems and replaced them with new democracies.

Post-Cold War Era: New Challenges, Globalization, and the War on Terrorism

In 1992, shortly after the formal implosion of the USSR, Francis Fukuyama wrote that history as we have known it so far has come to an end and that, with the spread of liberal democracies coupled with free market capitalism, we now face a sociocultural evolution that makes these forms of government and economic approaches the final type of human government. Linz and Stepan (1996) alternatively argued that consolidation of democracies in the newly-freed countries can happen only after democracy is the "only game in town," and it becomes such when other versions of government are frowned upon and chased "out of town" immediately. Today, both statements have found valid criticisms and opposition, although at the time—the beginning of the 1990s—an attempt at democracy in the former Soviet Union occurred, with the fifteen former republics gaining independence. Besides the three Baltic states, the rest reorganized themselves into the Commonwealth of Independent States (CIS). The process of democratization adopted in the former communist states was not easy, but the CIS countries—and especially Russia—did not enjoy the expected support from the old democracies of the West and instead had to fight their way through harsh economic transitions and lower standards of living. Although Russia claimed to be attempting democracy, its behavior towards nations and countries in the neighborhood argued otherwise. They brutally intervened and stopped secessionist movements, for instance, in Chechnya in 1995 and 1999. It also annexed the Crimea from Ukraine in 2014 and altered its consolidation in the direction of democracy by changing the laws of the land to accommodate the reelection of the former KGB operative Vladimir Putin, who has been in power at the top of the executive branch, as prime minister or president, since 2008.

While the tone of the 1990s was positive and optimistic, the world was headed toward a different direction, where liberal values of cooperation, international laws, and respect for sovereignty replaced the old Cold War values. The **Gulf War** (1990–1991) demonstrated this change when Saddam Hussein, encouraged by the instability that came after the Cold War and demanding historical territorial rights, coupled with disagreements over usage of common oil resources, invaded the small nation of Kuwait and, for a few hours, claimed ownership of over 20% of the world's oil reserves. Consequently, the U.S. and its allies asked the United Nations' Security Council (comprising five permanent members: U.S., China, the Russia Federation, the UK, and France) for the first time ever to give mandate to military forces to invade Iraq and push them out of Kuwait.

The international coalition that successfully freed Kuwait imposed sanctions against Iraq but did not overthrow its government since that was not part of the original mandate. The cost of the war was shared by the coalition members. For the first time, it used NATO troops, thereby giving this military security organization a new role, one that, again, was mandated and agreed upon with no opposition by the UN. It was thus a great success of a new liberal world order. Russia and the U.S. had a better relationship based on cooperation and agreements. For example, they agreed to consult with each other, and NATO would not expand to the east and the U.S. would include Russia in all decision-making processes that pertained to its interests (Tsygankov, 2016). This honeymoon soon ended, though, and the **Yugoslav Wars** (1991–2001) caused the first post-Cold War frictions between the former two superpowers. This complicated war began in 1991 in the Balkans.

To briefly summarize, complications began in 1991, when Slovenia and Croatia declared independence, followed by Bosnia, which had a mixture of Serbs, Muslims, and Croats. The Bosnian Serbs, helped by the Serbians and the Yugoslav army, resisted the calls for independence and opted for a "Greater Serbia." This triggered a war between the Serbs, who were Orthodox Christians, the Bosnian Muslims, and the Croats, who wanted their independence. The newly formed Bosnian Serb Army enacted ethnic cleansing and drove away millions of Muslims and Croats from their homes. NATO bombed Serbian military forces, civilian facilities, and cities in an effort to weaken their stance and force them to negotiate a peace agreement (*Balkans War: A brief guide*, 2016). In 1995, a peace agreement was finally reached when, in Dayton, Ohio, Richard Holbrooke's American-led delegation negotiated a cease fire and a peace agreement endorsed by the rest of the world powers.

Contrary to what happened in the Gulf War, this time the interests varied (Holbrooke, 1999). The Western powers did not burden share the crisis in Bosnia, preferring instead a more neutral role. The Russian interests defending the Orthodox Serbs were obvious and deeply hurt when the NATO allies bombarded the Serbs without ever consulting Russia as promised. A new crisis was triggered when ethnic Albanians declared the independence of Kosovo in 1999. The Serbs pushed back by then, committing ethnic cleansing. Ultimately, NATO forces launched air attacks and forced the Serbs to withdraw, allowing Kosovo to declare its independence. A different set of attitudes was revealed as a result of this conflict. Large powers like China and Russia considered the intervention in Kosovo illegal because it did not have a UN Security Council mandate. Ultimately, Kosovo declared its independence in 2008, but not all UN members recognized it. By 2019, 100 out of the 193 members of the UN, just slightly over 50%, recognized its independence. Notable absentees were Russia and Central Eastern European states, which did not desire to allow this regional and nationalistic conflict to create a precedent that could eventually force them to grant the same type of autonomy to their minorities if faced with the same internal and international pressure.

This was not the only international intervention that failed the people on the ground and showed that the politics of the great power interests were back. The U.S. intervened with humanitarian purposes in Somalia and was drawn into its internal conflict. When American soldiers from a downed Black Hawk helicopter were killed and dragged onto the streets of Mogadishu, the U.S. decided to turn a blind eye to these types of interventions and thus joined the group of the large powers who failed to prevent the genocide that followed in Rwanda in 1994, when over a million people died in a civil war triggered by the political vestiges of Belgium's colonial power.

On September 11, 2001, the world watched in astonishment when the U.S., arguably the hegemon of the unipolar new world order, was successfully attacked on its own territory by a group of individual terrorists. Four attacks—two on the World Trade Center in New York, NY, the Pentagon in Washington, D.C., and (through failing to reach the intended target) Stoneycreek Township, PA—killed 2,977 people and injured over 6,000 others. Four planes were hijacked by nineteen terrorists coordinated by the now defunct Al-Qaeda. All planes were domestic air carriers, and citizens of sixty other nations were on one of these four flights.

The world was headed down a path of no return, with new enemies, new types of wars to fight, and a brand-new set of coalitions and interests (Morgan, 2009). We were entering the era of the "war on terrorism," the fight against a stateless enemy, and were confronting an international organization with tentacles reaching into friendly as well as unfriendly territories. It was no longer clear where exactly to wage war and bring the fight to in order to secure our future safety. The old definitions of war and attacks against a sovereign nation, principles that built the UN half a century before, became somewhat obsolete. Still, the U.S. enjoyed the unconditional support of all-important actors. For the first time ever, NATO invoked Article 5 of its charter, an article that defined its role as a collective security organization and called for action in case of an attack against any of its members. The initial support managed to assemble a coalition of states that fought terrorism in every way possible. More countries, including France, Spain, and the UK, also became victims of terrorist attacks, making the war on terror a comprehensive necessity. Al-Qaeda, led by Osama bin Laden, previously enjoyed safe haven in Afghanistan, sheltered by a sympathetic Taliban-led regime. By late 2001, U.S. and allied troops removed the Taliban regime and any remaining links with Al-Qaeda, and, in May 2011, Osama bin Laden was killed by American Navy seals in Pakistan, who was officially an American ally in the war on terror.

Eventually, the coalition formed around the events of September 11 started to erode, and the great powers' respective interests created divisions along the lines of actions against governments viewed as potential enemies. Notably, France, Germany, China, and Russia opposed the war in Iraq waged by the U.S. and its main ally, the UK. In order to remove Saddam Hussein from power, the U.S. and its allies waged war starting in 2003, despite the lack of a UN Security Council mandate. The removal of the government of Saddam Hussein was received by some with great enthusiasm. Yet, the failure of the American occupation to create a fair governmental structure that could mediate the millennia-long conflict between the Sunni and the Shia communities eventually resulted in a slow burning civil war with anti-American sentiments on the rise. The U.S. government decided to lower its engagement in the area and started to withdraw from Iraq between 2009 and 2011. Unfortunately, the American presence in Iraq again intensified when a new terrorist organization developed and gained control in Syria as well as in certain regions in Iraq. This terrorist organization became known as ISIS, which roughly translates as Islamic State of Iraq and the Levant. By 2015, ISIS conquered vast territories in eastern Syria and western Iraq; its ultimate goal was to add more territories to the already-declared caliphate begun in 2014. The large power interests once more fought together; Americans, Russians, Iraqis, and Iranians joined in an attempt to eliminate ISIS. Once ISIS was dismantled, the great power interests started to diverge again. Building upon the U.S. interests to secure democratization in the Middle East through U.S. involvement in the Arab Spring, the Americans continue to be focused on the removal of authoritarian regimes throughout the region. Its involvement with Bashar al-Assad in Syria and ISIS is an example of such.

Russia's interest, on the other hand, was to maintain at least one friendly government in the region in order to defend its presence there. These efforts were to counter the U.S.'s involvement in the region and their efforts through the Arab Spring **to** replace nondemocratic regimes with liberal ones. The new regimes resulted from a series of anti-governmental protests and uprisings supported by popular movements and street pressure and combined, at times, with armed rebellions. The support for democratically-elected governments versus support for old allies in the region and the great powers' interests in the area echoed the Cold War. The Middle East's way of life was seriously disturbed, leading as a direct consequence to our witnessing an alarming increase in the rate of illegal **migration**, asylum-seeking populations, and refugees. These displaced citizens of the countries that are currently experiencing civil war are seeking safe haven in their neighboring countries, which themselves are often in precarious economic and political situations, so the additional burden is extremely costly. Others, if they have any financial means, risk their lives and illegally cross the Mediterranean Sea in a desperate attempt to gain refugee status in any of the Western European countries.

The world does not seem to be headed towards more peaceful resolutions, and, despite the liberal view that argues we had fewer wars and decreased destruction in the past hundred years, the potential for devastation is more imminent, as nondemocratic regimes such as North Korea take action to realize their **nuclear ambitions**. Their research and development programs, as well as their attempts at purchasing technology, enriched uranium and engineers in the world market, is well known. Once more, the great power interests converge when the issue of nuclear proliferation becomes a political reality. The "nuclear club" countries oppose horizontal and vertical proliferation, especially at the hands of hard to control, irrational leaders.

The characteristics of the international relations post-Cold War are summarized under the term **globalization.** This new term defines an international system that transcends the need for borders. Economic, political, and social relations among actors develop at a global scale, with very little concern for the old nation-state and its definitions. As Samuel Huntington (1993) famously wrote in *The Clash of Civilizations*, the post-Cold War era will be characterized by a clash of civilizations. Cultural and religious identities, he argues, will became the primary reason why people will engage in war, and he draws hypothetical maps showing the potential sources of the clash. Unfortunately, it seems that we are now experiencing a cultural clash of the Western culture and the rest of the cultures of the world. Globalization brought forward a great deal of benefits, but it also created a great deal of animosity between cultures.

Conclusion

This chapter briefly summarizes the events that characterized the international system since the Treaty of Westphalia to the latest events in the Middle East. It seems that, despite moments of hope and cooperation between actors at the international level, we have been predictably returning to the "bleak and anarchic" world described by realism. The liberal approach, that views the nature of the international system as "changing and evolving," can most definitely claim some triumphs in some battles, but it is clear that neither one of our international relations theories can explain away the entire evolution of the relations among states. Hence, it is extremely important to look at the historical moments, understand the context, and analyze the role of each actor. We must look at history to learn and to exercise caution, playing, if at all possible, a wise "what if" game. Individuals matter, presidents of democratic republics will act differently than irrational authoritarian leaders will, yet nondemocratic regimes will have the luxury of following one voice, one leader without running the risk of having a legislative branch strike down any decision. Individual and domestic actors matter just as much as intra-state relations, economic deals, tariff reductions, or reintroductions on the global level where the new war on terrorism involves absolutely all of us, more so than were all involved during the Cold War. The binary nature of the war on terror cannot be analyzed and forecasted for outcomes without taking a look at the history of the relations among actors in the areas where it operates now. We must understand our history if we want to be able to understand our current realities.

References

A Message to Putin from 42 Million Dead. (2017, May 10). Bloomberg. Retrieved from https://www.bloomberg.com/opinion/articles/2017-05-10/a-message-to-putin-from-42-million-dead

Balkans War: A brief guide. (2016, March 28) BBC News. Retrieved from https://www.bbc.com/news/world-europe-17632399

Blitzkrieg. (n.d.) Retrieved November 4, 2019, from https://www.history.com/topics/world-war-ii/blitzkrieg

Costs of the War: Killed, wounded, prisoners, or missing. (n.d.) Britannica. Retrieved November 4, 2019, from https://www.britannica.com/event/World-War-II/Costs-of-the-war#ref53608

Farr, J. (2005). Point: The Westphalia legacy and the modern nation-state. *International Social Science Review, 80*(3/4), 156–159.

First World War (1914-18): 15,000,000. (n.d.) Necrometrics. Retrieved August 1, 2019, from http://necrometrics.com/20c5m.htm#WW1

Fukuyama, F. (1992). *The end of history and the last man.* New York: Perrenial, HarperCollins Publishers.

Fursenko, A., & Naftali, T. (1997). *"One hell of a gamble:" Khrushchev, Castro, and Kennedy, 1958–1964.* New York. W. W. Norton and Company Inc.

Geggus, D. P., & Fiering, N. (Eds.). (2009). *The world of the Haitian revolution.* Indiana University Press.

Holbrooke, R. (1999). *To end a war.* Modern Library.

Kissinger, H. (2015). *World order.* New York: Penguin.

Knutsen, T. (1997). *A history of international relations theory.* Manchester: Manchester University Press.

Lamy, S. L., Baylis, J., Smith S., & Owens, P. (2013). *Introduction to global politics.* Oxford University Press.

Linz, J. J., & Stepan, A. (1996). *Problems of democratic transition and consolidation*. Johns Hopkins University Press.

Lisevey, J. (2001). *Making democracy in the French Revolution*. Harvard: Harvard University Press.

Morgan, M. J. (2009). *The impact of 9/11 on politics and war: The day that changed everything?* Palgrave Macmillan.

Rich, N. (1973). *Hitler's war aims: Ideology, the Nazi state, and the course of expansion*. New York, London: W.W. Norton.

Simms, B. (2008). *Three victories and a defeat: The rise and fall of the first British empire*. Penguin UK.

The Holocaust. (2009, October 9). History. Retrieved from https://www.history.com/topics/world-war-ii/the-holocaust.

Thirty Years' War. (2018, August 21). History. https://www.history.com/topics/reformation/thirty-years-war

Tsygankov, A. P. (2016). *Russia's foreign policy: Change and continuity in national identity* (4th ed.). Rowman & Littlefield.

UK National Archives, (n.d.) Retrieved August 1, 2019, from https://images.nationalarchives.gov.uk/assetbank-nationalarchives/action/viewFullSizedImage?id=30941&size=800.

Van Evera, S. (1984). The cult of the offensive and the origins of the First World War. *International Security, 9*(1), 58–107.

Wilson, P. H. (2010). *Europe's tragedy: A new history of the Thirty Years' War*. London: Penguin.

Wittner, L. S. (1980). The Truman Doctrine and the defense of freedom. *Diplomatic History, 4*(2), 161–188.

World War I. (2009, October 29). *History*. https://www.history.com/topics/world-war-i

Part II

Theories of Global Politics

Power Politics

Craig Greathouse

Abstract

This chapter examines the role of theory within international relations and focuses on the oldest school of thought, which is realism. The chapter starts by laying out what is a theory in international relations, why theory matters, and the importance of theory as an analytical tool which helps to simplify the field. Next, the chapter introduces students to realism, which shows the focus of realism as based on power, states, and the role of balance of power. It then highlights the differences of the four variants of realism addressed: classical realism, neorealism/structural realism, offensive realism, and neoclassical realism.

Learning Objectives

- Gain a basic understanding of what is a theory and its use within international relations
- Understand the core assumptions of realism which are shared by the different variants
- Able to describe different variants of realism

Within international relations, **theory** provides an important tool for understanding and processing the complexity of the field. As with other academic disciplines, limited agreement exists among scholars and researchers about which theoretical framework or approach is most appropriate to apply for understanding the occurrences in the international system. The next three chapters will address some of the most important theoretical frameworks to provide an understanding of the different approaches that can be taken to explaining how and why things occur in international relations.

This chapter will proceed with a brief overview of what theory is and how scholars and researchers use it within the field. It will then provide an overview of the theoretical school called realism. This school has been the most widely subscribed to approach for explaining the international system. However, it is also the mostly widely critiqued approach, given the length of time it has existed and the general focus of this school of thought. In laying out realism, this chapter will provide generalizations without delving into significant detail about the different variants of realism.

What is Theory?

What is theory? Why should I care? These are probably two of the most difficult questions a student will ever have to deal with in terms of academic theories. Thinking "theoretically" about a topic is something with which many students have a problem, in that they probably have heard over and over in class "Don't focus on the theory; focus on the real world." The problem is one of complexity. Without some sort of device to limit the amount of information one has to examine, explanation becomes very difficult or impossible. Our goal within international relations theory is to describe, explain, and predict (Singer, 1961). Theory is the tool that will allow us to engage in those actions.

Knowing what theory is provides scholars and researchers the critical capacity for addressing the array of questions and issues with which one has to deal for understanding international relations. If theory did not exist or was not applied, trying to understand international relations would mean that the researcher would have to study every event, occurrence, or interaction which ever happened within the system in order to understand it. This is not viable given the amount of interactions that occur in a single day within the system. For example, the Bank of International Settlements estimated that, in 2016, the **foreign exchange market**—trading of different currencies—saw about 5.1 trillion dollars of value-a-day traded (Bank of International Settlements, 2019). While currency trading is an important economic occurrence, it is but one type of interaction in the international system. Other interactions include trade between states, the movement of people and services, transfer of information, conflicts, and border disputes.

Another example of the amount of information being overwhelming without a framework for simplification would be war. Wars are critical events in international relations, so understanding a conflict like World War II is essential. Without a theoretical framework, researchers would have to study every interaction and nuance that led up to the start of World War II for each unique actor in the system. While not exhaustive, the previous list illustrates the fact that trying to understand international relations without something to simplify the amount of data generated on a daily basis would be futile.

As an abstraction from reality, theory does not intend to provide a one-to-one match with what occurs in the real world. Theory simplifies reality in order to help us understand it. (Waltz, 1979) The simplification theory provided allows the user to focus on specific variables which the theory's founder argues create or cause specific outcomes in the international system. The use of theory in the field of international relations is no different than the use of theory in the hard sciences. Authors create theories based on certain logical criteria and based on empirical and factual evidence. These theories can then be tested to see if their explanatory capability holds. Theories are not just random ideas thrown together. Rather, they are based in reality but focus on specific elements which the authors argue are the most important causes of a particular outcome.

There are three critical acts that theories help us perform within the field of international relations: describe, explain, and predict (Singer, 1961). These three elements help us articulate what the world is, explain how and why it operates, and then—if we are successful at the first two steps—we can predict what may happen going forward. The first step, description, means having the capacity to describe the world or parts of the world that the theory addresses. Since theory is an abstraction of reality, it does not have to describe every element; it must, however, be able to effectively describe elements in the world it claims are important.

The second step a theory must achieve is explanation. Once it provides a description of the concept, a theory should then explain the relationships between these concepts and why things happen. The step between description and explanation is significant. If a theory cannot explain, then it is not useful. Theories are judged on their explanatory capability about what they claim they explain. If it lacks explanatory capability, then a theory is not useful in providing a framework for looking at the world. Accurate theoretical prediction is something with which the entire field of international relations has struggled, which is why we are continually trying to improve our theories.

The idea behind the next step of prediction is that if theories can describe and explain phenomena, then they can effectively take that understanding and make predictions about the occurrences of those issues in the future. International relations is still working on building theories with enough descriptive and explanatory capacity to allow us to make accurate predictions about the phenomena. To be most effective, then, a theory must be able to describe, explain, and predict.

Within the field of international relations, we use both mid-range theory and grand theories, or **paradigms**. Unlike mid-range theory, a grand theory tries to explain everything that is going on in one framework. For example, the field of physics is working towards a unified theory that, once reached, would be a grand theory comprehending the entirety of physics. If they can develop this theory, and it holds over time with repeated tests, then physicists will have an increased capability to describe, explain, and predict the world around us. Mid-range theory in international relations focuses on addressing only areas or issues which pertain to a subset of actors within the field of international relations; it does not claim the capacity to address everything that occurs in international relations. While some mid-range theories will effectively address security issues, for example, they probably will not to be as effective in addressing economic issues in the system, and vice versa.

Theories in social science, and especially the theories we address in this book, are built on certain assumptions. You must find the assumptions of each theory. You cannot challenge or change the assumptions; you must either accept them across the board or reject the theory. If you accept them, you can use that theory. If you reject them, you have to move on and find a different explanation about why and how things occur in the system.

Waltz (1979) describes assumptions as theoretical notions. Assumptions are the logical elements that connect the different parts and concepts of a theory together and provide a foundation from which to use the theory as a lens for understanding and explanation. Assumptions cannot be randomly changed or ignored within a theory without destroying that theory. This is why the rejection of an author's assumptions for their theory, within international relations, will force the reader to move on to a different theory. Another thing to remember is that different theories cannot be easily combined due to the fact that they are based on different assumptions. Assumptions are not guesses but logically deduced ideas and themes that the author asserts in order to connect their different variables, particularly independent variables.

Theories will tell us which variables are important to consider and which ones are not. Theories are like sunglass lenses that let through the important information while blocking the unimportant. One theory, based on its assumptions, variables, and focus, may explain events very differently than might another. For example, applying one of the realist theories to the cause of World War II would result in a very different explanation than if we applied either one of the liberal theories or one of the constructivist approaches to explain the same event. The differences in assumptions, variables, and focus of the different schools of thought—especially when we get down to individual theories—provide for a range of explanations about the international system. Some theories or schools of thought will explain certain types of events or situations much better than others. For example, realism is stronger in terms of its explanation about issues related to security, defense, and war as compared to the liberal school of thought, which more effectively looks at economics, government types, and cooperative activities in the system. The limitations of theory in international relations is an important element to understand.

One thing to make perfectly clear is that mixing and matching ideas from different theories does not work and will likely lead to misinterpretations of political phenomena. A correctly built theory will have an internal logic that connects assumptions to the hypothesis, to the variables, and to the outcomes and explanations. If any part of that logical chain is missing, the theory is non-existent. Trying to pull elements from one theory and connect it with elements from another means no logical coherency will exist between theories arrived at through such piecemeal efforts. This is why the realist, liberal, and constructivist schools of thought cannot be blended together into a grand theory achieving a singular explanation for international politics.

Theory is designed to assist the researcher by focusing them on particular types of information rather than on looking at everything. There are always advantages to focusing on particular types of information, just as there are drawbacks to focusing on one element but not on other types of influences. If you understand the foundations of theory, you effectively gain the explanatory power a theory provides while being able to acknowledge there are weaknesses in that particular approach.

Realism

The first school of thought, or paradigm, we will explore is that of **realism**, which is the oldest of the theoretical traditions. It traces its origins back about 2,500 years to the conflict between ancient Athens and Sparta. Realism is *not* a theory in and of itself but is a school or related group of theories that share certain elements. These shared elements are unique and create links between different theorists within this tradition. Realism traditionally has provided the best explanations related to why wars occur, why states use or threaten the use of force in the system, and how actors worry about their basic existence. This focus is not only a strength but also a weakness of realism. While it has worked well in explaining war and conflict historically, it does not work as well in addressing more mundane day-to-day activities within the international system. Issues of trade, social interactions, societal groups, and other issues which might be considered "low politics" are not what realism has focused on explaining. While realism might, for example, do very well at explaining the Cold War period in general, it does not succeed well at explaining the creation of the European Union. One of the legitimate criticisms of realism is that it does not explain the totality of interactions in the system, but realists will argue that they focus their explanations on those types of interactions which are most important, that is, security and war.

This chapter focuses on the four most prominent variants which fall within realism. This list is not nor is intended to be exhaustive. Instead, it represents the major developments within realism over its history and the most important advancements. The four specific types of realism that we will address include classical realism, neorealism (structural realism / defensive realism), offensive realism, and neoclassical realism. The oldest version of realism is classical realism, which is then followed by neorealism, offensive realism, and then neoclassical realism. Realist theories are based both at the systemic and state levels of analysis. In general, realism focuses on the system and state actions within the system.

As discussed above, every theory has assumptions, or theoretical notions according to Waltz, which provide the foundation on which it operates. Assumptions are elements which are not tested. They are elements which are accepted within the context of the theory. What makes theories a part of realism is that they share certain assumptions. These shared assumptions are a thread which connects the most current version of neoclassical realism to the oldest version of classical realism.

The first of the shared assumptions, and the most important one, is that realism is predicated on **power** (Morgenthau, 1948; Waltz, 1979; Keohane, 1986; Holsti, 1995; Mearsheimer, 2001). Power is defined by realists as the ability of one actor to make another actor do something they would have otherwise not done, or, adversely, to stop another actor from taking an action they would have otherwise taken. Realist explanations based on power go back to Thucydides (1996), specifically, the Melian Dialogue; and to Machiavelli in *The Prince* (1961). Each includes a discussion on the role of power within the international system. Realism focuses on the power of the system's primary actors and how that power, in turn, is used and affects actions in the system. Traditionally, when we examine power in realism, we are talking about **hard power**. Hard power focuses on the use, or threat of use, of military capabilities. Each particular theorist may have their own specific measure of power. For many realists, the military component is one of the biggest elements of the state. While economic elements of power are important for realists, they are not more important than the military element. Economic elements of power play into how a state may act and in providing the assets for creating military capabilities (Organski, 1958). Interactions in the system under realism are influenced, affected, and created by power and its usage in the system.

The focus on power also allows realists to compare states based on their respective power. These comparisons can be either absolute or relative. Depending on the author's particular theory, they will use power to classify states. Neoclassical realists (Rose, 1998) focus on a *relative* comparison to power, as opposed to others who look at power in an *absolute* sense. The more power a state has, the more they can do within the system. Realists often categorize actors as superpowers, great powers, middle powers (regional powers), and those with little or no power (Schweller, 1998). Realism tends to focus on those states at the higher end of the power spectrum, on those that are hegemonic, superpowers, unipolar powers, or great powers. The argument is that those states with more power can do more things in the system and therefore have a bigger impact. Examples include the British Empire at the height of its power, which would be considered a hegemonic power. A simple definition of a **hegemonic power**, as presented in this chapter, is a state that has 50% + 1 of all power in the system. A **unipolar power** is a state that has a lot of power in comparison to others and is dominant but does not reach the level of a hegemonic state. The U.S., for about a decade or so after the collapse of the USSR, would exemplify a unipolar power. Superpowers only existed in one era: the Cold War. The U.S. and USSR were, by comparison, so much stronger than the other states in the Cold War system that they were considered the dominant concentrations of power within that system, or **poles**. This system with two concentrations of power is a **bipolar system.**

Great powers have historically dominated the international system. Great powers are the strongest powers in a given system, and they characterize a multipolar system. A **multipolar system** is defined by the presence of more than two states defined as great powers. The period before World War I had five great powers, including Russia, Germany, the Austro-Hungarian Empire, France, and the United Kingdom (UK). One element that differentiates a great power from a regional or middle power is the capacity to project power beyond their region. A regional or middle power is a state that is powerful in their region but cannot effectively project power outside their region. Given their power, Brazil, for example, matters in their region but cannot effectively project that power beyond the area of Latin America to effectively influence the international system. Those at the bottom of the power pyramid are in many ways at the mercy of larger powers and must operate differently than do those who have more and stronger power.

The second assumption of the school of realism is that states are the **primary actors**. (Morgenthau, 1948; Waltz, 1979; Gilpin, 1981; Keohane, 1986; Holsti, 1995; Mearsheimer, 2001; Ripsman, Taliaferro, & Lobell, 2016) Given that realism reaches back over 2,500 years, this assumption gets somewhat stretched to include city-states in Ancient Greece. But the idea is similar in that we are talking about an actor that has a specific defined territory, government, and sovereignty. **Sovereignty** is critically important in that a sovereign actor is one that makes the final decisions about its own actions. These actions do not have to effect good results for the actor, but they must derive from choices the actor can make itself. If, for example, a state decides to invade or go to war with a stronger state, then they are allowed to make that choice even if negative consequences ensue.

Realism looks at states as the primary actors in the system but not as the only actors. Realists do not claim that other types of actors in the system do not exist; they do, however, argue that states are the driving force within the system and that states can generate the most power of any of the actors in the system. This assumption gives the realists explanatory power when dealing with state interactions, but it affects their explanatory power when other types of actors, like international organizations or non-governmental organizations, are in play. In some versions of realism, the focus is on the "great powers" (Waltz, 1979; Mearsheimer, 2001) of any particular period in international relations. During the Cold War, for example, many realist writers of that time focused on the competition between the U.S. and the USSR.

The third of the shared assumptions of realism is that the system is **anarchic** (Hobbes, 1996; Morgenthau, 1948; Waltz, 1979; Gilpin, 1981; Mearsheimer, 2001). Realists assume there is no world government and no power beyond states that can dictate to states in terms of making decisions about how they operate within the international system. The only limitations on states in an anarchic system are the state itself in choosing not to take an action or other states in the system intervening to prevent a state from undertaking an action. An anarchic system means not that a state of war is in existence at all times but that war or conflict between states may break out at any time. This "reality" requires states to be vigilant and concerned about the actions of other states in the system.

The final shared assumption of realism is the **balance of power**. (Morgenthau, 1948; Waltz, 1979; Gilpin, 1981) The balance of power is a concept that has been widely used within the field of international relations, not only as an analytical concept but also critiqued as an ineffective means of explaining state action (Wohlforth, 1993). The simple idea behind the balance of power is that states with roughly equal power will not fight because neither side knows who will win. Therefore, if a state is unsure of an outcome, the uncertainty may limit that state's choosing to act, especially in terms of security issues or war. Part of this limitation is due to the possibility that, without knowing the outcome, a state could lose and therefore either put itself in a very difficult position in the system or be completely destroyed. Thus, according to realists, when states are roughly balanced in terms of power, the chances of war between them decreases. However, when power between two states is out of balance, the chances of war occurring increases, as one state has a significant advantage in terms of its power. A state that is stronger does not have to engage in war, but in an anarchic system, the choice remains the state's. Thus, when the international system is balanced, there will be less war in the system as opposed to when the system is out of balance. However, different versions of realism argue different variants of the balance of power. Morgenthau (1948) focused on balance of power in a multipolar system, Waltz (1979) focused on balance in a bipolar system, while Mearsheimer (2001) looked at issues of balance at a regional level.

For states to create balance versus other states, they traditionally have two options. The first option is to increase their own power, usually through generating more income which can then be transformed into military assets. Past examples would be moving to a war economy in which fewer resources are directed towards the civilian economy and more into the military. Another option is to gain more territory or area and then exploit that new area's resources to generate more power. This could be done through conquering another state and then taking its resources or through the colonization and creation of an empire, which has occurred often in world history. The second way realists have argued that states work to create a balance of power is in creating alliances. **Alliances**, defined as defensive or security alliances, are designed to allow states to connect with each other in order to present a combined front of higher power to achieve balance versus a potential threat.

For example, if state A had 100 units of power and was possibly threatening states B and C, who each had 45 units of power, states B and C are vulnerable individually to state A. However, by creating an alliance, states B and C now have power of 90 units, which will change state A's calculations. Does state A still win versus these two states' combined power, as compared to when they operated individually? In this scenario, state A will have to calculate rationally the conflict's potential outcome. Historical examples of alliance behavior in the system include the Triple Alliance and Triple Entente, which were formed prior to the start of World War I to try and prevent the occurrence of that war. Another example would be the creation of **NATO** and the **Warsaw Pact** in order to balance out the power of the U.S. and the USSR.

Alliances are a major area of debate within the field. For the balance of power to effectively operate, alliances and their participating states must understand the total sum of their power and their limitations. Certain areas of debate include whether balances of power operate independently of state actions and come into being because of systemic pressures, whether the balance of power must actively be pursued by states, or whether or not states always balance (Elman & Jensen, 2014; Walt, 1987; Schweller, 2006).

The next debate questions whether the balance of power works best, as Morgenthau (1948) argues, in a multipolar system (three or more great powers, or a regional setting with three or more regional powers) or in a bipolar setting, as argued by Waltz (1979). Most realists argue that the balance of power system operates best in a multipolar setting, but several prominent realists have argued that the balance of power is more stable in a bipolar setting. Another debate among realists considers whether states always balance or whether at times they instead **bandwagon** (ally or join) with a stronger state (Schweller, 2006). Some realists argue that states make decisions at times to join with stronger states rather than to balance. A significant argument is that states do not balance against power; rather, they balance against threat (Walt, 1987).

Realism shares four general assumptions: power, states as primary actors, anarchy, and a balance of power. A power assumption is not the only factor that determines if a theory falls into the realist school of thought, but if a theory does not have power as an essential element, it will not be a realist theory. The following sections will provide some overview of the main approaches of realism.

Classical Realism

Classical realism is a variant of realism which developed over two and a half centuries ago. It can be traced to Thucydides, a Greek historian who wrote about the Peloponnesian War between the city states of Athens and Sparta. In his work *The Peloponnesian War* (1996), Thucydides laid out the fundamental themes that still exist today at the heart of realism. Ideas like the importance of power, the balance of power, and anarchy all show up within his writings, specifically in the section on the Melian Dialogue. Other classical realists would include Machiavelli and the philosopher Hobbes. Machiavelli (1961) is best known for his book *The Prince*, which uses many of the ideas laid out by Thucydides and expands on them. In his classic work *The Leviathan*, Hobbes (1996) explicitly addressed the anarchic system and the importance of power. Many realists argue that these core ideas have been important in the system since the beginning of human society and must be used to understand the ideas of conflict between states in the system.

More modern classical realists include E. H. Carr (1939), whose book *The Twenty Years' Crisis* directly lays out the difference between realist thought and utopian ideas. The book was written to explain the period between the two World Wars and shows the importance of the ideas laid out by the historic classical realists. The most important modern classical realist is Hans Morgenthau. Morgenthau was the first to mold classical realism into a mostly social scientific theory. His book *Politics Among Nations* (1948) was the core text for studies in international relations into the 1980s.

One element of classical realism that sets it apart from other variants of realism is that of normative assumptions, which are difficult to quantify. Thus, classical realism, while it is theoretical, cannot be used and tested in the same ways that we test more recent variants of realism because classical realism includes the normative assumptions that humans are evil or bad. This is a value judgement made by classical realists that allows the other variables to effectively operate and explain the system. Because humans are bad, they will take advantage of situations within the international system. Therefore, if one state is stronger than others, it makes sense if that state chooses to invade the weaker. The issue of values and human nature comprises important characteristics found in Morgenthau, Carr, Hobbes, Thucydides, and Machiavelli.

For classical realism, the level of analysis is normally at the state level, with a focus on foreign policy. It looks at the specifics within the state and argues that those specifics are important to understanding how and why the state acts the way it does and determines the choices it makes. States are believed to be making rational decisions, which means that they utilize a **cost-benefit analysis** to choose the option which they believe will offer them the highest reward at the lowest possible cost. However, states may not always get the best outcomes due to the fact that there exists unknown information or that it made a calculation which does not hold within the context of the international system.

Classical realism is foundational to understanding realism and future variants of the theory. In recent years, many scholars have returned to the classic realist writings to pull core ideas and themes which have seemed to hold for hundreds, if not thousands, of years in the international system.

Neorealism

Another variant of realism is based on the work of Kenneth Waltz, whose 1979 book *Theory of International Politics* is groundbreaking. In many ways, Waltz is responsible for moving realism from a theoretical framework with a normative basis into a social scientific theory. Waltz also shifted realism from focusing on the state level of analysis to focusing on the systemic level of analysis. Waltz is the foundational author for everything that comes after him in realism. Theorists in the realist tradition, therefore, must address the ideas that Waltz advanced, either to develop them further or to move away from them.

Waltz's (1979) approach is completely systemic and does not look at states as unique actors. His approach differentiates states only by their relative power, as they all pursue the same goal of survival. It focuses on the issues of anarchy as the ordering principle of the system and a state's focus on survival to understand why the system works the way it does. Waltz focuses on the stability of the bipolar system and the role of the balance of power in shaping the system. Unlike previous variants of the balance of power, which focused on the multipolar system, Waltz argues that a bipolar system is more stable, given the focus on the other great power. Waltz (1979) further argues that states are unitary rational actors who, within the anarchic system, must engage in self-help behavior with the primary goal of ensuring survival. Given the nature of the system, states cannot be assured that others will come to their defense, so they must address the relative power of other states in the system to be able to ensure their survival. Waltz does not focus on the foreign policy outcomes of individual states. According to Waltz, states will act using the balance of power to ensure survival before they engage in the pursuit of any other goals within the system. Waltz's formulation of neorealism in this way moved realism away from a normative approach that was at the heart of classical realism into the realm of explicit social science theory.

The one element that makes neorealism confusing is that researchers could refer to it by any of three names. The initial name applied to Waltz's theory was *neorealism* or new realism. This name then morphed, depending on who was writing about Waltz's work, into *structural realism*. The name structural realism comes from the fact that Waltz's theory is, as discussed above, entirely at the systemic level and argues that the structure of the system determines how states act. Neorealism and structural realism for many are interchangeable terms. The tag of *defensive realism* is more problematic in many ways and is of much more recent vintage. Defensive realism was coined by John Mearsheimer, the creator of offensive realism—a theory we will address below—and applied to Waltz's work retrospectively. The context of defensive realism argues that systemic theories in the realist tradition assume that states have a status quo bias and work to maintain the system rather than change it and so are defensive in nature; i.e., they defend the system. Waltz was, in this way, classified as a defensive realist two decades after he wrote *Theory of International Politics*. A number of academics and researchers explicitly work within the vein of defensive realism, arguing that numerous states do try to protect the status quo. Many authors today include Waltz within this classification but, as one may see in reading Waltz's book, it does not explicitly focus on the status quo as a driving element. The status quo bias was applied retrospectively by others and has been debated as to whether Waltz's approach actually follows this idea. Anyone interested in defensive realism—again, a more recent offshoot of neorealism—can search specifically for authors who work within that theoretical framework.

Offensive Realism

This variant of realism originates with John Mearsheimer (2001) and was published in his book *The Tragedy of Great Power Politics*. The foundation of offensive realism comes from Waltz's neorealism but with a couple of significant assumption changes. The assumptional changes that Mearsheimer implements create a much more aggressive form of realism, which is focused on great power dominance. Mearsheimer's approach is still systemic, but he applied certain assumptions about states that are very different from Waltz's. First and foremost, Mearsheimer assumes that states seek security rather than survival as their primary goal. According to Mearsheimer

(2001), achieving only survival is not enough; states must also seek complete security. The only way to become completely secure would be to achieve the position of the hegemonic state in the world. However, Mearsheimer argues that achieving world hegemony is almost impossible in the current system. States can achieve security most effectively by pursuing regional hegemony. Achieving regional hegemony will ensure a state's security within that region. To achieve the goal of security, then, states will seek to maximize their power within the system. Only through maximizing their power can a state potentially reach the level of regional hegemon.

Given the focus on maximization of power, offensive realism at times sees the balance of power system operating differently. Unlike Waltz (1979), who argues that states will balance against rising states, offensive realism argues that states may opt for bandwagoning—rather than balancing—with a rising power. Another option for a state looking to maximize its power may be passing the buck and letting others balance against a rising state in order to preserve its power. The assumption change from survival to security creates significant predictive differences in how a state will act, if viewed from a neorealist lens as compared to an offensive realist lens.

States in offensive realism are much more aggressive and seek power to revise the system in their interests. The core ideas of realism exist within offensive realism, but how they are applied is what makes this variant unique when looking at other versions of realism. The focus and drive for security, the primary goal of the state, and how states engage in the balance of power all work together to provide an explanation of the international system which other versions of realism do not provide.

Neoclassical Realism

This is the newest variant of realism, which was first coined by Rose in a 1998 review article. The first and most important thing to understand about this approach is that it crosses the levels of analysis.

Unlike the other recent realist variants, it is both a systemic and a state level theory. Its goal is to explain not the international system but the individual foreign policies of states in the system. This takes neoclassical realism back in many ways to classical realism for parts of it. Neoclassical realism argues that, in focusing on systemic level influences to understand the international system, realism has lost its ability to understand the actions of individual states, which was the focus of many of the authors of classical realism. The neoclassical approach consequently works to combine the systemic influences that are emphasized by Waltz and other more recent realists with state level concerns of classical realism. Some researchers argue that neoclassical realism is an evolution of neorealism; others argue it is a reaction to neorealism's going too far in making the states unitary actors (Ripsman, Taliaferro, & Lobell, 2016).

Neoclassical realism argues that the primary independent variable is relative material power, which is found at the systemic level of analysis. The outcome, or dependent variable, is the foreign policy actions of each individual state. However, there is no direct path between relative material power and the state's foreign policy. Neoclassical realists argue that relative material power is processed by the state apparatus to determine what foreign policy decisions are made (Rose, 1998). Each state provides a unique set of intervening variables through which the systemic influence is processed at the domestic level. Some of these intervening variables include the leader's image of the situation, the state's strategic culture, and its ability to connect with and receive support from the domestic society, among other elements (Ripsman, Taliaferro, & Lobell, 2016) Thus, the unique elements of a state will influence how a state will respond to systemic stimuli. Waltz (1979) could not explain why all states did not actually act in the ways expected, given systemic constraints. Opening up the black box of the state, however, allows for unique influences within each state to have an impact.

While neoclassical realism crosses levels of analysis, it still falls firmly into the realist school of thought. The core assumptions of power, anarchy, balance of power, and states as the primary actors still hold. Of all the variants of realism, this version has received a great deal of attention since the Rose (1998) article coined the term (Ripsman, Taliaferro, & Lobell 2016).

Game Theory and Prisoner's Dilemma

Realism as a grand theory relies on rational choice. In order to better understand rational choice, international relations theorists have adopted **game theory**. This approach was developed in mathematics and then applied to predicting outcomes in international relations. One of the most popular games is the **prisoner's dilemma**. In this game, rational players choose the outcome which they find beneficial in the short term, if they do not understand the benefits of cooperation. The best outcome for the two parties in discussion would be if they cooperated and got out with the least amount of punishment. However, they often choose noncooperation, hoping to gain the highest payout resulting in the betrayal of the other player.

Another game that is often mentioned in international relations is the chicken game. This is just what the name says: the old challenge between rivals. The first to "swerve" to avoid a clash is the loser, while the winner should be the one courageously continuing to drive forward. Unfortunately, a positive outcome can only happen if both players calculate the outcome and realize that cooperation alone can bring positive results. Often these "games" are explained as zero-sum or non-zero-sum outcomes. A **zero-sum game** is defined as a situation where the gain of one player is only possible if the other player loses. A **non-zero-sum game** occurs when it is possible for both players to gain smaller yet more achievable shared outcomes.

Realism is the first theoretical approach established in international relations and was dominant in the field for many centuries. More recently, this theory has been attacked by many in the field for its limited explanatory capacity. However, the ability of realism to address security issues maintains its important role among international relations theories with many authors working on more effectively explaining the impact of power, anarchy, states, and the balance of power on political outcomes.

References

Carr, E. H. (1939). *The twenty years' crisis: An introduction to the study of international relations*. St. Martins Press.

Elman, C., & Jensen, M. A. (2014). *Realism reader*. Routledge.

Gilpin, R. (1981). *War and change in world politics*. Cambridge University Press.

Hobbes, T. (1996). *Leviathan*. R. Tuck (Ed.). Cambridge University Press.

Holsti, O. R. (1995). Theories of international relations and foreign policy: Realism and its challengers. In C. W. Kegley, Jr. (Ed.), *Controversies in International Relations Theory: Realism and the Neoliberal Challenge*. St. Martins Press.

Keohane, R. (1986). *Neorealism and its critics*. Columbia University Press.

Machiavelli, N. (1961). *The prince*. Penguin Books.

Matthews, E. G., & Callaway, R. L. (2017). *International relations theory: A primer*. Oxford University Press.

Mearsheimer, J J. (2001). *The tragedy of great power politics*. W.W. Norton and Company.

Milner, H. (1991). The assumption of anarchy in international relations theory: A critique. *Review of International Studies, 17,* 67–85.

Morgenthau, H. J. (1948). *Politics among nations: The struggle for power and peace*. Knopf.

Organski, A. F. K. (1958). *World politics*. Knopf.

Ripsman, N. M., Taliaferro, J. W., & Lobell, S. E. (2016). *Neoclassical realist theory of international politics*. Oxford University Press.

Rose, G. (1998). Neoclassical realism and theories of foreign policy. *World politics, 51,* 144–172.

Singer, J. D. (1961). The level-of-analysis problem in international relations. *World politics, 14,* 77–92.

Schweller, R. L. (1998). *Deadly imbalances: Tripolarity and Hitler's strategy of world conquest.* Columbia University Press.

Schweller, R. L. (2006). *Unanswered threats: Political constraints on the balance of power.* Columbia University Press.

Thucydides. (1996). *The Peloponnesian War.* In Robert B. Stressler (Ed.), *The landmark Thucydides: A comprehensive guide to the Peloponnesian War.* Free Press.

Walt, S. M. (1987). *The origins of alliances.* Cornell University Press.

Waltz, K. N. (1979). *Theory of international politics.* McGraw-Hill.

Wendt, A. (1992). Anarchy is what states make of it: The social construction of power politics. *International Organization, 46,* 391–425.

Wohlforth, W. C. (1993). *The elusive balance: Power and perceptions during the Cold War.* Cornell University Press.

Liberalism and Alternatives to Power Politics

4

Dlynn Armstrong Williams

Abstract

This chapter will be separated into alternative explanations to realism. These theories will include liberalism, the English School, constructivism, and poststructuralism. Each of these theories approaches the interaction between state and non-state actors in a unique way. It is the viewpoint of those who challenged realism that the world is much more cooperative than what the realists envision. Upon examining their viewpoints of the system, we see opinions range from an arrangement built on norms and principles and international organizations bound together by trade, to a much more complex system constructed on shared values and priorities of states as well as global citizens. The field that was once confined to only explaining the actions of states was expanded to looking at non-state actors as well as threats to humanity rather than just threats to the ongoing survival of the state. This expansion allows us to look more deeply into environmental threats, globalization, and the growing influence of non-state actors in the system, which will be covered later in this text.

Learning Objectives

- Explain how the world perspective or paradigm sets the parameters of our understanding of global politics and changes how we view the international system

- Identify the influences of the major thinkers that form the foundations of classical liberalism, and the role of economic liberalism within overall liberal theory
- Examine the emergence of neoliberalism and the importance of regimes as well as soft and smart power in the continuance of the neoliberal world order championed by the United States
- Explore the role of constructivism and how it influences the behavior of actors within the international system

While **realism** provides one world view, this chapter discusses alternative explanations for what we see as the interactions between global actors beyond realism. These differing world views are often also referred to as **paradigms**. Paradigms are also referred to as a grand theory. A paradigm is a singular overarching theory which can provide a framework for the study of international relations.

This chapter discusses the basic alternative explanations to realism. These theories, as ordered below, include liberalism, the English School, constructivism, and poststructuralism. Each of these theories approaches the interaction between state and non-state actors in a unique way. It is often helpful to see theories as highlighting certain elements of world politics, each through their different lens. These highlights emphasize differing elements of human nature and put a stronger emphasis on particular elements of politics.

Liberalism

Liberalism began as a type of thought during the Enlightenment of the eighteenth century. During this era, philosophers began to examine the role of man as the center of the universe and man's ability to learn and have an impact on the world around them. Liberalism as a paradigm is really the threading together of various philosophical views of numerous philosophers explaining the nature of humankind and our place in the role of governance. Each of the philosophers helped shape many of the ideas that we take for granted as rights or privileges of individuals today. First and foremost, liberalism focuses on the importance of the freedom of the individual. M. W. Doyle outlines three sets of rights or freedoms which are the foundation of liberalism (1997, p. 207). These freedoms are freedom from arbitrary authority, which includes the freedom of speech and equality under the law; the freedom to promote capacity and opportunity, such as education, health care, and self-expression; and the right to democratic participation or representation. These freedoms, however, can only be truly enacted if they come from a shared global commitment to four essential institutions. These institutions include the following:

- Citizens must possess fundamental civic rights, such as freedom of religion and the press
- The sovereigns of a state must derive their authority from the consent of the electorate, and the state is not subject to external authority and remains sovereign
- The economy rests on a recognition of the rights of private property and individual acquisition or by social agreement
- Economic forces are predominantly shaped by forces of supply and demand and are free from strict governmental control

How did these overarching elements of liberalism become so foundational, and how do these elements affect how we view the world today? For answers, we need to examine briefly some of the earlier theorists and their contributions.

One of the earliest influences on this type of thought was Hugo Grotius. Grotius's work *On the Law of War and Peace* was originally published in 1625. At that time in history, the only entity possessing the right to wage war was the state. However, Grotius (1901) helps us understand the role of the state by providing us definitions of war *more solemn* and of war *less solemn* (p. 55–57). Grotius helps us determine that individual redress of a grievance, such as the war that breaks out between the families of the Montagues and Capulets in *Romeo and Juliet,* is not permissible in the international system. This less solemn type of war is no more than vigilante justice so has no place in statecraft. Instead, it is the formal war, or war more solemn, that is the role of states. The authority of the state, according to Grotius, should never be entrusted to individuals but instead to the laws of the state and the sovereign entrusted as its moral power (p. 61). This power is called **sovereign**, which means that the actions of the state are not subject to the control of any other power (p. 62). While this idea is foundational in our understanding of world politics today, during Grotius's time, this was somewhat revolutionary. This assertion allowed the authority of the state to stand apart from the church and to be legitimized through international law.

While Grotius helped us understand the foundations of sovereignty and international law through a liberal perspective, John Locke allowed us to see the liberal viewpoint of humanity. Locke stands in stark contrast to Thomas Hobbes and his vision of human nature that became so foundational to realism. Locke provides a much more cooperative viewpoint of the state of nature. In his work *Of Civil Government: Two Treatises,* originally published in 1689, Locke outlines a state of nature that provides perfect freedom for equality between people as well as the personal liberty for someone to make their own decisions about property (1924, p. 118–119). This individual freedom drives the individual to not only protect themselves but also do all they can to preserve the rest of humankind (p. 120). Locke's state of nature is, therefore, very cooperative. However, it is cooperation directly linked to self-preservation. The good of the individual becomes intrinsically linked to the good of the group.

As liberal theory continued to progress, the need to define exactly who that "group of humankind" was became critical to the theory. While Locke sees theory through the eye of the individual,

Immanuel Kant helps us view theory through the lens of both the domestic society and the interstate system (Doyle, 1997, p. 252–253). Kant focuses on building an understanding between states which are naturally in a state of war. However, Kant believes that, through the broadening of a **liberal pacific union**, we can bring about global peace. Kant argues that because of the inherent dangers found in the state of war, it is "necessary to establish a federation of peoples [to] protect one another against external aggression . . . [going beyond an] alliance which can be terminated at any time, so that it has to be renewed periodically" (Kant, 1970, p. 165). According to Kant, this alliance, or pacific union, should be made up of **republics**. A republic, according to Kant, is a state that provides for the legal equality of citizens on the basis of a representative government with a separation of powers (Doyle, 1997, p. 257). Kant's viewpoint is that these republics will then establish peace among themselves. They will become, therefore, a pacific union. Scholars and researchers often refer to this union today as the international community. In the context of Western republics, the international community represents those republics that stand together to condemn an action, such as a human rights violation which goes against the ideals of the democratic republics that Kant envisions. This Kantian argument was later tested in democratic peace theory. **Democratic peace theory** contends that democracies do not go to war with one another. Although empirical evidence seems to support this theory, this argument has limitations. While democratic states, or republics, do not go to war with one another, they will go to war with non-liberal or non-democratic states.

Kant also provided the foundations of cosmopolitan law (Kant, 1970, p. 106). This law sets the conditions of universal hospitality. This right allows for conditions to make it possible for the foreigner to be allowed the opportunity to enter into trade relationships with native inhabitants of a state (p. 106). The integration of trade into the foundations of a pacific union allows us to integrate economic liberalism into our overall understandings of liberalism. This three-part structure of the international system becomes foundational to all discussions of liberalism and is based on international organizations, economic cooperation, and an international community based on republics or states with democratic values. Doyle, in his work *Ways of War and Peace* (1997, p. 286–287), helps simplify Kant's three conditions which provide the foundations for ongoing peace. Kant outlines these conditions as the following:

- Representative, republican government (a government responsible to its citizens)
- A principled respect for non-discriminatory human rights (a commitment to respect the rights of fellow liberal republics)
- Social and economic interdependence (interdependence beyond simple military cooperation for security)

While liberal theorists focus on each of these elements which form the foundation of Kant's work, the free trade principles are foundational to economic liberalism. These principles are critical to the establishment of economic interdependence discussed by Doyle. **Economic liberalism** supports individual autonomy within the economy and the role of free trade for increased prosperity. The two individuals most associated with economic liberalism are Adam Smith and David Ricardo. Smith is best known for his text *An Inquiry into the Nature and Causes of the Wealth of Nations*, originally published in 1776. He advocates for free market exchange that will ensure the consumer is "led by an invisible hand to promote an end which was no part of his intention" (Smith, 1981, p. 443). This "invisible hand" of the market drives the economy, as each individual makes rational choices for their own betterment. Individuals are, therefore, free to make their own choices economically. In other words, the government should have limited interference in the market or should follow a **laissez-faire** policy. Laissez-faire refers to limited governmental involvement in the market.

Building upon the notion of a person's independence in the economic sphere as espoused by Smith, David Ricardo introduces the concept of **comparative advantage**. Ricardo outlines in his work *The Principles of Political Economy and Taxation*, first published in 1817, that states are most efficient when they produce goods in which they have an economic advantage and import goods where they do not have an economic advantage (2004, p. 70–72). In other words, the U.S. should produce commodities that are well suited to its climate or labor strengths, such as wheat, and then trade with another country, perhaps India, for rice, which is more suitable to India's climate and topography. For this reason, states should allow themselves to specialize in certain goods in which they are most efficient and trade for goods which they are less efficient in producing. However, this economic efficiency can only occur within a system that supports global trade without any taxes or extra costs imposed by states. This freedom to trade without taxation or barriers is known today as **free trade**. Free trade policies support a free and open market between states, which leads to further economic integration.

While the ideas surrounding liberalism and free markets were foundational to enlightenment thinking, World War I shifted the discussion away from the thought that peace was a natural condition. Following the horrific implications of the first global war, leading statesmen came to understand that peace had to be constructed and secured with international organizations. This peace would be based on the respect for human rights, which was foundational to classical liberalism, as well as the support for governments which were responsive to the needs and input from their citizens or the republics which were so foundational to Kant's ideas. President Woodrow Wilson led the call to codify these ideas through an international organization in his famous Fourteen Points speech to the U.S. Congress in 1918. Wilson advocated for a general association of nations to be formed. This association, the

League of Nations, supported concepts such as collective security. **Collective security** was an arrangement where "each state in the system accepts that the security of one is the concern of all, and agrees to join in a collective response to aggression" (Roberts & Kingsbury, 1993, p. 30). This new cooperative vision of the world system was quickly overturned by world events. While founded on liberal ideals, the League of Nations was soon overwhelmed with the political and economic realities of the rise of Hitler in Germany and the governing structure of the Soviet Union, which clearly placed it outside the Kantian community of republics.

While there were forces that impeded the implementation of the League of Nations framework, the desire for cooperation had not disappeared from the international system. In fact, liberals rethought cooperation and transitioned from the imposition of one strong international organization to the creation of numerous organizations and linkages between like-minded republics. In the wake of World War II, liberals pushed this concept of multifaceted cooperation that became known as **functionalism**. Functionalism, introduced by D. Mitrany (1943), argues that transnational cooperation can be used to solve shared concerns, and this cooperation between states can lead to further cooperation in the future. It is the foundation of functionalism that agreements in a very small area lead to further and further cooperation. This cooperation can become so valuable for both parties that it may even lead to integration between states. This integration also leads to increased cooperation, both within and beyond the states themselves. This type of cooperation is central to understanding liberalism.

The English School

Hedley Bull in his work *The Anarchical Society: The Study of Order in World Politics* (originally published in 1977) grapples with the evolving nature of the liberal pacific union first mentioned by Kant. Bull's work responded to a world that had changed significantly since the time of Kant and which had extended the concepts of the global community well beyond the selective club of European states that Kant first envisioned. Bull, whom scholars and researchers consider the founder of the English School of thought, tried to grapple with these changing realities—to the point that he considered himself a bridge between realist and liberal schools of thought. Bull's greatest contribution to the field is his creation of **world society**. World society refers to "the common interests and values of all mankind" (Bull, 278). These common interests of all people include economic and social justice concerns for all individuals (Bull, 1995, p. 279). These concerns include things such as human rights, humanitarian law, and protections for indigenous peoples (Dunne, Kurki, & Smith, 2010, p. 150). All of these liberal values now extend beyond those guaranteed by states. Rather, they have simply seeped into the collective consciousness of world society. These transnational values are a product of the environment in which further cooperation between states and individuals is valued and pursued.

Neoliberalism

While Bull was writing about the foundations of world society, others were also grappling with the liberal international system constructed at the end of World War II. The classic liberalism discussed by Kant was not sufficient to explain the complex realities and the increased number of participant states in the international system created in the wake of this war. While the structural realists focused on the increased chance for conflict in the system, neoliberals contended that international cooperation was much easier to achieve in this new system through the creation of international institutions. Robert Keohane in his work *After Hegemony* (1984) highlights the importance of cooperation in the system. He contends that cooperation occurs when "policies actually followed by one government are regarded by its partners as facilitating the realization of their own objectives" (Keohane, 1984, p. 51). Rather than deeming conflict as the "natural state" of being within the system, Keohane argues that neoliberal institutions can cause cooperation to become the most natural outcome of rational participants. This cooperation can occur between states, non-state actors, or any combination of actors within the system. This cooperation is predicated not on the moral characteristics of the actors but on the fact that they are "rational devils" and that cooperation best serves the interests of all. Neoliberals share the Enlightenment viewpoint of other liberal thinkers, that it is possible for humanity to progress to promote freedom, democratization, and prosperity.

One of the most foundational and transitional works in neoliberal theory is *Power and Interdependence* (originally published in 1977), written by Robert Keohane and Joseph Nye. This work cedes realism's foundational view that the international system is anarchic and full of self-interested actors. Within this system, however, cooperation is often more rational than non-cooperation. Cooperation, therefore, can be a natural result of the system if institutions can be built that will support and facilitate this cooperation. Indeed, neoliberals view these realist (and neorealist) premises—that actors within the system are self-interested and that anarchy is the given state of the system—as an opportunity for institutions. Cooperation occurs in the form of a **regime.** Ruggie (1982) defines international regimes as the social institutions around which actor expectations converge in a given area of international relations (p. 380). As Ruggie states, international regimes consist of principles, norms, rules, and procedures. These norms and rules, if supported strongly by the community of states, can be further developed into an international organization. However, not all regimes become international organizations, and they are just as valuable in facilitating cooperative behavior among states.

The neoliberal view of cooperation in the system is linked to historical and technological changes which pushed states toward cooperation. These arrangements focus at the system level on the interdependence of states. This interdependence is a type of mutual dependence system where the interests and concerns of states are intertwined. Through a growing and deepening web of both political and economic interaction, states increasingly view a threat to overall stability in any state as costly to their own interests. This mutual dependence has a pacifying impact on the international system. Keohane explains in his work *After Hegemony* (1984) that even after the decline of U.S. dominance in the world, there will remain a strategic incentive for states to continue to cooperate within the international organizations and regimes constructed by U.S. dominance. The support of these structures provides the stability states need in order to prosper economically and politically, which in turn structures future cooperation (p. 215). Regimes do not disappear; rather, they transform.

The question for many neoliberals then becomes how this cooperation can be structured to continue. What incentives can be placed into the system to increase the chances for enhanced and continual cooperation? One of the greatest challenges to cooperation is the power of defection. Individuals and states defect from agreements if they feel that they can get a better deal elsewhere— or if they fear that the other state or entities may "cheat" in some way. This fear can cause states to defect or stop cooperating rather than be left "holding the bag" when cheated. The goal, therefore, is to try to find strategies to increase the chances for ongoing cooperation. Robert Axelrod in *The Evolution of Cooperation* (1984, p. 134–147) provides strategies that can help create conditions where cooperation can flourish even in an anarchic environment. He outlines the following strategic actions:

- Enlarge the shadow of the future
- Change the payoffs
- Teach people to care about each other
- Teach reciprocity
- Improve recognition abilities

In order to enlarge the shadow of the future, the actor must realize that they will need to interact with the other actor again in the future. The more ongoing and continuous this engagement, the more likely both actors will be to cooperate more. For example, if you go to your favorite restaurant and your server, Aliah, gets your order wrong, you will most likely continue to come back to that restaurant. You might determine that Aliah is having a tough day or that you would like to continue to go to this restaurant because it is convenient to your job. However, if you are at a restaurant while on vacation and so are unlikely to return, it is much easier to sever this relationship and never return if the server brings you the wrong order. Actors in the international system act similarly. If they know that they will need to cooperate in the future again, they will tend to be more cooperative. In fact, the more frequent and durable the interactions, the more likely cooperation will be successful (p. 129).

The second successful strategy to enhance cooperation is to change the payoffs for cooperation (p. 133). In the attempt to encourage cooperation, you can either increase the benefits for further cooperation or increase the punishments for a lack of cooperation. For example, if your professor would like you to attend an event, they can either offer you extra credit for your attendance (increasing the benefits of your attendance), or they can count the event as a regular class and doc your participation grade for lack of attendance (increase punishment). States can use similar strategies. States can enact sanctions for a lack of cooperation with international norms, or they can incentivize cooperation with grants, aid, or more open trade policies. The purpose of both tactics is to increase the target's desire to cooperate.

Axelrod's third discussed strategy is to teach people to care about each other. He bases this strategy on the concept of altruism, which is the utility of one person's being positively impacted by another person's welfare (p. 135). Altruism between individuals or states can be taught and reinforced. This strategy, however, can be reinforced by what Axelrod introduced as the fourth strategy, which is to teach reciprocity to all participants. Reciprocity is often seen as tit for tat and quid pro quo. The strategy of "if you do something to benefit me, then I will do something to benefit you" is **specific reciprocity**. Two participants assist each other but only in equal measure. However, the more effective system is one of **diffuse reciprocity**. This is when a community of individuals or states creates an environment where cooperation is expected. In your classroom, for example, a student, Irina, comes to class without a pen. If the student next to her, Carlos, lends her a pen, he exhibits altruistic behavior. However, if Carlos comes to class in a few days without a pen and expects only Irina to assist him, then reciprocity is specific. If, however, Irina does not have an extra pen on that particular day, most often another classmate will step in and help. This behavior exemplifies diffuse reciprocity. The environment of the class is one that leads to cooperation between all members rather than just between those who have benefitted in the past or those who have benefitted from a particular transaction.

The final strategy Axelrod discusses is for the participants to recognize the relevant and previous interactions between themselves and other participants (p. 139–140). This knowledge of past behaviors can build trust and eliminate the misinterpretation of signals from other actors that can lead to conflict. For example, if you have enough interactions with your best friend, when you suggest a burger place downtown for lunch and they say "that would be fine," then you know from those previous interactions whether that choice is actually fine or instead an undesirable lunch location.

While Axelrod highlights the construction of interaction between partners that can lead to success, Joseph Nye in his work *The Future of Power* (2011) focuses on strategies that will support the continuance of the liberal system based on liberal values. Nye focuses on the role of the U.S. in continuing the liberal world order through the exercise of several types of power. He views power as multidimensional and broadens our discussions of power into the realm of soft and smart power. Nye defines **soft power** as the second aspect of power. It is the type of power that "occurs when one country gets other countries to want what it wants" (1990, p. 166). This type of power stands in contrast to "hard or command power of ordering others to do what it wants" (Nye, 1990, p. 166). Nye contends that to assess the effectiveness of soft power, we must understand the basic resources upon which it depends. Soft power depends on a state's culture (in places where it is attractive to others), political values (when it lives up to them at home and abroad), and its foreign policy (when others see them as legitimate and holding moral authority) (Nye, 2001, p. 84). Importantly, in addition to his discussions of soft power, Nye also coined the phrase **smart power**. Smart power is the ability to combine soft and **hard power** resources into effective strategies (Nye, 2004, p. 32). Nye's definitions of power, along with his desire for a continuance of the liberal world order espoused by the U.S., places his work squarely in line with liberalism. Nye discusses the importance of the continuance of international organizations and other structures that can assure the perpetuation of the soft power influences of the U.S.

Beyond liberalism, we must ask why the concept of a liberal world order is desirable. What elements created that world order? Why is the Kantian vision of a community of states the way that the international system should be organized? These questions lead us to yet another paradigm, or perspective in international relations theory, and that is constructivism.

Constructivism and Poststructuralism

Constructivism sees international relations as a social construction. In other words, constructivists perceive a difference as existing across contexts and perspectives so that we do not share a single objective reality. Have you ever been in a situation where you thought that an interaction was very positive, but the other individual thought, "I wonder what their problem is?" How could the two of you have such differing perspectives of the situation? The main reason for this disconnect is that both parties are not viewing reality the same way. For example, the U.S. could see an action taken by Iran as highly aggressive, while the Iranians might see that same action as being provoked and entirely of a defensive nature.

Constructivists also highlight the social dimensions of the international system. They share with liberalism an interest in norms, rules, and the language of the world of international relations. The emphasis on particular norms or values depends on the perspective of the state or international relations scholar at the time. The state can choose to focus on a strict definition of sovereignty if, for example, they do not want other states to influence their domestic politics. However, that same state could counter that strict definition of sovereignty if they feel the human rights of citizens within another state are threatened.

The challenge for constructivism focuses on the interaction between the individual or state and the social construction of the international system. For example, what does it mean for a state to be a rational actor? Constructivists discuss what makes the action of the state or individual acceptable socially. Two differing elements often guide individuals and states: the **logic of consequences** and the **logic of appropriateness.** According to the logic of consequences, a state will take any action needed that will maximize its interests. For instance, the logic of consequences occurs when you resist stealing a loaf of bread even if you are hungry to avoid the high level of punishment you would endure for that theft. If stealing the bread would lead to long imprisonment time, then you would not steal. In terms of the state, if a war projected to incur an acceptable level of casualties will achieve the state's goals, then the state will decide to go to war. However, with **the logic of appropriateness**, the question is different. The question becomes, is it appropriate to steal the bread in this situation? Will my stealing the bread save my child's life? Will the international community support the U.S. interests in going to war? The question thus becomes, do my actions fall within the shared values of the group? If the answer is yes, then military action or stealing could be deemed appropriate.

Constructivists then also consider how the individual or the state crafts a social construction. The social construction of the international system is mutually achieved by the individuals, states, and non-state actors within the system. "We" agree upon concepts such as sovereignty, power, cooperation, force, and trade. Because we agree upon these concepts and we agree upon their meanings, these concepts now have meaning and value for all of us. For a constructivist, our interests are determined not by our actions but by our **identity**, that is, by how we identify ourselves. Identity can be a tricky thing for both states and individuals. For example, if being a University of Georgia (UGA) fan is part of your identity, then do you automatically view the Georgia Institute of Technology (GA Tech) and the University of Alabama as rivals? Does your identity keep you from attending Alabama, even though they offer you a $25,000 scholarship? How deeply does your definition of identity go? States are somewhat similar. Does the U.S. always see itself as having a special relationship with the UK? Will that relationship continue even long after the economic, political, and cultural ties dwindle between those two states?

Identity is developed over time through mutual interactions between states or players in the system. For example, how did you become a UGA football fan in the first place? Were you influenced by family, friends, or others? Did you buy merchandise, like t-shirts or keychains, to further broadcast that identity? Are your earliest memories fishing with a UGA fishing pole? Do those memories of UGA blend with your concepts of being a good son or daughter? In the same way, states have shared histories. Alliances between states develop over time, and they build upon shared histories and common enemies. These identities can cause states to see other states as natural allies or natural enemies.

A. Wendt (1992) explains in his article "Anarchy is What States Make of It" that states and individuals have agency. Therefore, individuals and states can influence the system as well as be influenced by it. In many ways, states have the choice to see others' actions as aggressive or premeditated. However, this choice must be mutually constituted. For example, the U.S. could view itself as the dominant power in Europe, but if this perception is not widely supported or shared by other European states, then it is not a mutually-constructed reality. Consequently, it does not have the same degree of validity as would something shared between states. My perception; my reality.

Researchers continue to disagree on whether constructivism is a theory or an approach. However, in general, researchers and scholars see constructivism as a middle ground between rational theories, such as realism and liberalism, and **poststructuralist theories**. Poststructuralist theories differ from constructivism in that, within poststructuralism, the states and individuals do not have agency. This view means you would have been socialized so that your only choice is to be a UGA football fan; it would be unthinkable to be something else. Even the concept that there were other possibilities, such as Alabama or GA Tech, would be simply inconceivable. Poststructuralism, then, is when the states and individuals in the system just accept the structures of the system as "natural" or unchangeable.

Each of the paradigms or world views discussed in this chapter helps the student understand the perspective from which an international issue can be addressed. Consider how different an analysis of China's aggression in the South China Sea might look through each of the perspectives discussed above. The student of international politics must ask several questions: Is China a part of the group of Kantian republics? If not, how does that impact our expectations? Is the real threat to our shared "construct" on how states should act? Is the international system one that was mutually constructed with China's input, or was it imposed upon them as the "natural" state of things? The purpose of this chapter is for students to begin to broaden their understanding of international politics, including realism, but also extend their understanding to other theories that include elements of reciprocity and identity in our understanding of global politics. As we navigate these global problems together, it is critical that we understand the perspectives of the other players so that we can forge joint solutions even in an environment of anarchy and endless challenges.

References

Axelrod, R. M. (1984). *The evolution of cooperation*. New York: Basic Books.

Bull, H. (1995). *The anarchical society: A study of order in world politics* (2nd ed). New York: Columbia University Press.

Doyle, M. W. (1997). *Ways of war and peace: Realism, liberalism, and socialism* (1st ed). New York: Norton.

Dunne, T., Kurki, M., & Smith, S. (Eds.). (2010). *International relations theories: Discipline and diversity* (2nd ed). New York: Oxford University Press.

Grotius, H., & Tuck, R. (2005). *The rights of war and peace*. Indianapolis, Ind: Liberty Fund.

Kant, I. (1970). *Kant's political writings*. Hans Reiss (Ed.). Translated by H. B. Nisbet. Cambridge, England: Cambridge University Press.

Keohane, R. O. (1984). *After hegemony: Cooperation and discord in the world political economy*. Princeton, NJ: Princeton University Press.

Keohane, R. O., & Nye, J. S. (2012). *Power and interdependence* (4th ed). Boston: Longman.

Locke, J. (1924). *Of civil government: Two treatises*. London, England: J. M. Dent & Sons, LTD.

Mitrany, D. (1943). *A working peace system*. London: RIIA.

Nye, J. S. (1990). Soft power. *Foreign Policy*, (80), 153–171. https://doi.org/10.2307/1148580

Nye, J. S. (2004). *Soft power: The means to success in world politics* (1st ed). New York: Public Affairs.

Nye, J. S. (2011). *The future of power* (1st ed). New York: PublicAffairs.

Ricardo, D., & Kolthammer, F. W. (2004). *The principles of political economy and taxation*. Mineola, N.Y: Dover Publications.

Roberts, A., & Kingsbury, B. (1993). Introduction: The UN's roles in international society since 1945. In A. Roberts and B. Kingsbury (Eds.), *United nations, divided world*. Oxford: Clarendon Press.

Ruggie, J. G. (1982). International regimes, transactions, and change: Embedded liberalism in the postwar economic order. *International Organization, 36*(2), 379–415.

Smith, A. (1981). *Wealth of nations*. R. H. Campbell and A. S. Skinner (Eds.). Oxford: Oxford University Press.

The philosophy of Kant: Immanuel Kant's moral and political writings. (1949).

Wendt, A. (1992, Spring). Anarchy is what states make of it: The social construction of power politics. *International Organization, 46*(2), 391–425.

Wendt, A. (1999). *Social theory of international politics*. Cambridge, UK; New York: Cambridge University Press.

Wendt, A. (2006). *Constructivism and International Relations*.

Williams, P., Goldstein, D. M., & Shafritz, J. M. (Eds.). (2006). *Classic readings and contemporary debates in international relations* (3rd ed). Belmont, CA: Thomson Wadsworth.

Social and Gender Theories

5

Dlynn Armstrong Williams

Abstract

As international relations theory evolved, critical theories emerged. These theories questioned the foundational assumptions set out by both the realist and liberal thinkers. These critical theories asked if the real structures of power were housed in states or if there were other constructs, such as economic class or gender, that drive our understandings of world politics. While there are many critical theories, the most dominant of these theories are Marxism and feminism. These theories question the underlying assumptions of international relations and force the student to examine the ability for states to truly make rational, objective decisions. The role of critical theory is not necessarily to offer another theoretical perspective but rather to ask us to question the theoretical assumptions of the foundational theories of realism, liberalism, and constructivism. The purpose of this chapter is to explore these criticisms and to expand our understandings of international relations. Critical theory pushes our discussions of international relations into the realm of economics, social constructs, and gender. This expansion helps us understand the impact of these elements on the international system and adds a level of complexity that could not be found through the use of previous theories.

Learning Objectives

- Identify the role of critical theory within international relations
- Understand the influences of the major thinkers which form the basis of a Marxist approach to international relations theory
- Evaluate the impact of feminist interpretations of international relations theory and different strains of thought within feminism

Social and gender theories are often lumped together into the term critical theories. These approaches contend with the fundamental assumptions of **realism** and **liberalism**. While both realism and liberalism see a world based on the rational self-interest of actors within the system, social and gender theories question these concepts of rationality as well as the basis of the self-interest argument. Social and gender theories ask the students of global politics to imagine a different set of assumptions about the state and the system. These other assumptions could provide a stronger explanation for how we understand struggles for power and control.

Chapter 4 discussed the basic outlines of the **constructivist** approach. This chapter examines theories that question our understandings of that construction. The first critical theory that focuses on society rather than on the state is **Marxism**. This chapter discusses the impact of Marxism on how we understand the international system and how Marxism evolved from a domestic theory to one that is used to explain the structure of global power. Marxism originates from the work of the nineteenth century German philosophers, Karl Marx and Friedrich Engels. In addition, this chapter also examines **feminist theory**. Within international relations, feminist theory attempts to broaden our understanding of state actors and the subjects that we should study that fall under the umbrella of global politics. Feminists broaden the inquiry within the field to areas previously unexplored in international relations, such as the autonomy of "political man" so often discussed by the realists.

Marxism

Marxism views the development of political and social structures within a historical context. This viewpoint differs greatly from the early work of those who favored a movement away from a state-controlled economy to one that placed the authority in the hands of individuals. In our discussion in Chapter 4, you might remember the importance of Adam Smith in the development of liberal economics. Adam Smith focused on the importance of individuals through their creative abilities being active participants in a vibrant and free market. The individual's talents, strengths, or tenacity would allow them to achieve their full creative and economic potential if they were permitted to freely engage within the market, and the market would determine the value of their work. In this view, individuals are almost hard-wired to be self-interested. Their personal drive leads to their success. While Smith sees individuals as economic generators, Marx views individuals as more multifaceted. Marx views individuals economically and as social beings, as well as agents that can shape and reshape social institutions and structures.

The question then becomes, how do human beings change both politically and economically? For Marx, this development is a relational process; that is, individuals evolve their political and economic ideas through the process of a dialectic. A **dialectic** is the science that explains the general evolution of human nature, human society, and thought (Heinrich, 2012, p. 37). Inherent in a dialectic is the role of contradictions. For example, I might enter into a conversation in which I believe the best band of all time is the Beatles. You would disagree with me and provide counterevidence regarding why your favorite band, Led Zeppelin, is the best of all time. Through our discussion (conflict), my understanding of music would deepen as would yours, and I might contend that your band had a better guitarist or had stronger performances at live shows, while you might agree that the Beatles were stronger in the studio and had a deeper cultural influence for their time. Through our dialectical discussion, both of our understandings of music would evolve and deepen. We would become more informed.

Imagine ongoing dialectical opportunities in which we interacted and talked about music every day for five years. After five years, we would have perhaps developed into experts on the music of both eras. For Marx, it is through these repeated social interactions that both individuals and societies change. This process-oriented approach for understanding starts to allow societies to even change the basic definitions of social and political institutions. For example, our conversations about the best band ever could evolve our understandings of what a band is or what instruments are. In our discussion, synthesizers, sound effects, or even household implements such as spoons could be redefined as instruments. In this same way, Marx felt that through dialectics, human society could evolve beyond the institutions of capitalism and the individualism that forms the foundations of our viewpoints of the international system.

Marx is best known for his critique of capitalism. Capitalism was a structure that was imposed on society due to the need of the individual to sell their labor on the open market. While Smith viewed this individual autonomy over their labor as freeing, Marx saw this as trapping individuals within a system in which they were compelled to sell their labor to those who owned capital in order to be able to provide for themselves and their families. For Marx, those who were forced to sell their labor were the **proletariat**, or wage dependent workers (Heinrich, p. 14). In contrast, those who owned capital or were the propertied class were known as the **bourgeoisie** (Heinrich, p. 14). For Marx, the relationship between these two classes was fraught with exploitation. While the proletariat class performed the majority of the labor, the bourgeoisie class gained the majority of the wealth. Marx viewed the individual's use of their personal labor as both freeing and constraining. While the proletariat was free to increase their skills and generate more income, they always found that they spent most of their time working for their own survival; therefore, they did not have the time or energy to join together to get more of the **surplus value** that their work generated for the bourgeoisie. Surplus value was the money generated by the worker beyond what they earned in wages (Foley, 1986, p. 49). Due to this reason, workers did not develop a **class consciousness** and rebel against the system. Class consciousness indicates that workers develop an understanding that they are part of the proletariat and their allegiance should be to that social class.

For Marxists, individuals see the capitalist system as natural, necessary, and universal. They cannot imagine that society could produce another structure. Because they cannot imagine change, they give up their own personal power and give into the capitalist structures that support their daily life. Additionally, capitalism by its very nature is exploitative. The only way for capitalism to grow is to continue to increase the surplus value created by labor for increased profits for the owners of capital. The capitalist class harnesses the use of social pressure to keep workers in a position to be continually exploited. The social influencers in society measure success by wealth, property, and other economic means. For the Marxist, capitalism then becomes much more than simply an economic process. It is also part of the social structure of society and the state. As someone with a retirement account, for example, you are now part of the system that wants stability, ever increasing rates of return, and the continuation of economic growth. Capitalism becomes an overarching social theory that confines our understanding of politics and human agency.

From Marxism to Imperialism and World Systems Theory

Classical Marxism was focused predominantly on class conflict that could expand beyond the borders of the state. The strain between the proletariat and the bourgeoisie within the state could boil over into class conflict and could then cause this conflict to be picked up across state lines and form a type of global revolution, but the start of the conflict would be domestic. Classical Marxism pushes the concept of economic determinism. **Economic determinism** posits that the economic structure of a system determines all other elements of political and social life. It wasn't until the 1970s that international relations theorists emerged to push Marxist theories into the international realm. Immanuel Wallerstein, in his work *The Modern World System* (1974), started to view capitalism as a system, an overarching global phenomena, with its own structure. Wallerstein, the father of the world systems theory, shared with Marx the view that capitalist society was based on exploitation. However, Wallerstein saw this exploitation on a more global scale. Within Wallerstein's viewpoint, the world was not divided into the proletariat as a global working class and the bourgeoisie as a global capital owning class; rather, states took on these identities. He saw a global division of labor where the core (wealthy, developed states such as the U.S. and Europe) controlled the research and development and held the capital within the system (Wallerstein, p. 63). The semi-periphery (developing countries) held manufacturing and could act as markets for finished goods (Wallerstein, p. 63). And finally, the periphery (lesser developed countries) provided raw materials to the system for a low cost and provided markets for finished goods (Wallerstein, p. 63). In effect, Wallerstein's theory took the traditional Marxist concept of exploitation and placed it on a global scale. Similar to Marx's viewpoints of the bourgeoisie protecting the capitalist system, Wallerstein views states in the core as perpetuating the system of exploitation and doing all that they could to assure that European states or allies could not "fall out of" the core. A critical element of the world systems argument is that states within the core are only advanced and wealthy because they were able to exploit the other states within the system (Hobson, 2000, p. 136).

How did these core states become strong through exploitation? From a Marxist perspective, the answer is colonialization and imperialism. Initially through colonialization, where resources were forcibly removed from the periphery, and later through imperialism, where resources were removed at an extraordinarily low cost, core states slowly built their wealth and influence throughout the world. In fact, Vladimir Lenin articulated the idea that this reliance of the core, or the West, on low cost materials and labor draws it into conflict. In his pamphlet, *Imperialism: The Highest Stage of Capitalism* (originally published in 1916), Lenin attempts to produce an account of war that is driven by capitalist exploitation. Lenin's **imperialist theory of war** contends that strong capitalist states need markets for their goods and that domestic markets in these countries are "over-ripe" (Lenin, 1939, p. 58). In other words, wealthy states need the markets of developing countries to purchase goods. Lenin contends that capitalist states need to go to war to protect the interests of the capitalist class. They need to make sure that the lesser-developed states remain open to buying their goods and the source of low-cost efficient labor. They also need to ensure that these states continue to be exploited for the betterment of the capitalist state. If the lesser developed country in the periphery or semi-periphery rebels, increases the compensation for their workers, or destabilizes what we would refer to today as the "supply chain" of goods and services, then strong capitalist states will go to war with these countries to assure the stable flow of low-cost goods and labor.

Feminism Within International Relations and Critical Theory

While Marxists highlighted the fact that realism and liberalism did not take into account the strong role of the economy as a determinant of both political and societal relations, feminism contended that both of these theories similarly ignored gender. Feminists contend that if we viewed the world through a gendered lens, we would see international politics quite differently (Peterson & Runyan, 2015, p. 6). Feminism tends to be categorized into three different groups: **liberal feminism, difference feminism, and poststructural (postmodern) feminism**. Liberal feminism emerged out of a long historical tradition of feminism and sees all human beings, male or female, as rational, isolated individuals with no necessary connection to one another (Tickner, 2001, p. 12). Liberal feminists contend that whereas men have been judged based on their individual merit, women have been judged as a group, and only in a society where the legal barriers to women are removed can they then move forward to full equality (Tickner, 2001, p. 13).

Liberal feminists are often referred to as "same" feminists. If you can treat men and women as the same, then the gender differences between men and women are trivial or non-existent. *Difference feminists* come out of a more sociological perspective. Rather than women aspiring to be equal to men, they should celebrate the unique virtues of women that have been devalued in patriarchal societies (Tickner, 2001, p. 14). These unique qualities should then form the foundation of a different way of understanding international politics. *Socialist feminists* focus their work on the interactions between men's control of the labor power of women and issues surrounding the removal of women from the public sphere of paid work and into the private sphere of caretaking of the young and elderly which, in general, receives no economic compensation (Tickner, 2001, p. 16).

Poststructural (postmodern) feminists focus on gender as a source of power and hierarchy in order to understand how we shift from "words" and "understandings" to actual power relationships (Tickner, 2001, p. 19). In other words, have you ever heard of the phrase, "You throw like a girl"? Is that a compliment? More likely than not, when you heard that phrase, you envisioned a ball headed straight into the ground and not making its target. In this way, the phrase "you throw like a girl" comprises a group of words that have a greater understanding. The understanding is that you have a weak arm or that the throw is weak and you are not that athletic. In a similar way, postmodern feminism looks for the meanings that underlie our words in such phrases as "not-electable" and doesn't have "the makings to be commander-in-chief." Words take on meanings that then underlie gendered understandings for the post-modernist feminist.

For a difference feminist, gender is a social construct that defines "proper" behavior for both men and women. Men are often associated with strength, charisma, rationality, independence, protection, war, and the public sphere, while women are associated with weakness, the need for protection, emotionality, and the private sphere. These underlying assumptions linked to gender have caused political science and, in particular, the study of power, war, and force to be considered under the dominion of men. While Western symbolism has viewed the qualities of unity, stability, identity, and self-mastery as masculine, these qualities have contrasted with those we see as feminine, which are seen as spontaneity, multiplicity, and the loss of self (Peterson, 1992, p. 13). Feminists view that these factors, which have become so embedded into realist thinking, have caused realists to define a world from a completely masculine perspective.

J. Ann Tickner, in her ground-breaking article "Hans Morgenthau's Principles of Political Realism: A Feminist Reformulation" (1988), directly challenged the foundational concepts of realism and its limitations in understanding the feminist viewpoint. First, while Morgenthau views power as control of man over man—which is considered an agreed-upon definition of power by realists—

Tickner points out that this is inherently masculine. Consequently, rarely have women been able to exercise legitimate power in the public domain (p. 434). However, feminists agree upon a different definition of power. They view power not as control but as mutual empowerment or the ability to act in concert, or in connection, with others who share similar concerns (Arendt, 1970, p. 44).

Second, in terms of an objective reality—which is also foundational to realist thought—feminism introduced the concept that objectivity is really culturally defined. In fact, the "objective" laws of human nature are, in fact, based on the masculine view of human nature. Feminists argue that there needs to be room for a dynamic objectivity based more on the concept of actual objectivity than on cultural or political domination (Tickner, 1988, p. 437).

Third, the feminist perspective believes that national interest is multidimensional and cannot be defined solely in terms of power (Tickner, p. 438). In the current international system, states are often more successful seeking out cooperative solutions to deal with issues such as nuclear war, economic well-being, or environmental degradation (Tickner, p. 438).

Fourth, feminism contends that it is impossible to separate moral command from political action (Tickner, p. 438). This means that it is impossible for the feminist to take a political action without taking into account the moral impact of that political action. While the realists see the international political realm as an area of amorality (simply without morality), the feminists see morality embedded into all political decision making. To ignore a famine in a state or a major health emergency is just as much a moral decision as is the decision to get involved or the decision to send troops to war.

Fifth, feminism asserts that because there is morality in politics, it is possible to find common moral ground across a variety of cultures and perspectives (Tickner, p. 438). This quest for common moral ground is then seen as an area for cooperation rather than an area for the continuance of conflict. Finally, while the realists see "political man" as autonomous, meaning that our political selves are not necessarily integrated with the other elements of self, feminists see a world that brings together the concerns of both women and men and views the political realm as a much broader and more inclusive place (Tickner, p. 248).

The broader question remains. What is the role of women in both war and peace? Jodi York, in her article "The Truths(s) about Woman and Peace," examines the emphasis in Western culture between "women's peace" and "men's war" (1996, p. 323). In Western tradition, war was antithetical to women's natural or biological role of bearing and nurturing children or "feminine" traits such as cooperation, caring, and nurturing, which were seen as superior to male values of dominance and violence (York, p. 323). Therefore, peace can be attained through the revaluation of feminine traits. This emphasis on feminine traits would lead to a decline of war and violence. Women, therefore, are seen as the virtuous moral guides for their children and, as such, take on the need to defend their children and advocate for peace (York, p. 324).

Difference feminists contend that this very construct of women as nurturers helps utilize them in the larger narrative of war. In fact, the role women play as the protectors of moral virtue in particular fits well with the western concept of **just war**. Just war is an attempt to distinguish between legitimate and illegitimate violence in the international system (Elshtain, 1985, p. 44). War, according to St. Augustine, may be just if it is waged in defense of a common good and to protect the innocent from death (Elshtain, p. 44). In the construct of just war, men are constituted as Christian warriors, fighters, and defenders of righteous causes, while women fall into the category of culturally-sanctioned virtuous, non-violent womanhood (Elshtain, p. 45). Women cannot put a stop to suffering and cannot effectively fight. She therefore becomes the weeper, the occasion for war, and the keeper of the flame of non-violence (Elshtain, p. 45). Difference feminists contend that in order to break this narrative leading to the justification of war, we need to question the very premise of the argument. Is it even possible to protect women in war? Are they in need of protection? Should they be used for the justification for the war that a state would like to pursue? As we look at the dilemma of nuclear weapons, which can be aimed at a major city with the push of a button, is there really a "home front" where women and children are safe?

The answer for feminists is that there is no safe space, so women should no longer be utilized as the constructed "innocent" in order to justify military action. Instead, women should be seen as citizens within the state which often becomes combatant out of desire or necessity in support of state goals. Our "war stories" should then glorify the acts of not only men in battle but also women who contribute to state goals.

Feminists also expanded notions of security. In comparison to realism, which focuses on the security of the state, feminism in particular focuses on the security of individuals within the state as well as on the victimization of individuals due to actions of the state or societal constructs supported by the state. Feminists added to the discussion of security the concept of structural violence. **Structural violence** is a term used to "denote the economic insecurity of individuals whose life expectancy was reduced not by the direct violence of war, but by domestic and international structures of political and economic oppression" (Tickner, 1992, p. 69). Since Tickner's initial work, others have also highlighted the role of structural violence. V. Spike Peterson adds to the discussion of security and structural violence by identifying that such violence is not considered a matter of importance by security scholars (Peterson, 1992, p. 49). The major question that the scholar and student of international relations must ask is, "how has the systematic exploitation and degradation of human lives . . . become so acceptable, so apolitical, so natural" (Peterson, p. 49). Peterson questions the need to protect women as a type of protection racket. Protection leads to the structural dependency of women on the protection of men, which forces women to cede their own agency and control of future change. Through their laws and policies, states then codify this "protection" into laws which make the decisions regarding women's access to education, bank accounts, and work opportunities in the public sphere. These activities then might require that women have the permission of the men in their lives.

Individual women then buy into these systems in many ways. Women might make the "rational" choice to accept the protection because without it, they might feel that they cannot generate their own income or that they will face strong cultural and societal punishment if they act on their own outside the protection of men (Peterson, p. 51). Secondly, the perpetuation of structural violence depends on the decentralization of women within the security arrangement (Peterson, p. 52). Women cannot see themselves as sharing a collective interest in that they can join together and assure their own security. They must continue to see the system as one in which women must compete or fight to assure the security that can only be provided for them by men in the system. For example, if a woman's access to education depends on the support for said access to that education by her husband, father, or uncle, then that woman would concentrate all her energies on these men to assure her being allowed access to the education she desires. She would, therefore, redirect her energies which otherwise could be used to form a women's interest group to push for collective access to educational opportunities. If men hold the keys to power in the system, then women have essentially allowed men to control the "rules of the game" regarding economic, political, cultural, and social power.

The third element of this type of protection system, according to Peterson, is the ability to obscure accountability of protectees for maintaining boundaries (p. 52). Many actions then can be taken for "women's own good," wherein the women have no input in the decision-making process. Decisions can be made regarding child rearing, reproduction, and a variety of topics which have the implied consent of the protected because of the assumption that men are acting in women's interest. Finally, Petersen states that "while we can acknowledge the structural asymmetry of protection rackets, we cannot ignore the reality of threats; once institutionalized, protection systems render disengagement risky at best, and possibly devastating (Peterson, p. 52). A woman's pushing the boundaries of the arrangement or rejecting the arrangement can be portrayed as selfish, counter-cultural, unpatriotic, or heretical, depending on the level of state buy-in to the structure.

Structural violence from the feminist perspective, then, is the state's utilizing such structures in a way that notably perpetuates ongoing violence or the limitation of opportunities economically, politically, or educationally for a portion of the population, which in this case is women. While structural violence comes out of feminist theory, it has broad applications to other underrepresented populations. For example, individuals in poor communities might have access to lower quality education, undrinkable water, and fewer job opportunities due to the zoning laws that ensured a low tax base in these communities and has kept them perpetually underfunded.

As the difference feminists tried to broaden the definition of security through the creation of the concept of structural violence, they also shifted some of the focus of the act of warfare itself. War—which was often visualized as male-based forces clashing in the air, land, and sea—also created realities that directly had an impact on the lives of women. Feminist scholars push for an examination of the use of rape as a tool of warfare. Numerous wars have included cases where rape was perpetuated by numerous armies. For example, "a World War I French poem boldly states 'Germans we shall possess your daughters,'" with possession referring to rape. A German soldier describes how Turkish soldiers traveling with the Germans abducted 200 Armenian women and girls, raped them all night, then cut their throats (Goldstein, 2001, p. 363). According to Goldstein, in Bosnia, rape was used as a tool of ethnic cleansing to both humiliate and terrorize the enemy to get them to abandon territory (p. 363). The number of women raped (mostly Muslims raped by Serbian forces) has been estimated by the European Commission as at a minimum of 20,000 (Goldstein, p. 363). The Bosnian case is not unique. Mass rapes were also perpetuated against women during the Bangledeshi War of Independence (200,000 cases), the Berlin area after World War II (100,000 cases), and the Japanese "rape of Nanking" (over 20,000 cases) (Goldstein, p. 363). In her work, Tickner also discusses the Rwandan Civil War example where more than 250,000 women were raped and, as a result, were then stigmatized in their communities (Tickner, 2001, p. 50). The children from these unions were also labeled as "devil's children" and became outcasts.

Often these incidents of rape could not be dismissed as a lack of troop discipline. According to Goldstein, military governments in Latin America during the 1980s "developed patterns of punishment specifically designed for women" who opposed the regime (2001, p. 364). Individual women were identified by the government as enemies and then were jailed and sexually tortured (p. 364). Gang rape was the "standard torture mechanism" used to break the spirit of these women by destroying their sense of self and any idea that they were morally or spiritually superior to men (p. 364). The use of rape to break the spirit of the victim causes war rapes to frequently go unreported, especially in traditional societies (p. 365). The issues of shame connected to family honor stigmatizes the male members of traditional societies, which can result in honor killings of the female members of the family. Rape then is a violation of men's cherished property rights or, as Susan Brownmiller (as cited in Rejali, 1996, p. 366) contends, "sexual trespass on the enemy's women is one of the satisfactions of conquest."

Both social and gender theories contend that the world of international relations is much larger than what is studied by those who utilize both realist and liberal theories. Social and gender theory examines the larger societal and economic constructs that have an impact on which problems are studied and expands the borders of traditional international relations. While Marxist interpretations look at the intersections between the fields of politics and economics, feminist interpretations delve more deeply into the intersections between sociology, psychology, and international relations. Although this expansion is troublesome to some who would prefer the field to be narrower and more clearly defined, this broader understanding allows for more extensive cross-disciplinary examinations of global problems.

References

Arendt, H. (1970). *On violence*. New York: Harcourt, Brace & World.

Elshtain, J. B. (1985). Reflections on war and political discourse: Realism, just war, and feminism in a nuclear age. *Political Theory, 13*(1), 39–57.

Elshtain, J. B. (1987). *Women and war*. New York: Basic Books.

Foley, D. K. (1986). *Understanding capital: Marx's economic theory*. Cambridge, U.S.: Harvard University Press.

Goldstein, J. S. (2001). *War and gender: How gender shapes the war system and vice versa*. Cambridge: Cambridge University Press.

Heinrich, M. (2012). *An introduction to the three volumes of Karl Marx's Capital*. New York: Monthly Review Press.

Hobson, J. M. (2000). *The state and international relations*. Cambridge, UK: New York: Cambridge University Press.

Iadicola, P., & Shupe, A. D. (2013). *Violence, inequality, and human freedom* (3rd ed). Lanham, MD: Rowman & Littlefield Publishers.

Lenin, V. (1939). *Imperialism: The highest stage of capitalism*. Retrieved from https://books.google.com/books?id=HwRwDwAAQBAJ

Peterson, V. S. (Ed.). (1992). *Gendered states: Feminist (re)visions of international relations theory*. Boulder, CO: Lynne Rienner.

Peterson, V. S. & Runyan, A. S. (2015). *Global gender issues in the new millennium*. Oxfordshire, UK: Taylor & Francis.

Rejali, D. M. (1996). After feminist analyses of Bosnian violence. *Peace Review, 8*(3), 365–371. https://doi.org/10.1080/10402659608425981

Tickner, J. A. (1988). Hans Morgenthau's principles of political realism: A feminist reformulation. *Millennium, 17*(3), 429–440. https://doi.org/10.1177/03058298880170030801

Tickner, J. A. (1992). *Gender in international relations: Feminist perspectives on achieving global security.* New York: Columbia University Press.

Tickner, J. A. (2001). *Gendering world politics: Issues and approaches in the post-Cold War era.* New York: Columbia University Press.

Tickner, J. A. (2014). *A feminist voyage through international relations.* Oxford, UK; New York: Oxford University Press.

Wallerstein, I. (1974). *The modern world-system I: Capitalist Agriculture and the Origins of the European World-Economy in the Sixteenth Century.* New York: Academic Press.

Wallerstein, I. (1980). *The modern world-system II: Mercantilism and the consolidation of the European world-economy, 1600-1750.* New York: Academic Press.

Wallerstein, I. M. (1989). *The modern world-system III: The second era of great expansion of the capitalist world-economy, 1730-1840s.* San Diego: Academic Press.

York, J. (1996). The truth(s) about women and peace. *Peace Review, 8*(3), 323–329. https://doi.org/10.1080/10402659608425974

Part III

Global Structures and Processes

Foreign Policy

Jonathan Miner

Abstract

Foreign policy exists to achieve national interests abroad. A state's leader often directs the process of making these policies, yet many other domestic actors involved complicate the process even before a state's foreign policy comes into competition with that of another state. This chapter investigates the major actors of the foreign policy process, including national leaders, diplomats, militaries, the intelligence community, lawmaking bodies, judiciary, and such societal actors as the media, the public, and interest groups. This chapter also applies the major theories in foreign policy analysis to illustrate the many complexities that emerge when states build their foreign policy. Extending the analysis of foreign policy making to China, Germany, Iran, Mexico, Russia, and the U.S., the chapter illustrates the similarities and differences in how states make foreign policy. The process of foreign policy making is a complicated one, designed to safeguard the citizenry, develop a strong economy, and manage relations with the states of the world. This chapter intends to clarify this process and enable students to understand how states around the world interact to achieve their often-conflicting national goals.

Learning Objectives

- Explain the specific actors that contribute to the process of making foreign policy

- Ability to introduce theoretical tools to enable an analysis of the foreign policy-making process
- Analyze and recognize the different ways states make foreign policy around the world
- Appreciate the complexity and challenges states face in achieving national foreign policy goals in a diverse and competitive international system

What are the foreign policy positions on international trade between the U.S. and the People's Republic of China at a given moment in time? As the two largest global economies, the decades-long trading relationship between the U.S. and China establishes each country as its largest trading partner (Kiernan & Debarros, 2019). Yet during the last three years, news broadcasts across the world report that a trade war between the two countries threatens that trading relationship. As people watch these reports, many ask if is this an unfair trade relationship? Is there actually a trade war? When did these disagreements begin?

The U.S. administration of President Donald J. Trump argues the Chinese are taking advantage of the American economy and their trade practices unfairly prejudice American businesses and consumers by creating a trade imbalance in their favor. President Trump argues, "We have been ripped off by China, an evacuation of wealth like no country has ever seen before, given to another country that's rebuilt itself based on a lot of the money they've taken out of the United States, and that's not going to happen anymore" (Reuters, 2018). The Chinese Commerce Minister, Zhong Shan disagrees in his reply:

There is a view in the U.S. that so long as the U.S. keeps increasing tariffs, China will back down. They don't know the history and culture of China . . . this unyielding nation suffered foreign bullying for many times in history, but never succumbed to it even in the most difficult conditions. China doesn't want a trade war, but would rise up to it should it break out. (Lee, 2018)

While these quotes illustrate the recent hostility between the U.S. and China on international trade, an investigation of the issue is complex. Is China "taking advantage of the U.S.?" Does the U.S. seek to gain an economic or political advantage against China? What is a trade imbalance? Has a trade imbalance existed for a long time, and does it hurt U.S. or Chinese national interests? The two countries have a beneficial, decades-long trading relationship, producing significant benefits for both economies (Council on Foreign Relations, 2019), so what are the reasons for the recent dispute?

After collecting facts and evidence regarding the issues behind the U.S.-China trade dispute and current relationship, students should next ask about who controls the foreign policy making process on each side. Which actors in the U.S. and China have the power to make foreign policy? Do citizens and policymakers across society have input in making governmental policy as in a democracy? Or do authoritarian leaders and small, powerful groups in society make policy alone? How can leaders and citizens understand the complex strategy needed to make foreign policies that enable a state to achieve its national interests and "win" an issue such as a trade dispute? Why is this process important to me as an individual citizen?

This chapter intends to help answer many of these questions by clarifying the process of making foreign policy. The first part of the chapter introduces the concept of a state's foreign policy and looks at the types of national interests built into a policy that achieves that country's goals abroad. The second part of the chapter surveys the prominent actors and complexities of the foreign policy-making process, introducing concepts and theories the student can use to explain and analyze its prior foreign policies and understand how actors inside the state construct current and future policies. The third part of the chapter surveys the foreign policy-making process in some important countries around the world, including China, Germany, Iran, Mexico, and Russia, enabling students to compare, contrast, and appreciate the different ways these states develop foreign policy from the process in the U.S.

At the end of the chapter, students will gain the tools needed to understand how a foreign policy is made and the challenges states face when their policy competes on the world stage with states whose national interests and policy-making processes are different. Students will gain an appreciation for how much easier it is for authoritarian states to make foreign policy, in contrast to democratic governments who must respond to their citizens' desires, constitutional separation of powers, and the interests of their trading partners. States that partner with many others in **intergovernmental organizations (IGOs)** such as the **World Trade Organization (WTO)**, **European Union (EU)**, and the U.S.-Mexico-Canada Agreement (USMCA) face a significantly more complex process in developing foreign policy, as their complex, domestic policy-making process must find common ground with international partners before being finalized.

What is Foreign Policy?

Foreign policy, or foreign relations, is "the scope of involvement abroad and the collection of goals, strategies, and instruments selected by governmental policymakers" (Rosati & Scott, 2014; see Rosenau, 1976). In other words, foreign policy represents the different needs, interests, and reasons for a state's involvement abroad and the ways and means chosen to achieve those goals. Foreign policy contains the specific national interests of a particular country. Whether these interests involve the export of products, concerns about terrorism, global pollution, or the drug trade, the issues and concerns most important to our country as a whole determine its foreign policy (Greathouse & Miner, 2017).

At its core, foreign policy often has several important general issues influencing decision-making that help to prioritize the policies created. These issues—security, trade and economic growth, morality and human rights, and isolationism versus internationalism—define a state's policies to the outside world and continue to influence how each state collectively makes foreign policy (Greathouse & Miner, 2017). Different actors within each state possess different views on these issues, often complicating the process leaders go through to decide a specific foreign policy to enact in a particular situation.

While it appears that governments are a single actor and make foreign policy alone, this chapter illustrates that this is not nearly the truth. Government leaders are the primary but not the sole creators of foreign policy. The president, prime minister, king, or dictator often leads in foreign policy making but they are influenced and supported by the state's legislative body, diplomats, the military, the media, the intelligence community, interest groups, bureaucracy, and the public, among others. It is often a bargaining process in which, depending on a state's governmental structure, interested groups and individuals participate in the making of a foreign policy on a particular issue, using all their power and persuasive skills to shape a policy in their combined best interests (Allison & Zelikow, 1999). One might think of this process as a board meeting; the leader often sits at the head of a conference table, and all around him sit representatives of interested parties on a given issue, and discussions occur to determine the national interests and a foreign policy to achieve them. The leader often announces the new policy, but all the interested actors around the table participate in the formation and implementation of that foreign policy.

It is also important for students to understand that each country has a unique way of making such policies, and part of the foreign policy process is to understand other countries' policies within the context of these differences. Americans misunderstand the foreign policies of other countries when they assume their national interests and policy-making processes are the same as the U.S.'s (Rosati & Scott, 2014). For example, while Canada and Mexico are both democracies and U.S. neighbors in North America, each has different national interests and political systems with a different distribution of decision-making powers. The states of Russia, Iran, and China are not democratic like the U.S., Mexico, and Canada, and while many of their national interests are similar in aiming to possess an economically vibrant and secure country, their national goals and policy making processes are very different and present challenges when attempting to understand the differences in how they interact with one another.

Who Makes Foreign Policy?
The Executive Branch

The leader of the executive branch is often the undisputed leader in making foreign policy. Each country's constitution regularly grants the national leader the powers of chief-of-state, commander-in-chief, chief diplomat, chief administrator, chief legislator, chief judicial officer, and voice of the people (Rosati & Scott, 2014). These powers establish a legal basis for the leader to direct overseas matters, such as fight wars; negotiate treaties, trade agreements, and diplomatic relations; and also "organize the chain of command" of making foreign policy, appointing cabinet leaders and ambassadors to represent them overseas (Hook, 2013).

In addition to this legal basis, the leader also derives a great deal of this power from professional reputation, public prestige, and the ability to persuade others to their line of thinking (Neustadt, 1960). The national leader is only one individual, but one who often has the most power and influence of any member of the government, and the entire country will listen if they choose to exercise those powers (Neustadt, 1960). Frequently, leaders make foreign policy during times of crisis (Lebow, 1981)—such as war or natural disaster—and it is at these times when citizens "rally around the flag" of national solidarity and a leader's power is at its maximum (Rosati & Scott, 2014). Each country usually possesses a national security council, a group of state leaders that collaborate with the national leader in making and carrying out foreign policy decisions (Rothkopf, 2005). It is at these "boardroom" meetings where leaders make the tough decisions necessary during times of crisis.

In addition, executive branch decision-making depends upon the personality, beliefs, and leadership style of the leader and the supporting people and institutional departments at the "boardroom" meetings (Rosati & Scott, 2014). The beliefs and leadership style of U.S. President George W. Bush, German Chancellor Angela Merkel, and Chinese President Xi Jinping differ from one another (Elovitz, 2008; Holsti, 2006; Allison & Zelikow, 1999), as do the opinions of the cabinet secretaries, military leaders, and other members of each state's executive branch and bureaucracy. When students of foreign policy consider a specific policy, they must also consider what specific national leader directs the process; the leader's beliefs, opinions, leadership style; and what other advisors were present in the process of developing the policy. How leaders make policy is as important as the success or failure of the resulting foreign policy itself (Rosati & Scott, 2014). Later, we will discuss the differences between a logical, unbiased, and thorough foreign policy-making process and one damaged by decisions taken during periods of high stress, anger, and bias. These problems affect both the ability to make quality foreign policy decisions and the content of those policies.

The Bureaucracy

Decision-making is a crucial part of the foreign policy making process, but implementation by the governmental bureaucracy is what actually makes policy a reality by putting policy into practice. Without the bureaucracy, foreign policies remain words on executive letterhead (Allison & Zelikow, 1999). Each senior leader heads a specific body of its state government, and whether it is defense, diplomacy, security, treasury, or another department, each has a bureaucratic staff in charge of carrying out the specific foreign policies.

The implementation of leadership decisions sounds simple, but the reality is far from it (Allison & Zelikow, 1999). The bureaucracy is immense and complex, comprising different organizations with their own work cultures and individuals with their own career goals. Bureaucracy consists of many layers necessary to carry out foreign policy decisions. It also provides the opportunity to modify or even change the original presidential decisions from their originally intended form (Rosati & Scott, 2014).

Diplomats are part of this bureaucracy and figure prominently in the making of foreign policy. A state's diplomatic corps provides the most public and visible part of the foreign policy process, charged with taking the directives of the government to the peoples of the world. Located in embassies and consulates worldwide, a state's diplomatic representatives communicate and implement foreign policy to both its allies and enemies overseas (Rosati & Scott, 2014). Diplomats also analyze policy positions of other countries and provide policy advice to their state's leaders and other relevant actors who make foreign policy (Rosati & Scott, 2014).

The Secretary of State or Foreign Minister is the top international diplomat and appointed by the executive, a person whose actions and words communicate these views as they travel the globe (Rosati & Scott, 2014). An effective, influential chief diplomat understands the views of their national leader, all of the issues that are important to a state's foreign policy, and has hundreds of diplomats around the world assisting them in communicating and achieving those national interests (Gvosdev, Blankshain, & Cooper, 2019). Often the first to respond to an international crisis, a chief diplomat is responsible for sending state representatives to coordinate aid, negotiate, and generally influence the outcome. Whether dealing with the security, economy, treaties, or other political issues, diplomats regularly take the lead (Hook, 2013).

The Military and Intelligence Community

Since the technological revolution of the twentieth century, the military and intelligence communities are a part of the bureaucracy that have increasingly taken power and influence away from a state's diplomats. With a vast military and intelligence budget and advanced weaponry enabling the ability to implement policy directly, the military is often the first choice of the modern executive in carrying out foreign policy (Rosati & Scott, 2014).

Each state also has a series of intelligence agencies working together to protect its citizens and gather information on both its enemies and friends. The intelligence agencies are government led, funded, and often a part of the state's bureaucracy or armed forces (Rosati & Scott, 2014). As the technological revolution enables them to gather information about their allies and enemies abroad and respond quickly with force as needed, the military and intelligence agencies continue to gain influence in making a state's foreign policy (Hook, 2013).

Legislatures

Like a state's diplomatic corps, the legislative branch also continues to lose influence in making foreign policy to the executive branch, military, and intelligence agencies. Legislatures pass laws and budgets, approve international agreements, and often can withhold funds for use in foreign policy and act as a check on the power of the executive (Rosati & Scott, 2014). This enables influence in the making of foreign policy, as a unified legislature can block executive branch actions in a political system with an effective separation of powers (Hook, 2013).

Just as often and especially in authoritarian states, the legislature is of the same political party as the executive branch and does not possess the power to go against the national leader. If there is no balance of powers in the political system, the legislature will "rubber stamp" the policies of the leader, dramatically reducing the legislature's power in the making of foreign policy (Stent, 2014; Lust, 2013, Shambaugh, 2013). In the end, legislatures retain crucial powers in the making and implementation of U.S. foreign policy (Rosati & Scott, 2014)—a power to make foreign policy that is often undermined by non-democratic political systems.

The Judiciary

The judiciary often provides a useful check on the executive power as well, but as with the legislature, this power is dependent on the balance of power within the particular political system. In a democratic system, the state courts adjudicate disputes among the other branches of government, intervening when necessary to, for example, prevent the executive branch from launching an unnecessary invasion abroad or implementing a policy deemed illegal by the state's constitution (Rosati & Scott, 2014; Hook, 2011; Henkin, 1996).

However, as is more often the case in non-democratic systems, the courts lack independence and exhibit bias towards the powerful groups in the state. In such cases, powerful leaders appoint judges based upon loyalty, not adherence to the rule of law, tying court decisions to the leaders who appoint them and make national and foreign policy decisions (Stent, 2014; Lust, 2013, Shambaugh, 2013). In these cases, the dependent nature of the judiciary renders the institution an inefficient check on national power in making foreign policy. In sum, the power of courts to review actions by the executive branch can be significant but is dependent upon the political structure of the country.

The Public, Media, and Public Opinion

The public, media, and interest groups also have a crucial role to play in making foreign policy making as the national barometer of public interest. Students may wonder, how much does the public care about foreign policy? Scholars argue there are two types of publics, an *elite* public of opinion leaders and citizens with keen interest and who participate in and shape the making of foreign policy and the *mass* public, the rest of society whose only interest occurs when directly affected (Gvosdev, Blankshain, & Cooper, 2019; Rosati & Scott, 2014). Public media outlets, talk radio, and network and cable news programs are influential in communicating foreign policy to the public at large. In today's world, citizens receive their news from countless online and written sources, and this information comes with every conceivable opinion and bias. From conservative to liberal, anti-war to pro-business, news media and interest groups seek to inform ordinary citizens using their own unique take on the issue and to motivate them to support or oppose the government policy (Hook, 2013).

Whether voting, picketing, protesting, or resorting to letter-writing campaigns and petitions, ordinary citizens have a direct impact on making foreign policy and the ways the government implements them. Each of these groups has an almost symbiotic relationship with their government, as national leaders cannot win election to a governmental seat without constituents (the voting public) and interest groups, and these three groups cannot communicate without a third party, the media.

Traditionally, scholars, policymakers, and observers see the public as uninterested and uninformed in foreign affairs, with opinions based upon "dubious [factual] foundations" and ultimately having little impact on the making of foreign policy (Holsti, 1992). Due to the increasing impact of globalization on information access, this traditional, elitist view known as the Almond-Lippmann consensus has largely been replaced by an argument that sees the public interest and impact on foreign policy to be more complex and consequential (Holsti, 2004; Jentleson 1992; Page & Shapiro 1992; Popkin, 1991; Gelb, 1972). The constant and real-time access to news through the internet heightens daily interest in foreign affairs, enabling the creation and accuracy of reputable, up-to-date, influential public opinion polls about the beliefs of the mass public.

Organizations such as the Pew Research Center, Eurobarometer, and the American National Election Studies, pollsters such as Monmouth University, and companies like Investors' Business Daily generate data each day illustrating public opinion on an issue and its impact on the content of the foreign policy policymakers create. The rise of internet communication and social media enables increasing involvement among the mass public, deepening their awareness and understanding of international issues and increasing their influence on foreign policy making (Gvosdev, Blankshain, & Cooper, 2019).

The Complexities of Making Foreign Policy

The following sections illustrate the many actors contributing to the process of making foreign policy, resulting in a complex, difficult, and often contentious process. Each collective actor, whether the executive, diplomatic corps, legislature, or public, comprises many individuals whose combined interests are collectively advanced through each actor as a potential foreign policy. These interests are often different and conflict with one another, resulting in vigorous negotiations by actors to determine the eventual foreign policy.

The aim of political science is to explain and analyze past political events and to generate conceptual patterns suggesting useful ways for policy makers to manage similar political issues in the future. The most prominent and groundbreaking analysis of a foreign policy event is a study of the 1962 **Cuban Missile Crisis**. Graham Allison's foundational study—*Essence of Decision: Explaining the Cuban Missile Crisis* (1972)—established the theoretical basis for the analysis of foreign policy making still utilized today. Allison devised three conceptual patterns that explain the different paths U.S. foreign policy makers might have taken during the Cuban Missile Crisis: the Rational Actor, Organizational Behavior, and Governmental Process models (Allison & Zelikow, 1972). Since that time, scholars of foreign policy analysis apply these conceptual patterns to foreign policy making in states around the world.

The Rational Actor Model

The **Rational Actor Model (RAM)** suggests a centralized policy making process directed by the executive branch and assumes the state acts as a unified whole. In an event such as the Cuban Missile Crisis of 1961, the Rational Actor Model argues President John F. Kennedy controlled, created, and implemented the U.S. foreign policy response to Soviet placement of nuclear missiles in Cuba (Allison & Zelikow, 1999). In this model, the executive branch acts rationally and correctly in response to a full understanding of the crisis and is in sole control of the policy-making process. The RAM conceptual pattern argues the U.S. successfully defused the international crisis because its leaders developed the correct policy and were able to lead and control its implementation in response to the Soviet threat (Allison & Zelikow, 1999). This model is the most succinct of Allison's theories, enabling students of foreign policy analysis to develop a simplified, clear explanation of the process of making any specific foreign policy.

Students quickly understand that not all decision-making is rational, based on a full understanding of a crisis, and developed without stress or time limits. In this more common situation, Allison developed a related **Bounded Rationality Model** in which expected human error occurs but does not result in a flawed policy-making process (Allison & Zelikow, 1999). In this model, President Kennedy successfully discussed, negotiated, and created a U.S. foreign policy response to Russian aggression in Cuba under tremendous stress in a short time and without full information and evidence but within the bounds of rational, effective decision-making (Allison & Zelikow, 1999).

What happens when the decision-making process is irrational, based upon flawed evidence, and devised under excessive stress and inadequate time? Allison's **Groupthink** describes a policy making process in which rational, unbiased, evidence-based opinions forced out of the negotiating process are justified using irrational reasoning

(Allison & Zelikow, 1999). Illustrated by the psychological concept of cognitive dissonance, Groupthink theory is further extended to the idea of **Palace Politics** in which a leader's advisors act less as unbiased contributors to a rational policy-making process than as opportunities to rise to a higher position of influence in the game of "palace intrigue" (Gvosdev, Blankshain, & Cooper, 2019).

A great deal of additional conceptual research followed the introduction of human psychological processes into the study of foreign policy analysis. Robert Jervis' study, *Perception and Misperception in International Politics* (1976), creates a two-step model to explain both accurate and inaccurate processes of the human perception of crisis during decision-making. O. Holsti pioneered the psychological study of national image formation and belief systems in the 1960s (1962), and L. Johnson explores national level misperception for reasons of ignorance, arrogance, lack of empathy, unilateralism, isolationism, and excessive emphasis on the military and executive branch dominance (2007). Doris Kearns Goodwin extended these studies to individual analyses of specific policy makers such as President Lyndon Johnson (1976), the Fitzgeralds and Kennedys (1987), Abraham Lincoln (2005), and Theodore Roosevelt (2013). Scholars now individually analyze national leaders around the world such as Saddam Hussein of Iraq (Post, 2005) and Slobodan Milosevic of Serbia (Wedgewood, 2003) to determine how their personal history, upbringing, and belief systems affect their decisions in making foreign policy.

The Organizational Behavior Model

Allison's second conceptual idea, the **Organizational Behavior Model**, explains situations when government bureaucracy takes the lead in the process of making foreign policy (1972). Each country faces international issues and crises simultaneously around the world, and the executive branch cannot lead the process of policy making on everyone, often choosing to address issues of high politics with vital importance to particular state. In these situations, other actors take the lead on international issues comparatively deemed low politics, such as communications, transportation treaties, and economic harmonization policy. While still important aspects of a state's foreign policy, these less-pressing issues fall under the leadership of different bureaucratic organizations with the government, while the executive branch continues to address ongoing crises such as military conflict, natural disaster, or human rights policy.

The Governmental Politics Model

Allison's third conceptual idea, the **Governmental Politics Model,** explains foreign policy decision-making in situations when many different actors in the process of making foreign policy wish to include their interests in the final product, resulting in a highly political and often contentious negotiation. During these prominent high politics crises (such as military conflict, nuclear weapons proliferation and testing, and trade disputes), many different actors seek policy input in the foreign policy-making process. The more attention paid to an issue, the more difficult and contentious the process of negotiation and the greater the likelihood of failure to develop a unified foreign policy.

These difficulties are even more apparent when students of foreign policy realize there is both a domestic and international level of negotiation. Robert Putnam's concept of foreign policy making as a two-level game illustrates the simultaneous international negotiation between leaders of foreign countries as well as the domestic political views in response to any policy agreed upon between countries on the international stage (Putnam, 1988). The international and domestic views on a policy often conflict and thus explain the inability of a state to develop effective foreign policies on some of the most important issues it currently faces.

Foreign Policy Making around the World

Political scientists apply many of these analytical concepts to foreign policy making around the world, generating the field of comparative foreign policy analysis and adding detailed understanding to the two-level game devised by Putnam (1988). As the goal of foreign policy making is to achieve a state's national goals, foreign policy makers must analyze the process of foreign policy decision making in other countries to gain a better understanding of how to develop their national negotiating strategy. An accurate understanding of the political, social, cultural, and historical bases for the policy put forward by a foreign state increases the likelihood of achieving a state's own policy goals (Rosati & Scott, 2014).

Democracies and authoritarian systems each have different governmental structures, centers of power, political and cultural histories, and shared experiences that combine to reveal unique ways of making foreign policy. In this final section, a brief analysis of the processes of foreign policy making in China, Germany, Iran, Mexico, Russia, and the United States illustrate some of the differences in how countries create their foreign policy and the complexities foreign policy makers face when engaging in international negotiation. These differences include, but are not limited to, governmental structure, geographic location, history, culture, language, religion, and relative economic and military power.

Foreign Policy Making in Democracies around the World

The United States of America

The United States is a state with which most students are familiar, having been raised to understand and appreciate its governmental structure. Most Americans believe the president is the leader in making U.S. foreign policy, and it is true that Article II of the Constitution places a vast amount of that power in the president and the executive branch (Rosati & Scott, 2014). As the chief of state, chief diplomat, and commander-in-chief, the U.S. president does wield considerable power in making foreign policy (Hook, 2013). It is, however, a more complex picture, with the U.S. separation of powers giving the Congress and Judiciary specific powers in making foreign policy, including passing budgets and ratifying treaties (Congress) and deciding legal disputes as to the limits of executive power (Judiciary) (Rosati & Scott, 2014).

While true that the power to make U.S. foreign policy is increasingly in the hands of the president and executive branch, other institutions of government retain some power and influence. Its legislature, Congress, retains the constitutional powers of the purse (annual budget), oversight of actions by the executive branch, and the ratification of treaties (Rosati & Scott, 2014). Congress has a legal duty to exercise oversight of the executive branch when seen to be contrary to the interests of the American public. As a result of the Vietnam War, the War Powers Resolution of 1973 placed a series of reporting limitations on actions of the president overseas, requiring him to report back to Congress every 90 days to receive authorization for a further dispersal of funds and political permission to continue its activities overseas (Bowen, 1973). Public hearings investigated government failures after 9/11 in the "Final Report of the National Commission on Terrorist Attacks upon the United States" (Kean & Hamilton, 2004). Lastly, the U.S. Senate ratifies (or formally approves) treaties, having famously rejected the 1919 Versailles Treaty, ending President Woodrow Wilson's hopes of American membership in an organization he founded (Miner, 2019). While not as influential as in centuries past, Congress continues to influence the foreign policy making process in the United States.

The separation of powers in the U.S. flows further down in its governmental structure. While the executive branch appoints leaders to run the State Department and Departments of Defense, Treasury, and Homeland Security, among others, these actors possess their own internal goals, ways of operating, and career government officials that often contest the power of the president and executive branch (Rosati & Scott, 2014). In addition, the media, public, and interest groups participate freely in the process of making foreign policy, requiring the executive branch to incorporate their views— unless they wish to risk losing the next election (Hook, 2013). As seen in Figure 6.1 below, many different actors contribute to making foreign policy in the United States, although it remains true that the Constitution endows the president the most power in this process. The United States political system attempts to provide some checks on the power of the president to make foreign policy, with each of these actors described above possessing power to influence this process.

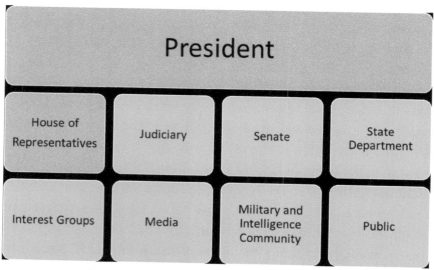

Figure 6.1: Foreign policy making in the United States

The United Mexican States

The United Mexican States is geographically adjacent to the United States and a fellow democracy with a similar governmental structure. Mexico is a federal state, has a president, legislature, political parties, free and fair elections, a military and intelligence community, active media, attentive and mass publics, and many other characteristics similar to the U.S. It differs in its unique history, political culture, geographic location, and modest military and economic power when compared to the U.S. A significant difference is that the Mexican president wields more power than their U.S. counterpart, dominating the policy making process (Kesselman, Krieger, & Joseph, 2007).

As seen in Figure 6.2, there are fewer actors making significant contributions to the foreign policy process in Mexico due to the prominent position of its president. In addition, the office of the president more directly influences these actors through their leadership of the ruling political party and the influence of their office (Kesselman, Krieger, & Joseph, 2007). Many scholars study Mexican foreign policy and its relation to the U.S. and its neighbors, reaffirming the top-down policy making structure and foreign policy patterns towards its neighbors (O'Neill, 2013; Smith, 2007). Mexico is in many ways similar to the U.S., yet its different distribution of political and legal power and its unique national interests, goals, and streamlined policy making process generate a foreign policy significantly different to its northern neighbor.

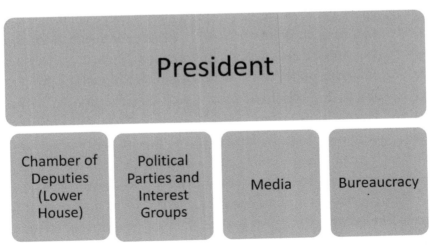

Figure 6.2: Foreign Policy Making in the United Mexican States

The Federal Republic of Germany

The Federal Republic of Germany is a close ally of the U.S. It is a federal, democratic state with strong global economic reach and has many of the same governmental and societal actors that make foreign policy in the U.S. and Mexico. Important differences include the German historical experience since the creation of the Federal Republic of Germany in 1871, its twentieth-century involvement in two World Wars, and its status as a founding member and leader of the European Union (Almond, Dalton, Powell Jr., & Strøm, 2006). To safeguard stability and democracy and to discourage aggression, the German constitution intentionally creates a weak leader, called the Chancellor, placing additional power in its individual states, called länder, than do the political systems of the U.S. and Mexico (Kesselman, Krieger, & Joseph, 2007).

While the Chancellor remains the prominent leader in the German foreign policy process, as seen in Figure 6.3, German foreign policy is a collective, national process. The federal government, länder, and a strong, independent bureaucracy share power in the decision-making process to safeguard stability and democracy so no single political actor can acquire excessive power as in times past (Kesselman, Krieger, & Joseph, 2007). Scholars of German foreign policy also stress a reliance on international, collective decision making in foreign policy and adherence to international law through IGOs, such as the North Atlantic Treaty Organization (Almond, Dalton, Powell Jr., & Strøm, 2006; Kashmeri, 2011) and European Union (Almond, Dalton, Powell Jr., & Strøm, 2006; Caporaso, 2000). German foreign policy decision-making is therefore much more of a multi-state, group effort than in the United States and Mexico, illustrating a more complex process for its government to make foreign policy.

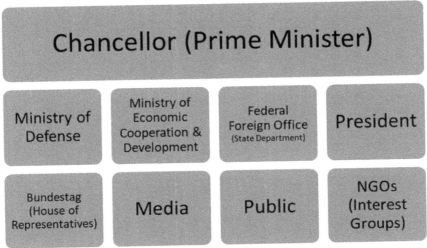

Figure 6.3: Foreign Policy Making in the Federal Republic of Germany

Foreign Policy-Making in Authoritarian Systems

Common among authoritarian systems in the twenty-first century, Russia, Iran, and China possess democratic structures, hold elections for active legislatures, and use a political structure borrowed from traditional western democracies. In daily governance, however, a smaller group of actors utilizes ideas such as nationalism, religion, political ideology, or other tools to dominate policy making. Therefore, while the states appear democratic, they are actually **illiberal democracies**, that is, states that use the structures of democracy to disguise an authoritarian system (Almond, Dalton, Powell Jr., & Strøm, 2006). This section illustrates several of the ways authoritarian political systems use these approaches to dominate the policy-making process at home and abroad: nationalism in Russia, religion in Iran, and political ideology in China.

The Russian Federation

The Russian Federation is a federal system just as the United States, Mexico, and Germany, and has a president, legislature, media, political parties, and almost all of the same governmental bodies as a democracy. These structural similarities disguise the authoritarian system leading the country and the few actors that dominate its foreign policy making process. In Russian domestic politics, "the power vertical" creates this dominance, a top-down system where the executive branch controls the actions of almost all other domestic political actors (Brown, 2001). The Russian executive appoints the Federation Council, the Minister of Foreign Affairs, and exercises an overriding influence over the media, military, and intelligence community with its allies in economy, industry, and politics, known as oligarchs (Kesselman, Krieger, & Joseph, 2007). Political parties exist, and annual elections do occur, yet no elected body or other actor is a check on presidential power.

As seen in Figure 6.4, the "power vertical" in the Russian Federation consists of actors under the direct and indirect control of a superior, all-powerful presidency. Vladimir Putin continues to lead Russia as president from 2000–2009, indirectly as prime minister from 2009–2012, and again as president since 2012 (BBC, 2019). In the summer of 2020, Putin held a popular vote to secure approval for a constitutional change enabling him to be President of Russia until 2036 (Hodge & Ilyushina, 2020). Whether leadership takes the form of czar (tenth to nineteenth centuries), Soviet Premier (twentieth century), or the twenty-first century President of the Russian Federation, the executive branch utilizes Russia's extensive and proud history as a unifying nationalist tool to dominate both domestic politics and the foreign policy-making process (Tsygankov, 2016; Stent, 2014; Mandelbaum, 1998).

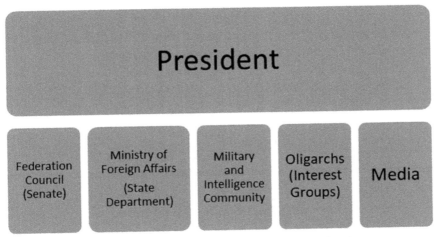

Figure 6.4: Foreign Policy Making in the Russian Federation

The Islamic Republic of Iran

The 1979 Islamic Revolution in Iran ushered in a new political system with some democratic elements, including direct popular elections of the president and legislature. Iran has a president, a leader that is the international face of the country. Simultaneously, however, a parallel, unelected set of institutions possesses absolute power and authority to make decisions (Lust, 2013). Like Russia, a few powerful actors control the foreign policy making process in this authoritarian system. Instead of the president, that person is the Ayatollah, or Supreme Religious Leader. Regardless of the structure of the political system as viewed from the outside, the Supreme Leader is the top political and religious leader in the country (Bill & Springborg, 2000).

As seen in Figure 6.5, the vertical power structure of foreign policy making in Iran is similar to Russia's, with a hierarchical system and subservient structures below. The Islamic Revolution of 1979 removed the secular authoritarian monarchy of the shah (king), replacing it with a religious authoritarian system ruled and directed by Shiite religious leaders (Pollack, 2013; Owen, 2000). The Supreme Leader and ruling religious oligarchy select all leaders for important political positions, vetting candidates who stand for popular election by the people and disqualifying those deemed insufficiently loyal to the regime. (Lust, 2013; Eickelman & Piscatori, 1996).

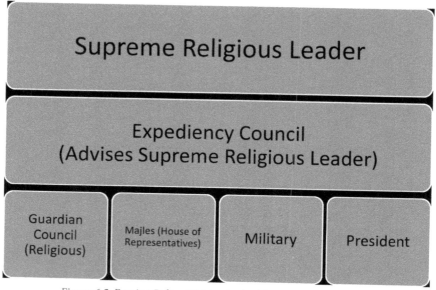

Figure 6.5: Foreign Policy Making in the Islamic Republic of Iran

The People's Republic of China

The People's Republic of China is a global superpower like the U.S. with a powerful economy and far-reaching regional and international influence. China's 4,000-year history, unique culture, and sheer population size are under the direct, absolute control of the Chinese Communist Party. This ideological political party took control of China following a 1949 civil war between the nationalist Republic of China and the communist People's Republic (Kesselman, Krieger, & Joseph, 2007). As seen in Figure 6.6, the structure of foreign policy decision making in the People's Republic of China is vertical as in Russia and Iran, with ideological leadership through the Communist Party as well as Chinese national identity. While a similar authoritarian result exists in the Russian Federation and Iran, China's leaders utilize ideological nationalism through the patron-client networks of the Chinese Communist Party. Both formal and informal, these arrangements trade power and influence for employment and wealth among the Chinese population, a system that also dominates the foreign policy making process (Kesselman, Krieger, & Joseph, 2007). China's position at the summit of the global economy and its important global trading influence generate much research on the process of making Chinese foreign policy and how its partners and adversaries can best negotiate in support of their own national interests (Campbell, 2016; Shambaugh, 2013).

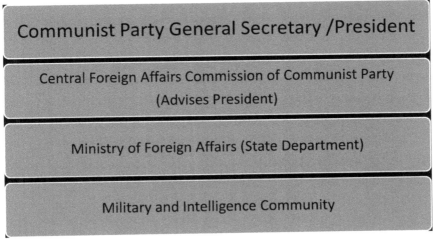

Figure 6.6: Foreign Policy Making in the People's Republic of China

Conclusion

This chapter endeavors to clarify the process of making foreign policy. The first part of the chapter introduced the concept of a state's foreign policy and looked at the basics of a state's national interests in making a foreign policy that achieves its goals abroad. The second part surveyed the prominent actors and complexities of the foreign policy-making process, introducing concepts and theories the student can use to explain and analyze how prior policies were made in the past, are made in the present, and will be made in the future. The third part surveyed foreign policy-making process in several important countries around the world—China, Germany, Iran, Mexico, Russia, and the United States—enabling the student to compare and contrast how these states' policy-making processes are both similar and different.

Students should now be more familiar with foreign policy, the influential actors that compete to make it, and several of the theoretical tools that help explain its complexity. Students should also be able to compare and contrast that process in the United States with several influential countries around the world and be better able to appreciate the complexities that exist for states to develop an effective foreign policy, as described in the ongoing trade dispute between the United States and China presented at the beginning of the chapter. The national interests of China and the U.S. are different, as are the powerful government and societal actors that make the foreign policy in each state. While serving as an introduction to the process of foreign policy making, students should now appreciate the competitive process of making foreign policy in a given state and recognize the complexities that exists in achieving that state's national goals in a competitive international system.

References

Allison, G. (1972). *Essence of decision: Explaining the Cuban missile crisis* (1st ed.). Boston, MA: Little Brown Publishers.

Allison, G. & Zelikow, P. (1999). *Essence of decision: Explaining the Cuban missile crisis* (2nd ed.). New York, NY: Longman.

Almond, G. A., Dalton, R. J., Powell, G. B. & Strøm, K. (2006). *European politics today* (3rd ed.). New York, NY: Pearson Longman Publishers.

American Election Studies (2020). "Data Center." Retrieved July 6, 2020, from https://electionstudies.org/data-center/

BBC. (2019). "Russia Profile—Timeline." Retrieved August 18, 2019, from https://www.bbc.com/news/world-europe-17840446

Bernstein, C., & Woodward B. (1974). *All the presidents' men.* New York, NY: Simon & Schuster.

Bill, J. A., & Springborg, R. (2000). *Politics in the Middle East* (5th ed.). New York, NY: Addison, Wesley, Longman.

Bowen, G. L. (2019). *War powers resolution of 1973.* Salem Press Encyclopedia.

Brown, A. (2001). *Contemporary Russian politics: A reader.* New York, NY: Oxford University Press.

Campbell, K. M. (2016). *The pivot: The future of American statecraft in Asia.* New York, NY: Twelve Publishers.

Caporaso, J. A. (2000). *The European Union: Dilemmas of regional integration.* Boulder, CO: Westview Press.

Central Intelligence Agency (CIA). (2019).Retrieved August 16, 2019, from https://www.cia.gov/library/publications/the-world-factbook/geos/us.html

Council on Foreign Relations. (2019). "U.S. Relations with China: 1949–2019." Retrieved August 19, 2019, from https://www.cfr.org/timeline/us-relations-china

Department of Defense. (2011). Retrieved from http://www.defense.gov/

Eickelman, D. F., & Piscatori, J. (1996). *Muslim politics*. Princeton, NJ: Princeton University Press.

Elovitz, P. H. (2008). Presidential responses to national trauma: Case studies of G. W. Bush, Carter, and Nixon. *Journal of Psychohistory, 36*(1), 36–58.

Eurobarometer (2020). "Public Opinion." Retrieved July 8, 2020, at https://ec.europa.eu/commfrontoffice/publicopinion/index.cfm/Archive/index

Gelb, L. H. (1972). "The essential domino: American politics and Vietnam." *Foreign Affairs, 50*, 459–75.

Goodwin, D. K. (1976). *Lyndon Johnson and the American dream*. Ann Arbor, MI: University of Michigan Press.

Goodwin, D. K. (1987). *The Fitzgeralds and the Kennedys*. New York, NY: Simon & Schuster.

Goodwin, D. K. (2005). *Team of rivals: The political genius of Abraham Lincoln*. New York, NY: Simon & Schuster.

Goodwin, D. K. (2013). *The bully pulpit: Theodore Roosevelt, William Howard Taft, and the golden age of journalism*. New York, NY: Simon & Schuster.

Greathouse, C. B., & Miner, J. S. (2017). United States foreign policy. In C. Cavalli (Ed.), *The Basics of American Government* (3rd ed.). Dahlonega, GA: University of North Georgia Press.

Gvosdev, N. K., Blankshain, J. D., & Cooper, D. A. (2019). *Decision making in American foreign policy: Translating theory into practice*. Cambridge, UK: Cambridge University Press.

Henkin, L. (1996). *Foreign affairs and the constitution* (2nd ed.). New York, NY: Oxford University Press.

Hodge, N., & Ilyushina, M. (2020, July 2). Russian voters overwhelmingly back a ploy by President Vladimir Putin to rule until 2036. *Cable News Network (CNN)*. Retrieved July 6, 2020, at https://www.cnn.com/2020/07/01/europe/russia-referendum-putin-power-2036-intl/index.html

Holsti, O. R. (1962). The belief system and national images: A case study." *Journal of Conflict Resolution, 6*(3), 244–52.

Holsti, O. R. (1992). Public Opinion and Foreign Policy: Challenges to the Almond-Lippman Consensus. *International Studies Quarterly, 36,* 439–66.

Holsti, O. R. (2004). *Public opinion and American foreign policy.* Ann Arbor, MI: University of Michigan Press.

Holsti, O. R. (2006). *Making American foreign policy.* New York, NY: Routledge.

Hook, S. W., & Spanier, J. (2013). *American foreign policy since World War II* (16th ed.). Thousand Oaks, CA: Sage Publishers/ CQ Press.

Hook, S. W. (2011). *U.S. foreign policy: The paradox of world power.* Washington, DC.: CQ Press.

Howell, W. G. & Pevehouse, J. C. (2007). *While dangers gather: Congressional checks on presidential war powers.* Princeton, NJ: Princeton University Press.

Investor's Business Daily/TIPP Online (2020). "TIPP Online: Home." Retrieved July 6, 2020, at http://www.tipponline.com/

Jentleson, B. W. (1992). "The pretty prudent public: Post Vietnam American opinion on the use of military force. *International Studies Quarterly, 36,* 49–74.

Jervis, R. (1976). *Perception and misperception in international politics.* Princeton, NJ: Princeton University Press.

Johnson, L. K. (2007). *Seven sins of American foreign policy.* New York, NY: Pearson Longman Publishers.

Kashmeri, S. A. (2011). *NATO 2.0: Reboot or delete?* Potomac Books, Washington D.C.

Kean, T. H., Hamilton L. (2004). *The 9/11 commission report: Final report of the national commission on terrorist attacks upon the United States.* (Official government edition). Washington, D.C.: U.S. Independent Agencies and Commissions.

Kesselman, M., Krieger, J., & Joseph, W. A. (2007). *Introduction to comparative politics,* (4th ed.). Boston, MA: Houghton Mifflin Company.

Kiernan, P., & Debarros, A. (2019, August 4). Top U.S. Trading Partner is no longer China, Thanks to Tariff War. *The Wall Street Journal.* Retrieved August 19, 2019, at https://www.marketwatch.com/story/top-us-trading-partner-is-no-longer-china-thanks-to-tariff-war-2019-08-04

Lebow, R. N. (1981). *Between peace and war: The nature of international crisis.* Baltimore, MD: The Johns Hopkins University Press.

Lee, A. (2018). China won't back down in trade war with U.S: commerce minister. *South China Morning Post.* Retrieved October 22, 2019, from https://www.scmp.com/economy/china-economy/article/2167715/china-wont-back-down-trade-war-us-commerce-minister

Lust, E. (2013). *The Middle East.* (13th ed.) Washington, D.C.: CQ Press.

Mandelbaum, M. (Ed.). (1998). *The new Russian foreign policy.* New York, NY: Council on Foreign Relations.

Mead, W. R. (2002). *Special providence: American foreign policy and how it changed the world.* New York, NY: Routledge.

Miner, J. S. (2019). One hundred years on: The shadow of League of Nations failure on American support for international law. In C. Cavalli (Ed.), *The Basics of American* Government (3rd ed.). Dahlonega, GA: University of North Georgia Press.

Monmouth University Polling Institute (2020). "All poll reports." Retrieved July 6, 2020, at https://www.monmouth.edu/polling-institute/reports/

Neustadt, R. (1960). *Presidential power: The politics of leadership.* New York, NY: John Wiley & Sons, Inc.

O'Neill, S. K. (2013). *Two nations indivisible: Mexico, the United States, and the road ahead.* New York, NY: Oxford University Publishers.

Owen, R. (2000). *State, power and politics in the making of the Middle East* (2nd ed.).New York, NY: Routledge.

Page, B. I., & Shapiro, R. Y. (1992). *The rational public: Fifty years of trends in Americans' policy preferences.* Chicago, IL: University of Chicago Press.

Pew Research Center (2020). "Home." Retrieved July 8, 2020, from https://www.pewresearch.org/

Pollack, K. M. (2013) *Iran, the bomb, and American strategy.* New York, NY: Simon & Schuster.

Popkin, S. L. (1991). *The reasoning voter: Communication and persuasion in presidential campaigns.* Chicago, IL: University of Chicago Press.

Post, J. M. (Ed.). (2005). *The psychological assessment of political leaders: With profiles of Saddam Hussein and Bill Clinton.* Ann Arbor, MI: University of Michigan Press.

Putnam, R. P. (1988). Diplomacy and Domestic Politics: The Logic of Two-Level Games. *International Organization, 42*(Summer), 427–460.

Reuters. (2018). Trump: China, other nations have become spoiled on trade. Retrieved August 19, 2019, from https://www.reuters.com/article/us-usa-trade-china-trump/trump-china-other-nations-have-become-spoiled-on-trade-idUSKCN1II2MD

Rosenau, J. N. (1976). *The study of foreign policy.* In J. N. Rosenau, G. Boyd, & K. W. Thompson (Eds.), *World Politics.* New York, NY: Free Press.

Rothkopf, D. J. (2005). *Running the world: The inside story of the National Security Council and the architects of American power.* New York, NY: Public Affairs.

Rosati, J. A. & Scott, J. M. (2014). *The politics of United States foreign policy* (6th ed.). Boston, MA: Wadsworth Cengage.

Rourke, J. T. (2007). *International politics on the world stage*. New York, NY: McGraw Hill.

Shambaugh, D. (2013) *Tangled titans: The United States and China*. Boulder, CO: Rowman & Littlefield.

Shapiro, R. Y., Kumar, M. J., & Jacobs, L. R. (Eds.). (2000). *Presidential power: Forging the presidency for the twenty-first century*. New York, NY: Columbia University Press.

Smith, P. H. (2007). *Talons of the eagle: Latin America, the US, and the world*. New York: NY: Oxford University Press.

Stent, Angela. (2014). *The limits of partnership: U.S.-Russian relations in the 21st Century*. Princeton University Press.

Tsygankov, A. P. (2016). *Russia's foreign policy: Change and continuity in national identity* (4th ed.) Lanham, MD: Rowman and Littlefield.

Wedgwood, R. (2003). The fall of Saddam Hussein: Security council mandates and preemptive self-defense. *American Journal of International Law, 97*(3), 576–585. doi:10.2307/3109842

Woodward, B. (2002). *Bush at war*. New York, NY: Simon & Schuster.

Woodward, B. (2010). *Obama's wars*. New York, NY: Simon & Schuster.

Woodward, B. (2018). *Fear: Trump in the White House*. New York, NY: Simon & Schuster.

Yergin, D. (1978). *Shattered peace: The origins of the Cold War and the national security state*. Boston, MA: Houghton Mifflin.

State and Non-State Violence: War and Terrorism

7

Samuel Rohrer

Abstract

This chapter provides an overview of the evolution of the terms *war* and *terrorism*. In addition to outlining the development of these terms, it provides contemporary definitions that are applied in the public and academic spheres. It will also address the nebulous origins of these concepts and describes the tensions between common understandings and an academic approach to these ideas.

Learning Objectives

- Be able to analyze and assess the origins of the term war
- Gain an understanding and ability to differentiate between types of warfare
- Outline the evolutionary change of terrorism as a concept
- Identify the central components of the contemporary definition of terrorism
- Be able to analyze and assess the distinctions made between state and non-state violence

The objective of this chapter may at first seem straightforward, as it is devoted to addressing two terms that we frequently use in our daily parlance. Most people feel that they have a solid grasp on the terms *war* and *terrorism*. Yet both terms can be applied to a shockingly-wide variety of acts and actors. In international relations, we find that there is important nuance applied to both of these terms. In order to investigate and develop appropriate policies, we must craft definitions that separate war and terrorism as distinct acts. This chapter will first consider the topic of war, highlighting the multiple forms of this conflict, depending on the parties involved. It will then address the vague, but commonly used, term terrorism. Over time, this term has been applied to numerous distinct acts and actors. While this complicates our ability to hone in on a contemporary definition, our doing so is not an impossible task. The ways in which these terms are utilized by international relations and within a government indicates the different ways that common terms can be used in our day-to-day lives versus how they might be used in a more academic manner and in policy formation.

What is War? Classifications of a Slippery Concept

Before discussing different forms of war, first we must establish the term's exact origin as well as meaning. *Bellum* is a Latin phrase the Romans used to describe a state of war. The combative nature of this word remains reflected in contemporary terms such as belligerent, which describes a combative person or state. The usage of *bellum* to describe war declined over time, as it was notably close to the term *bellus*, which referred to beauty (Freedman, 2014; S. W. Smith & Lockwood, 1994). Later, in the evolution from Old English into German, terms like *war* transition into our more contemporary usage. In Old English, the term *werre* referred to a large military conflict. The term *gewinn*, which referenced the seizing of a prize or profit, was commonly used to translate *bellum* into Old

English. The German term *werran*, which refers to a confusing or perplexing state, perhaps accurately referring to the complexities of the battlefield, also began to be associated with conflict. This term underwent a gradual transition, becoming *weeorre*, and later *warre*, in English (Freedman, 2014; Harper, 2001). Like many terms, war has a complex origin, and the modern term would not immediately be recognizable in conversation during earlier points in history. The common element shared by all of these terms is a focus on attempting to seize a prize, a large-scale organized conflict, and the presence of an aggressor.

Despite reaching this preliminary definition, the word *war* can be applied to a wide range of activities that do not involve sovereign states or formal militaries. For example, the "War on Drugs" is a phrase used in American politics and policy discussions for decades. Clearly, there are organized actors and conflict in this war, yet this "conflict" does not consist of anything as structured as one state versus another state or a declaration requiring authorization from Congress. Rather, the "War on Drugs" was a public policy and cultural battle declared by President Richard Nixon and strengthened by President Ronald Reagan (Paterson & Robertson, 2014; United States Congress Office of Technology Assessment, 1987). As Black (2019) notes, the term war applied to a wide range of concepts, including a medical campaign; an education campaign; an effort to increase policing; a conflict that is armed, nuclear, or biological; and a battle involving sovereign states or not involving any sovereign states. This variety of applicability creates a challenge to those seeking to study war. Common usage of the term implies that it may be applicable to everything and, therefore, potentially to nothing.

This brief look at the etymology of *war* demonstrates how it can be a slippery concept. However, the question that remains is "What exactly is war?" As political science seeks to apply the scientific method to a social field, it is important for the discipline to apply reasonably-consistent terminology to its study. Without this consistency, scholars and students will face a challenge in developing testable hypotheses. Published material in international relations show that several forms of conflict are commonly researched: inter-state wars, extra-state wars, and intra-state wars. While definitions of these acts may vary slightly, one of the most widely accepted classification systems comes from the Correlates of War data collection project which was founded in 1963 and housed out of Penn State University.

Inter-state War

Inter-state wars are the types of conflict that come to mind most frequently associated with the term war. They are the conflicts studied in history books, conflicts that militaries prepare to engage in, and events that policymakers play a large role in initiating and resolving. Prominent examples would include the Napoleonic Wars, World Wars I and II, and the Invasion of Iraq in 2003. The common elements used to define an inter-state war are as follows: the conflict must involve at least two actors that possess territory, a population, and the ability to engage in diplomacy and that are considered to be members of the international system. In order to be a member of the international system, a state simply must be recognized as sovereign by other states. Unfortunately, the study of war is the study of a violent act. As a result, this definition must also include sustained combat involving two regular armies that results in 1,000 battle deaths within a 12-month period (Sarkees, 2010). These criteria define an inter-state war as an actively prosecuted act of violence engaged in by sovereign states. There is a real cost in terms of committing manpower and casualties. These criteria will also differentiate an inter-state war from extra-state or intra-state wars.

Extra-state War

The **extra-state war** is a category that does not come up much in a general conversation or on your favorite 24-hour news network.

An extra-state war differs from an inter-state or intra-state conflict in that it only involves one sovereign state or a collection of sovereign states on the same side of the conflict. It occurs when a sovereign state's army engages in sustained combat with a force representing a political entity that does not meet the requirements for sovereignty. Again, this is a violent act, and one of the hallmarks of an extra-state war is, unfortunately, the loss of life. To be classified as an extra-state war, the state must incur 1,000 battle-related deaths in a 12-month period (Sarkees, 2010).

There are two types of extra-state conflict. The first is a **colonial conflict**, in which a state finds itself in conflict with a colony, dependency, or protectorate; any of these classifications must fall short of being a sovereign state at the initiation of hostilities. A theoretical example would be if the U.S. engaged in a conflict with Puerto Rico or the U.S. Virgin Islands. Both of these are political actors that fall short of being sovereign states and are tied to the U.S. While an internal component exists, this conflict differs from an intra-state war, also known as a civil war.

The second classification is an **imperial extra-state conflict**. This occurs when a state finds itself in conflict with an actor that does not qualify as a state due to not controlling territory or possessing a population or by failing to receive recognition from existing sovereign states (Sarkees, 2010). A good example of this form of conflict would be the efforts of the U.S. to contain, reduce, and eliminate the capabilities of the Islamic State or the Al-Qaeda network of terrorist organizations.

In short, in an extra-state conflict, a state finds itself involved in a sustained conflict—either colonial or imperial—against a non-state entity. A colonial conflict is between a state and a dependent territory, while an imperial conflict is between a state and a non-state actor that does not have ties to the sovereign state and is not recognized as a sovereign state in its own right; the primary distinction here is that it is not a conflict between two recognized sovereign states.

Intra-state War

The last category of war we will address is an **intra-state war,** commonly referred to as a civil war. What makes a civil war? On one hand, we can see that it differs from an inter-state conflict in that it is not waged by two independent, separate, and recognized sovereign states. On the other hand, it sounds like a concept that might be close to the previous definition of an extra-state war, specifically, a colonial extra-state war. The Correlates of War project provides generally-accepted categories for the definitions of warfare. Scholars and analysts may differ regarding how many injuries or battle deaths are required for the conflict to qualify as war, but that is a more technical debate for a later time.

An intra-state war can be identified by a national government becoming actively engaged in combat with a lower level of government or a competing element within the government that seeks to seize control of the government or secede from a sovereign state. It is not a conflict between two existing sovereign states, which differentiates an intra-state conflict from an extra-state conflict as well. It is akin to the Civil War that the U.S. experienced. During that war, the federal government was engaged in conflict not with a dependency or a colony but with internal states. While they designed a flag, drafted a constitution, held elections, and commissioned distinct military uniforms, the Confederate States remained a largely-unrecognized entity and fell short of sovereignty in the international system. An intra-state conflict means the national government is actively involved in prosecuting the war, and the challengers should be actively engaged as well. The threshold of 1,000 battle deaths is also common in identifying an active intra-state conflict (Sarkees, 2010).

Yet, a conflict can slide across the categories of inter-state, extra-state, and intra-state wars. A conflict that begins as an intra-state conflict could become an inter-state conflict if the challenger in an intra-state conflict becomes widely recognized as sovereign by other states. One theoretical example of such an event would have occurred if the Confederate States of America had succeeded in gaining recognition as a fully sovereign states from a majority of major powers in Europe. A second theoretical example of a potential drift across categories would have occurred if the Islamic State had been widely recognized as a sovereign state. If this had occurred, an imperial extra-state conflict would have transitioned to an inter-state conflict. Nevertheless, being able to separate these categories helps researchers and policymakers better understand what causes these forms of conflict to occur. This is especially noteworthy if different forces drive different wars.

But these general classifications can miss the occurrence of certain wars. A common question that emerges is, "What happens if there are 999 battle-related deaths? It still sounds a lot like a war happened." This can happen, and a conflict with fewer than 1,000 battle deaths is still researched. The primary goal of maintaining the battle death threshold of 1,000 is to identify that the conflict is real and not something that merely existed on paper as a declared, but unexecuted, conflict. A newer area of research in international relations is a militarized interstate dispute, which is a conflict that falls short of being a full-scale war.

An Overview of Modern Terrorism

Apart from war, another common act of political violence that scholars and analysts frequently discuss and study is **terrorism.** Unfortunately, terrorism is not unique to the twentieth or twenty-first centuries. Across human history, we find examples of groups that have engaged in spectacular and strategic violence against an adversary in order to achieve a political objective that cannot be gained through more traditional forms of conflict or political efforts. There have occurred outbreaks of violence commonly referred to as terrorist acts that are geographically dispersed among numerous distinct cultural settings. This section provides a brief introduction to notable organizations that have engaged in modern acts of terrorism. While not discussed, we should note that terrorism was a strategic choice used by groups resisting Rome's control of Palestine and the United Kingdom's colonial administration of British India. The term "modern terrorism" generally applies to the start of the **French Revolution** (1789) and beyond. This examination of contemporary terrorism will ground its discussion in Bruce Hoffman's seminal work *Inside Terrorism*, James Forest's *The Terrorism Lectures*, and an array of case-specific material.

Origin and Ideological Links: From Protecting the Democratic Revolution to Anarchist Tool

In examining terrorism in the modern era, scholars consider the French Revolution a defining moment in the modern age of terrorism. Contrary to the contemporary image of terrorism, which is focused on non-state actors generally having anti-democratic goals and utilizing religious imagery, terrorism was quite different in the late 1700s. Rather, terrorism was closely linked to the ideals of virtue and democracy and was utilized as a morally just action to confront an illiberal political force and protect a newly-democratic state from a counterrevolution. This concept motivated Robespierre's Reign of Terror in Revolutionary France (Palmer, 2014). At this originating point for modern terrorism, it was considered an act organized and conducted by the state, especially an aspiring liberal and democratic state, that was willing to use domestic violence and fear to ensure the survival of that state.

Late in the eighteenth century, we see terrorism continue as an act that remained associated with aspirational democratic values. However, the legacy of Robespierre in Imperial Russia during the 1870s shows a noticeable shift where terrorism becomes a tool utilized by those dissatisfied with the state. Narodnaya Volya ("The People's Will") was a political organization that sought to establish an expansive list of government reforms that do not sound outlandish to a supporter of modern democracy. They sought to establish a democratic parliament, universal suffrage, freedom of speech, the abolishment of a permanent army, and the transfer of land to the people (Hoffman, 2017). Unfortunately, these goals ran contrary to the governing norms of Imperial Russia at the time, and there was no avenue by which to easily advance these proposed democratic reforms within the existing governing structure. I ✓ left off

In an attempt to force change onto an unreceptive state, Narodnaya Volya resorted to conducting high profile assassinations in order to raise awareness of their group with the wider public and to advance their objectives. When planning attacks, they favored targets that symbolically represented the government they opposed. They hoped that, if successful in carrying out attacks targeting these individuals and institutions, the state would be willing to make some concessions or the wider populace would be moved to revolt against the state (Law, 2016). The expected revolt of the public was linked to the theory of Propaganda by Deed which proposed that "ideas result from deeds, not the latter from the former, and the people will not be free when they are educated but when they are educated to be free" (Woodcock, 1983, p. 43). If the terrorist actions were violent, high profile, and persistent enough, the state would grow weary of the attacks or the wider public would thereby come to understand the objectives of the group and so join the terrorist organization's cause. More importantly, the public would learn how they would benefit from a change in government.

The notable questions here are, what was the role of terrorism? Who conducted the acts? Rather than preserving the state, terrorism was becoming a tool for attempting to change the state. In less than a century, terrorism transitioned from being a tool of the state to protect itself to a tool used by non-state actors seeking to dramatically reshape the state. However, in both of our cases of modern terrorism thus far, terrorism was an act tied to protecting or advancing liberal political values within a lone state.

In the late nineteenth century, we see terrorism shift from being associated with both state and non-state actors focused on establishing or protecting liberal political values to an action associated with anarchism. From the 1880s to the 1920s, anarchist groups resorted to terrorism in the hopes of sparking a revolt that would lead to the overthrow of an existing government. Rather than establishing a liberal government like their predecessors, the anarchists believed that any type of formal government was harmful, so it needed to be dissolved (Forest, 2015). A common thread that tied the anarchist movements to Narodnaya Volya was their desire to exemplify "propaganda by deed," or to engage in political action that would create dramatic political change and allow the message of the terrorist organization to reach the general public. Over barely a century, the groups that engaged in political terrorism evolved quite dramatically.

Rather than seeing terrorism as an act constrained to a specific state or form of political movement, it has continued to be used by a wide range of shifting movements either preserving the state, attempting to reform the state, or trying to dissolve any form of government. This begins to raise questions about who commits modern terrorism, and why?

Terrorism and Nationalism: Let me out of this Empire!

As nationalism and separatism from imperial states developed in the 1800s and 1900s, terrorism began to be associated with nationalist movements. Rather than protecting a revolutionary liberal state or trying to gain reforms within an imperial state, terrorism began to be employed by groups seeking to leave a previously-existing state or, more specifically, by nationalist groups that were too weak to confront their perceived oppressors in a traditional conflict (Forest, 2015). This is another significant shift in terrorism that makes it more challenging to associate terrorist acts with a clear set of actors. This change sets the stage for the challenges that states in the twentieth and early twenty-first century faced when they tried to consistently utilize the term terrorism and apply it to groups in a logical manner.

The Fenian Brotherhood, Irish Revolutionary Brotherhood, and Clan na Gael (later rebranded the Irish Republican Brotherhood) represented a noteworthy step in the development of modern terrorism. The first change is that these organizations actively drew support from citizens in both the U.S. and Ireland, a harbinger of modern transnational terrorism. The second notable shift was in the scale of attacks these groups sought to carry out. Rather than targeted assassination like Narodnaya Volya's, these organizations considered a wide array of other strategies when debating potential targets. These strategies ranged from an attempted invasion of Canada by former Irish Civil War veterans to a series of transnational bombing campaigns intended to damage the British economy and, ideally, gain full Irish independence (Hoffman, 2017; Klein, 2019; Law, 2016). With the bombing campaigns, the attacks launched by these groups became more indiscriminate in terms of collateral damage; public locations and buildings were targeted more than were specific individuals. This is a significant deviation from targeting lone individuals who represent the state (Hoffman, 2017). These changes in strategy adopted by the various Irish groups represented a rational attempt to damage the British government, to convince the British populace that maintaining control of Ireland came at too high a cost (and was potentially dangerous on a personal level), and to ensure a string of running engagements that Irish nationalists could utilize as propaganda to encourage future recruitment. In many ways, these strategies are still current, as exemplified, for instance, by the Palestinian groups' struggles with contemporary Israel.

State Terrorism? Soviet and Nazi Oppression

During World War II, the perpetrators of terrorism noticeably shift again, and terrorism seems to become an action organized and perpetrated by a state. This historical drift introduces a notable challenge in defining modern terrorism. Terrorism scholars and analysts consider this divide between terrorism conducted by a formal state, and terrorism that is not conducted as a tool of state policy, a topic of concern. In an attempt to understand how the state-based violence of the early twentieth century aligns or deviates from the actions of non-state actors, Hoffman argues,

> state sanctioned or explicitly ordered acts of *internal* political violence directed mostly against domestic populations—that is rule by violence and intimidation by those *already* in power against their own citizenry—are generally termed "terror" to distinguish that phenomenon from "terrorism," which is traditionally understood to be violence committed by non-state entities.(Hoffman, 2017, p. 16)

With this perspective in mind, many works refer to the acts of Robespierre as the "Reign of Terror" and not the "Reign of Terrorism." Between the 1930s and 1950s, the Soviet Union and Nazi Germany engaged in systematic state-organized violence directed against their domestic populations, which would fall under this definition.

Thus far, across our historical arc we find many groups, states, and movements associated with the term terrorism. Even as the field attempts to separate state and non-state actors, it is challenging to ignore the acts conducted by states in the early twentieth century. In many ways, these acts appear to be descendants of the actions of Robespierre. Similar to Robespierre's desire to prevent a counterrevolution, for example, the Soviet Union and Nazi Germany sought to enhance their grip on power and discourage any challenges to their political rule through domestic violence and fear.

Soviet Union

Similar to Revolutionary France, the early Soviet Union felt that it existed in a perilous state of being. Soviet leadership believed they were surrounded by forces seeking counterrevolution that would restore the capitalist bourgeoise to power in Russia. In response to this perceived threat, an organized campaign against enemies of the state was launched and dubbed the Red Terror. In executing this campaign, the secret police were authorized to shoot all counterrevolutionary enemies of the state (Figes, 1998). The implementation of the Red Terror was a deliberate and purposeful act. When Revolutionary Russians reflected on the experience of Revolutionary France, they believed the French were on the correct path but had made a critical error. The Jacobins in France slowly developed a policy of terror that created an environment that permitted adversaries to gain strength and challenge the revolutionary state (Law, 2016). Vladimir Lenin attributed the failure of the Paris Commune to its "excessive generosity . . . it should have exterminated its enemies" (Pipes, 1990, p. 790). Under his leadership, Lenin intended to learn from this example and improve the efficacy of state-based terror.

In such an environment, one likely did not want to qualify as a counterrevolutionary and hence be subject to terror from the state. However, this term was left vaguely defined by the Soviet state, which allowed the Red Terror to be applied to anyone who resisted the state or plausibly could do so at a later time. Within the context of these lax guidelines, the former royal family was executed, mass executions were committed, and thousands of bourgeois hostages were taken. Many arrests and executions were also considered to be arbitrary, though deliberate (Law, 2016). As noted by a Soviet Commissar of Justice, "We must execute not only the guilty. Execution of the innocent will impress the masses even more" (Pipes, 1990, p. 822). This chilling statement exemplifies the extent of the terror employed by the early Soviet State in order to consolidate power. Following this consolidation, violence within the state decreased for a few years.

Unfortunately, the Soviet Union experienced a second wave of state-based terror under Joseph Stalin. This violence differed from the previous example. Rather than consolidating a Revolutionary State against a counterrevolution, Stalin's Great Terror was designed to bend government instruments and the populace to his personal will (Hoffman, 2017). Creatively, Stalin's terror campaign was organized around an effort to counter a campaign of terrorism that was allegedly being waged against the state. In 1934, a disenfranchised Communist assassinated Sergei Kirov, head of the Leningrad branch of the Communist Party. This event led the police to arrest, try, imprison, and execute thousands and, eventually, millions. With each conviction, a complex web of relations and professional organizations traced their way back to the assassination of Kirov. Between 1934 and 1953, an estimated 786,098 people were executed and seventeen million were imprisoned (Law, 2016). While the Red Terror was directed at consolidating a revolutionary state and removing non-Communist challengers, the Great Terror served as a way for Stalin to remove potential challengers from within a consolidated Communist state.

State-based terror, or terror conducted and organized by a government, was a tool employed by political movements of the revolutionary left and the revolutionary right. There is a noteworthy commonality with the rise of Nazism in Germany. In this case, a political party—arguably a non-state actor—employed terrorism to co-opt the state and then later formed a state that formally engaged in campaigns of terror. It can be argued that the actors and actions remain the same, which raises questions regarding why these actions would be divided into the separate categories of terrorism and terror. As such, this case is worth keeping in mind when debating the difference between acts of terrorism and acts of terror.

Nazi Germany

Before gaining control of the German state, the Nazi Party utilized violence intended to create an atmosphere of fear while providing a way for the party to gain greater public support. The Nazi Party organized the Sturmabteilung (SA), or Brownshirts, which were used as a tool to recruit and organize those disenfranchised by Germany's decline following World War I. It also promoted a narrative that the nation was endangered by the extreme left of the political spectrum. The SA promoted what could arguably be called **domestic terrorism**. Domestic terrorism can be defined as acts of terrorism organized by domestic groups and aimed at changing policy of the domestic government. Throughout the 1930s, the SA engaged in hundreds of attacks against political parties opposed to the Nazi Party. As noted by R. D. Law in *Terrorism: A History*, "During the first three weeks of June, 1932, police recorded, but were unable to stop, 461 battles between the Red Front and the Brownshirts in the state of Prussia alone" (Law, 2016, p. 165). These clashes led to substantial death tolls and a widespread increase in public fear. The violence linked to the Brownshirts extended far beyond political brawls and included physical attacks and acts of intimidation against government officials considered hostile towards the Nazi Party (Siemens, 2017). This wave of violence destabilized Germany. At the time, public sentiment generally blamed this instability on the Communists and the political left more than they did the Nazis and the political right. This attitude created an opening that allowed the Nazis to present themselves as the force with the capacity to confront the domestic challenges facing Weimar Germany, even though they were, in fact, the source of much of these challenging and destabilizing activities.

After gaining control of the state, the Nazi Party continued to use acts of violence and political intimidation against the German populace, transitioning from being what could be called domestic terrorists to becoming perpetrators of state-based terror. The Nazi state developed a complex prison camp system and encouraged citizens to inform on friends and family who were viewed as insufficiently loyal to the Nazi state. In addition, many Brownshirts became members of the Gestapo, or secret police, an organization that used fear and violence to solidify the Nazi Party's hold on the German state. The attitude towards domestic terror was perhaps best expressed by Nazi Party leader Hermann Göring when he said,

> My measures will not be crippled by any judicial thinking. My measures will not be crippled by any bureaucracy. Here I don't have to worry about justice; my mission is only to destroy and exterminate, nothing more. (Bullock, 1958, p. 239)

The application of domestic terror was deliberately designed to dismiss existing legal and bureaucratic norms, thus adding another dimension of fear. Regardless of societal rules or norms, the Nazi Party, now empowered, would punish and terrorize any and all potential ideological opponents.

Nationalist Terrorism in the Twentieth Century: Palestine

Post-World War II, the pendulum swings yet again, and acts of terrorism are associated once more with non-state actors. The most common association is with terrorist organizations seeking independence from a colonial power, an association that introduces the somewhat nebulous term "freedom fighter." Primary examples from this period include the anti-colonial struggles in the Mandate of Palestine and, later, the Palestinian fight against the state of Israel.

These ethno-nationalist struggles share similarities with previous cases, as do the efforts of the Irish to gain independence from the British. However, these cases do not support a consistent definition of terrorism. It appears that, every three-to-four decades, there occurs a sudden alternation between state and non-state actors using violence to create an atmosphere of fear to achieve a political goal. When this swing occurs, the primary actor at the time tends to be labeled as a terrorist.

Israel and the Mandate of Palestine

A common perception views Israel as a state that struggles against the threat of terrorism. Yet the state of Israel was born, in part, by terrorism carried out by Jewish settlers against the United Kingdom. Following the defeat of the Ottoman Empire in World War I, the territory that is Israel today was part of the British Mandate of Palestine. The mandate system was intended to assign territory to a state that would guide the mandate territory towards independence and self-governance. In that role, the British proposed several different forms of government in attempting to create a governing structure that would appease Palestine's Arab, Jewish, and Christian populations. Unfortunately, no proposal ever won over these competing groups. As time went on, the Arab populace, as well as the Jewish settler populace seeking to create a Jewish homeland, came into increasing conflict with each other as well as with the local British administration (Fromkin, 2009).

The Mandate of Palestine, consequently, was a powder keg of competing nationalist identities. Disagreements and hostility became more common between the Arab and Zionist communities. Following a riot incited by the Islamic Mufti of Jerusalem who encouraged a year of conflict that resulted in the deaths of at least 120 Jews, the Zionist community organized the Haganah, or "the defense," in 1929. During this period, a rift emerged in the Haganah as it considered how the organization should defend the Zionist community and effectively gain autonomy for the Jewish residents. At the time, it faced two primary adversaries: the British administration and the Palestinian Arab community (Fromkin, 2009). A splinter group emerged that called itself the Irgun Zvai

Leumi. The Irgun believed that a campaign of terrorism was the only way to remove the British and secure a Jewish state despite Palestinian Arab opposition (Burleigh, 2009).

The Irgun and their struggle against the British show how organizations that adopt terrorism can draw inspiration from each other. The Irgun maintained links with active and former Irish Republican Army (IRA) personnel and based their structure on that of the IRA. In devising their campaign, the Irgun considered the IRA's bombing campaign against the United Kingdom and developed several strategies that would, in turn, be copied by later terrorist organizations. The car bomb was pioneered by the Irgun. They also encouraged their members to join the local British administrative services to collect intelligence and assist in staging attacks (Walton, 2013).

Classifying the Irgun is tricky. Supporters view the group as a liberating force, while opponents view it as a violent terrorist organization. It was indeed an independence movement that utilized terrorism; both of these descriptions were true. This complexity continues to be illustrated by the later terrorist organizations in the twentieth century, as the ability for an organization to be viewed in such starkly different ways continues to complicate objective and consistent use of the term terrorism.

The Irgun's campaign against the United Kingdom escalated following the end of World War II. During this time, thousands of Jews migrated to the Mandate of Palestine after being displaced by the Holocaust and a continent-spanning war. Formally, the British had banned Jewish migration to Palestine, but in the aftermath of war, there was little they could effectively do to control migration. As the Jewish population grew, the demands for an independent state for the Jewish people grew as well. The end of the war and increased demand for independence encouraged the Irgun to launch a full-scale terrorist assault on the United Kingdom in order to exploit a potential moment of weakness (Cleveland & Bunton, 2016).

The strategy of the Irgun was to focus on an urban campaign. They attacked urban centers with the two-fold goal of forcing the British to commit a large number of troops to anti-terror operations in city centers and of terrorizing the urban Arab populace. Similar to previous nationalist campaigns, the Irgun actively sought overseas support. These efforts not only raised funds but also successfully fostered sympathetic communities in the U.S. and Europe. When members of the Irgun were captured, tried in court, and executed as criminals by the British, the Irgun retaliated by kidnapping and executing British soldiers. The Irgun's campaign came to a climax with the bombing of the King David Hotel in Jerusalem (Burleigh, 2009; Cleveland & Bunton, 2016).

This brief description cannot fully convey the importance of these acts. The impact of the Irgun bombing of the King David Hotel was substantial, as British offices managing the Mandate of Palestine were housed on the hotel's upper floors, thus making the act akin to bombing a government building. The Irgun effectively inspired urban terror while targeting British personnel. Given that the Irgun could not confront the British Army, their ability to wage asymmetric attacks on the British Empire and destabilize society within the Mandate of Palestine proved quite effective. In 1947, the British turned to the newly-formed United Nations (UN) to solve their problems in the Mandate of Palestine, and the UN advocated a partition between the Arab and Jewish populations. On May 14, 1948, the state of Israel was formed, substantially influenced by the United Kingdom's realization that they could not defeat a long-running and consistently-executed campaign of terrorism.

The Palestine Liberation Organization and its Origins

Despite efforts to create a Jewish and a Palestinian state out of the Mandate of Palestine, this territory became rife with conflict almost immediately. Zionist groups moved to secure the borders outlined as belonging to Israel. Following Israel's formal declaration of independence on May 15, 1948, every neighboring Arab state declared war on the new state. The newly-formed Israel Defense Force (I.D.F.) was organized and martialed around 30,000 soldiers. The combined Arab forces consisted of around 21,500 soldiers operating under multiple command structures, both factors that contributed to their defeat. A large population migration followed the I.D.F.'s victory; approximately 500,000 Palestinians were displaced from the conflict and forced to seek shelter in refugee camps in neighboring states (Cleveland & Bunton, 2016). This sizable displaced population served as the seed that grew into the creation of a Palestinian liberation movement.

Initially, the displaced Palestinians maintained hope that Arab states neighboring Israel would mount a counterattack and allow the Palestinians to return to their homes. But as time passed, this seemed less and less likely to occur in the immediate future. As a result, Palestinians began organizing into a series of independence-oriented groups based within Palestinian refugee camps, and these organizations began launching raids into Israel from bases in refugee camps in Egypt and Jordan with the aim of weakening the Israeli state. As a result of being expelled from their homes—paired with Egypt and other Arab states being unprepared for a large-scale conflict with Israel—the Palestinians continued to develop their own independence organizations. However, the frequent raiding of Palestinian organizations in Israel proved inconvenient for the Arab states bordering Israel. In response to these attacks, Arab states formed the Palestine Liberation Organization (PLO) in 1964 as an umbrella organization tying together various Palestinian independence movements. Rather than simply offering more effective organization, the formation of the PLO intended to help restrain and limit Palestinian attacks, thus improving the governing capabilities of Arab states neighboring Israel (Cleveland & Bunton, 2016).

Law (2016) succinctly notes the three primary events that created the PLO as an active terrorist organization and champion of the

Palestinian cause. The first component was the rise of Yasser Arafat, a displaced Palestinian studying engineering in Cairo who formed "Fatah," an inverted acronym for the Palestinian National Liberation Movement. As an organization, Fatah intended to serve as part of an ongoing armed struggle against Israel, aimed at triggering a regional war between Israel and her reticent Arab neighbors. Once triggered, this conflict would ideally lead to an Israeli defeat and a liberated Palestine. The second component was financial support and access to weapons from Syria. At the time, the Syrian government was unstable and unpopular, but their one source of public support was providing aid to Palestinian independence groups. The third trigger was the Israeli success in the Six-Day War in 1967, a conflict that resulted in a staggering defeat of Arab armies. Consequently, Palestinians began to transition away from the idea that Arab states would willingly intercede on their behalf.

The PLO used terrorism to challenge Israel and to influence her Arab neighbors. Despite the prominent role of Arafat, the terrorist attacks attributed to the PLO were committed by a series of Palestinian groups that only nominally belonged to the PLO. Groups like the Popular Front for the Liberation of Palestine (PFLP), a Marxist Palestinian group, sought to strike at Israeli interests wherever they could be found on a global battlefield. These attacks were designed to confront Israel in a new way and raise global awareness of the Palestinian independence cause (Rubin, 1994). The attacks possessed tenuous ties to Israel, but these actions are frequently considered one of the origin points of international terrorism during the twentieth century (Hoffman, 2017). Despite the change in how these attacks were carried out, their objective remained similar to their historical predecessors, such as Narodnaya Volya, the IRA, and the Irgun.

In their quest to draw media attention to the Palestinian cause, the PLO factions saw a terrorism arms race emerge among them. In 1968, an Israeli national El-Al airliner was hijacked, diverted to

Algeria, and held hostage until Israel completed a prisoner exchange. As no one was hurt and no property was destroyed, the success of this attack led to additional airline hijackings. A year later, a TWA flight was hijacked by the PFLP and diverted to Damascus where passengers were offloaded before the plane was destroyed with explosives. This attack drew a high level of media attention (Jenkins & Johnson, 1975). These acts inspired a PLO group called Black September—a group determined not to be outdone by the PFLP—to attack a Swissair flight bound for Tel Aviv. In this case, however, the plane was destroyed mid-flight by a bomb with a barometric trigger (Rubin, 1994). Following this event, the PFLP increased the scale of their plane hijackings in order to continue to attract media attention that was always drawn to the most spectacular acts of violence. In 1970, the PFLP hijacked four planes simultaneously; when one of these hijackings failed, a fifth plane was taken hostage. The four successfully-hijacked flights were flown to Jordan and held hostage until the failed PFLP hijackers were released. The captured planes were then offloaded and destroyed (Hoffman, 2017). This escalation continued through the kidnapping and subsequent massacre of the Israeli Olympic Team by Black September (Reeve, 2000). Each act aimed to be more spectacular than the last in order to garner as much media attention as possible.

The international terrorism carried out by the PLO drew on many earlier influences. The scale of the attacks spanned multiple states and was similar to the wide-targeting objectives conducted by Irish independence groups. During this period of PLO attacks was when the nebulous term "freedom fighter" emerged, in part due to the fact that terrorism was only partially effective for the organization. While their primary goals were not achieved (that is, Israel was not removed from the map and an independent Palestine does not exist), the PLO's actions raised the profile of the Palestinians enough that Arafat realized a global platform and a chance to fill the role of Palestinian statesman.

Following the increasingly dramatic terrorist attacks carried out by PLO factions, Arafat was invited to speak before the United Nations. There, he said, "Today I have come bearing an olive branch and a freedom fighter's gun. Do not let the olive branch fall from my hand" (United Nations Information System on the Question of Palestine, 1974). With this statement, he made an interesting attempt at positioning. On one hand, he does not deny the extent of the violence that has been carried out, since this very violence is what landed him on the international stage. Once there, he sought to further advance the Palestinian cause by attempting to rebrand them as a legitimate independence movement, no different than the American revolutionaries, despite their having adopted a different primary tool. The widespread use of the term freedom fighter shows the effectiveness of Arafat's pivot in terminology. The acceptance of freedom fighter as a term generally used in daily discourse rendered the term terrorism nearly useless, as it became subjective and seemingly dependent on one's opinion of the justness of the cause.

The history of modern terrorism shows a common thread: including a state or a non-state actor, violence is used to encourage a political outcome. An effort is made to differentiate acts of the state (terror) from those of a non-state actor (terrorism). Yet in the case of the Nazis, some movements have morphed from one category to the other. The use of violence by these organizations at both levels was aimed at gaining and consolidating power. The types of acts that a group labelled as "terrorist" can carry out has ranged from specific assassination or targeting symbolic buildings to widespread, indiscriminate violence that could potentially qualify as a form of war. With this nebulous combination of events, states have a clear problem. Can the term terrorism maintain a consistent meaning for policymakers? Or is it simply a label for any group that is challenging your state?

Can Contemporary Terrorism be Defined?

As the preceding historical examination highlights, terrorism is a challenging topic to define. While a familiar term, terrorism has had many different meanings over time. For many, the term terrorism is similar to an ink blot test. The term can represent different activities to different people examining a common event. This subjectivity is reflected in a quote from Bruce Hoffman noting that "most people have a vague idea or impression of what terrorism is but lack a more precise, concrete, and truly explanatory definition of the word" (2017, p. 1). This imprecision presents numerous theoretical problems for the public, those who study terrorism, and those who seek to develop and implement policies to limit or prevent terrorism. Between the 1800s and 2000s, terrorism was conducted by anarchists, liberals, conservatives, nationalists, religious organizations, atheists, the state, and non-state actors. The following section examines how the contemporary academic debate seeks to define this ambiguous term. It will consider these underlying contradictions in definitions, as well as common elements that can be used to define contemporary terrorism.

In recent years, one way to classify acts of terrorism has been by attempting to classify the organizations that engage in these violent acts. In doing so, scholars have hoped to discover how one terrorist group differs from another—a substantive step that seeks to examine the possible homogeneity or heterogeneousness of terrorist organizations. Recent literature that examines the motivation and actions of various groups provides such classifications as religious terrorism, ethno-nationalist terrorism, and suicide terrorism. Religious terrorism is primarily motivated by a prominent faith. **Ethno-nationalist terrorism** is motivated by a traditional sense of Westphalian nationalism. It is terrorism conducted along traditional nationalist identities. Suicide terrorism applies to organizations, that can be either religious or nationalist, that engage in attacks where the perpetrators do not intend to survive (Forest,

2015; Hoffman, 2017; Pape, 2003, 2005). While these classifications provide constructive differentiation for examining the activities of specific groups, they do not move us towards a straightforward definition of the term terrorism. Rather, they leave us with a constellation of types of terrorism.

It is perplexing that a term seemingly so central to our political experience in the twenty-first century can be so difficult to define. A partial explanation can be found in the work of H. Smith (2008). During the Global War on Terrorism of the early 2000s, Smith argues that the Bush administration intentionally obfuscated and conflated terrorism and rebellion. During this period, the U.S. military was confronted with an insurgency in Iraq and Afghanistan, but the American public responded more emotionally to the term terrorism as a result of the terrorist attacks of September 11, 2001. Hoffman (2017) also lays a portion of the blame for inconsistent usage and understanding on the media. This apportionment attributes no nefarious intent on the part of the media. Hoffman notes that the need for print and televised media to convey complex messages in a brief amount of space has led to careless labeling of various acts as terrorism. This inconsistency has created a "perfect storm," making it challenging for the public to consistently apply the term terrorism at a time when doing so is increasingly relevant to foreign policy debates.

Despite this murkiness, attempts at crafting a common and consistent definition of terrorism have been a recurring goal in terrorism literature. Most researchers agree on certain common elements as hallmarks of terrorism, the most central of which is the combination of notable violence with political motivations. However, this element alone could explain a number of actions that are not terrorism. David Rapoport argued that terrorism is violence with distinctive properties used for political purposes both by private parties and states (Hoffman, 2017). This definition reiterates the idea that violence is used to achieve a political objective, yet the inclusion of public or private actors is an interesting addition.

Rapoport is debating whether or not a formal state can be classified as a perpetrator of terrorism. Ricardson (2007, p. 4–5) defines terrorism by saying, "terrorist organizations have a political objective that they seek to obtain through violence or the threat of violence." Combs (2003) highlights similar components, outlining terrorism as dramatic violence that targets innocent victims with some form of political objective.

Returning to the definition of terrorism, additional expert views still remain to be considered, as well as does the formal position of the U.S. government. By examining these perspectives, academic definitions can continue to be compared as well as a more broadly-applicable definition. Again, Hoffman (2017) discusses terrorism as a deliberate act committed by a group with the intention of taking advantage of the fear created by acts of violence, or fear from the potential exposure to violent acts, in order to force a political change. Even more than the actual attacks, terrorists are focused on creating an environment of fear. Finally, the U.S. Code of Federal Regulations defines terrorism as "the unlawful use of force and violence against persons or property to intimidate or coerce a government, the civilian population, or any segment thereof, in furtherance of political or social objectives" (Cornell Law School—Legal Information Institute). This definition notes violence for political change but differs from previous work with the addition of unlawful violence. This strongly suggests that the violence is not state-conducted.

Therefore, a unified definition that covers the most common ground in the literature is that terrorism is a (1) collection of symbolic violent acts (2) conducted by non-state actors (3) to influence the public or state to adopt new policies. It is a weapon of the weak, an act of desperation from an organization that lacks strength or public support. In this sense, it is likely not a group's first choice. If they could seize control of the government or force their desired change in another manner, they would do so. An additional element that generally separates a terrorist group from other forms of violence is that terrorist organizations generally avoid seizing and holding land and generally seek to avoid engaging a formal military force in combat due to their comparative weakness (Hoffman, 2017).

This definition draws a distinction between contemporary groups such as the Taliban and Al-Qaeda. Al-Qaeda is a non-state actor consisting of a series of loosely affiliated terrorist organizations. The Taliban is a body that controls and governs territory. One is a terrorist organization, the other is not. In the case of the Islamic State of Iraq and al-Sham (ISIS), the organization had aspirations of statehood. However, the classification of this entity as a terrorist organization allowed governments to clearly signal that they did not accept it as a sovereign entity.

A common theme in this chapter is trying to establish clear and investigable definitions of terms that are commonly, but loosely, used in our daily conversations and on the media. This is a challenge commonly faced by the social sciences. The term *war* evolved over centuries. Within the political science literature there are clearly identifiable forms of war, including inter-state war, intra-state war, and extra-state war. The development of the commonly used term *terrorism* has evolved dramatically over the past few centuries. As such, the term terrorism has been applied to a shockingly large number of activities. As a result, its use frequently lacks specificity. Academic and professional literature on terrorism has sought to identify consistent forms of violence that fall under the label of terrorism, making a distinction between state and non-state actors: state-based actors commit acts of terror while non-state actors commit acts of terrorism.

In a classroom, a reasonable question encouraged by historical examples and this definitional debate is, "These are all violent acts seeking to force people to behave in a certain way. What's the real difference?" This sparks the terror versus terrorism debate. It's true that this dividing of terrorism and terror into distinct categories can feel arbitrary when first introduced. In fact, the emergence of the modern usage of terrorism frequently focuses on the French Revolution and government acts as the starting point. From the perspective of a policymaker or researcher, separating these acts nevertheless serves a meaningful purpose: how a state would attempt to combat or deter a state vs. a non-state actor varies greatly. There is real value in understanding when a state would resort to terror to shape domestic opinion. When this occurs, the state utilizing terror offers a more tangible target than does a non-state actor. In order to deter state-based terror, sanctions can be leveled; coercive force—such as military strikes—can be directed at fixed targets; and pressure can be brought to bear at international forums, such as the United Nations or an economic summit.

When a state seeks to deter terrorism, it faces a different set of challenges. A non-state actor may be non-responsive to pressure from an international organization and it may prove a more challenging target for the application of coercive force than can a formal state. In fact, terrorist organizations frequently seek to goad a state into responding with a large-scale coercive action so that they can depict the state as an aggressor to the wider public and thereby gain followers. The two acts are unique in their goals, and a state seeking to confront terror and terrorism would find it challenging to address them in the same manner. After all, the IRA and the French Revolution, while both employed violence, possess fundamental strategic and tactical differences. Hence, separating terror and terrorism is vital to developing a thorough understanding of the acts, why they occur, and how to address them. At times, an alternative option can appear on the international stage. **State-sponsored terrorism** occurs when one state provides aid to a terrorist organization that seeks to exert pressure on an adversary of the funding state.

The categories of war introduced earlier in this chapter provide a similar function when examining the act of war. Again, the term "war" has been applied to a seemingly endless series of acts and entities, including illiteracy, crime, drugs, cancer, terrorism, poverty, fascism, Communism, and so on. For the purposes of international relations, this diffuseness makes war too nebulous a concept to be completely useful. If it is to be studied, and states are to adequately prepare for war, then we must parse one act from another. In doing so, we see three common categories.

The classic inter-state war is engaged in by sovereign states, with formal militaries, rules, and some form of an authorization. These acts differ substantively from intra-state, or civil wars, where two factions within a lone state engage in a struggle to seize control of the state or secede from the state. Perhaps one of the most apt but underutilized categories of war is the extra-state war, when a state finds itself engaged in a conflict with a dependency, such as a commonwealth, colony, protectorate, or a non-state actor. When we think about the War on Terrorism that the U.S. has waged since the dawn of the twenty-first century, we see it as an extra-state conflict. When we consider the efforts of the U.S. to deter the Islamic State, here again we see an example of a potential extra-state conflict. These non-traditional wars are clearly different from inter- and intra-state conflicts, and overlooking these distinctions would ignore their unique features and so hinder researchers and policymakers from pursuing targeted solutions.

A good tool when wrapping up a topic, especially a topic with so many contemporary and historical examples, is to consider cases that might fall under these varying categories of violence. This process can help build a personal understanding of what can otherwise feel like distinctions without a difference. As a thought exercise, you might also consider what steps you would take to deter, or perhaps encourage, these acts as the leader of a state or non-state entity.

References

Agenda Item 108: Question of Palestine, United Nations General Assembly, 29th Session (1974).

Black, J. (2019). *War and its causes*. New York: Rowman & Littlefield.

Bullock, A. (1958). *Hitler: A study in tyranny*. New York, New York: Harper.

Burleigh, M. (2009). *Blood and rage: A cultural history of terrorism*. New York, New York: Harper.

Cleveland, W., & Bunton, M. (2016). *A history of the modern Middle East* (6th ed.). Boulder, CO: Westview Press.

Combs, C. (2003). *Terrorism in the 21st century*. New Jersey: Prentice Hall.

Cornell Law School—Legal Information Institute. Electronic Code of Federal Regulation. Retrieved from https://www.law.cornell.edu/cfr/text/28/0.85

Figes, O. (1998). *A people's tragedy*. New York, New York: Pengiun Books.

Forest, J. J. F. (2015). *The terrorism lectures: A comprehensive collection for students of terrorism, counterterrorism, and national security* (2nd ed.). Santa Ana, CA: Nortia Press.

Freedman, L. (2014). Defining war. In J. Lindley-French & Y. Boyer (Eds.), *The Oxford Handbook of War*, 17–29. London: Oxford University Press.

Fromkin, D. (2009). *A peace to end all peace: The fall of the Ottoman Empire and the creation of the modern Middle East*. New York, New York: Holt Paperbacks.

Harper, D. (2001). "War." Retrieved from https://www.etymonline.com/word/war

Hoffman, B. (2017). *Inside terrorism* (3rd ed.). New York City: Columbia University Press.

Jenkins, B., & Johnson, J. (1975). *International terrorism: A chronology*. Santa Monica, CA.

Klein, C. (2019). *When the Irish invaded Canada*. New York, NY: Double Day.

Law, R. D. (2016). *Terrorism: A history*. Malden, MA: Politiy Press.

Palmer, R. (2014). The age of democratic revolution: A political history of Europe and America 1760–1800. Princeton, NJ: Princeton University Press.

Pape, R. (2003). The Strategic Logic of Suicide Terrorism. *American Political Science Review, 97*(3), 343-361.

Pape, R. (2005). *Dying to win: The strategic logic of suicide terrorism*. New York City: Random House.

Paterson, P., & Robertson, K. (2014). *Measuring success in the war on drugs*. Washington, D.C.: William J. Perry Center for Hemispheric Defense Studies.

Pipes, R. (1990). *The Russian revolution*. New York Knopf.

Reeve, S. (2000). *One day in September: The full story of the Munich Olympic Massacre and the Israeli revenge operation "Wrath of God"*. New York, New York: Arcade Publishing.

Ricardson, L. (2007). *What terrorists want*. New York: Random House.

Rubin, B. (1994). *Revolution until victory? The politics and history of the PLO*. Cambridge, MA: Harvard University Press.

Sarkees, M. R. (2010). The COW typology of war: Defining and categorizing wars. Retrieved from http://www.correlatesofwar.org/data-sets/COW-war/the-cow-typology-of-war-defining-and-categorizing-wars/view

Siemens, D. (2017). *Stormtroopers: A new history of Hitler's Brownshirts*. New Haven, Connecticut: Yale University Press.

Smith, H. (2008). Defining terrorism: It shouldn't be confused with insurgency. Retrieved from http://www.unc.edu/depts/diplomat/item/2008/1012/comm/smith_defining.html

Smith, S. W., & Lockwood, S. J. (1994). *Latin-English dictionary*. London: Chambers.

United States Congress Office of Technology Assessment. (1987). *The border war on drugs*. Washington, D.C.: Congress of the United States.

Walton, C. (2013). *Empire of secrets: British intelligence, the Cold War, and the twilight of empire*. New York, New York: Harper.

Woodcock, G. (1983). Anarchism: A historical introduction. In G. Woodcock (ed.), *The Anarchist Reader*, 11–56. Glasgow: Fontana.

Security and Military Power

8

Seyed Hamid Serri

Abstract

This chapter provides a general definition of security. It argues that any security analyst needs to decide on three topics. They first need to determine their preferred conception of security: objective, subjective, or discursive. They should then choose their referent object of security, or whose security they are studying: a state's, a society's, a gender's, an economic class's, or the individual's. The third decision that a security analyst should make is their preferred sector of security. The most frequently studied areas of security are military, environmental, economic, political, societal, and cyber sectors. The analyst should decide whether they want to focus on one, a few, or all of the above sectors. After introducing the reader to the three essential components of security analysis, this chapter ends with a review of security arguments by the three most popular international relations theories: realism, liberalism, and constructivism.

Learning Objectives

- Define security and its main components
- Compare the three conceptions of security: objective, subjective, and discursive
- Compare the security of nation-state and individual as the two main referent objects of security studies

- Discuss six security sectors: military, environmental, economic, political, societal, and cyber
- Compare and discuss security arguments in realism, liberalism, and constructivism

What is security? You might find it interesting to know that, until the 1980s, this question was not discussed much. Scholars and practitioners talked about security issues and problems but not security as a concept. Instead of talking about security, scholars wrote about concepts such as war (Wright, 1942) or power (Morgenthau, 1948). Security was seen as a consequence of having power: those who have power are secure. Or it was seen as the consequence of peace: when you are not at war, you are secure. In other words, security was regarded as a self-evident concept (Buzan, 1983).

This chapter discusses security in five sections. The first section is the definition of security and its main components; the second covers the three conceptions of security, and in the third section, two of the main referent objects of security studies will be discussed. The fourth section is dedicated to the discussion of security sectors. Finally, section five reviews the security arguments from the perspective of realism, liberalism, and constructivism.

What is Security?

Security is about protecting the survival of someone or something, that is, the **referent object of security**. The more the survival of a referent object is at risk, the more that referent object is under security threat. Security is about extraordinary measures that one adopts to confront urgent threats and vulnerabilities that put the survival of a referent object at risk (Buzan, Waever, & de Wilde, 1998). Students and readers might ask if there are many issues that can endanger the survival of a referent object; are they all considered security threats? For instance, according to the National Center for Health Statistics (Kochanek, Murphy, Xu, & Arias, 2019), in 2017 alone, there were more than thirty-six thousand deaths in the U.S. due to unintentional falls. Should we consider accidental falling a security threat to a nation-state? Not necessarily.

For an existential threat to be considered a security threat, there should be a sense of urgency about it as well. In other words, relevant authorities should come to the conclusion that an existential threat is so urgent that they have to address it right away. Another characteristic of security issues is that they are usually resolved through extraordinary measures. The moment someone declares that a security problem threatens a referent object, they imply that they can go beyond regular norms and rules to address that security problem. For instance, in times of war, when terrorist attacks are imminent, or when diseases are pandemic, governments resort to policies that are not part of the day-to-day practice of their respective societies. They may adopt such policies as declaring mandatory conscription, imposing curfews, or issuing travel restrictions (Buzan, 1983; Buzan, Waever, & de Wilde, 1998).

Security Studies

Textbooks on security studies usually cover theories like strategic studies, peace research, human security, feminist security, critical security, environmental security, regime security, energy security, and cybersecurity (Collins, 2019; Williams & McDonald, 2018). Why are there so many theories in security studies? It is because different theories use different conceptions of security, prioritize different referent objects of security, and choose different sectors of security. What follows expands on these differences.

Three Conceptions of Security

Buzan and Hansen (2009) argue that one of the reasons that scholars subscribe to multiple theories in security studies is that they hold different understandings of security. A literature review shows that difference as being according to the following conceptions: objective conception, subjective conception, and discursive conception. Any security studies analyst implicitly or explicitly chooses one of these three understandings of security, with this choice having fundamental impacts on their definition of threat and their policy recommendations.

Objective Conception of Security

An objective approach focuses on the absence or presence of concrete threats (Buzan & Hansen, 2009). For the **objective conception of security**, one of the most important factors would be the military expenditure and capabilities of other countries. For instance, it would be essential for those taking the objective approach to know that, in 2018, the six countries with the highest military spending were the U.S. ($649 billion), China ($250 billion), Saudi Arabia ($68 billion), India ($67 billion), France ($64 billion), and Russia ($61 billion) (Stockholm International Peace Research Institute, 2019). From the objective conception of security perspective, because Russia, China, India, Saudi Arabia, and France spend a lot on their military, the U.S should be worried about all these countries and should have contingency plans for confronting their respective military powers.

Subjective Conception of Security

While the objective conception of security defines security as the absence of threat, the **subjective conception of security** defines security as the absence of fear. In other words, what is important is not only the material capabilities of other countries but also the fear generated from those capabilities (Buzan & Hansen, 2009). A good way to differentiate between the objective conception and the subjective conception of security is to consider weapons of mass destruction as a case in point.

Weapons of mass destruction (WMDs) refers to a class of weaponry that intends to harm and kill a large number of people.

When they are used, WMDs usually have massive and longstanding impacts on the environment and future generations. WMDs are divided into four categories: biological, chemical, nuclear, and radiological (UNRCPD, 2019). Of the different types of WMDs, atomic weapons are infamous for their destructive powers. To offer a brief review, nuclear weapons create a massive amount of energy by splitting a heavy atom, like uranium-235 (fission weapons) or by joining smaller atoms, like hydrogen (fusion weapons). In the process of splitting or joining atoms, some mass turns into energy, and creates a large amount of energy. For example, though the nuclear bomb that the U.S. dropped on Hiroshima, Japan on August 6, 1945, was a relatively small nuclear weapon and only had a blast yield equivalent to 15 kilotons of TNT, it killed and wounded about 135,000 Japanese people (Avalon Project, 2008). The massive destructive power of nuclear weapons and the fact that there is little their targets can do in defense against them make atomic weapons a frightening existential threat to states and individuals. However, fear of countries with nuclear weapons is not uniform.

According to the Federation of American Scientists (Kristensen & Korda, 2019, July), nine countries have nuclear weapons in the world: Russia (6,500), the U.S. (6,185), France (300), China (290), the United Kingdom (215), Pakistan (150), India (140), Israel (80), and North Korea (25). France and the United Kingdom have far more nuclear weapons than North Korea does, yet the U.S. is not worried as much about the United Kingdom's 215 nuclear weapons as it is about North Korea's 25 nuclear weapons.

The above example shows that material capabilities alone are not enough to define a security problem. The subjective conception of security argues that security should be defined not as the absence of threat but as the absence of fear. Therefore, in order to choose the subjective conception of security, analysts must compare not only the material powers of countries but also the history of relations between states. For instance, the difference in the history of U.S.

relations with the United Kingdom and North Korea helps explain why their respective number of nuclear weapons does not make the United Kingdom a perceived threat to U.S. security, while the opposite proves the case regarding North Korea.

Discursive Conception of Security

Compared to the objective conception of security, the subjective conception provides a more nuanced and practical approach and is, therefore, more capable of explaining the security policies of countries. However, the subjective conception of security is still tied to the objective conception because it only adds an interpretative filter to the objective approach. The discursive approach, on the other hand, is not tied to the objective conception of security. Instead, it argues that threats are "'objective' when they are accepted by significant political actors, not because they have an inherent threatening status." (Buzan & Hansen, 2009, p. 34). The **discursive approach to security** studies the process through which security problems are created by speech acts. (Buzan & Hansen, 2009, p. 34). This process is called the **securitization** process. Securitization refers to the process whereby a securitizing actor convinces an audience that someone or something is an existential threat to a referent object. (McDonald, 2013, p. 73). Let's examine the discursive approach and its securitization process using three examples.

On June 5, 1981, the U.S. Center for Disease Control (CDC) reported that a disease had severely compromised the immune systems of five young men in Los Angeles. This announcement was the first official reporting of a disease that was later named the Acquired Immunodeficiency Syndrome (AIDS). Soon, AIDS became a dangerous existential threat to many societies. In 1994, AIDS became the leading cause of death for all Americans between the ages of 25 to 44. In 1999, AIDS was the fourth largest cause of death worldwide and the number one cause of death in Africa (HIV. gov). One of the reasons behind the HIV/AIDS pandemic in the world and its high casualties was that it took the governments and the public some time to accept health professionals' warnings about this disease. While HIV/AIDS was lethal, it only became a security issue after the general public and politicians accepted the narrative by health professionals that AIDS is an existential threat to society.

The second example is about the "missile gap" debate during the Cold War. During the Eisenhower and Kennedy administrations, perception in the U.S. was that there was a missile gap between the Western bloc and the Eastern bloc. People and policymakers in the U.S. had accepted the narrative that Soviet missile power was greater than that of the West. In reality, however, the Soviet missile capability was not as powerful. Despite this fact, Western policymakers and the public treated the missile gap as a real security threat and tried to tackle the perceived danger by allocating more resources to their military (Central Intelligence Agency, n.d.). The missile gap example shows how a nonexistent threat can become a significant security issue when the relevant audience accepts a securitizing actor's narrative.

The third example is about the end of the Cold War. The **Cold War** (1946–1991) was a geopolitical and ideological competition between the U.S. as the leader of the Western bloc and the Soviet Union as the leader of the Eastern bloc. Scholars and analysts have discussed at length the reasons behind the end of the Cold War. Some argue that the main reason that the Cold War ended was that Soviet military spending could not keep up with military spending in the West. One would argue, however, that if nuclear weapons were the main reason for parity between the two superpowers, that material parity between the U.S. and the Soviet Union never changed. Even at the end of the Cold War, the Soviet Union had a mighty nuclear force that was well capable of creating parity between the U.S. and the Soviet Union (Defense Intelligence Agency, 1989).

In explaining the end of the Cold War, the discursive approach points to the change in the Soviet elite's perception of the competition between East and West. During the 1980s, a new Soviet elite came to power that had different views about the West. The leader of this new Soviet elite was Mikhail Gorbachev, who became the General Secretary of the Communist Party of the Soviet Union. In the following passage, Gorbachev describes the transformation of the Soviet elite's worldview:

> We in the Soviet Union began by looking at ourselves. Four years ago in April 1985 we made a choice, asking ourselves the most difficult questions. We have tried to answer them honestly and straightforwardly. We have set out to reappraise our experience, our history, the world around us and our own position in it. We have firmly opted for overcoming ossified dogmas and stale patterns of thinking and stereotypes. This has produced perestroika and the new thinking and the domestic and foreign policies based on them. (Gorbachev, 1989b)

Because of this change in the Soviet elite's belief system, the Soviet Union eventually announced that it no longer regarded the U.S. as an enemy. The Malta Summit between Gorbachev and President George H. W. Bush in December 1989 is regarded as the event at which Gorbachev announced the end of the Cold War:

> First and foremost, the new U.S. president must know that the Soviet Union will not under any circumstances initiate a war. This is so important that I wanted to repeat the announcement to you personally. Moreover, the USSR is prepared to cease considering the U.S. as an enemy and announce this openly. We are open to cooperation with America, including cooperation in the military sphere. (Gorbachev, 1989a)

The **discursive conception of security** argues that, if relevant actors accept something as a threat to the survival of a referent object, then that issue becomes a security threat. On the other hand, when they cease to see an issue as a threat, that issue no longer is considered a security threat. According to the discursive conception of security, the Cold War ended because the new Soviet elite chose not to see the U.S. as an existential threat to the Soviet Union. The Cold War ended, consequently, with the end of the Soviet Union's perceiving the U.S. as a security threat.

Referent Objects of Security

After choosing the conception of security, the second decision analysts must make concerns the referent object of security. The referent object of security is the answer to the question of "whose security?" During the Cold War, the majority of scholarly works in security studies focused on the security of nation-states. As the Cold War came to an end, scholars began to cover other referent objects, including individual, gender, society, region, regime, civilization, and environment (Buzan, 1983, p. 13). Table 8.1 shows the referent objects of the most important theories in security studies. As this table indicates, the most common referent objects are the nation-state and individual, which are discussed below.

Security Theory	Referent Object of Security	Security Sector
constructivism	state, collectivities	military
Copenhagen School	collectivities, environment	all
critical security studies	individual	all
feminist security studies	individual, women	all
human security	individual	all
liberalism	state, individual, collectivities	all
peace research	state, societies, individual	all
post-colonial security studies	state, collectivities	all
realism	state	military, political
strategic studies	state	military

Table 8.1: Referent Objects and Security Sectors in Security Studies. Modified from Buzan and Hansen (2009, p. 38)

The Individual and Security

An individual might be threatened by physical threats, economic threats, threats to their rights, and threats to their status. Therefore, security for individuals includes such factors as protection of life, health, status, wealth, and freedom. But who provides such security for individuals? Most of the time, the state protects individuals and provides them with all sorts of protections. Accordingly, some scholars argue that, if the state is secure, then so are the individuals. In other words, they reduce the security of individuals to the security of states. However, as we can see in the following examples, a state can also become a source of insecurity for individuals. The security of the state and the security of individuals may not be the same.

During Saddam Hussein's rule in Iraq (1979–2003), the security of Saddam's regime was not tantamount to the security of many Iraqi citizens, including Iraqi Shias and Kurds. Saddam invaded Iran in 1980, which resulted in a bloody eight-year war between Iraq and Iran. During that war, known as the Iran-Iraq War (1980–1988), Iraqi Kurds on many occasions sided with Iran, and this angered Saddam's regime. In March 1988, in the battle of Halabja, which is a Kurdish town in Iraq, Saddam's forces used mustard gas and chemical weapons against the Iraqi Kurdish population, killing thousands (Central Intelligence Agency, 2007).

Saddam also used chemical weapons against the Iraqi Shias after the invasion of Kuwait (August 2, 1990). After his invasion of Kuwait failed in 1991, Saddam faced a popular uprising by Shias in southern Iraq. Iraqi forces fought the Shia uprising by using nerve agents and chemical weapons against them (Central Intelligence Agency, 2007). Saddam's use of chemical weapons against the Kurdish and Shia population shows how some governments pursue their security at the expense of the security of their citizens.

The U.S.-Soviet competition during the Cold War provides a second example of the possible misalignment of the security of states and individuals. During the Cold War, the principal strategy of the U.S. and the Soviet Union was nuclear deterrence based on mutually assured destruction (MAD). The logic behind MAD was that, as long as both sides' civilian populations were vulnerable at all times, neither side would initiate a nuclear war. In other words, for the sake of state security, both countries agreed to keep their civilian populations vulnerable (Buzan, 1983, p. 33–34).

State Security, National Security

For many scholars, the nation-state is the main referent object of security. The most important components of a state are its people, political system, territory, and sovereignty. Therefore, threats to state security are threats that impact these elements. Of the above components, states are especially sensitive to threats to their **sovereignty**, which has two parts: **internal sovereignty** and **external sovereignty**. Internal sovereignty refers to the degree of control and governance a state has over its citizens and its territory. A state's external sovereignty, on the other hand, is the degree of its independence from other states.

States face multiple sources of threats. Other states, especially those within close geographic proximity, usually pose the biggest threats to the survival of states. Individuals can also become a source of threat to a state's security. In fact, threats by individuals to the national security of states are growing every day. Individual empowerment, along with easier access to lethal technologies, such as precision strike capabilities, cyber instruments, and bioterror weaponry, have increased states' security vulnerabilities to individuals (National Intelligence Council, 2012).

Another factor that affects the security of states is the anarchic nature of the international system. In an anarchic international system, no higher authority exists to regulate relations among sovereign states. Scholars disagree on the exact impact of the anarchic international system on the security of states. Realists argue that this lack of central authority, or anarchy, in the international system makes the international system a self-help system riddled with security problems for countries.

In contrast to the realist analysis, constructivists argue that the anarchic nature of the international system does not necessarily create a security challenge for the states. Instead, constructivists contend that anarchy is what states make of it (Wendt, 1992). Constructivists argue that, based on the degree of positive identifications between countries, states can interact as enemies, rivals, or friends. In an anarchic international system where there is no positive identification between states, they will be each other's enemies and will only care about their respective self-interests. This type of international system poses a significant security threat against the survival of states. On the other hand, if states have positive identifications with each other, they will interact as friends, with their interactions based on collective interests. For many years, Germany and France, for instance, did not have positive identifications with each other. As a result, they fought multiple wars, including the two World Wars. Today, Germany and France have a much more positive identification with each other; consequently, they cooperate on issues such as Common Security and Defense Policy in Europe.

Security Sectors

After deciding on the preferred conception of security (objective, subjective, or discursive) and the referent object of security (such as state, individual, society, gender, or environment), the third topic is the choice of the security sectors. Many security theories, especially those associated with strategic studies, prefer to focus on the military sector, while others, like scholars of human security, include multiple sectors of security in their analysis (see Table 8.1). The next section provides a brief discussion of the following security sectors: military, environmental, economic, political, societal, and cyber.

Military Security

Of all sectors of security, the military sector is the most studied. That is because security studies, as a subfield of international relations, started at the beginning of the Cold War and focused primarily on the military competition between the U.S. and the Soviet Union. The military sector is mainly concerned with addressing internal and external military threats to states. Examples of internal threats to states include separatist movements, terrorist organizations, and militant drug cartels. Examples of external threats to states include occupation by other states and loss of territory or resources to foreign countries.

States allocate resources to their ground, naval, air, and nuclear forces to achieve **military security**. One could argue that other tools of military power are effective in as much as they support the land power missions. Victories at sea, air, or space are significant if they have an impact on what is occurring on land. Some strategists, like the British geographer Halford John Mackinder, therefore believe that the control of territory is the essential element of a state's power.

The three main types of operations by ground forces are **offensive**, **defensive**, and **stability operations**. Countries use offensive operations to destroy, dislocate, disintegrate, or isolate enemy forces and get control of population centers, terrain, and resources. Defensive and stability operations usually follow a successful offensive operation. The primary purpose of defensive operations is to counter the enemy's offense and create conditions favorable for future offensive operations against the enemy or the stability operations (Department of Army, 2011). Countries use stability operations to "re-establish a safe and secure environment, provide essential governmental services, emergency infrastructure reconstruction, and humanitarian relief" (U.S. Marine Corps, 2018, p. 1). Scholars or analysts usually compare the ground forces of countries according to the number of active and reserve military personnel in the army, armored vehicles, tanks, and artillery (Institute for International and Strategic Studies, 2019).

The navy is used for control of the sea, providing or denying maritime access and security, sea transport, and projection of power. Some scholars, like the American strategist Alfred Thayer Mahan, have argued that the national greatness of countries is achieved through the command of the sea and naval power. Based on their operational environment, navies can be divided into the three categories of **blue water**, **brown water**, and **green water navies**. The three metaphorical colors "denote generally the proximity of land: 'blue' water, the oceanic, reaches farthest from land; 'green' water is the oceanic littoral; and 'brown' water comprises rivers, bays, and estuaries" (Rubel, 2010, p. 44). Scholars and analysts usually compare the naval power of countries according to the number of active and reserve military personnel in the navy, aircraft carriers, submarines, cruisers, destroyers, frigates, and amphibious ships (Institute for International and Strategic Studies, 2019).

The air force is used for control of the skies, support of ground forces, strategic bombardment, air transport, reconnaissance, and air defense. The advantage of airpower over land and naval power is that it can bypass the enemy's navy and army and get to places where land and naval forces usually cannot reach. Airpower has more fluidity and flexibility than do land and naval forces (Mueller, 2017). Scholars and analysts usually compare the airpower of countries according to the number of active and reserve military personnel in the air force, tactical and strategic aircraft, unmanned aerial vehicles, transport aircraft, long-range missiles, and air defense systems (Institute for International and Strategic Studies, 2019).

With advances in technology, countries have started investing in their space force as well. The U.S., Russia, and China are investing in such space-related capabilities as space reconnaissance and surveillance; counterspace capabilities like jamming capabilities, directed energy weapons, and ground-based antisatellite missiles;

and their overall ability to locate and assess other countries' space capabilities (Defense Intelligence Agency, 2019).

The nuclear power of countries comprises two types of nuclear weapons and three types of delivery systems. The two types of nuclear weapons are **strategic nuclear weapons** and **tactical nuclear weapons**. Strategic nuclear weapons are delivered via long-range delivery systems, and their primary use is to attack the war-making capabilities of the enemy, including the military and industrial centers. Tactical nuclear weapons, on the other hand, are short-range nuclear weapons for attacking military forces of the enemy on the battlefields. Scholars and analysts usually compare nuclear forces of countries according to the number of strategic and tactical nuclear weapons and the three delivery systems known as the **nuclear triad**: bombers, ballistic missiles, and submarines.

Among the strategies that states use to tackle internal and external military threats are annihilation, dislocation, attrition, exhaustion, deterrence, and coercion. The main goal of the **annihilation strategy** is to destroy an enemy's material strength by defeating it in a decisive battle. An example of an annihilation strategy is the U.S.'s military strategy in the Spanish-American War of 1898, when it defeated the Spanish fleet at Manila Bay in the Philippines and Santiago Bay in Cuba. In contrast to annihilation strategy, a **dislocation strategy** is mainly about the war of movement, or maneuvering, and achieving victory through knocking an adversary off-balance psychologically. German lightning war, or blitzkrieg, which resulted in the collapse of the French military in 1940 is an excellent example of a dislocation strategy (Echevarria, 2017).

When a state adopts an **attrition strategy**, its primary goal is to destroy an enemy's physical capacity to fight. The U.S. strategy against Japan during the World War II was mainly based on the attrition strategy. The **exhaustion strategy** targets the enemy's willingness to fight. Historically, states resort to guerrilla warfare, siege, and blockade to exhaust their enemies. An example of exhaustion strategy occurred with Britain's blockade of Germany during World War I (Echevarria, 2017).

Deterrence strategy is when states dissuade others from changing their policies. States that choose deterrence strategy adopt policies that send the message to their rivals that they are capable of and willing to inflict pain on their rivals and even suffer pain if it becomes necessary. An excellent example of deterrence is the nuclear deterrence between the U.S. and the Soviet Union during the Cold War. In contrast to deterrence, the main goal of **coercion strategy**, or compellence, is to persuade an adversary to change its policy, either through show of force or limited use of force. An example of a successful coercion strategy is the U.S. military threat in 1994, which reversed the coupe in Haiti and brought Jean-Bertrand Aristide back to power (Echevarria, 2017).

Environmental Security

In 1972, Sweden hosted the United Nations Conference on the Human Environment which started many of the discussions on **environmental security**. According to Buzan, "Environmental security concerns the maintenance of the local and the planetary biosphere as the essential support system on which all other human enterprises depend" (Buzan, 1991, p. 433). Since 1972, states have signed more than 500 agreements about environmental security. As of 2019, the most important environmental agreement is the 2015 Paris Agreement, with 186 members (Mitchell, 2019).

One of the main questions in environmental security is about the referent object of security. Should humans care about environmental security because of its impact on their lives, or should they care about it because of its impact on the lives of all the species that share this planet? For instance, should humans care that one in four species in the world is at risk of extinction (United Nations, 2019)? Depending on the answers to the above questions, different issues can be included in environmental security.

According to Buzan, Wæver, and de Wilde (1998), some of the environmental security issues are:

- disruption of ecosystems, such as climate change and deforestation (Busby, 2007)
- energy problems like depletion of natural resources, or the problems of nuclear waste (Hargreaves, 2011)
- population problems, such as the question of sustainable development (Hartman, Butts, Bankus, & Carney, 2012)
- food problems, such as loss of fertile soil (National Intelligence Council, 2015)
- economic problems due to global sea level rise (Lindsey, 2019)
- war-related environmental damages, such as the impact of use of depleted uranium on the environment (International Atomic Energy Agency, 2009)

Economic Security

Economic security is about protecting access to markets and resources, financial stability, and trade. The scope and definition of economic security very much depend on the relations between politics and the market. Mercantilists, for instance, argue that the state is more important than the market; therefore, they see economic security as an element of national security. For mercantilists, economic interaction among states is a zero-sum interaction, in which someone's gain is another's loss. Liberals, on the other hand, argue that a state's interference in the market should be minimal. According to liberals, economic interactions are not zero-sum games; therefore, an economic gain by a country will not necessarily create security problems for others (Buzan, Wæver & de Wilde, 1998).

Political Security

Political security discusses non-military threats to a state's internal and external sovereignty. It is about "the organizational stability of states, systems of government, and the ideologies that give them legitimacy" (Buzan, 1991, July 1, p. 433). The legitimacy of a state can be threatened internally by secessionist movements, revolutions, and coups. External legitimacy of countries can be challenged when other countries do not recognize them as a legitimate government. For 16 years, the U.S. refrained from recognizing the Soviet regime as the legitimate government of Russia, only extending its recognition to the Soviet Union in 1933 (Department of State, n.d.). External actors can also play a role in challenging the internal legitimacy of states. An example of such a threat by external actors is the Soviet Union's manipulation of Communist parties around the world to challenge other countries' policies.

Societal Security

Societal security is about protecting the identity and cohesion of societies. The recent surge in nationalist, anti-globalization movements in the world is a reaction to societal insecurities created by globalization. Because of its cultural homogenization tendencies, globalization has weakened local identities and replaced them with global identities. These changes have created societal security challenges (Buzan, Wæver & de Wilde, 1998).

One of the important topics associated with societal security is the security of minorities in society. Many societies have ethnic, religious, and linguistic minorities, and security for those minorities is not always tantamount to the security of the majority. Indeed, some may see the security of minorities as contradictory to national security. During World War II, for instance, thousands of people of Japanese descent (many of whom were citizens) were put in internment camps in the U.S. (National Archives, 2020) and Canada (Marsh, 2020) in the name of national security.

Alternatively, since 2017 the Chinese government has adopted a program called "Regulations on De-extremification," resulting in the internment of millions of Chinese Muslims in Xinjiang Uygur Autonomous Region. The Chinese government is accused of trying to erase the identity of ethnic Muslim groups and stop them from practicing their religion (Amnesty International, 2018).

Cybersecurity

Cybersecurity is defined as the "activity or process, ability or capability, or state whereby information and communications systems and the information contained therein are protected from and/or defended against damage, unauthorized use or modification, or exploitation" (National Initiative for Cybersecurity Careers and Studies, n.d.). It is about reducing the insecurity of the physical and virtual aspects of cyberspace. The physical aspect of cyberspace includes computers, servers, satellites, and undersea data cables while the virtual aspect of cyberspace refers to the data and protocols for processing, sharing, storing, and protecting the information.

The referent objects of cybersecurity include computer networks, individuals, companies, and the critical infrastructure of states. For computer experts, the referent objects of cybersecurity are computers and computer networks. For those who deal with crimes and espionage, such as law enforcement and intelligence agents, the referent objects of cybersecurity are business and government networks. From the perspectives of national security experts, the referent objects of cybersecurity are military networks and the critical infrastructure of states (Cavelty, 2019).

The most common types of cyberattacks include malware, phishing, man-in-the-middle, denial of service (DOS), SQL injection, and zero-day exploit attacks (IBM Services, 2018). Cyberattacks can be either targeted attacks, like spear-phishing attacks, or untargeted attacks, like ransomware attacks. Some of the motivations behind cyberattacks are financial gain, access to restricted information, disruption of infrastructure, and even bringing awareness to a political or social cause. Perpetrators of cyberattacks are cyberterrorists, cybercriminals, state-sponsored actors, and hacktivists (Ablon, 2018). Cybersecurity operations against cyber threats include "threat reduction, vulnerability reduction, deterrence, international engagement, incident response, resiliency, and recovery policies and activities" (National Initiative for Cybersecurity Careers and Studies, n.d.).

Security Studies and Theories of International Relations

Many theories of international relations address security. The following section reviews security concepts from the perspective of the three best known theories of international relations: realism, liberalism, and constructivism. Each of these three theories differs from the others on the most important referent object of security, security sectors, and conceptions of security.

Realism and Security Studies

From the perspective of **realism**, the most appropriate referent object of security is the nation-state. Realism also primarily focuses on the military sector. Even though some realists use the subjective conception of security in their analysis (Walt, 1985), many realists choose the objective conception of security. Realists argue that states interact in a self-help system, which is based on the conflict of interests among states. According to realism, power is the primary tool for states to achieve security in an anarchic international system.

When it comes to nation-states and power, there are three typologies of realism. Human nature realists argue that states, like humans, have a lust for power; therefore, they look for maximization of their relative power. Defensive realists, on the other hand, argue that states do not seek to maximize their relative power. States instead strive for as much power that does not disrupt the balance of power in the international system. Finally, offensive realists argue that, because states interact in an anarchic world, they seek to maximize their relative power and their ultimate goal is to achieve hegemony (Mearsheimer, 2001).

One of the key security concepts in realism is the concept of the **security dilemma**. The main idea behind the security dilemma is that, when a state increases its power to achieve more security, other countries feel threatened by it, so they increase their power as well. As a result, all countries end up feeling less secure. Some realists argue that a security dilemma is more conducive to war if offensive military capabilities are more advantageous than are defensive capabilities and when it is not easy to distinguish between offensive and defensive capabilities. In contrast, a security dilemma is less conducive to war if defensive capabilities have the upper hand and offensive and defensive capabilities can be distinguished from each other (Jervis, 1978).

Liberalism and Security Studies

In contrast to the realism, **liberalism** considers multiple referent objects of security and does not explicitly prioritize any of the security sectors or any of the three conceptions of security. Liberalism believes in the harmony of interests among states and argues that interactions among states can result in non-zero-sum games. Liberalism provides several solutions to the problems of the security dilemma and war. Liberalism's democratic peace theory, for instance, argues that the nature of governments has a direct impact on the security dilemma in the world. According to liberals, the historical evidence has shown that democracies do not go to war with each other (see Chapter 4 about the democratic peace theory). According to other proponents of liberalism, international regimes and institutions help nation-states find solutions to collective good problems, such as the problem of collective security. Liberalism also argues that an increase in international commerce and interdependence among states contributes positively to peace and security in the world.

Those liberals, whose referent object of security is the individual, focus on issues such as human rights and argue that when confronted with gross violations of human rights, such as ethnic cleansing and genocide, the international community has the Responsibility to Protect (R2P) and should intervene. **Ethnic cleansing** refers to policies that render "an area ethnically homogeneous by using force or intimidation to remove persons of given groups from the area" (United Nations Security Council S/25274, 1993, February 10). **Genocide** refers to any "acts committed with intent to destroy, in whole or in part, a national, ethnic, racial or religious group" (United Nations General Assembly No. 1021, 1948).

Constructivism and Security Studies

The referent object of security for **constructivism** is the nation-state and other collectivities. Like realism, constructivism focuses on the military sector. When it comes to conceptions of security, constructivism chooses the discursive approach (Buzan & Hansen, 2009, p. 38). Constructivism's main argument is that humans make the world what it is through interactions with each other. If the world is a self-help and war-prone world, that is because humans made it that way (Onuf, 1989). Positive or negative identifications of people with each other create different types of worlds. If people positively identify with each other, they perceive others' interests and security concerns as theirs. The more people positively identify with others, the more they interact based on collective interests. On the other hand, the more people, states, races, and civilizations have negative identifications with others, the more they are prone to consider only their self-interests. The more actors consider their self-interests, the more they exploit others (Wendt, 1999).

One of the main contributions of constructivism in security studies is the **securitization theory**. Securitization theory talks about the process through which someone or something is considered a threat to the survival of a referent object. Successful elevation of an issue to the level of security issues enables the securitizing actor to go beyond the usual norms and rules of the game and adopt extraordinary measures. For instance, a successful securitization process during the COVID-19 pandemic enabled authorities around the world to shutdown economies, issue travel bans, require wearing masks, and quarantine people. Sometimes a successful securitization of a group as a threat to the survival of a state can lead to extraordinary measures that result in gross human rights violations, such as ethnic cleansing and genocide.

Conclusion

This chapter provides some necessary analytic tools for making a decision concerning a preferred conception of security, a referent object of security, and security sectors that put the survival of a referent object at risk. The three conceptions of security are objective, subjective, and discursive. The objective approach to security defines security as the absence of threat, and it mainly cares about threats that emanate from material capabilities. The objective approach does not differentiate between the capabilities of friends, rivals, and enemies. For a scholar with an objective conception of security, the capabilities of enemies, rivals, and friends are all threatening. The subjective approach to security is more nuanced than is the objective approach. The subjective approach defines security as the absence of fear. It argues that states are not worried about the capabilities of other states equally. They are more worried about the capabilities of enemies than of friends. The discursive approach to security looks at the process through which someone or something is perceived as a security threat to the survival of a referent object.

After the conception of security, the scholar must determine the referent object of security. The two common referent objects of security are the individual and the nation-state. It must be followed by a decision regarding the security sector that is the most important for the survival of the referent object. For instance, if the referent object is the nation-state, then the military, societal, economic, or political security sectors should be studied.

Based on the above three choices, scholars and analysts land in either traditional or nontraditional camps in security studies. Traditional security studies mainly focus on military competition among states. The nontraditional camp, on the other hand, has a wider approach (that is, more security sectors) and a deeper approach (that is, more referent objects of security) to security studies. The nontraditional camp includes non-military security sectors, such as the environmental, economic, societal, and political sectors. Furthermore, the referent object of nontraditional security studies goes beyond the states and includes individuals, genders, societies, and economic classes.

From the above three choices, one can see how the choice of a conception of security has a fundamental impact on analysis and on policy recommendations. The policy recommendation of an analyst relying on the objective conception of security might be the creation of a deterrence force against all the powerful countries, regardless of whether they are allies, rivals, or enemies. For an analyst with the subjective conception of security, a deterrence force capable of deterring rivals and enemies would be sufficient. An analyst with the discursive conception of security can challenge the list of enemies and allies and ask why they have been considered as such in the first place. This last analyst has a longer list of policy alternatives and is more capable of thinking outside the box.

References

Ablon, L. (2018, March 15). Data thieves, the motivations of cyber threat actors and their use and monetization of stolen data [PDF File]. *RAND Corporations*. Retrieved from https://www.rand.org/content/dam/rand/pubs/testimonies/CT400/CT490/RAND_CT490.pdf

Amnesty International. (2018). China: "Where are they?" [PDF File]. Retrieved from https://www.amnesty.org/download/Documents/ASA1791132018ENGLISH.PDF

Avalon Project. (2008). The atomic bombings of Hiroshima and Nagasaki: Chapter 10 - Total Casualties. Retrieved from https://avalon.law.yale.edu/20th_century/mp10.asp

Busby, J. W. (2007, November). Climate change and national security: An agenda for action [PDF File]. *Council on Foreign Relations*. Retrieved from https://cfrd8-files.cfr.org/sites/default/files/report_pdf/ClimateChange_CSR32%20%281%29.pdf

Buzan, B. (1983). *People, states, and fear: The national security problem in international relations*. Brighton: Wheatsheaf Books.

Buzan, B. (1991, July 1). New patterns of global security in the twenty-first century. *International Affairs*, 67(3), 431–451.

Buzan, B., & Hansen, L. (2009). *The evolution of international security studies*. Cambridge: Cambridge University Press.

Buzan, B., Wæver, O., & de Wilde, J. (1998). *Security: A new framework for analysis*. Boulder, Col: Lynne Rienner.

Cavelty, M. D. (2019). Cyber-security. In A. Collins (ed.), *Contemporary Security Studies*. Oxford: Oxford University Press.

Central Intelligence Agency. (n.d.). What was the missile gap?. Retrieved from https://www.cia.gov/readingroom/collection/what-was-missile-gap

Central Intelligence Agency. (2007) Iraq's chemical warfare program. Retrieved from https://web.archive.org/web/20200802012241/https://www.cia.gov/library/reports/general-reports-1/iraq_wmd_2004/chap5.html

Collins, A. (2019). *Contemporary security studies.* Oxford: Oxford University Press.

Defense Intelligence Agency. (1989). Chapter IV - Nuclear, strategic defense, and space programs. *Federation of American Scientists.* Retrieved from https://fas.org/irp/dia/product/smp_89.htm

Defense Intelligence Agency. (2019, January). Challenges to security in space [PDF File]. *Defense Intelligence Agency.* Retrieved from https://www.dia.mil/Portals/27/Documents/News/Military%20Power%20Publications/Space_Threat_V14_020119_sm.pdf

Department of Army. (2011, October 10). Unified land operations [PDF File]. Retrieved from https://www.army.mil/e2/downloads/rv7/info/references/ADP_3-0_ULO_Oct_2011_APD.pdf

Department of State. (n.d.). Recognition of the Soviet Union, 1933. *Department of State Office of the Historian.* Retrieved from https://history.state.gov/milestones/1921-1936/ussr

Echevarria, A. J. (2017). *Military strategy: A very short introduction.* New York: Oxford University Press

Gorbachev, M. S. (1989a). Soviet transcript of the Malta Summit December 2–3, 1989 [Transcript PDF File]. *The National Security Archive.* Retrieved from https://nsarchive2.gwu.edu/NSAEBB/NSAEBB298/Document%2010.pdf

Gorbachev, M. S. (1989b, April 7). Text of Gorbachev speech [Transcript]. *AP NEWS.* Retrieved from https://www.apnews.com/9f9af12bfbeda79deebc76e1423b8ba8

Hargreaves, S. (2011, April 1). Nuclear waste: America's 'biggest security threat'. *CNN Money*. Retrieved from https://money.cnn.com/2011/04/01/news/economy/nuclear_waste/index.htm

Hartman, J., Butts, K., Bankus, B., & Carney, S. (Eds.). (2012, January). Sustainability and national security [PDF File]. *United States Army War College*. Retrieved from https://csl.armywarcollege.edu/usacsl/publications/SustainabilityandNationalSecurity(webversion).pdf

HIV.GOV. (n.d.). A Timeline of HIV and AIDS [PDF File]. Retrieved from https://www.hiv.gov/sites/default/files/aidsgov-timeline.pdf

IBM Services. (2018, October 2). Learn about cyber attacks and how to defend against them. Retrieved from https://www.ibm.com/services/business-continuity/cyber-attack

Institute for International and Strategic Studies. (2019, February 15). Chapter One: Sixty years of The Military Balance. *The Military Balance, 119*(1), 9–20. https://doi.org/10.1080/04597222.2019.1561024

International Atomic Energy Agency. (2009, April). Assessing effects of depleted uranium: The IAEA role [PDF File]. Retrieved from https://www.iaea.org/sites/default/files/iaearole.pdf

Jervis, R. (1978, January 1). Cooperation under the security dilemma. *World Politics, 30*(2), 167–214.

Kochanek, K. D., Murphy, S. L., Xu, J., & Arias, E. (2019, June 24). Deaths: Final Data for 2017 [PDF File]. *National Vital Statistics Reports, 68*(9). Retrieved from https://www.cdc.gov/nchs/data/nvsr/nvsr68/nvsr68_09-508.pdf

Kristensen, H. M. & Korda, M. (2019, July). Status of world nuclear forces. *Federation of American Scientists*. Retrieved from https://fas.org/issues/nuclear-weapons/status-world-nuclear-forces/

Lindsey, R. (2019, September 19). Climate change: Global sea level. *NOAA Climate*. Retrieved from https://www.climate.gov/news-features/understanding-climate/climate-change-global-sea-level

Marsh, J. H. (2020, June 12). Japanese Canadian internment: Prisoners in their own country. *The Canadian Encyclopedia, Historica Canada*. Retrieved from https://www.thecanadianencyclopedia.ca/en/article/japanese-internment-banished-and-beyond-tears-feature

McDonald, M. (2013). Constructivism. In P. D. Williams (ed.), *Security Studies an Introduction*. (2nd ed)., p62–75. New York: Routledge Taylor & Francis Group.

Mearsheimer, J. (2001). *The tragedy of great power politics*. New York: Norton.

Mitchell, R. B. (2019). International Environmental Agreements Database Project (Version 2018.1). Retrieved from http://iea.uoregon.edu

Morgenthau, H. J. (1948). *Politics among nations: The struggle for power and peace*. New York: A. A. Knopf.

Mueller, K. (2017, November 20). Air power. *Oxford Research Encyclopedia of International Studies*. Retrieved from https://oxfordre.com/internationalstudies/view/10.1093/acrefore/9780190846626.001.0001/acrefore-9780190846626-e-1

National Archives. (2020, March 17). Japanese relocation during World War II. *National Archives*. Retrieved from https://www.archives.gov/education/lessons/japanese-relocation#documents%20

National Initiative for Cybersecurity Careers and Studies. (n.d.). Cybersecurity glossary. Retrieved from https://niccs.us-cert.gov/about-niccs/glossary

National Intelligence Council. (2012). Global trends 2030: Alternative worlds [PDF File]. Retrieved from https://www.dni. gov/files/documents/GlobalTrends_2030.pdf

National Intelligence Council. (2015). Global food security [PDF File]. Retrieved from https://www.dni.gov/files/documents/ Newsroom/Reports%20and%20Pubs/Global_Food_Security_ ICA.pdf

Onuf, N. G. (1989). *World of our making: Rules and rule in social theory and international relations.* Columbia, SC: University of South Carolina Press.

Rubel, R. C. (2010). Talking about sea control. *Naval War College Review, 63*(4), 38–47.

Stockholm International Peace Research Institute. (2019). Data for all countries 1949–2018 [Excel File]. Retrieved from https://www.sipri.org/sites/default/files/SIPRI-Milex-data-1949-2018_0.xlsx

United Nations. (2019, May 6). World is 'on notice' as major UN report shows one million species face extinction. Retrieved from https://news.un.org/en/story/2019/05/1037941

United Nations General Assembly No. 1021. (1948, December 9). Convention on the Prevention and Punishment of the Crime of Genocide. Retrieved from https://treaties.un.org/doc/ publication/unts/volume%2078/volume-78-i-1021-english.pdf

United Nations Security Council S/25274. (1993, February 10). Interim Report of the Commission of Experts Established Pursuant to Security Council Resolution 780 (1992). Retrieved from https://undocs.org/S/25274

UNRCPD. (2019). Weapons of mass destruction. Retrieved from http://unrcpd.org/wmd/

U.S. Marine Corps. (2018, April 4). Stability operations [PDF File]. *Department of the Navy.* Retrieved from https://www.marines. mil/Portals/1/Publications/MCWP%203-03.pdf

Walt, S. M. (1985, April 1). Alliance formation and the balance of world power. *International Security, 9*(4), 3–43.

Wendt, A. (1992, January 1). Anarchy is what states make of it: The social construction of power politics. *International Organization, 46*(2), 391–425.

Wendt, A. (1999). *Social theory of international politics.* Cambridge, U.K: Cambridge University Press.

Williams, P., & McDonald, M. (2018). *Security Studies: An Introduction.* London: Routledge, Taylor & Francis Group.

Wright, Q. (1942). *A study of war.* Chicago: University of Chicago Press.

International Organization, International Law, and Human Security

9

Scott Meachum

Abstract

An important aspect of international politics is international organization based on international cooperation. While there is justifiable emphasis placed on the causes and consequences of international conflict, it is just as important to understand the foundations and results of international cooperative efforts. States and other actors consistently work with each other to achieve common goals, but they do so within an environment that makes organization difficult. Yet evidence of successful cooperation is readily apparent from the presence of intergovernmental organizations to the continued growth and development of international law. One of the areas where this development has taken on significant relevance is in the establishment of human rights and humanitarian interventions. The key to understanding and explaining the success of cooperation—or lack thereof—lies in recognizing the inherent difficulties of collective action. Organization does not occur by accident, and it is most useful to view international cooperation as a process undertaken by international actors.

Learning Objectives

- Know and explain the difference between international organization/cooperation and between international organizations and intergovernmental organizations

- Identify and describe key obstacles that obstruct international cooperative efforts
- Understand how international law differs from domestic law and explain the nature and sources of international law
- Describe the development and the failures of international organizations and international law with respect to human rights

Textbooks on international politics treat the topics of international organization, international law, and human security in a variety of manners. Some give each topic its own chapter while others group them together in various ways, focusing on different aspects of each. Still others omit one or more entirely. While each deserves its own fuller treatment, insofar as concerns their introduction, there are common themes that link the topics and provide a useful framework for study. Foremost among the many themes is the notion of cooperation, which is how states and other actors work together for a common purpose. Focusing on cooperation, this chapter illustrates how states organize themselves, examine the rules and laws that shape behavior, and how international organizations and international law have both succeeded and failed in one important aspect of human security: human rights.

An initial challenge when studying these particular topics is understanding the vocabulary discipline-specific scholars and analysts use. For instance, **international organizations** are bodies or agencies that are tasked with addressing a particular issue or topic. Examples of such include the United Nations (UN), the World Trade Organization (WTO), the International Court of Justice (ICJ), and many hundreds more. Because these and other organizations are created, financed, and controlled by their member states, scholars and analysts often refer to them as **intergovernmental organizations (IGOs)**. Meanwhile, *international cooperation* will refer more generally to the collective actions of states and nonstate actors to address common problems in international politics. An example of such cooperation would be when states and other actors work together to address the threat of climate change.

Cooperation is not often easy. Recall that the defining characteristic of the international system is anarchy. This does not mean chaos or disorder; rather, it refers to the fact that, unlike domestic politics where a country's government is the highest authority over a given area, there is no supranational authority that controls international politics. Another way to say this is that states are sovereign. They have ultimate authority over their domestic territory and are treated as equals in the international system. This notion of sovereignty is one of the many rules and norms that shape and sometimes constrain behavior in the international system. Over time, through either explicit agreement by states or by customary practice, some of those rules have attained the status of law. In that way, international law, which is discussed in the second part of this chapter, is distinct from domestic law. There is no world government to pass or enforce laws. Instead, international law has developed over centuries from many different sources.

The third part of this chapter examines a topic that sits squarely at the intersection of international organization and international law. Especially since the end of World War II, there has been a broadening of what "security" means in international politics. While once it almost exclusively referred to the sovereign rights of states, as the United Nations and other organizations began to focus on relief efforts and humanitarian concerns, the notion of human security—including the protection of individuals from violence, environmental concerns, and health disasters—has come to prominence in recent decades. A significant portion of human security is the human rights regime that has built up to protect certain rights that everyone possesses. However, cooperation is difficult even in this context, and there is a significant gap between what international organization and international law can provide.

International Organization and Cooperation

On April 4, 1949, representatives from twelve countries in North America and Western Europe signed the Washington Treaty and established the **North Atlantic Treaty Organization (NATO)**. Known best for the language in Article 5 of the Charter that declares an attack against one as an attack against all, the initial focus of NATO was the commitment of its members to collective security. Meant to act as a counterweight to the Soviet Union and as a bulwark against the tide of the perceived threat of global communism, NATO served this purpose through the Cold War. With the fall of the Berlin Wall in 1989 and the dissolution of the Soviet Union in 1991, many questioned the continued need for the organization.

While questions about its continued existence remain to be answered, it is important to remember the international environment at the time of NATO's founding, as it is hardly surprising that states sought some form of collective security after World War II. For centuries, states and their predecessors had signed treaties and formed alliances meant to prevent wars, but the alliance system broke down with disastrous consequences ahead of World War I. That conflict saw the worst fighting the world had known, and, seeking to forestall a similar occurrence and to prevent future wars, the League of Nations was a collective security organization tasked with maintaining world peace using dispute resolution mechanisms like negotiation and arbitration. That hopeful peace was never realized, though, as within twenty years of the League's founding the world was at war for a second time. Though historians and other scholars correctly identify a myriad of complex factors that led to the outbreak of World War II, a general lack of commitment to collective security—exemplified by the United States refusing to ratify the League's treaty after being championed by President Woodrow Wilson—certainly compounded issues. More horrific than World War I, World War II once more spurred a consensus that some form of collective security was required to prevent a third world war.

In 1945, the United Nations was formed as both a successor to and an improvement on the League of Nations. Created with six principal organs—the General Assembly, the Security Council, the Economic and Social Council, the International Court of Justice, the Secretariat, and the Trusteeship Council—the UN serves multiple roles. Meant to be an inclusive organization, the UN boasted fifty-one member-states at its inception and has grown to include 193 members as of 2019. According to Chapter V, Article 24 of the UN Charter, the Security Council is tasked with maintaining international peace and security. To achieve this goal, the Security Council is empowered to take a number of actions up to and including armed force, which it has invoked on a limited number of occasions.

If the UN was created to act as a collective security organization, why then did the countries in the north Atlantic region form another organization four years later? If there was a broad, international consensus that collective security was an important goal, is a second organization not redundant? Moreover, why would states that have to provide funding for IGOs be willing to spend twice for the same outcome? There are many correct answers to these questions, but any full explanation must begin with an understanding of the possibilities for and difficulties with international cooperation more generally.

The Logic of International Cooperation

Politics is frequently described as the process through which individuals and groups in a society decide on a particular course of action. For instance, the decisions to form the UN and NATO were the result of a number of countries responding to a perceived threat and creating organizations to deal with it. Another way to think of the study of politics, then, is that it is the study of the collective action of various groups of actors. Those actors might have different goals and motivations, and there are certainly external influences that shape events, but the results we see are the consequences of the interactions of the various actors. It is thus particularly useful to think of international cooperation through the lens of collective action.

The **prisoners dilemma**, which has been discussed in previous chapters, illustrates how actors might be drawn towards defection or cooperation based on calculated outcomes founded in their self-interest. What does the outcome of the prisoners dilemma mean for international cooperation? Potentially a great deal. Consider an arms race between two fictitious countries: Country A and Country B. Each country spends huge amounts of money every year to try and ensure that it has more missiles than the other. After some time, each country has enough missiles to destroy the other, but each keeps building because there is no guarantee that the other will stop. Even if the two countries sign an agreement that would limit the number of missiles produced, there is a perceived advantage to be gained by either country in defecting from the terms of the agreement and continuing to build up its stockpiles. Indeed, many scholars pointed to the nuclear arms race between the U.S. and the Soviet Union during the Cold War as an actual prisoner's dilemma. Both countries would be better off agreeing to stop producing missiles and nuclear weapons, but non-proliferation treaties were difficult to negotiate as the stakes were so high.

The prisoners dilemma is not the only way to examine the difficulties that exist for international cooperative efforts. In the 1960s, biologist G. Hardin introduced what he called the **tragedy of the commons**, which is a situation in which individuals who would benefit from a common resource nevertheless destroy that resource by acting in their own self-interest. Hardin's example focused on a "common," which was public pastureland once prominent in Great Britain where herders could let their animals graze. For each herder, it makes sense to increase the size of their own herd because they benefit from having more animals that they can sell at the market. However, all herders have the same incentive to grow their herd, and over time, as more and more animals graze in the commons, the pasture is unable to support the larger number of animals. Thus, while the herders tried to maximize their own individual profits, their actions had a detrimental effect on the collective whole (Hardin, 1968).

Both the prisoner's dilemma and the tragedy of the commons speak to a set of concerns that are known as **collective action problems**. Put simply, collective action problems arise when actors (individuals or states) try to work together for a common goal but face obstacles due to their own self-interest. In the prisoner's dilemma, the incentive is for each prisoner to defect and confess and ensure a lighter sentence. In the tragedy of the commons, the incentive is for each herder to add to their herd, as one more animal means more profit. In both instances, though, the group is worse off than if everyone had worked together.

Collective action problems arise frequently in international politics. The arms race during the Cold War undermined international security while the U.S. and the Soviet Union each tried to make themselves safer. In order to engage in collective security, states must invariably allow their militaries to be directed by foreign commanders and that implicates sovereignty concerns. Free trade is shown to increase the global standard of living, but many domestic constituencies will suffer by eliminating trade barriers. The environment would be better off if global carbon dioxide emissions were curbed and the reliance on fossil fuel was lowered, but oil producing countries would lose revenue and the cost to shift to clean energy is deemed prohibitive by many. Virtually all topics in international politics are subject to collective action issues.

Organizational efforts around global environmental concerns underscore one other significant obstacle that is endemic to collective action. Things like clean air, the ozone layer, and the global eradication of diseases are **public goods**. Public goods, sometimes referred to as *collective goods*, are those things that no one can be prevented from using or enjoying once they are created or provided. Moreover, one person's use does not reduce the amount available for others. That is, when one person breathes in clean air, their doing so does not take away clean air for others to breathe. The crucial issue associated with public goods is that everyone wants to use them, but no one wants to pay for them. This introduces the incentive to free ride, wherein individuals benefit but do not want to contribute. This tendency can make cooperation that much more difficult.

If the prospects for cooperation look bleak, it is for good reason. Cooperation in international politics is hard. First, states often have conflicting preferences. They might not even want to work towards the same goal. Second, even if they generally agree on a potential outcome, there may be individual incentives that compel states to act in their own self-interest and not the group's. Finally, there is a possibility that other states will free ride on the efforts of a few, which can create a disincentive to act. Yet cooperation is possible and happens frequently in the international system. Both Hardin and Olsen suggest that coercion is a means to force cooperation and avoid collective action issues. The lack of a supranational government makes this difficult, but it is not an impossible task. Moreover, states utilize a number of other mechanisms to aid cooperation, and it is to those efforts that we now turn.

Designing Cooperation

The previous description and examples of collective action underscore two fundamental obstacles associated with cooperation in the international system. The first is enforcement and relates to the fact that states often struggle to make credible commitments to abide by their agreements. In the prisoner's dilemma, the suspects might have agreed with each other to stay quiet, but once they are at the police station, there is no way to guarantee their behaving accordingly. Likewise, in an arms race, how does one country convince the other that it will actually limit its arms production? Compounding the enforcement and credibility issue are difficulties associated with information. In a perfect world where every state knew everything, including the goals and motivations of every other state, there is still the possibility of miscommunication or misunderstanding. Where states have private information, and incentives to keep that information private, uncertainty must enter the calculus of states as they make decisions.

With that said, cooperation does not happen by chance. The UN was created only after states addressed the specific and general failings of the League of Nations and sought to correct them. The **World Trade Organization (WTO)** evolved from the **General Agreement on Tariffs and Trade (GATT)** and only after decades of negotiated trade discussions by member-states. Even setting aside formal IGOs, cooperative efforts like the Convention Against Torture and other Cruel, Inhuman or Degrading Treatment or Punishment (CAT) and other human rights agreements represent the concerted efforts by states and other actors toward a goal. Thus, the important takeaway is this: cooperation is possible and happens when states take intentional steps to address specific collective action issues.

Koremenos, Lipson, and Snidal (2001) theorize about this approach to cooperation and suggest that states meticulously and carefully design institutions to help them overcome obstacles. In particular, states can limit the size of organizations, define the scope of issues that organizations address, determine whether the activities of the organization are diffused or centralized, control the decision-making processes that the organization will use, and regulate the amount of flexibility that the organizations allow their members. Each one of these areas offers possibilities to address collective action issues; therefore, it should not be surprising that organizations vary greatly in their design. For instance, with regard to any international issue, an increase in the number of states involved is likely to make cooperation more difficult. More voices and opinions mean the possibility of more conflicting views and opinions. The more states that are involved increases the difficulty of monitoring all of the participants. Larger numbers increase the likelihood for miscommunication or misunderstanding, both of which can cause cooperation to break down. One solution, then, is to limit the membership of the organization to help prevent those problems.

Just as the size of an organization affects how well it can facilitate cooperation, so too does the number of issues it deals with. The UN addresses security concerns, development concerns, environmental concerns, and more. It is far broader in scope than the WTO, for example, which focuses exclusively on free trade. A singular focus might allow for more coordinated efforts on a particular topic, while a broad organization can address multiple issues but without the same depth. Will an organization have a centralized focus, or will its tasks be decentralized and left to its member-states? In the case of the WTO, there is a centralized dispute settlement mechanism that rules on trade disputes, but enforcement of the decision is then left up to members. This is an example of both centralization and decentralization that encourages states to participate but does not threaten their sovereignty too greatly.

Likewise, the structure of the decision-making process can inhibit or encourage cooperation. In the **UN General Assembly**, all 193 countries have an equal vote and decisions are majority rule. The **UN Security Council**, meanwhile, is limited to fifteen members, five of which are permanent members with a veto. Finally, flexibility refers to whether or not an organization will impose punishments or sanctions on members who cannot or will not meet its obligations. Consider an environmental agreement in which states agree to limit their emissions of carbon dioxide. If a state fails to meet its goal, should it be removed from the treaty or perhaps forced to pay a penalty? Would imposing such a condition make states less likely to agree in the first place?

That question speaks to a deeper lesson regarding international cooperation. Koremenos et al.'s design characteristics are useful to highlight the tradeoffs that come with designing cooperative efforts. For instance, depending on the issue or issues, states might want a broad consensus from countries around the world. This might lead to more superficial cooperation, like a treaty that condemns genocide but provides no mechanisms to prevent it. Conversely, a smaller organization or a narrower institution that comprises only a few members might allow for more preference alignment and deeper cooperation. No matter which decisions they make about cooperation, states, as we can clearly see, purposefully design organization to achieve different outcomes. This explanation also offers answers to the questions surrounding the need for two collective security organizations formed in the wake of World War II.

Since its founding, the UN Security Council has had difficulties reaching a consensus about how to respond to security threats and, in many cases, identifying whether particular security threats even exist. The reality that permanent members of the Security Council frequently disagree in their assessments and their vetoes ensures that nothing of substance occurs without near unanimous consent. The veto itself represents a tradeoff between an interest in bolstering global support for the UN and acknowledging the sovereignty concerns of the five most powerful countries, without which the organization would never last.

NATO, on the other hand, represented a far more cohesive group of countries. With all its members facing a security threat from the Soviet Union, consensus was easier to achieve. Yet even within that context, representatives of the original twelve members struggled to cooperate. The U.S. emerged from the Second World War as the dominant military and economic power in the world, and a strong history of isolationism would prove difficult to overcome. Meanwhile, some proposed continental European members had very different visions of an integrated Europe, especially from a military perspective. France was wary of German involvement given the history between the two countries, while the Benelux countries of Belgium, the Netherlands, and Luxembourg saw German integration as a prerequisite for any agreement and for future European economic stability (Kaplan, 2007).

NATO and the UN are two very different organizations with the same broad goal that were formed within four years of each other and were viewed very differently by their members. Each serves the particular needs of their respective members, and each organization is carefully designed in its own mission manner. Cooperation takes many forms, from a formal organization to a signed treaty to a simple agreement to act in a particular way. In all cases, though, it takes effort and planning to overcome the obstacles of collective action.

International Law

International organizations, particularly in the form of IGOs and NGOs, are a relatively recent addition to international politics. Likewise, international organization as a field of study in international relations dates back only a few decades. In both practical and scholarly terms, however, international law has a much longer tradition. Generally considered the father of international law, Hugo Grotius (1583–1645) wrote on the laws of war, the laws of the sea, and, most importantly, the law of nature as far back as the seventeenth century. Grotius conceived the law of nature as based in human reasoning and rationality. It exists separate and apart from any religious or political structures. We should not be surprised that legal scholars following this particular tradition would form a "naturalist" school of international law that focused on rules, laws, and norms derived completely from the laws of nature. Many modern human rights proponents point to natural law theories to support their arguments for universal human rights.

As the naturalist movement developed, so too did a competing school of thought that argued that international law comprised and was defined by state practice. This "positivism" emerged at the same time as the modern nation-state system, following the Peace of Westphalia in 1648. With the emphasis that Westphalia placed on nation-states as the dominant actors in international politics, positivist thinkers argued that the focus should be on the rules that states developed to govern themselves. That is, what states ought to do did not matter much, as they were not bound by any higher law. Instead, international law developed as states created it, and any individual or natural rights yielded to the supremacy of the state.

Generally, legislatures make laws, executives enforce those laws, and judiciaries interpret those laws. In international politics, no government exists to serve those functions. The lack of a central authority is an important distinction, but it should not obscure the fact that, even though international law is qualitatively different in its creation and enforcement from its domestic counterparts, it serves the same fundamental purposes as domestic law. All societies adopt rules and norms that provide order, offer stability and predictability, afford a means for conflict resolution, and promote conformity with a society's values. International law can and does give that structure to the international system.

Sources of International Law

As students of American or comparative politics realize, the basic three branch system of government wherein each branch has its own limited role as described above does not always exist in practice. For instance, although we may commonly assume that legislatures make laws, we can clearly see that, in countries around the world, coordinate branches also perform this task. In common law legal systems, precedent, that is, how a court decides a case and interprets the law, establishes law that future courts and other branches of government must follow. Likewise, executives and executive agencies frequently issue rules and regulations that have the same force and effect as legislative statutes. In short, in domestic systems of government, laws come from a variety of sources; international law is no different in this regard. Specifically, Article 38 of the Statute of the **International Court of Justice (ICJ)**, which scholars and analysts view as the most authoritative and complete account of the sources of international law, outlines four separate sources: (1) international custom, (2) treaties and agreements, (3) general principles of law, and (4) judicial decisions and statements and teachings on the law (UN, *Statute of the International Court of Justice*, Art. 38, Cl. 1). What follows expands on each of these sources.

Customary International Law

As a source of international law, customs are behaviors that have been so consistently practiced by states that they are ingrained as habits. Initially, the rules governing those behaviors are not likely written down and are more likely reinforced through societal pressures. Over time, though, more and more states follow the same habits to the point that they are universally practiced. Then the common practice is for customary law to be codified, that is, written down in a treaty; however, this usually only occurs after a considerable period of time. A good example of the application of customary international law, how it develops, and how courts deal with it comes from the U.S. Supreme Court case The Paquete Habana.

During the Spanish-American War, the U.S. imposed a blockade around Cuba, which was then a Spanish colony. Two Cuban fishing vessels that were unaware of the blockade were caught by American warships and captured as prizes of war. The captains of the ships argued in U.S. court that fishing vessels were exempt from capture under customary international law. To answer the question of whether that exemption did in fact exist, the U.S. Supreme Court traced the history of the rule as far back as 1400. The Court found that it had been the practice of France, England, Spain, Germany, and others to exempt coastal fishing vessels from being captured as prizes of war. The Court cited treaties, other court rulings, and other evidence to support its holding that states had, for a long period of time, acted in such a manner so as to establish the existence of a rule to apply to all states in the international system. In the words of Justice Horace Gray, "But the period of a hundred years which has since elapsed is amply sufficient to have enabled what originally may have rested in custom or comity, courtesy or concession, to grow, by the general assent of civilized nations, into a settled rule of international law" (The Paquete Habana, 1900, p. 694).

While an important part of international law, customary law has certain drawbacks. Because it relies on the practice of states over time, customary international law takes decades, if not longer, to develop. Both international and domestic courts have failed to recognize certain rules as customary laws if they have not been practiced for a sufficient time. Likewise, because customary law is rarely written down until it is recognized as such, confusion can arise as to whether and how a rule applies. This is particularly problematic as one of the hallmarks of law is to provide order and predictability. If there is uncertainty about whether a rule is in fact a law that applies to everyone, then states may not be able to sufficiently rely on it. Finally, when determining whether a particular custom has become so ingrained as to rise to the level of law courts, jurists and others typically look at the actions of the dominant states in world affairs. Thus, the law of the sea developed largely based on the habits and customs of the British and American navies. This means that not all states participate equally in the development of international law. Given the nature of the system for the last few centuries, many of the customs that have been recognized as law have a very Western-centric orientation.

Treaties

International agreements between states are known by a host of names, including treaties, conventions, accords, pacts, charters, protocols, and more. No matter the label, the key defining characteristic of international treaties is that states that sign them agree to "bind themselves legally to act in a particular way or to set up particular relations among themselves. A series of conditions and arrangements are laid out which the parties oblige themselves to carry out" (Shaw, 2017, p. 69).

Unlike custom as a source of international law, treaties are explicit regarding to what and to whom they apply. Think back to the North Atlantic Treaty discussed previously. The Charter was originally signed by twelve countries that mutually agreed to certain conditions: chiefly, to marshal a collective defense should one of the signatories be attacked. Following the 9/11 attacks in the U.S., the American government and its allies invoked Article 5 of the Charter, and NATO forces went on to fight in Afghanistan alongside U.S. forces against the Taliban government. This is exactly how treaties should function. The parties to them, having agreed to certain obligations, fulfill those obligations when the terms of the treaty require it. Unsurprisingly, treaties are the most common source of contemporary international law. Because they are negotiated between states, treaties allow less room for ambiguity than exists with customary international law, which is certainly a positive when it comes to identifying legal obligations.

Of course, the fact that treaties are voluntary means that states do not have to sign them at all. If a state views a particular obligation as too onerous, it can simply refuse to be a part of the agreement and will not be subject to any of its provisions. Indeed, many major international agreements lack a full consensus, as many states have refused to sign on to them. Moreover, it is important to note that merely signing a treaty does not indicate a state's full commitment or intent to comply with its terms. Before a treaty is binding on a state, it must be ratified. **Ratification** is the domestic process by which a state formally agrees to a treaty's terms. For instance, a U.S. trade delegation might negotiate a trade agreement with another country and provisionally agree to it, but the U.S. Senate has to vote on and approve any treaty before it becomes law. We can find many instances—particularly with respect to human rights agreements—of states signing international agreements but never ratifying them and, therefore, not being bound by them. For instance, the Office of the United Nations High Commissioner for Human Rights records that of eighteen major human rights treaties, the United States has signed and ratified only five, has signed but not ratified another four, and has refused to sign and ratify the remaining nine (United Nations Office of the United Nations High Commissioner for Human Rights).

Finally, if signing and ratifying a treaty was not already a complicated enough process, states frequently attach reservations to treaties, even as they ratify the agreements. Reservations are objections to particular provisions of a treaty. A state might disagree with how certain terms are defined or applied or might agree with the general text of a treaty but not with each and every clause. By tendering a reservation, a state can agree in principal but try to limit certain provisions. For instance, the International Covenant on Civil and Political Rights (ICCPR) prohibits the use of the death penalty on any individual under the age of eighteen. When it ratified the ICCPR in 1992, the U.S. included a reservation that would allow the death penalty to be imposed in a manner that was consistent with U.S. law, even if that conflicted with the terms of the treaty. Specifically, the U.S. stated "[t]hat the United States reserves the right . . . to impose capital punishment on any person (other than pregnant woman) duly convicted under existing or future laws permitting the imposition of capital punishment, including such punishment for crimes committed by persons below the age of eighteen years of age" (ICCPR, Declarations and Reservations).

While Article 38 of the ICJ's Statute lists two more sources of international law, scholars and analysts widely hold the view that custom and treaties are the two main sources. The general principles of law are frequently evidentiary or procedural rules found in many national legal systems that have not necessarily been established in an international court. They often fill in gaps in international jurisprudence that simply have not been developed. For instance, the Permanent Court of International Justice, which was the predecessor to the International Court of Justice, adopted the widely practiced principle that for every legal wrong there must be a legal remedy (Epps, 2014, p. 30). The final listed source of international law is that of judicial opinions and scholarly writings, and those come with an important caveat. They are described in the Statute as "subsidiary" sources of law, which essentially means that they are not sources themselves but, when taken together with international custom or general principles of law, they may prove that a particular law exists. That judicial opinions do not operate to create international law might seem confusing. However, when considered in the context of compliance and enforcement, it is easier to understand.

Compliance and Enforcement in International Law

From actual events, we can see and widely acknowledge that states follow, or comply with, international law most of the time. This may not seem a significant fact, but given the anarchic nature of the international system and the lack of a supranational authority to enforce laws, it should at least be surprising to many. Why would states obey laws if there is nothing that is actually making them comply?

Scholars have suggested a number of explanations to that question, and the explanations largely align with the major theories of international relations. For instance, the first accounts draw on realist theories of power politics and suggest that states comply with international law because other, more powerful states, make them. Through various coercive means, those with power are able to force those without it to do what the powerful want. A second category of explanations suggests that states follow international law out of a sense of obligation that stems from a fidelity to the liberal order and the legitimacy of rule-based governance. An emphasis on representative government, respect for civil and political rights, and regard for the rule of law exemplify a shared liberal identity that encourages compliance. The third group of explanations maintains that states obey international law because of their status as members in international society. Peer pressure induces compliance as states want to act as good neighbors to one another. Finally, some scholars argue that states obey international law because it is in their self-interest to do so. Based in cooperative and rational theory, these explanations focus on the benefits that states can attain when following laws that are in their joint interests.

Each of these explanations is supported by various historical and contemporary examples, and the point here is not to champion one approach over others. Rather, the key lesson to take away from this brief discussion is that most of the explanations focus on state-to-state relationships. This is because the international system largely lacks vertical enforcement mechanisms, which would allow international organizations or bodies to ensure compliance with international law via their own authority over states. Indeed, compliance is predicated on horizontal enforcement between the states themselves, as sovereignty concerns dictate that states should generally be unwilling to ever grant that authority to third parties.

A good example of the distinction between vertical and horizontal enforcement is the International Court of Justice (ICJ). Often called the world court, the ICJ is a part of the United Nations tasked with hearing disputes between states. Yet, the ICJ does not function as many domestic courts do, primarily because of the restrictions on its jurisdiction or power to hear cases. Specifically, the ICJ Statute specifies three ways that the court can assert its jurisdiction, and each relies on states granting the court that authority (UN, *Statute of the International Court of Justice*). First, states can voluntarily recognize the court's compulsory jurisdiction, meaning they agree to be brought before the court by any other state that has likewise agreed to compulsory jurisdiction. States can also bring a case to the court via a special agreement, which is simply an understanding that the parties accept the court's jurisdiction with regard to a specific issue. Finally, states may include jurisdiction clauses in treaties that the court can enforce.

States do not have to submit to the court's jurisdiction, and they frequently do not. In a stinging rebuke to the ICJ specifically and to the notion of vertical enforcement more generally, the U.S. once withdrew from a pending case. Accused of violating Nicaraguan sovereignty by providing support to rebels, the U.S. simply refused to participate in the merits stage of the case after the court ruled that it had jurisdiction. Moreover, after the court ruled against it, the U.S. blocked enforcement of the judgment in the United Nations Security Council.

In terms of explaining compliance and enforcement in international law, one must also consider the fact that not all international law is qualitatively equivalent. That is, not every law imposes the same level of obligations or duties as every other law. The idea that laws can vary based on certain characteristics is known as legalization, and the degree to which a particular law is legalized can help explain compliance and enforcement (Abbott, Keohane, Moravcsik, Slaughter, & Snidal, 2000). In plainer language, that means that some laws impose greater obligations or address more specific issues, while others are less demanding in what they require. Abbott and Snidal (2000) describe the varying degrees of legalization as either hard or soft law, and this is a useful conception to understand how law varies.

Hard law refers to laws, agreements, and more that exhibit high levels of obligation, delegation, and precision. Obligation is the level of commitment required by a legal rule or agreement. For instance, a treaty may require that states cut their carbon emissions 50% over the next decade or dictate a reduction of tariffs on foreign goods by a specified amount. In tandem with the rigorous legal commitments, laws that exhibit high levels of obligation commonly include stringent legal remedies in case a state breaches its responsibilities. **Precision**, meanwhile, means that a rule or law defines in clear terms what is expected so that there is no ambiguity or room for interpretation or disagreement about what the law requires. An agreement that calls on states to condemn violence against civilians versus one that requires an armed intervention to protect civilians when a population is threatened by government violence is an example of one that lacks precision and one that is far more precise. Finally, **delegation** is defined by how much or how little authority states are willing to relinquish to designated third-parties. The ICJ is an example of low or weak delegation, while the World Trade Organization's dispute settlement mechanism is an example of a higher or stronger degree of delegation.

Why is this particular distinction worth examining? First, when people discuss whether international law is useful or effective or whether or not states comply with it, it is important that they understand what exactly international law is. International law varies in both how it is created as well as its level of legalization. Customary international law develops based on state practice over decades and years. Treaties and agreements are specifically negotiated by states to suit their particular purposes. This suggests that, in some circumstances, states might want hard law that sets clear obligations that can be enforced. Other instances might require a softer approach that provides more flexibility at the expense of firm commitments and obligations. Viewed in this manner, international law fits into the broader framework of international cooperation in the same manner as do international organizations. It can shape and regulate the behavior of states, but in many ways it is limited by its very nature.

Human Security and Human Rights

One of the main areas in which international cooperation and international law have had both successes and failures is **human**

security, which is an all-encompassing phrase that refers to the idea that every individual has a right to be protected from systemic violence related to inter- and intra- state conflicts, environmental threats and disasters, and medical crises. An important part of human security is the recognition of human rights that are intrinsic and universal. That is, certain rights are inherent to all human beings and exist regardless of citizenship or nationality. A relatively recent development is the increased focus on human rights law that shows both the promise and the difficulties for international cooperation.

For centuries, international law dealt mostly with regulating state-to-state behavior. The Peace of Westphalia in 1648 that ended the Thirty Years' War introduced the modern nation-state system with an emphasis on state sovereignty, or the right of states to be free from interference in their internal affairs. For the next three centuries, states would assume the dominant role in world politics, and among their primary concerns was their own security. As such, international laws of war developed that largely structured how and when states could go to war and how those wars would be conducted. Jus ad bellum, often referred to as **just war**, is a phrase that literally means "right to war" and is the part of the laws of war that outlines when it is appropriate for states to fight. Born out of the just war tradition, jus ad bellum stresses that, in certain circumstances, states are justified in their use of armed force against other states, even though such use of force clearly violates notions of sovereignty. The UN Charter even recognizes that armed intervention is a sometimes necessary and appropriate response to acts of aggression (United Nations Charter, Art. 42).

In the midst of these developments regarding when the use of force was appropriate, an important movement began to take shape. By the middle of the nineteenth century, international law began to evolve to regulate how wars were conducted and not just when states could use force. Jus in bello refers to the conduct of parties during hostilities and addresses the treatment of prisoners of war, of civilians that are present in war zones, and more. Horrified by the suffering of wounded soldiers, social activists—including a group that would go on to become the International Committee of the Red Cross— advocated for limitations on state conduct during wartime. These activists believed that, even during conflict, there should be a place for humane treatment; the result was the first Geneva Convention, signed in 1864, that dealt with the treatment of wounded soldiers during wars. This was followed by the second Geneva Convention in 1906 that addressed service members at sea, a third Geneva Convention in 1929 regarding prisoners of war, and, finally, the fourth Geneva Convention in 1949 on the protection of civilians during wartime (Shaw, 2017, p. 892). To this day, those treaties are among the most respected agreements in international law.

While the original emphasis of those agreements was on state action, they also represent huge steps forward for the rights of individuals under international law. In particular, the fourth Geneva Convention was born directly out of the civilian suffering of World War II and focused on protecting individuals who were present during international conflicts. In the decades that followed, additional protocols were added to provide for humane treatment of individuals during civil wars and other internal conflicts. Those rights included protections against murder, mutilation, torture, and other inhumane acts. By 1977, the Conventions and the additional protocols formed the basis of what is now known as international humanitarian law.

Growth and Development of Human Rights Law

Humanitarian law is now a key component of human security, and its evolution in recent decades is a testament to a growing emphasis in the international community of the rights of individuals. It is not alone in this regard. Just as the collective efforts of individuals, activists, organizations, and states have led to further protections for people during wars and other conflicts, so also is a complementary expansion of human rights law evidence of the importance of human security. Arguments for human rights are not new. Religious and moral writers and scholars have for centuries acknowledged basic human dignities that ought to be respected. It was, however, the collective experiences of the horrors of World War II that provided the impetus to protect those basic human rights in international law.

To date, the UN has identified a number of significant international agreements that codify various rights, including the Convention on the Prevention and Punishment of the Crime of Genocide, Convention against Torture and other Cruel, Inhuman or Degrading Treatment or Punishment (CAT), and more. Of particular note is the Universal Declaration of Human Rights (UDHR), which was the first step in forming the International Bill of Human Rights. The UDHR was adopted by the UN General Assembly in 1948 and specifies a diverse set of rights, including everything from a prohibition against slavery and torture to the freedom of thought, conscience, and religion. It is extraordinary in its scope and ambition and to this day is viewed as comprising the most authoritative lists of human rights in international law. Unfortunately, many of the skeptics of human rights law—or at least skeptics of the effectiveness of human rights law—claim that the UDHR is little more than a catalogue of rights. None of the thirty articles in the agreement contains enforcement provisions or establishes how states will be bound to it. In terms of the hard/soft law dichotomy discussed in the previous section, the UDHR falls squarely in the soft law category, and that fact frustrates many who would like to see the rights fully protected.

Enforcement is always going to be an issue with human rights law, but two of the other main UN human rights agreements highlight other difficult aspects of developing and protecting rights. Together with the UDHR, the International Covenant on Civil and Political Rights (ICCPR) and the International Covenant of Economic, Social, and Cultural Rights (ICESCR) complete the International Bill of

Human Rights. The ICCPR and ICESCR were both completed in 1966 and entered into force in 1976. They contain virtually the same rights as listed in the UDHR but attempt to more narrowly define the rights, as well as include more binding legal obligations for the signatories. Given the potential for intrusion into state sovereignty, it is hardly surprising that it took nearly two decades to draft those agreements. For instance, the ICCPR includes a provision that defines the scope of when countries can impose the death penalty. While it does not prohibit the practice, it does restrict it to serious crimes. Moreover, it forbids the punishment for anyone under the age of eighteen. The U.S. did not prohibit use of the death penalty against minors until 2005.

This is just one example of how an international treaty can shape state behavior. Consider that the ICCPR also calls for due process of law, protections for the right to vote, equality from discrimination, freedom of expression, and more. Many of these rights are open to interpretation as, for instance, states often disagree about what should actually be included in the right of due process. Does that include a right to hearing before a neutral judge? What about states that do not recognize or provide for an independent judiciary? Should every person be provided an attorney? It is not surprising that countries are hesitant to adopt international commitments that might go beyond what they recognize and provide for their own citizens.

Beyond disagreeing about the definitions of key terms and what rights are included within them, there are also fundamental disagreements about what rights should be protected. The first half of the UDHR and the entirety of the ICCPR recognize rights that are often identified as core liberal democratic rights. The right to freedom of speech, religion, movement, and to participate in the political process are all included. In short, they are the type of rights that are more strongly recognized in Western countries than elsewhere. The second half of the UDHR and the ICESCR, meanwhile, focus on economic and social welfare. The ICESCR includes the rights to education and healthcare, along with an adequate standard of living and more. These particular values are emphasized in socialist and socially democratic countries, while frequently viewed as entitlements rather than rights in many states. In fact, this divergence regarding what constitutes fundamental human rights led to two separate treaties for fear that one treaty that included all rights would not be universally ratified. The U.S. ratified the ICCPR in 1997, while attaching certain reservations; it signed the ICESCR in 1977 but has yet to ratify that agreement.

The story of the development of human rights law is similar to the more general problems associated with international cooperation. States often agree about a particular issue in a broad context. When it comes to organizing around a solution, though, the process often breaks down entirely or results in an outcome that is short of an ideal. An example of this particular pattern is in respect to the international community's efforts regarding humanitarian interventions.

Humanitarian Intervention and the Responsibility to Protect

On August 4, 1993, the Arusha Peace Agreement was signed between the government of Rwanda and representatives of the Rwanda Patriotic Front (RPF). The agreement was meant to end the Rwandan Civil War that had been fought since 1990; the accords provided for a transitional government ahead of general elections. Soon after the agreement was signed, the UN Security Council passed Resolution 872 establishing the UN Assistance Mission for Rwanda (UNAMIR). Specifically, the mission was tasked with overseeing the implementation of the accords, supporting the coordination of humanitarian assistance programs, and monitoring the ceasefire (United Nations Security Council Resolution S/RES/872). On April 6, 1994, Rwandan President Juvenal Habyarimana's plane was shot down while landing in the capital of Kigali. The peace was shattered, and over the next 100 days, approximately 800,000 ethnic minority Tutsi and politically moderate Hutus were murdered in a systematic fashion throughout the country (United Nations Security Council Report S/1999/1257).

Even while it was occurring, the Rwandan genocide was generally acknowledged and recognized by the international community. Though the word genocide was conspicuously absent from their pronouncements, government representatives from countries around the world denounced and condemned the violence. While they would later dispute knowledge of the severity of the violence, it was understood that mass atrocities were taking place. No country sent troops or supplies to help. Whether states did not want to set a precedent for military intervention, whether they deemed the fate of people in a remote African country as less important than other concerns, or whether they justified not acting on some other grounds, the fact remains that the states failed to collectively act to stop the genocide. Indeed, accounts of the U.S. response during and after the genocide reflect a reticence of administration officials to even use the word "genocide" so as to avoid legal obligation (Power, 2002).

The UN force on the ground was similarly ineffectual at stopping the violence, but for different reasons. Under UN regulations, **peacekeeping** forces are incredibly restricted by their rules of engagement. Peacekeepers are not a fighting force and cannot engage military operations unless they are attacked. In fact, peacekeeping forces are only deployed with the permission of the government where they will be deployed and are limited to what their mandate allows. These points are underscored in the official inquiry into the UN's failure to prevent or stop the Rwandan genocide; they also emphasize the organizational obstacles that prevented collective action (United Nations Security Council S/1999/1257).

The Rwandan Genocide served as a catalyst for international efforts to acknowledge and affirm the principle that state sovereignty also included a **Responsibility to Protect (R2P)** a state's citizens from genocide, war crimes, ethnic cleansing, and other humanitarian crises. R2P also demanded action should a state fail its obligations, as advocates argued that the international community should be required to intervene militarily to stop or prevent crises. Initially the idea received support from states and organizations, and observers were hopeful ahead of the World Summit in 2005 that the principle would be codified by the UN. Supporters were left disappointed when R2P was simply recognized by states; states left any major action to the discretion of the UNSC. The consensus was simply not strong enough to overcome states' sovereignty concerns.

The international community's response to humanitarian crises is a stark reminder of the fundamental lesson regarding international organization. Cooperation is a difficult task. Whether viewed through the lens of organizations created by states to deal with particular problems or the development of international law—both in a general context and with respect to more narrow issues—it is readily apparent that there are significant barriers to collective action. Sovereignty concerns are a very real impediment. Frequently, states do not agree on a preferred outcome, much less what the preferred method to achieve any particular goal should be. In the instances that there is agreement, self-interest can inhibit cooperative efforts.

Yet, there are examples everywhere in international politics of successful cooperative efforts. The United Nations, the World Trade Organization, and other organizations represent purposeful action by states to address issues in international politics. The continued development of international law, particularly in the areas of humanitarian and human rights law, exemplifies collaborative efforts of members of the international community both broadly and with respect to particular issues. The key to effective organization hinges on the ability and willingness of states and other actors to identify and overcome collective action problems. Cooperation does not happen by accident, but it does, in fact, happen, and its implications for international politics can be profound.

References

Abbott, K. W., Keohane, R. O., Moravcsik, A., Slaughter, A. M., & Snidal, D. (2000). The Concept of Legalization. *International Organization, 54*(3), 401–019.

Abbott, K. W. & Snidal, D. (2000). Hard and soft law in international governance. *International Organization, 54*(3), 421–456.

Epps, V. (2014). *International law* (5th ed.). Carolina Academic Press: Durham, NC.

Hardin, G. (1968). The Tragedy of the Commons. *Science, 162*(3859): 1243–1248.

ICCPR, Declarations and Reservations. United Nations Treaty Collections. Retrieved from https://treaties.un.org/Pages/ViewDetails.aspx?src=TREATY&mtdsg_no=IV-4&chapter=4&clang=_en

Kaplan, L. S. (2007). *NATO 1948: The birth of the transatlantic alliance*. Lanham, MD: Rowman and Littlefield.

Koremenos, B., Lipson, C., & Snidal, D. (2003). The rational design of international institutions. *International Organization, 55*(4), 76–99.

Olson, M. (1971). *The logic of collective action: Public goods and the theory of groups*. Cambridge, MA: Harvard University Press.

The Paquete Habana. 175 U.S. 677. 1900.

Power, S. (2002). *"A problem from hell": America and the age of genocide*.. Philadelphia, PA: Basic Books.

Shaw, M. N. (2017). *International Law* (8th ed.). Cambridge, UK: Cambridge University Press.

United Nations. (1946a, April 18). *Charter of the United Nations*. Retrieved from https://www.un.org/en/charter-united-nations/index.html

United Nations. (1946b, April 18). *Statute of the International Court of Justice*. Retrieved from https://www.un.org/en/charter-united-nations/index.html

United Nations Office of the High Commissioner for Human Rights. Status of Ratification: Interactive Dashboard. Retrieved from https://indicators.ohchr.org

United Nations Security Council Resolution 872. *Rwanda.* S/RES/872 (1993, October 5). Retrieved from https://undocs.org/S/RES/872

United Nations Security Council Resolution 1999/1257. (1999, December 16). *Report of the Independent Inquiry into the actions of the United Nations during the 1994 genocide in Rwanda.* S/1999/1257 Retrieved from https://undocs.org/S/1999/1257

NGOs and World Politics

Laurel Wei

Abstract

This chapter is about nongovernmental organizations (NGOs) and world politics. It includes five major sections: (1) Defining NGOs; (2) Types of NGOs; (3) NGOs' power and strategies; (4) NGO's role and influence in world politics, including perspectives of realism, liberalism, and constructivism; and (5) NGOs' critiques and challenges to efficacy.

Learning Objectives

- Know the definition of non-governmental organizations (NGOs)
- Understand NGOs' historical development and the formation of "NGO" as a concept
- Describe different types of NGOs
- Explain NGOs' power and influence in world politics
- Explain the different tactics used by NGOs in their worldwide activities
- Analyze the contending perspectives international relations theorists bring to their analysis of NGOs
- Understand and critically evaluate the phenomenon of NGOs

On February 27, 2014, world leaders gathered in Helsinki, the capital of Finland, to celebrate the first World NGO Day, which, by 2018, had been marked by eighty-nine countries across six continents (World NGO Day). Clearly, states commonly understand that NGOs are active and influential players in international society. World politics would be much less dynamic without NGOs' involvement, and most global issues today need NGOs' involvement in one way or another.

The term **nongovernmental organization (NGO)** is defined in Article 71 of the UN Charter in 1945. Under the UN-led system of international institutions, an NGO can be any kind of citizen-based group that is non-profit, private, voluntary, and functions independently from government. Because NGOs form an essential part of civil society, they are also referred to as civil society organizations (CSOs) or non-profit organizations (NPOs). In every country, there are numerous NGO entities, ranging from nationwide organizations, professional associations, and religious orders to small local charities, grassroots organizations, and community services.

The number of NGOs has grown dramatically each year, according to the annual editions of *The Yearbook of International Organizations* (1948–2018). Today, there are an estimated 10 million NGOs worldwide. In the U.S. alone, there are approximately 1.5 million NGOs in operation (The US Bureau of Democracy, Human Rights, and Labor, 2017). The thriving global civil society, ongoing globalization, and spread of democracy, along with progress in education, technology, and innovation, have led an increasing number of NGOs to flourish at local, national, and international levels. The activities, services, and projects that NGOs have carried out have won them a positive overall image. Their increasing value appears in a number of NGOs having been awarded the Nobel Prize for Peace, including the International Committee of the Red Cross (1917, 1944, and 1963), Amnesty International (1977), International Physicians for the Prevention of Nuclear War (1985), the International Campaign to Ban Landmines (1997), and the Intergovernmental Panel on Climate Change (2007). Most recently, the prize was awarded in 2015 to the National Dialogue Quartet, a coalition of civil society organizations in Tunisia (Encyclopaedia Britannica, 2019). Although they represent a multitude of interests, sectors, and activities, the better-known international NGOs, such as the Red Cross, Greenpeace, and Amnesty International, have successfully demonstrated to the world that NGOs stand for altruistic and humanitarian purposes.

Defining NGOs

NGOs as an analytical category remains complex and broad. It is difficult to formulate a standard definition as to what constitutes an NGO. One reason for this difficulty is that the extreme diversity and extensive reach of NGOs preclude any form of generalization. Another reason is that NGOs play different roles and take different forms within and across different societies. Therefore, it may be more accurate to describe NGOs as a cluster of concepts sharing certain commonalities.

Different versions of the definition of NGOs can be found in various authoritative sources. The United Nations first coined the term "NGO"—which first came into use in the UN Charter—when organizations that were neither governmental entities nor member states were needed for a consultative status in the UN. In February 1950, the United Nations Economic and Social Council (ECOSOC) defined an **international NGO (INGO)** as "any organization which is not established by inter-governmental agreement" [Resolution 288 (X), February 27, 1950], "including organizations which accept members designated by government authorities, provided that such membership does not interfere with the free expression of views of the organizations" [Resolution 1296 (XLV), June 25, 1968] (Union of International Associations, n.d.A). Global NGOs, then, are broadly defined as anything that is not an **intergovernmental organization**

(IGO) or a government. An IGO is an organization whose members are states' governments. The World Bank defines NGOs as "private organizations that pursue activities to relieve suffering, promote the interests of the poor, protect the environment, provide basic social services, or undertake community development." In the broadest sense, an NGO can be "any non-profit organization which is independent from government" (Malena, 1995, pp. 13-14).

In addition to the emphasis on the nature of NGOs as private autonomous organizations free from government intervention, the World Bank version also outlines the major areas NGOs generally focus on. Based on the above explanations, we define an NGO as an autonomous and voluntary legal entity that is noncommercial, nonviolent, and independent from both the government and the business sector, established by private individuals under a common cause or a set of common interests, maintained through a formal or semi-formal structure with regular membership, and aimed at making positive social change by collective action. NGOs are active at local, national, and international levels. Although they are a diverse body of social organizations, NGOs generally share seven common characteristics:

1. They are tax-exempt legal entities with a relatively high level of autonomy.
2. They are non-profit organizations at least partially supported by private funding.
3. They can hire professionalized staff, but almost all NGOs use volunteers.
4. Their relationship with the government is complicated. Although some are set up or sponsored by governments, they are not governmental agencies.
5. NGOs are nonviolent and do not use or support any form of violence.
6. Most NGOs work in one or more of these areas: charity, conservation, disaster relief, education, literacy, public

safety, religion, science and technology, and violence-prevention. They intend to maintain peace and bring about positive change to the world.

7. At least in the U.S., NGOs are also called nonprofit organizations (NPOs). The two terms are often used interchangeably, although not all nonprofits are NGOs.

NGOs tend to work in areas where a government may also be involved, such as poverty alleviation. They are supposed to stay neutral in politics, although some do join lobbies or interest groups and take sides when contending issues. While the concept of NGOs is fairly recent, the phenomenon of their activities is not new in international politics.

History of NGOs

The history of NGOs can be traced back to ancient times. For example, humanitarian groups were found to have been active in China around the thirteenth century (Davies, 2013). In the West, entities such as religious orders, fraternities, missionary groups, and scientific societies had engaged in nonprofit and charitable activities across continents; many are still in operation to the present day. In the eighteenth and nineteenth centuries, independent humanitarian societies and organizations were established in such areas as rescue, disease control, and anti-slavery, and many had eventually grown into INGOs with branch offices all over the world. Many anti-slavery groups, for example, in their advocacy for the abolition of slavery, influenced not only national legislation, such as The British Slavery Abolition Act (1833), but also international negotiations. In spite of the fact that most of the NGOs in the 1830s later ceased to exist, the British and Foreign Anti-Slavery Society, established in 1839, has survived and become the world's oldest international human rights organization. Now under the name Anti-Slavery International, it continues to combat slavery and related human rights abuses (Anti-Slavery International, 2019).

Another well-known example is the International Committee of the Red Cross (ICRC) founded in 1863 by Swiss philanthropist Henri Dunant. The initial Red Cross movement was developed to provide neutral assistance to the wounded in conflict, and, over time, the Red Cross has grown into one of the most active and influential INGOs operating worldwide to help people affected by conflict and to promote the laws that protect victims of war (International Committee of the Red Cross, 2019).

From the late nineteenth century to World War I, accompanying the expansion of the world market and the second industrial revolution, INGOs mushroomed in number and variety across the globe, as they called for awareness on health, human rights, and intellectual development. Notable examples include the Universal Scientific Alliance (1876), the International Commission on Occupational Health (1906), the International Alliance of Women (1902), Society for the International Exchange of Children and Young People (1903), and the International Olympic Committee (1894) (Union of International Associations, n.d.B). They were active in areas that paved the way for modern-day social movements, such as gender, labor rights, conservation, public health, culture, and education. The exponential growth of NGOs led to vibrant inter-NGO cooperation since the early 1900s. In 1910, at the First World Congress of International Organizations in Brussels, representatives from 137 international civil society bodies and thirteen governments formally agreed to establish the Union of International Associations to provide services in regulating and advancing cooperation among international organizations (Union of International Associations, n.d.C). Again, the term NGO did not exist back then; instead, those bodies called themselves alliances, associations, federations, societies, unions, or institutes. In the years after World War I, NGOs became more prominent during the existence of the League of Nations. However, with the League's decline and the subsequent onset of World War II, they faded into obscurity.

After World War II, the establishment of the UN revitalized NGOs' development. Not only have they flourished since, but the term NGO also came into popular usage. For the purpose of strengthening and formalizing ties with private organizations, the UN decided to include in its Charter a provision specifying rules relevant to them. Attention was turned to world economic and social issues, and the **Economic and Social Council (ECOSOC)** became an essential designated UN agency to work with NGOs. Under Article 70,

> The Economic and Social Council may make arrangements for representatives of the specialized agencies to participate, without vote, in its deliberations and in those of the commissions established by it, and for its representatives to participate in the deliberations of the specialized agencies (Charter of The United Nations, 1945).

And under Article 71,

> The Economic and Social Council may make suitable arrangements for consultation with non-governmental organizations which are concerned with matters within its competence. Such arrangements may be made with international organizations and, where appropriate, with national organizations after consultation with the Member of the United Nations concerned (Charter of The United Nations, 1945).

ECOSOC remains the only main UN body with a formal framework for NGO participation. This cooperative framework benefits both the UN and NGOs. On the one hand, ECOSOC benefits from NGOs' valuable information and expert advice; on the other, NGOs have the opportunity of influencing the work of ECOSOC, engaging in events for capacity-building and fostering a closer relationship with the UN and its extensive global network (ECOSOC, 2018, pp. 16–17). By 1992, over 700 NGOs had attained consultative status; by 2018, the number had increased to more than 4,900 (p. 2). These NGOs enjoys various types of status at the UN, including consultation, association, and accreditation.

Those registered with the UN are the better-resourced, more influential INGOs, comprising a small minority of the group. Most NGOs are domestic and only operate within their respective home countries. It is difficult to know precisely how many NGOs are present today, perhaps because of varying definitions and a lack of comprehensive or reliable statistics. In non-democracies like China, many NGOs are unregistered, underground voluntary groups. If both formal and informal organizations are included, the estimated figure can be over a million. According to statistics, in the near future, the total number of INGOs could probably go well beyond 70,000 (Lamy, Masker, Baylis, Smith, & Owens, 2018, p. 199).

Types of NGOs

As discussed previously, the main purpose of the UN creating the term NGO and using it in the UN Charter was to distinguish private organizations from IGOs and member states in their status and relationship with the UN system. Therefore, NGO is a broad term that encompasses many different types of organizations. Accordingly, there are also multiple ways of categorizing them. This section looks at four common typologies of NGOs based on their levels of operation, issue areas of operation, nature of services, and relations with other state and non-state actors.

By levels of operation, NGOs generally fall into one or more of the following types: first, **community-based organizations (CBOs)**, also referred to as "grassroots organizations" or "people's organizations," are typically local community or neighborhood groups mostly concerned with community affairs. Members are usually those from within a community and are neighbors to one another. Membership base is relatively small and can completely depend on volunteers. Funding comes from voluntary donations. For example, the TLC Humane Society is a community-level NGO working to protect pets, facilitate their adoption, and promote responsible pet ownership in Dahlonega in north Georgia (TLC Humane Society, n.d.).

CBOs are distinct in nature and purpose from NGOs at other levels. While national and international NGOs are intermediary NGOs established to serve others, thus making them public-oriented NGOs, CBOs, in contrast, are normally membership organizations comprising a group of individuals coming together to further their own interests (e.g., women's groups, youth clubs, and farmer associations). Members are more likely to be both contributors and recipients of the goods and services provided, making those NGOs private-oriented.

Second, **municipal** or **provincial level organizations** are larger than CBOs in organization and membership, but they still usually operate at the local level and with local concerns. They can be established by private individuals, local businesses, or local governments. Many rely on membership dues and private donations, while others may also receive public funding. The purpose can be either advancing members' self-interests (like CBOs) or serving others. Depending on the scale, some may completely rely on volunteerism, while others may rely on paid memberships. Nowadays, the boundary between municipal or provincial level organizations and national organizations has been blurred. Local NGOs often actively get involved in issues of national importance. For example, The Bombay Natural History Society—one of the largest conservation and ecology oriented NGOs in India—is actively involved in biodiversity-related research projects, education program, and public awareness raising. (BNHS, n.d.)

Third, **national organizations** operate mostly within their countries of origin and reach into various subnational—that is, state, county, and city—levels. While some nationally-renowned and affluent NGOs may go global, most of them remain in the home country. Their membership base is normally larger than are subnational NGOs. Sources of funding include private donations, charity events, membership dues, and national or federal grants. Depending on their finances and network, national organizations conduct missions of national and even global importance. A typical example of national organizations is the Make-A-Wish Foundation of America, which helps to create and realize the life-changing wishes for children with a critical illness. Founded in Arizona in 1980, it has chapters throughout the U.S., serving communities across the nation and its territories (Make-A-Wish America, n.d.). Due to their size and nationwide presence, most national NGOs are created to serve others and typically carry altruistic and philanthropic missions.

Finally, **international NGOs (INGOs)**, also called transnational NGOs (TNGOs), are comparatively the largest in capacity, staff size, and funding level, and enjoy considerable publicity. Prominent INGOs, like Human Rights Watch, the Red Cross, and Greenpeace, have been acknowledged and endorsed for their good works. Many of them originated as INGOs in the late 1800s or early 1900s, while others, like Make-A-Wish International, were initially national-level NGOs that gradually expanded beyond their respective home country.

Working in multiple countries and continents, INGOs have numerous branch offices and professionalized staff, more generous donors, and long-term, active relationships with governments, the UN, IGOs, and other NGOs. Major sources of INGO funding include membership dues, the sale of goods and services, grants from international institutions or national governments, and private donations. An INGO may have annual budgets in the millions of dollars. For example, in 2018, Human Rights Watch spent over 81 million dollars in total expenses (Human Rights Watch, 2018, p. 3). According to the UIA's *Yearbook of International Organizations, 2018–2019*, most of today's INGOs are headquartered in the developed countries. Based on the region of origin, **Northern NGOs (NNGOs)** refer to those that are established in developed countries, whereas **Southern NGOs (SNGOs)** refers to those originated in developing countries (Lewis, 2018, p. 1057). The two often work together in partnerships.

By issue areas of operation, NGOs can be categorized into five major types (Lawry, 2009; Frandsen, 2002). Most of them today are dedicated to more than one of the following areas:

1. NGOs for international relief, emergency response, and development: e.g., International Red Cross, Doctors Without Borders, and Direct Relief International.
2. NGOs for social progress, including democracy promotion, human rights, and good governance, e.g., Human Rights Watch, the National Democratic Institute.
3. NGOs for conflict mitigation, management, and resolution, e.g., the Alliance for Conflict Transformation (ACT), Global Network of Women Peacebuilders (GNWP).
4. NGOs for education, medical help, and state service replacement or improvement, e.g., the Association for Sustainable Community Development (ASSCOD), Africare.
5. NGOs for civil society support and community-based services, e.g., Community Options, Inc., The Hong Kong Council of Social Service, and YMCA.

Based on the nature of their services, the World Bank suggests two main categories of NGOs: **operational NGOs** and **advocacy NGOs** (Malena, 1995, pp. 14–15). Both types widely exist in local, national, and international levels. Operational NGOs primarily focus on the design and implementation of development-related projects. Advocacy NGOs are organizations for empowerment, and their primary goal is to promote or defend a specific cause, such as social justice. Different from operational project management, they typically try to raise awareness, promote acceptance, and spread knowledge by lobbying, press work, activist events, and social movements, seeking to influence the policies and practices of various state and non-state actors. Whereas operational NGOs prefer to achieve small-scale and evolutionary change directly through relevant projects, programs, and services, their advocacy counterparts, in contrast, tend to embrace broader and more ambitious goals of promoting and realizing large-scale, fundamental change by exposing the deep-seated violence, oppression, injustice, and inequality in society. Advocates believe that developmental projects alone are not enough to cure social ills. Advocacy is necessary for addressing the deep roots of problems. It must be pointed out that the two categories are not mutually exclusive, and a growing number of NGOs have combined both operational projects and advocacy initiatives in their activities. Some advocacy groups, while not directly involved in designing and implementing projects, focus on advocacy for specific project-related concerns (Malena, 1995).

Finally, based on their relations with other social entities, there are five common types of NGOs that are also most influential; these types are expressed by the following various acronyms. **BINGOs** are business-oriented international NGOs or business-industrial NGOs that represent and work closely with businesses and industrial sectors. **GONGOs** are government-organized or operated NGOs, which may have been set up by governments to look like NGOs to promote governmental interests at home and abroad. Major NGOs in non-democracies are GONGOs established as facades to a closely-monitored civil society. A typical example is China Foundation for Poverty Alleviation (CFPA), one of China's largest NGOs regulated and supervised by the Chinese government **PANGOs** are political party NGOs, set up by political parties under the name of NGOs to serve their political purposes. **QUANGOs** are quasi-autonomous NGOs or refer to NGOs set up and funded (at least partially) by government but that still function as independent organizations. QUANGOs are particularly prevalent in the United

Kingdom, where their number is estimated to be in the thousands. **RINGOs** are religious international NGOs, such as the Catholic Relief Services and Medical Teams International. Also called faith-based organizations (FBOs), they are established and maintained by religious orders, churches, or missionary groups. Some were founded on religious principles, such as the Mercy Corps, but do not include evangelization as part of their mission. Many others, such as Samaritan's Purse, explicitly express a commitment to evangelism through aid, relief, and services.

Unlike sovereign states, NGOs are not legal entities under international law. An exception is the International Committee of the Red Cross, which is considered a legal entity under both international law and domestic law because it is based on the Geneva Convention. All the others possess a legal status under domestic law. When an NGO works in a country, it is usually required by law to register. Watchdog groups (NGOs and governmental agencies) and donors provide oversight for NGOs by monitoring their performance and responsibility. As voluntary, non-profit organizations, NGOs are often misunderstood as "toothless" and susceptible to political and economic realities. A closer look at NGOs, however, would suggest otherwise. Not only do NGOs have power, but also they can be powerful and influential.

The Power of NGOs

This section answers the following questions: Do NGOs have power? If so, where does it come from? How do NGOs use their power?

To begin with, NGOs' long history, their diverse types, and their abundant number have indicated that NGOs do have enough power for existence and development. As mentioned in the previous section, most NGOs are legal entities recognized by law, entitled to certain rights, and are able to carry out various responsibilities. However, unlike sovereign states, they do not have hard power to force compliance or punish violators. Instead, NGOs rely on **soft power**, also known as the power of persuasion, that is, the ability to persuade others to do what one wants without using force or coercion. Soft power can take the form of culture, ideals, beliefs, and values.

Where does such power come from? It can only come from an NGO itself. As independent organizations, NGOs must rely on their own material resources and human capital to maintain and execute power. Even those established or supported by the state—as long as they are NGOs in nature—are no exception. That explains why NGOs focus so intensely on fundraising and publicizing. A well-organized NGO is a brand of itself. It can take better advantage of available resources and grow in capacity, reach, and potential. A carefully-designed website can help achieve these ends, as well as can clear-set missions, professionalized staff, transparency, and efficacy. All of these factors can keep the NGO in good standing and make it more powerful. The role of founder(s) is essential in providing an NGO with a strong starting point. In addition, almost all NGOs today have social networks. It is very rare for an NGO to work completely on its own. A powerful social network proves to be an asset to an NGO, serving both as a source of power and a channel for exercising power. Therefore, developing an amicable relationship with other social forces—in particular, governments, businesses, and international institutions—is essential to NGOs.

Members and donors can provide sufficient and stable funding. As corporate social responsibility grows, businesses, especially multinational corporations (MNCs), have become more socially responsible and more willing to make donations to NGOs. In fact, multitudes of them have developed their own charities or foundations. Other than the support and contributions from members and donors, NGOs often work closely with governments as well. Their independent nature does not preclude their cooperating with state actors. Rather, many are established and maintained by the government, receive public funding, and accept members designated by governments.

An extensive social network benefits an NGO not only in resources and influence from members and donors, but also from its ambassadors, that is, one or more celebrities of good repute that voluntarily promote the NGO. The **celebrity diplomacy** is where a highly-respected and popular public figure acts as an NGO's icon and uses their status to lead major global campaigns, fund-raise for the NGO, and create other favorable conditions to facilitate the NGO in its projects or advocacy. In recent years, celebrities such as Taylor Swift, George Clooney, and Angelina Jolie have attempted to play an increasingly important role as NGOs' transnational activists in areas such as conflict resolution, humanitarianism, and developmental programs. In a similar case, celebrities from India's Bollywood have been successful in establishing and operating their own NGOs to address various social issues. Under NGOs, celebrity activism has become an ever-growing and internationally visible phenomenon. It remains debatable as to whether those celebrities have genuinely and effectively advanced those altruistic, philanthropic causes, or whether they are primarily motivated by self-interests (Tsaliki, Frangonikolopoulos, & Huliaras, 2011). However, it seems undeniable that celebrity activism has contributed to the growth of NGOs, making NGOs' role more evident and influential in world issues that deserve broader attention.

How do NGOs use their power? A short answer is through persuasion. An NGO can encourage, entreat, or urge people to act. An advocacy NGO can lobby, negotiate with, or petition to the authorities. There are multiple tactics by which NGOs may achieve their goals. A more specific explanation is developed by Keck and Sikkick (1999, p. 95), in which a typology was used to illustrate four major strategies that NGOs apply in their transnational advocacy network. Although the authors' focus is on INGOs, it is not uncommon for these tactics to also be used by national and local

NGOs. They include:

1. "**information politics**, or the ability to move politically usable information quickly and credibly to where it will have the most impact;

2. **symbolic politics**, or the ability to call upon symbols, actions, or stories that make sense of a situation or claim for an audience that is frequently far away

3. **leverage politics**, or the ability to call upon powerful actors to affect a situation where weaker members of a network are unlikely to have influence

4. **accountability politics**, or the effort to oblige more powerful actors to act on vaguer policies or principles they formally endorsed" (Keck & Sikkink, 1999, p. 95).

To make a change, an NGO must galvanize enough participation and resources to persuade those in power to take action. There are diverse power sources.

First, an NGO may use information politics to exercise its power. While NGOs must keep themselves well-informed of relevant events all the time, they themselves are also an important source of information. In other words, NGOs use their power to access, process, and disseminate information. Nowadays, sources of information have grown so diverse that it is no longer enough to follow news only from traditional media. NGOs not only work closely with newspapers, TV programs, and radio stations but also maintain considerable presence on the Internet and social media. Informal sources—like phone calls, email, social media posts, online chatrooms, and circulation of small pamphlets and flyers— provide NGOs information that would otherwise be unavailable, allowing activists and concerned people who may be geographically dispersed to stay informed and connected with one another. Once the information has been gathered, processing begins. Numerous NGOs, especially INGOs, have their own analysts and researcher teams and periodically publish analyses, reports, studies, and policy recommendations, which may in turn go public and become credible references for press use or further research. After selection and analyses, it is time to disseminate information. To impress the public, NGOs publish stories told by people whose lives have been changed by their efforts. Activists then move on to interpret facts and testimonies so that they become clear, powerful messages to promote the NGO's image and serve its cause(s).

Second, advocacy NGOs usually engage in leverage politics. Exerting material or moral leverage (or both) over more powerful institutions such as governments makes it possible for NGOs to gain influence far beyond their ability to directly influence policy practices. Identifying points of leverage is a crucial strategic step in NGOs' campaigns. There are two categories of leverage: material and moral. **Material leverage** generally involves issue linkage and distribution of money and goods (Keck & Sikkink, 1999, p. 97). For example, NGOs cannot force an authoritarian state to stop its human rights abuses in any direct way, but they can obtain leverage by providing domestic policymakers with relevant information and persuade them into imposing sanctions or diplomatic condemnations on that state. This is a way to "name and shame" the abuser and, in a best situation, the state's abusing practices can be deterred.

Moral leverage is used when an NGO takes an explicit attitude toward what is morally wrong, exposes it, and keeps it under continued press coverage. This can be damaging to a state's national image and credibility, and the international society can be motivated to condemn said immoral behavior. If the problem goes ignored, the state in question has to face rising outside pressure and be ready to bear any diplomatic consequences. This is another way of "naming and shaming" by NGOs. A typical example is human rights NGOs' close monitoring and constant strong criticism of China's so-called "Uygur camps" (see Chapter 8). In this case, NGOs such as Amnesty International have allied with governments of Western democracies in voicing their strong condemnation of this human rights abuse and call for correction. The result is that in addition to constant media exposure, the case has reached the U.N. Human Rights Council. Leverage politics requires an NGO to secure powerful allies, direct public opinion via the media, and maintain a unified and strong voice.

Third, NGOs use symbolic politics to identify a critical issue and frame it through analysis in such a way as to make it a catalyst for actions to be taken (Keck & Sikkink, 1999, p. 96). Symbols, banners, signs, colors, slogans, or images are heavily used to make an issue important and urgent. For example, in June 2019, Human Rights Watch intended to call for worldwide attention on the persistent violence against political dissidents and authoritarian resilience. This was done by bringing up the juxtaposition of China's grand celebration of 40 years' reform and the thirtieth anniversary of the violent crackdown of Tiananmen Square protestors. Images were used in the story to create dramatic visual effects of a formidable and inexorable statecraft versus the vulnerable but tenacious voices for freedom (Human Rights Watch, 2019).

Finally, NGOs use accountability politics to urge or push for a policy change. They hold a government or an entity liable for issues it caused and press it to become more answerable to the people. In this tactic, an NGO plays the role of a watchdog and helps to monitor the conditions of the people affected, implementation of a policy, or compliance with a treaty. They are quick to find any gaps or inconsistencies between a public commitment and actual practices, expose them, and spread the information in society (Keck & Sikkink, 1999, pp. 97–98). Embarrassed, a government may be prompted to save face by making a correction or adopting normative or policy change.

In reality, an NGO may employ one or more tactics at the same time. However, their efforts do not always produce the desired outcomes. After all, soft power works as far as an issue has been brought to decisionmakers' attention. In democracies, an accountable government and an active civil society usually provide NGOs with more resources, opportunities, and networks to obtain and use soft power, and NGOs can more likely make their voices heard or achieve the best intended outcomes. In contrast, in non-democracies, NGOs have a harder time just to maintain survival. If they manage to exist, they are more likely to get ignored or marginalized. In a worst-case situation, activists could even risk their freedom or lives to advance a cause. No matter what conditions they are in, NGOs are usually quick to formulate strategies and develop flexibilities that enable them to ensure their safety and carry on their agenda. Because of their diverse types and adept tactics, NGOs have grown into influential players of world politics. At the same time, however, their influence is perceived differently from the three mainstream international relations theoretical lens: realism, liberalism, and constructivism.

NGOs' Influence on World Politics

This section discusses the following questions: how influential are NGOs on global issues? Can they be treated as primary actors of world politics just the same as sovereign states? The three major theoretical perspectives of international relations (realism, liberalism, and constructivism) have offered different answers.

Realists are skeptical of the efficacy and impact of NGOs on world politics, although they do not completely disregard or negate them. The world system is in anarchy, so no overarching authority exists to maintain the world order, gauge justice or injustice, or enforce rules. The world, as structural realists see it, is primarily made up of sovereign states with a consistent set of national interests, of which survival and security come first. To this end, all states have a strong incentive to empower themselves, since more power provides them a more likely guarantee for survival. To the realist, the world is an arena of free competition among sovereign states who are self-interested bodies driven by their respective national interests. What they have in common is the willingness to do whatever they can to defend themselves. As opposed to the anarchical world system, every sovereign state is endowed with the legitimate use of force for defense and law enforcement. That is why we say that states have sovereign power, which is supreme and unique, without any higher world power above it.

NGOs are not sovereign entities and therefore do not have such power. All they have is the power of persuasion, or soft power, which realists criticize as inconsequential and as only able to help when backed by material strength, or hard power. As a result, NGOs' activities and impact can go only as far as states allow them. Ultimately, their capacity remains limited since they are subject to states' power and only sovereign states are the primary actors of world politics. If an NGO's activity goes against states' national interests, they will likely be ignored, resisted, or, even worse, banned. For realists, an NGO may encounter a predicament when it exposes an unacceptable practice, such as human rights abuses, but can do nothing if a state refuses to cooperate. NGOs intend to make the world better, but they have to rely on state authorities for policy change or approval of a program.

How, then, do realists explain the fact that most states' around the world work closely with NGOs? The answer is plain and simple: because they are motivated by national interests. For realists, states do not bother to invest in anything to promote altruism or some distant ideal. Rather, they have an essential interest in growing in power and cooperation with NGOs may contribute to that purpose. Governments need NGOs at various levels for information, improvement of national solidarity, and increase in global influence. Put differently, sovereign states use NGOs to strengthen power and because they can serve as effective helpers. At the domestic level, many NGOs are successful in mobilizing resources and people for their causes.

Explained in terms of power, neoclassical realists argue that effective mobilization can happen due to the support of powerful domestic interest groups that can exert more influence over society and politics. Well-resourced and affluent NGOs also have extensive social connections, giving them powerful allies and more leverage at home. In conclusion, realists argue that NGOs should not be treated as truly independent organizations because they cannot exist separately from the sovereign state and, more often than not, they are used by states as a convenient tool in furthering national interests. Their legal status is granted by governments, and the outcome of their activities also relies on state power and authority. NGOs cannot, and will not, replace sovereign states in world politics. Consequently, their role can only be small or supplemental. The realist view has been criticized, however, as having underestimated NGOs' importance.

Liberals take an optimistic view toward NGOs. Not only do they believe that NGOs are generating positive change to the world, they also predict that their global influence will go further and deeper in the future. The world system since 1945, according to the liberal lens, is a rule-based, open, and inclusive international system led by liberal democracies. Under this system, economic interdependence, international institutions, and international law, rules, and norms flourish. Mutual respect, reciprocity, and cooperation have become common understandings among countries around the world. Under these circumstances, states do come together with sincerity to seek peace and pursue common interests. Unlike what happened in the past when most issues could be resolved within state boundaries, today we are faced with a series of globalized issues requiring collective action, issues such as conflict resolution, cybersecurity, development, ecology, human rights, and social justice. These issues transcend national borders and cannot be tackled single-handedly by any state. That is why NGOs have become increasingly relevant and important.

Instead of seeing NGOs as tools for manipulation in the power game, liberals consider them as a natural product of modern world politics whose positive influence has been clearly evident. Sovereign states remain essential, but liberals explain that NGOs, given their sheer numbers and extensive reach, should be viewed as no less important than states, especially considering the "global" nature of most contemporary political issues. In the case of a weak or a failed state, NGOs' involvement can protect people and provide them with basic life necessities. In multiple cases, NGOs have managed to enter ISIS-controlled areas and in a timely manner brought goods and services to the people affected. These instances provide supporting evidence to the liberal view that NGOs can do what states are otherwise unable or unwilling to do, thereby giving liberals another reason for NGOs' having become more relevant and significant in world politics. In addition, liberals attribute the growing awareness and knowledge of human rights, rule of law, and social justice to the activities of NGOs. Their campaigns within a country and beyond are what lead to such constant world attention to these issues. In this sense, NGOs educate people and provide an effective alternative solution or venue for distributing resources and helping those in need.

As liberals believe, NGOs' remarkable achievement results from and contributes to the development of multi-layered global governance. Collective efforts by actors from the local, national, and international levels build up this system in which NGOs become prevalent and influential. Under global governance that fosters an open, diverse, inclusive, and peaceful world order, starting an NGO is a relatively easy process, and an NGO can act freely to develop goals and strategies, recruit members, and use various means to advance its cause. Together with global governance, an international society and global citizenry are also on the rise. As they become more prominent, so do NGOs. Therefore, the burgeoning multilateral global governance is yet another factor that both shapes, and is being shaped by, the increasing weight of NGOs.

From the liberal perspective, as helpers and partners to states, platforms of further cooperation, and alternative options to most global issues, NGOs form an integral part of the emerging global governance, and they do enjoy independence from state interference. It is the NGOs that choose whether to cooperate with state actors or not and, if so, how. They can help identify an issue, gather information, conduct research, and offer policy suggestions. Their dynamic activities also help strengthen repeated interaction among state and non-state actors. Because NGOs are run by voluntary individuals, they are more attentive to investing resources on an issue of their concern and to contributing strategies to make change happen. In areas where a government is weak or failing, NGOs can fill the gap and act as an alternative to state institutions to improve or replace insufficient or bad policies.

Although NGOs only have soft power, that power is enough to keep them independent and efficacious. Under a rule-based international society, most states voluntarily choose to cooperate with NGOs and to respect them as independent and private organizations entitled to rights and protection under law. NGOs, on their part, have developed multiple ways to strengthen their independent status and advance their goals, for example, by diversifying sources of funding, increasing transparency, and expanding their social network. INGOs tend to be adept at mobilizing their resources and utilizing their campaigns to induce or even press for compliance from governments. Liberals argue that NGOs' independence and autonomy are not negligible, and, as an essential part of global governance, they have played active and prominent roles in today's world.

Constructivists also acknowledge NGOs' relevance and achievements in various world issues, but they argue that their influence should be more accurately viewed in ideational terms. The world is socially constructed, and every participant engages in the construction of identities; so does an NGO. Through repeated interactions with others, actors acquire their own identities, interests, and roles, all of which serve to guide behavior. For constructivists, both realists and liberals err in describing the world system simply as an anarchy and thereby have overlooked the variety of choices and possible outcomes actors are faced with. The system and its composing actors mutually shape each other. To paraphrase Alexander Wendt, anarchy is what states make of it. Peace or conflict is determined by identities and interests flowing from constant interaction. The world will become more peaceful when actors' identities and interests converge, whereas war will arise out of divergent identities and conflicting interests. NGOs are built upon and represent shared identities and interests among individuals, and convergent ideas can make them dedicated and efficient. Through repeated interactions with other actors, an NGO may successfully engage more like-minded people, absorb new ideas from them, and strengthen existing identities and interests. Alternatively, an NGO may gradually be dissolved by diverging identities and interests.

An NGO's influence is also explained in terms of ideas. Powerful NGOs know how to lead in persuasive communication and frame information in such ways as to highlight and favor their very identities, interests, and roles. Some constructivists believe that NGOs' influence on world politics is getting stronger and remains positive overall. They represent the convergence of identities and interests among state and non-state actors, which fosters the development of commonly-recognized norms, rules, principles, and values. Human rights NGOs, for example, promote the recognition of universal human rights, while conservationist NGOs call for a shared awareness of the importance of nature to our civilization. More NGOs can bring us together to manage issues that require collective action. Through cooperation, we build up mutual trust and reduce misunderstandings, resulting in further convergence of ideas. In addition, NGOs provide learning and capacity-building opportunities for us all. The international norms a state acquired from interaction with INGOs, for example, can become internalized and lead to its policy and normative change. NGOs are essential to multilateralism, in which participants solve a problem through inclusive discussions and collective decision-making. NGOs also serve as facilitators in the exchange of ideas, by which they channel the grassroots' concerns upwards to higher level actors who may, in turn, respond correspondingly. Because of these reasons, many constructivists tend to view NGOs as important positive social forces that bring peace to the world through constructing shared identities and interests.

Some constructivists, in contrast, point out that, while many NGOs work to bridge differences, others widen them. Conventional views seem to assume NGOs as altruistic, caring, and philanthropic entities. Not all of them are so. Many, instead, are self-serving and established to enrich their members and reflect certain narrow self-identities and self-interests. These NGOs may be catalysts for regressive identity politics and resisting social forces against development, leading to deepening divergence in identities and interests. The result would be identity-based conflicts. For example, the Muslim Brotherhood, an NGO whose members have led various Islamist movements ranging from charitable organizations to political parties, caused controversies for its alleged ties with multiple terrorist groups, such as Hamas, a Palestinian terror group. Involvement in global conflicts and even terrorism, financial dependence, and political susceptibility have led observers to look closely at NGOs' weakness and room for improvement.

Critiques of NGOs

Just like other social organizations, NGOs have their weaknesses and challenges. First, realists and others have raised doubts about NGOs' nature as independent private organizations. Ideally, NGOs are supposed to maintain neutrality and keep themselves free from the interference of state actors. However, in reality, most are not truly independent, as those critics argue, and they act out of their own self-interests or become tools used by big donors for their personal enrichment.

While a state can collect taxes to guarantee its revenue, an NGO does not have any coercive or mandatory means of collecting funds. Unlike businesses, NGOs do not make a profit, so they are unable to support themselves. Instead, they have to rely on voluntary giving for their budget, including membership dues, donations, grants, and sponsorship. Such income sources can be unstable, subjecting NGOs' finances to fluctuation due to factors that may be beyond their control, for example, membership change, donors' wishes, and the like. Funding has been a constant concern for NGOs, for without funding nothing will be possible. In a society with limited resources and many other organizations asking for donations, NGOs are locked in a constant competition against one another for gaining more resources. Critics argue that it is therefore hard for NGOs to stay neutral, as they frequently find it necessary to give in to the pressure to please a donor or to exchange more benefits for their own development. Individuals, businesses, or governments can use their material leverage to force an NGO to shift its course or to make a compromise. Therefore, they tend to be more self-serving than other-serving.

Second, critics also point out that NGOs suffer a series of institutional and functional weaknesses, including lack of transparency, lack of accountability, and misinformation. The larger an NGO is, the more likely it will exhibit bureaucratic characteristics. Just like state agencies, they face challenges of low efficiency, redundant personnel, crisscrossing institutions, or corruption. Unlike an elected government accountable to the people, an NGO often does not have the same level of transparency. They are not required to publish expenditures or income, nor do they need to reveal their decision-making processes. The lack of transparency and the lack of accountability are mutually-reinforcing.

Community-level NGOs and grassroots organizations often tend to be more accountable since they are established by local members for their own common interests. Community members are asked to offer scrutiny, evaluation, and feedback to oversee an NGO's performance. National and international NGOs, in contrast, hardly ever get a chance to come face to face with those they are supposed to help and represent. Leaders and organizers are not elected and therefore do not have to be answerable to a populace. It is, instead, the major donors and sponsors that have the right to question and have access to information only available to insiders.

Once again, an NGO could face a predicament when it needs to speak out on issues unpopular with their patrons or governments. Material dependency, together with an often-hierarchical corporate structure, can erode and endanger an NGO's legitimacy and distort the purposes for its very existence. Liberals tackle these challenges by arguing that conscientious global governance can help to improve transparency and accountability in NGOs. Constructivists point out that shared ideas, especially commonly recognized rules, norms, and principles, will be more helpful than will institutional restraints.

Lack of transparency or accountability, or both, can possibly lead to misinformation. Misinformation can happen due to NGOs' unintentional mistake or bias. For example, an analysis from NGO Monitor (2012) finds that political advocacy NGO networks, partially funded by European governments, developed a selective and one-sided narrative against Israel. Steinberg (2009) similarly argues that some human rights NGOs have developed anti-Israel agendas in the UN. Most NGOs do not intentionally mislead the public. However, political advocacy NGOs can be controversial in that they carry certain political biases, so when they promote their agendas, their biases are automatically conveyed to the global society. The information gathered may be misleading, or the processing of information may be inaccurate. NGOs can manage these challenges by improving their handling of information. However, when misinformation occurs on purpose, it can be caused by corruption, a bad decision, self-interests, or some ongoing crisis. Since NGOs have specific purposes, they tend to treat information in ways that can help them. Scientific evidence can be abused by NGOs in pragmatic ways and for their own advantage. In practice, an NGO constantly needs to balance self-interests with those of beneficiaries. Deviating from a declared mission can lead to such problems.

Critics also question NGOs' helpfulness (Nunnenkamp, 2008; Alford, 2015; Banks, Hulme, & Edwards, 2015; Anderson, 2017). Their activities can be counterproductive. When superfluous NGOs are simultaneously working on an issue without enough coordination, they can lead to a waste of resources and distract the government's capacity to generate and implement policies in the same area. When a government makes a decision, it usually does so by balancing interests and concerns. An NGO, instead, only has to focus on its cause. While it has proven to be a notable advantage of NGOs, the lack of balanced concerns can bring benefit to some parts of society at the expense of others or emphasize short-term goals while neglecting long-term ones. Some critics even argue that NGOs from developed countries should be treated as colonizers of contemporary times, acting as foreign policy instruments for some countries. For example, as Easterly (2011) observes, in the past decade, partnerships between many NGOs and the USAid for humanitarian purposes have increasingly become attached to national security interests, such as nation-building in some failed states. The political failures had overshadowed successes in the traditional aid programs, like public health and poverty reduction. A suggested solution is for the Aid to be apolitical and focused on its original humanitarian missions (Easterly, 2011).

To sum up, NGOs are not immune from weaknesses and challenges, some of which cannot be easily solved in the short term. They are also aware of this situation, and action has been taken to reform corporate structure, staffing, fundraising, supervision, etc.

Some NGOs have been developed to undertake scrutiny missions. For example, the NGO Monitor, an independent global research institute that regularly publishes research and analyses of NGOs' human rights activities, primarily under the Arab-Israeli conflict, has been working since 2002 to urge improved accountability, transparency, and good governance among NGOs around the world (The NGO Monitor, n.d.). These critiques notwithstanding, most international relations scholars of all theoretical lenses recognize the charitable roles NGOs play in global governance. Despite various challenges, NGOs will continually be among the most active participants under globalization.

As nonprofit, independent, and private organizations, NGOs have been active around the globe for centuries. Since the UN coined the term NGO, it gradually became more popular until it is now a widely recognized idiom. Today, NGOs' positive role and importance in world politics have been widely acknowledged by various governments and non-state actors all over the world. Since the 2000s, NGOs have become more prominent, more active, and more responsible in almost every issue of global scope, ranging from conflict resolution to development to the protection of human rights. Over the past decade, not only have NGOs grown significantly in number but they have also developed into diverse types. Through developmental projects and persuasive communication, they have achieved successes in making the world happier and more peaceful. Nation-states are not the only actors, but NGOs have become increasingly influential in shaping the foreign policy of individual states and the future of international politics.

References

Alford, R. (2015, November 12). Bad aid: Should all NGOs close down? *The Guardian*. Retrieved June 30, 2020, from https://www.theguardian.com/global-development-professionals-network/2015/nov/12/aid-should-ngos-close

Anderson, M. (2017, November 19). NGOs: Blessing or curse? *The African Report*. Retrieved June 30, 2020, from https://www.theafricareport.com/777/ngos-blessing-or-curse/

Anti-Slavery International. (2019). About us. Retrieved July 13, 2019, from https://www.antislavery.org/about-us/

Banks, N., Hulme, D., & Edwards, M. (2015). NGOs, states, and donors revisited: Still too close for comfort? *World Development*, 66, 707–718.

Davies, T. (2013, January 24). NGOs: A long and turbulent history. Retrieved July 13, 2019, from http://www.theglobaljournal.net/article/view/981/

Easterly, W. (2011, November 21). A firewall should be built between USAid and the Defence Department. *The Guardian*. Retrieved from https://www.globalpolicy.org/ngos/role-of-ngos-in-the-international-arena/ngos-and-states/51096-a-firewall-should-be-built-between-usaid-and-the-defence-department.html

ECOSOC. (2018). *Working with ECOSOC: An NGO's guide to consultative status*. [PDF file]. New York: The United Nations. Retrieved from http://csonet.org/content/documents/ECOSOC%20Brochure_2018_Web.pdf

Human Rights Watch. (2018, June 30). *Consolidated financial report*. [PDF file]. Retrieved from https://www.hrw.org/sites/default/files/supporting_resources/financial_statement_fy18.pdf

Human Rights Watch. (2019, May 30). Human rights activism in post-Tiananmen China - A tale of brutal repression and extraordinary resilience. Retrieved July 13, 2019, from https://www.hrw.org/news/2019/05/30/human-rights-activism-post-tiananmen-china#

International Committee of the Red Cross. (2019). Who we are. Retrieved July 13, 2019, from https://www.icrc.org/en/who-we-are

Keck, M. E., & Sikkink, K. (1999). Transnational advocacy networks in international and regional politics. *International social science journal*, *51*(159), 89–101.

Lamy, S. L., Masker, J. S., Baylis, J., Smith, S., & Owens, P. (2018). *Introduction to Global Politics* (5th ed.). New York: Oxford University Press.

Lawry, L. (2009). *Guide to nongovernmental organizations for the military*. [PDF file]. Originally written by Grey Frandsen, Fall 2002. Retrieved from https://fas.org/irp/doddir/dod/ngo-guide.pdf

Lewis, D. (2010). Nongovernmental organizations, definition and history. *International Encyclopedia of Civil Society*, 1056–1062.

Make-A-Wish America. (n.d.). Our mission. Retrieved July 13, 2019, from https://wish.org/about-us/our-story/our-mission

Mingst, K. A., McKibben, H. E., & Arreguin-Toft, I. M. (2019). *Essentials of International Relations* (8th ed.). New York: W. W. Norton & Company.

Malena, C. (1995). *Working with NGOs: A practical guide to operational collaboration between The World Bank and non-governmental organizations*. [PDF file]. Washington, D.C.: World Bank. Retrieved from http://documents.worldbank.org/curated/en/814581468739240860/pdf/multi-page.pdf

Nau, H. R.. (2018). *Perspectives on international relations* (6th ed.). Los Angeles, CA: CQ Press.

NGO Monitor. (2012, November 26). Trading away peace: How biased political NGOs fuel conflict. Retrieved on June 30, 2020, from https://www.ngo-monitor.org/reports/_trading_away_peace_how_biased_political_ngos_fuel_conflict/

Nunnenkamp, P. (2008, April). Aid effectiveness: The myth of NGO superiority. *Global Policy Forum* (GPF). Retrieved June 30, 2020, from https://www.globalpolicy.org/component/content/article/177/31624.html

Steinberg, G. (2009). The centrality of NGOs in promoting anti-Israel boycotts. *Jewish Political Studies Review, 21*(1/2), 7–31. Retrieved June 30, 2020, from www.jstor.org/stable/25834823

The Editors of Encyclopaedia Britannica. (2019, July 8). National dialogue quartet. Retrieved July 13, 2019, from https://www.britannica.com/topic/Tunisian-National-Dialogue-Quartet

The NGO Monitor. (n.d.). About. Retrieved July 13, 2019, from https://www.ngo-monitor.org/about/

World NGO Day. (n.d.). Timeline. Retrieved July 14, 2019, from: https://worldngoday.org/timeline/

TLC Humane Society. (n.d.). About us. Retrieved July 13, 2019, from http://www.tlchs.org/about-us/

Tsaliki, L., Frangonikolopoulos, C. A., & Huliaras, A. (Eds.). (2011). *Transnational celebrity activism in global politics: Changing the world?* Intellect Books.

United Nations. (1945, October 15). Charter of United Nations Chapter X: The Economic and Social Council, Article 70. Retrieved from https://www.un.org/en/sections/un-charter/chapter-x/

Union of International Associations. (2018). *Yearbook of International Organizations, 2018–2019* [PDF file]. Brussels, Belgium: Union of International Associations. Retrieved from https://uia.org/sites/uia.org/files/misc_pdfs/pubs/yb_2018_vol4_lookinside.pdf

Union of International Associations. (n.d.). What is an international non-governmental organization (INGO)? Retrieved July 13, 2019, from https://uia.org/faq/yb4

Union of International Associations. (n.d.). Open yearbook. Retrieved July 13, 2019, from https://uia.org/ybio/

Union of International Associations. (n.d.). UIA's history. Retrieved from https://uia.org/history

U.S. Bureau of Democracy, Human Rights, and Labor. (2017, January 20). Non-Governmental Organizations (NGOs) in the United States: Fact Sheet. Retrieved July 13, 2019, from https://www.state.gov/non-governmental-organizations-ngos-in-the-united-states/

Global and Regional Governance

11

Nathan Price

Abstract

Driven by technological advancements, globalization has fundamentally altered international relations. Similar to other historical processes, globalization presents us with tremendous opportunities as well as costs, like the rise of transnational problems such as climate change, the threat of global terrorism, and the rapid spread of infectious diseases such as Covid-19. States are incapable of addressing these transnational problems alone and thus are increasingly working together—along with intergovernmental organizations, nongovernmental organizations, and multinational corporations—to ensure these issues are what Kofi Annan refers to as "problems without passports." This chapter identifies and describes the constellation of actors that work together in pursuit of global and regional governance. Additionally, it traces the evolution of global governance in the international system and discusses the challenges this diffuse network of actors faces as it seeks to confront twenty-first century challenges.

Learning Objectives

- Define global governance and identify and describe the various actors that work together in pursuit of global governance
- Analyze why global and regional governance are increasingly important in our efforts to confront twenty-first century challenges

- Identify and describe challenges associated with global and regional governance
- Describe the institutional structure of the United Nations
- Analyze the factors that contributed to the evolution of the European Union and describe the institutional structure of the contemporary European Union

Global governance is probably a term most new students of international relations have never seen before, let alone thought much about or analyzed. In order to get a better idea of what global governance is, we need first to discuss what it is not. While the terms are related, global governance is not synonymous with global government. In other words, "there is no top-down, hierarchical structure of authority," in regard to global governance. (Karns, Mingst, & Stiles, 2015, p. 2.) James Rosenau (1995) argues that governance is a broader, more encompassing term than government. Rosenau describes governance as a "system of rule" that exists without an authoritative document, such as a constitution that typically delineates what a government can and cannot do. Thomas Weiss and Rorden Wilkinson (2014, p. 211) state, "We understand global governance as the sum of the informal and formal ideas, values, norms, institutions, and procedures that help all actors— states, intergovernmental organizations (IGOs), civil society, and multinational corporations (MNCs)—identify and understand trans-boundary problems."

The last few words of Weiss and Wilkinson's definition encapsulates why global governance is on the rise. Transnational problems, such as climate change, global terrorism, and the spread of infectious diseases such as COVID-19, pose a serious threat to people living in all parts of the world. Nevertheless, states lack the capacity to address these challenges alone; therefore, they have an interest in cooperating with a constellation of IGOs, NGOs, and MNCs in order to address these problems that transcend state borders. These efforts aim to quarantine and mitigate problems at their source in order to ensure they do not become what former Secretary-General of the United Nations Kofi Anan refers to as "problems without passports."

Combatting transnational problems often entails partnerships between multiple numbers of the aforementioned entities. For example, the 2009 Great Recession wreaked havoc on the economies of European Union member states, and high budget deficits and levels of accumulated debt in countries such as Portugal, Italy, and Greece threatened to destabilize the Euro (the common currency) and the economies of other states in the Eurozone. A partnership of European institutions, including the Commission and the European Central Bank, teamed up with the International Monetary Fund (IMF), an independent specialized agency of the United Nations (UN), to manage the crisis. Similarly, the Bill and Melinda Gates Foundation, a nongovernmental organization funded and managed by private citizens, works closely with another UN program called the United Nations Capital Development Fund and MasterCard, a multinational corporation, to issue microcredit loans to spur development in forty-seven of the poorest countries in the world.[1] Just as Karns et al. stated, there is no top down hierarchy in these arrangements that resembles a typical domestic government.

Nevertheless, the de-centralized nature of global governance, the shifting of power in the international system, and the propensity for states—particularly the great powers—to fiercely guard their sovereignty all pose challenges to global governance. Additionally, the rise of global governance raises important questions about the responsiveness of such unelected entities as IGOs, NGOs, and MNCs to popular demands. On the other hand, critics often lambast the UN in particular for its perceived failure to solve such problems as the ongoing civil war in Syria, genocide, and nuclear proliferation. Nevertheless, the UN is powerless to act on its own

---

1   More can be read at the UN website: https://sustainabledevelopment.un.org/partnership/?p=7501)

and requires states—especially the great powers—to enforce its treaties and resolutions.

After World War II, the U.S. reversed the isolationist course it had taken for most of its history prior to that point, and began to promote greater cooperation between states through a series of multilateral agreements, including the **General Agreement on Tariffs and Trade (GATT)**, and intergovernmental organizations, including the **North Atlantic Treaty Organization (NATO)**. Crafted at the height of American power, many of these multilateral agreements and IGOs were critical to American efforts to promote free markets and liberal democratic values around the globe while geopolitically isolating the Soviet Union. However, scholars have long noted the presence of an elite-mass split in the U.S. in regard to foreign policy, with many academics and statesmen preferring deepening ties to the rest of the world and the masses preferring isolationism. Nevertheless, Miller and Stokes (1963) found that while the votes of members of Congress closely aligned with their constituents in regard to civil rights and social welfare issues, their votes were not as closely aligned on foreign policy. This has contributed to a sense that American foreign policy is elite-driven, and that the public has historically been more deferential in regard to international affairs than on domestic policy matters.

The 2016 presidential election in the U.S. and the 2016 Brexit vote in the United Kingdom exposed deeply divided electorates in two countries that have been staunch supporters of global governance since World War II. In the U.S., former Secretary of State Hillary Clinton was often on the defensive from attacks from her right—from former President Trump—and left—from Senator Bernie Sanders—over her support of the Trans-Pacific Partnership (TPP), which would have deepened the U.S.'s economic ties to such allies as Japan, South Korea, and Australia. One of the mantras for President Trump's successful 2016 campaign was "America First," and the campaign regularly maligned America's involvement in international accords, such as the Paris Agreement and the Iran Nuclear Deal. Additionally, Trump regularly took aim at regional trade pacts, such as the North American Free Trade Agreement (NAFTA), and intergovernmental organizations, such as NATO. Throughout his time in office, Trump has consistently been skeptical of **multilateralism**, or an alliance of multiple states working together in pursuit of a common goal. A common complaint Trump levies against multilateral agreements is that the U.S. is being taken advantage of or getting the raw end of the deal. Trump regularly speaks of renegotiating these deals bilaterally, or between two states, in hopes of leveraging the U.S.'s power and securing more favorable deals.

Trump's resistance to multilateralism has proven popular in some segments of the American society, but it often frustrates and confounds critics and many of America's closest allies who point to the successes of the liberal order, which Joseph Nye (2017) defines as "the loose array of multilateral institutions through which the U.S. provided public goods such as freer trade and freedom of the seas," that the U.S. created after World War II. The liberal order is essentially a rules-based international system intended to reduce the likelihood of states going to war through promotion of political and legal channels for settling disputes. Notable critics of President Trump's foreign policy have included French President Emmanuel Macron, who reportedly applied considerable pressure during a terse private phone call for Trump to reconsider his decision to withdraw the U.S. from the **Paris Climate Agreement**. Similarly, the leaders of many of the worlds' most advanced economies appeared quite frustrated during a heated 2018 **G7 (Group of 7)** in which Trump reversed course and refused to sign a statement of goals for the organization to which he had previously agreed.

The growing rift between the United States and international efforts to confront global challenges was also exposed by the COVID-19 pandemic. The Trump administration repeatedly criticized the World Health Organization's (WHO) response to the global pandemic, accusing the organization of being too closely aligned with China's interests. In April 2020, the United States declined to join the WHO's efforts to find a vaccine for COVID-19, instead opting to devote resources to a nationalist effort called Operation Warp Speed. In June 2020, the Trump administration began efforts to formally withdraw from the WHO, a move his opponent former Vice President Joe Biden vowed to reverse if elected.

While Americans continue to fiercely debate the role their country will play in global affairs in the twenty-first century, the rise of powers such as China, India, and Brazil will fundamentally alter the nature of global governance. While the U.S. is still the largest economy in the world and Americans spend more on their military than the next seven countries combined, the rapid economic growth of China and India will certainly increase the voice those countries will have in financial IGOs, such as the International Monetary Fund (IMF) and the **World Trade Organization (WTO)**. Additionally, China has worked to deepen its economic ties to other regional economies in the aftermath of the U.S.'s abandoning its efforts in regard to the Trans-Pacific Partnership, and the Chinese have been increasingly assertive in their territorial claims to disputed areas of the South China Sea. As the world gets smaller due to globalization, the proliferation of transnational problems—and consequently a demand for transnational solutions—increases. Thus, regardless of the decisions Americans make in their elections, there will continue to be demand for global governance and other entities who are willing to pick up the slack should the U.S. abandon its leading role.

Why Global Governance is on the Rise

The process of globalization has dramatically accelerated since the Soviet Union collapsed in 1991 and fundamentally altered international relations. **Globalization** can be defined as "a fundamental shift or transformation in the spatial scale of human social organization that links distant communities and expands the reach of power relations across regions and continents." (McGrew, 2008, p. 19) Driven by technological advancements in regard to communication and transportation, globalization has made the distance between people less important, as it allows for people and goods to rapidly travel great distances. Interconnection among states, cultures, and economic markets at unprecedented levels has contributed to the proliferation of new problems that transcend state borders. For example, the ongoing civil war in Syria has produced a flood of refugees seeking asylum in other states, an issue that rankled European politics.

Globalization has dramatically altered global politics and eroded some of the sovereignty of states in favor of a rise in intergovernmental organization, nongovernmental organizations, and multinational corporations. It presents us with tremendous opportunities, such as lowering the price of consumer goods through trade and providing American companies an opportunity to grow through expansion into foreign markets. Nevertheless, there is no perfect world, thus the benefits of globalization are offset by costs, such as the loss of many high paying American manufacturing jobs to cheaper labor markets and the opportunity for multinational corporations to exploit citizens of states with lax labor or environmental regulations.

Nevertheless, similar to the opening of Pandora's Box, the process of globalization is irreversible as it is largely driven by technological advancements. Thus, the question is not how to reverse this trend but how to manage it in order to ensure the benefits and costs are distributed equitably. The changing realities of the international system challenge world leaders to reform institutions and build new partnerships that are capable of confronting twenty-first century problems. In this way, the rise of global governance is our world's attempt to respond to ever-changing circumstances and ensure the twenty-first century is defined by progress, peace, and cooperation.

Theory and Global Governance

International relations scholars employ theories to describe, predict, and explain various aspects of our complex international system. The real international system is an extraordinary compilation of actions taken by states, **IGOs, NGOs, MNCs,** and individuals, and it is too large and complex in scope to study in its entirety. Therefore, we use theories in order to simplify the international system and clarify what matters the most. While none of the theories of international relations explains everything, we can gain insight by knowing the assumptions of these various theories and understanding the criticisms of each.

Our oldest theory of international relations, **realism,** can be distilled into Thucydides's observation recorded in the Melian Dialogue that power drives all decisions. Recall Hans Morgenthau's (1948) assumptions of realism from Chapter 3. Realists believe that states are the highest actors in world politics and thus the international system is anarchy. Realists see states as the primary actor in world politics and therefore IGOs, NGOs, and MNCs have a limited impact at best. Additionally, realists have a pessimistic view of human nature and view cooperation as hard to come by in an international system in which each state has a goal of maximizing its own self-interest.

Given these assumptions about the world, it will come as no surprise to most readers that realists generally are the most skeptical of the notion of global governance. Morgenthau (1967) believed that the great powers would manipulate IGOs into pursuing their own national interests. Furthermore, many realists believe that states are unlikely to join international agreements, such as The United Nations Convention on the Law of the Sea, which the U.S. has refused to ratify despite America's insistence that China abide by its provisions. Gruber (2000) argued that because IGOs have no enforcement mechanism, they have no authority and thus no real power.

Similar to other theories of international relations, realism has evolved into several different variations, including neorealism which places a greater importance on the structure of the international system than does classical realism, which was primarily concerned with human nature (Doyle, 1997). Neorealists are highly skeptical about the notion of international cooperation because of their belief that some states have more to gain from cooperation than do others. This disparity, which neorealists refer to as "relative gains," means that, over time, one state in an agreement will benefit to a greater extent than will its counterparts and thus will alter the power dynamics of the international system. Neorealists are particularly skeptical about the prospects for states to enter into these arrangements in regard to national security.

Classical **liberalism** maintains that human nature is inherently good and that inadequate or corrupt institutions are to blame when humans fall short of just and peaceful outcomes. Liberals believe humans are rational, that progress is possible, and that humans can reform political institutions to overcome the issues that often lead to injustice or conflict. A classic example of this notion can be found on the European continent in the aftermath of World War II. Jean Monnet, often regarded as the father of Europe, worried that conflict over coal resources could drag France and Germany into conflict once again, a fate that nobody who lived through the horrors of World Wars I and II wanted to repeat. Monnet, therefore, proposed creating the European Coal and Steel Community (ECSC), which would allow Germany and France to place their coal under the command of a high authority along with four other neighbors: Italy, Belgium, the Netherlands, and Luxembourg. At the first meeting of the Coal and Steel Community, Monnet told attendees that they were there to discuss not coal and steel but a peaceful and unified Europe. Sure enough, the European Coal and Steel Community paved the way toward the European Union, the strongest and most cohesive regional intergovernmental organization in the world.

Liberals believe that intergovernmental organizations play a key role in allowing states to negotiate to avoid conflict and work together in pursuit of solutions to common problems. Additionally, liberals are strong proponents of international law and the establishment of a rules and norms based international system that places constraints on states' actions. Furthermore, while neoliberals acknowledge that global governance is incomplete, they contend that realists exaggerate the extent to which the international system is anarchic. As Grieco declares, "Even if . . . anarchy constrains the willingness of states to cooperate, states nevertheless can work together and do so especially with the assistance of international institutions" (1993, p. 117).

Neoliberal scholars, including Robert Keohane, draw on game theory approaches, such as the classic prisoner's dilemma, to illustrate how cooperation can be in the state's best interest. Imagine two suspects are arrested for suspected involvement in a crime. As most readers know, the two suspects will be immediately separated by law enforcement in order to prevent the two suspects from working together to coordinate their account of pertinent events. Instead, law enforcement will separate the two prisoners and give them two choices: they can tell the truth in hopes of securing some sort of deal for leniency for themselves, or they can stay silent and hope that law enforcement is unable to connect all the details of the crime together, which could ultimately free the prisoners. Obviously, each prisoner is going to have to try to imagine what their counterpart is going to do when making their own decision. If both prisoners stay silent, then both could avoid the threat of a long prison term. If both confess, then they are both facing a potentially significant prison term. However, if Prisoner A squeals, and Prisoner B stays silent, then Prisoner B risks the potential of a very long prison term for not cooperating, while Prisoner A leverages their cooperation in exchange for leniency (or vice versa).

These hypothetical prisoners are states, and states have to make decisions every day with incomplete and imperfect information that will often have serious consequences. Realists believe that states are self-interested and that cooperation is hard to come by; therefore, realists would hypothesize that many states would pursue their own interests no matter what the consequence for the other state. However, neoliberals argue that this is not a one-stage game and that states can develop norms of cooperation and reciprocity that are mutually beneficial. Additionally, neoliberals argue that the focus should be on absolute gains accrued through cooperation and not dwell on the potential for one state to get more out of a deal. Furthermore, neoliberals contend that a long standing tradition of cooperation, such as in the special relationship between the U.S. and the United Kingdom, will deliver long-term benefits that states will want to preserve rather than backstab each other in pursuit of some short-term gain.

Constructivism is a newer theory of international relations but nevertheless is increasingly important for studying the role of intergovernmental organizations in the international system. Constructivists contend that the international system is essentially a construct, a byproduct of our perception of reality. Thus, while realists believe in the presence of fixed realities of the international system, the system is anarchy and composed of self-interested states, constantly seeking to maximize their power constructivists argue the patterns that often lead to conflict can be overcome by changing our perceptions.

A classic illustration of constructivism is to think about nuclear weapons arsenals of different states. As we've seen in Chapter 8, for most Americans, the idea of the United Kingdom's possessing 215 nuclear weapons is not a threat to Americans because of the long standing special relationship between the two states. However, when the same American thinks about North Korea possessing 25 of the exact same weapons, suddenly they perceive this arsenal as a threat due to the notoriously strained relationship between the two countries since the middle of the twentieth century.

Constructivists believe that, through interaction and dialogue, these threats can be overcome.

Constructivists argue that intergovernmental organizations can be very influential in the sense that they socialize states into accepting the norms and rules of the IGOs (Checkel, 2005). In the immediate aftermath of World War II, many people considered the Germans and Japanese to be warlike societies that posed significant threats to the prospects for peace moving forward into the twentieth century. However, the U.S. encouraged integrating the defeated Axis powers into various global and regional intergovernmental organizations, such as NATO for Germany and GATT for both, rather than repeat the mistake of imposing a humiliating settlement as the allies had done with the Treaty of Versailles in World War I. The result was two countries that enjoyed economic miracles and now have a seventy-five year track record of working together with other great powers in a wide variety of multilateral pacts and intergovernmental organizations.

The Evolution of Global Governance

The idea of global governance has been around since antiquity, although its actual iterations differ dramatically in response to changing times. The ancient Greek city states entered into protective alliances with one another in hopes of deterring potential enemy attacks. Similarly, the Romans promoted the idea of the Pax Romana (Roman Peace) and the notion that a world dominated by one great power would finally be at peace.

Often regarded as the father of international law, Hugo Grotius argued that states are bound by rule of law, that is, law made by man and natural law, and thus rejected the notion that states have a right to do whatever they want, including going to war. Several notable philosophers proposed institutions that they believed would promote cooperation and diminish the likelihood of states engaging in warfare. Writing against the backdrop of the Thirty Years' War in the early seventeenth century, the French writer Émeric Crucé proposed a world organization that would promote free trade and resolve international disputes. In 1693, William Penn proposed the idea of a European Confederation that could settle disputes by a three-fourths vote. The great German philosopher Immanuel Kant was one of the first thinkers to make a connection between democracy and peace, arguing that democratic states would exist in a "pacific union," working together to avoid war.

While each of these philosophers eloquently advanced ideas that were ahead of their time, the actual application of global governance was considerably less ideal. Following the Napoleonic Wars, Austrian Prince Klemens von Metternich established the Concert of Europe, the aim of which was to coordinate the European powers working together to ensure a delicate balance of power on the continent that was supposed to act as safeguard against war. While certainly a far cry from global governance in the twenty-first century, the Concert of Europe did facilitate multilateral negotiations in an attempt to avoid conflict between Europe's great powers. Nevertheless, the Concert of Europe proved untenable and collapsed with the breakout of World War I.

Before World War I ended, U.S President Woodrow Wilson outlined his vision for the post-war world in his landmark **Fourteen Points** speech. Drawing upon many ideas from classical liberalism, Wilson called for a reduction in national armaments and the removal of economic barriers between countries, urging European allies to relinquish their colonial claims in favor of self-determination. Also included in the speech is Wilson's call that "a general association of nations be formed under specific covenants for the purpose of affording mutual guarantees of political independence and territorial integrity to great and small states alike."[2]

Wilson's speech served as inspiration for the next iteration of the world's attempt to avoid conflict between the great powers in

---

2   Wilson's Fourteen Points speech

the **League of Nations**. Included as a provision in the Treaty of Versailles, the League of Nations was designed to establish the principle of **collective security**, or the notion that every member state's security is the responsibility of all the other member states. The principle of collective security is perhaps best illustrated by Article 5 of NATO's treaty: that an attack against one shall be considered an attack against all. The purpose of Article 5 is to drive up the cost of an attack on any NATO member state in order to deter would-be attackers. Consequently, even attacking tiny Luxembourg would impose high costs because it would serve as the *casus foederis* (case for the alliance) that would trigger a response from other NATO members, such as the U.S. and United Kingdom.

League of Nations members also agreed to not attack other members of the League. Should two members have a conflict, the League's Covenant mandated that the members bring their disagreement to the League of Nations in order to allow the intergovernmental organization an opportunity to try to mediate the dispute. Should a League member state fail to abide by this provision, the Covenant called for the other member states to impose either economic sanctions or the threat of military force on that member for failure to comply with the terms of the League's Covenant.

The League of Nations started in 1920 with forty-two original members, which ultimately grew to sixty. However, isolationists in the U.S. Senate refused to ratify the League's Covenant, thereby effectively blocking American participation in the intergovernmental organization that was born out of President Wilson's Fourteen Points. Historians and scholars of international relations have long debated the extent to which American membership could have buoyed the League's efforts to promote cooperation and peace, but the U.S.'s decision not to join certainly had deleterious consequences on the League's ability to navigate the security challenges of the interwar international system.

And those challenges would prove to be daunting, to say the least. In 1931, the Japanese began their conquest of Manchuria under the guise that China had set off a small bomb on some railroad tracks near Mukden. The League sent a council to investigate, but by time the investigation could be completed, the Japanese invasion of Manchuria was complete. (Roskin & Berry, 2014, p. 329–330) Four years later, the Italians decided to invade Ethiopia, but the British and French were afraid that coordinating a League effort to condemn the Italians would push Mussolini toward an alliance with Hitler. In this way, two members of the League of Nations had engaged in attacks on other members, and the League had failed to respond to these violations of the League's Covenant. Italy and Japan would then decide to leave the League of Nations altogether, and Hitler noted the League's tepid response as he began to violate the terms of the Treaty of Versailles and acquire more territory in the mid-1930s.

The League of Nations effectively dissolved when World War II broke out in Europe in response to the 1939 German invasion of Poland, which crossed a red line in the sand drawn by the United Kingdom and France. While the League ultimately proved incapable of preventing World War II, it nevertheless was an advancement in the notion of global governance, and the allies discussed working together to craft a new intergovernmental organization to promote dialogue and cooperation while the war was still raging.

The United Nations: The Centerpiece of Global Governance

The **United Nations** is the cornerstone of global governance. While often maligned for budgetary issues or the perception of ineffectuality, the UN is unmatched by any other intergovernmental organization in terms of the scope of its membership and the wide variety of issues it addresses. The UN is an important post for discussing and debating contemporary global issues and serves as hub for multilateral diplomacy. Additionally, the UN Security Council is an important venue for discussing strategies to deal with global security issues, and it is the primary source for obtaining international legitimacy for military action or peacekeeping missions. Specialized Agencies of the UN, such as the World Health Organization, take the lead in managing such issues as the recent Ebola virus outbreaks at their source, ensuring they do not grow into global pandemics. Finally, the UN works closely alongside regional organizations, such as the African Union, to ensure a strong relationship between global and regional governance.

The Organs of the United Nations

The **General Assembly** is the United Nation's main deliberative body. Like the League of Nations Assembly before it, each of the 193 states currently represented in the UN General Assembly has one vote, regardless of population. Additionally, the Holy See (the Vatican) and Palestine enjoy non-member observer state status, while regional IGOs, such as the European Union, African Union, and Arab League, are also observers. The General Assembly meets in New York City every year from September to December but can convene for special sessions at the request of the UN Security Council or by majority vote of the UN member states. The General Assembly serves as a hub for many activities, including debating matters covered by the UN Charter and supervising the subsidiary bodies of the UN. Additionally, the General Assembly elects the Secretary General of the UN, who essentially acts as the organization's spokesperson. The General Assembly also elects the nonpermanent members of the Security Council and appoints judges to the International Court of Justice (ICJ).

Karns et al. (2015) argue that the "UN General Assembly comes closer than any other international body to embodying what is often called the 'international community.' To paraphrase Shakespeare, if 'all the world's a stage,' the UN General Assembly is center stage"

(Karns et al., 2015, p. 113). Many readers have probably at one time or another witnessed highlights from a speech at the General Assembly. It is common to see one leader on stage and many members of the audience listening on devices that allowed for the speech to be translated into dozens of different languages. Sometimes speakers at the UN General Assembly have pointed criticism for other member states, including incidents when former President of Venezuela Hugo Chavez insinuated that President George W. Bush was the devil or when Trump derided North Korean Premier Kim Jong Un as the "little rocket man." Typical speeches are far less dramatic than those extreme examples, but many are devoted to calling out a specific state's actions, expressing frustration about the status quo, or urging other members to unite in pursuit of common goals.

Membership in the General Assembly grew dramatically during the middle of the twentieth century as the European empires collapsed and more states in Africa and Asia secured independence. Again, every state has exactly one vote in the General Assembly, regardless of its size or relative power, and most resolutions require a simple majority vote. Matters pertaining to security, budget, or new membership require a higher threshold of a two-thirds vote. For much of the Cold War, the primary cleavage at the General Assembly was East vs. West, with members from Western Europe and the Americas backing the U.S., while members from Eastern Europe backed the Soviet Union. However, the growth of membership from states in the developing world, along with the collapse of the Soviet Union, have caused the North vs. South schism to be the current primary division at the UN General Assembly.

Any state can propose a resolution to the UN General Assembly, and the body can address any matter within the purview of the UN Charter (Article 10). This includes such issues as global poverty, matters pertaining to de-colonization, environmental issues, human trafficking, women's rights, and many more. Additionally, the General Assembly does share some authority in regard to security, but much of the heavy lifting falls to the UN Security Council. While not a world legislature, UN General Assembly resolutions play an important role in crafting international law and are particularly influential in developing norms that represent international consensus referred to as "soft law" (Karns et al., 2015, p. 116)

Karns et al. (2015, p. 122) state that many of the critics who call for UN reform are really speaking about the need for reform of the General Assembly. The General Assembly has passed hundreds of resolutions per session in recent years, but many of them are so general that they are non-controversial and have little chance for implementation. Given this reality, much of the power at the UN has shifted in recent years to the UN Security Council and Secretariat (Karns et al., 2015, p. 122.)

The UN Charter grants primary responsibility for maintaining security to the **UN Security Council**. The Security Council exists to promote peace and conflict resolution through diplomatic channels. The UN has a peacekeeping force of roughly 100,000 soldiers (supplied by member states in exchange for the UN's paying their salaries) that is tasked with carrying out some Security Council resolutions. Peacekeeping forces are tasked with trying to create conditions on the ground that are conducive to establishing a lasting peace. They are officially neutral and are designated as non-combatants under international law. However, the UN Security Council primarily relies on its member states to support enforcement actions and impose and maintain sanctions.

The Security Council has fifteen members, ten of which serve on a rotating basis for two-year terms. The ten rotating members of the Security Council come from five regions: Africa, Asia-Pacific, Eastern Europe, Latin America and the Caribbean, and Western Europe. Every region gets two seats. The remaining five members of the Security Council are permanent and possess the ability to exert **veto** power over all Security Council resolutions. The permanent members include: the U.S., the United Kingdom, France, Russia, and China, or, in other words, the victorious Allied powers in World War II. Fearing that the Soviet Union would consistently get outvoted at the UN Security Council, Joseph Stalin insisted at Yalta that each permanent member would enjoy veto power, and Winston Churchill and Franklin Delano Roosevelt acquiesced to Stalin's request. This provision is perhaps the most controversial of all topics that pertain to the Security Council.

The U.S. and the Soviet Union (now Russia) account for more than 75% of the vetoes of UN Security Council resolutions since its inception in 1946. In recent times, the U.S. has often vetoed resolutions that are critical of Israeli policies, such as building settlements on territory that is disputed with the Palestinians. Meanwhile, Russia has used its position on the Security Council to protect a close ally—Syria's Assad regime—from UN Security Council resolutions critical of the ongoing Syrian civil war. These individual instances of vetoes are often met with condemnation and frustration. However, the concept of the veto itself has drawn considerable scrutiny in recent years.

One common complaint regarding the five permanent members of the Security Council is that they gained this status because of power dynamics from 75 years ago. President Barack Obama asserted that India should be granted veto power to reflect its status as an emerging power in the international system. Others argue that adding new permanent members will just invite more opportunities for vetoes and imperil the UN Security Council's ability to act cohesively. Finally, other observers, such as Amnesty International, argue that no state should enjoy veto power at all, arguing that the permanent member states regularly veto resolutions that condemn violations of human rights.

Nevertheless, the true nature of the Security Council might be more collaborative and inclusive than some critics imagine. The Security Council has approved over 90% of proposed resolutions since 2000 (Karns et al., 2015, p. 126). Furthermore, nonmembers are regularly invited or permitted to sit in on meetings and informal sessions of the Security Council. Additionally, non-members may be invited or permitted to address the Security Council. As Johnstone writes, "The Security Council is not a sealed chamber, deaf to voices and immune from pressure beyond its walls" (Johnstone, 2008, p. 88–89).

The **Economic and Social Council (ECOSOC)** has emerged as one of the key organs of the UN, despite the fact that the Charter establishes a relatively skeletal framework. The ECOSOC is responsible for coordinating all of the economic and social policies of the UN, thus it works closely alongside various UN specialized agencies, programs and funds, and regional organizations.

A substantial portion of the UN's focus is on reducing poverty in the developing world, curbing the threat of climate change, preventing the spread of infectious diseases, and promoting human rights around the globe. To that end, the UN has a multitude of different funds, programs, and specialized organizations devoted to helping the intergovernmental organization achieve those lofty goals. This includes the United Nations Children's Fund (UNICEF), the World Health Organization (WHO), the United Nations Development Program (UNDP), the United Nations Environmental Program, and dozens more. Given the multitude of different agencies and programs working toward these goals, the ECOSOC is needed in order to coordinate their actions. This means the ECOSOC is responsible for overseeing 70% of the UN's human and financial resources (Karns et al, 2015, p. 129).

The **International Court of Justice (ICJ)** is the judicial branch of the UN and comprises fifteen judges from different states who are elected by the General Assembly and Security Council. The ICJ gives states an opportunity to adjudicate disputes according to international law; however, the ICJ can only issue binding decisions if the states that are party to the case agree to accept the decision beforehand. Additionally, no state can be forced to appear before the ICJ, and powerful states such as Russia and China have recently declined to allow the ICJ to settle cases brought against them by other states. As with the Security Council, the UN relies on member states to enforce ICJ rulings in contentious cases. The ICJ can also issue advisory rulings that often pertain to the functioning of the UN.

The ICJ is generally well-respected and stands to grow in importance, given the ongoing development of international law. Nevertheless, a key structural weakness is that the ICJ may only hear contentious issues cases involving states and cannot adjudicate matters involving non state actors in land disputes—such as the Palestinians or Kurds—nor matters pertaining to individuals, terrorist organizations, or nongovernmental organizations.

The **Trusteeship Council** was created at the end of World War II to assist former colonies as they transitioned toward independence. Although the organization once played an integral role in assisting various colonies make their transition to self-government, the Trusteeship Council suspended operations in 1994 after helping over seventy countries transition to independence, but it can reconvene should the situation require it to do so.

The **Secretariat** is the sixth and final main organ of the UN. With a total of approximately 43,000 professional and administrative staff members hailing from 175 countries, the Secretariat is responsible for compiling reports, facilitating communication between various UN entities, and carrying out the UN's administrative work under the direction of the General Assembly and UN Security Council.

The Secretariat is headed by the **Secretary-General** of the UN. Nominated by the Security Council and elected by a two-thirds vote in the General Assembly, the Secretary-General serves for five-year renewable terms. The UN Charter is very vague in regard to the office of the Secretary-General, but the position is highly important both in terms of management of such a complex intergovernmental organization and the necessity for its chief spokesperson to possess a certain degree of gravitas. According to Karns et al., "the

Secretary-General is the manager of the organization, responsible for providing leadership to the Secretariat, preparing the UN's budget, submitting an annual report to the General Assembly, and overseeing studies that are conducted at the request of the other major organs" (2015, p. 134). Additionally, the Secretary-General is authorized to present information about threats to global security to the UN Security Council. Finally, the UN Secretary-General serves as the most visible spokesperson for the entire organization and, in that sense, is "the representative of the community's interests or the defender of the values of the international community" (Barnett & Finnemore, 2004, p. 23).

Regional Governance

Globalization and the rise of new transnational problems have spurred a rise in regional governance as well as the growth of global governance. Regional governance is driven by all the same issues that gave rise to global governance: security issues, economic issues, environmental issues, humans rights issues, and others. The European continent, in particular, is densely populated and comprises many states that are in close proximity to one another. These states had desperately tried to maintain their security through a complex series of ever-changing alliances since the seventeenth century. The result was a series of increasingly catastrophic wars that many believed would ultimately threaten human existence.

Following World War II, Italian politician and political theorist Altiero Spinelli proposed an ultimatum to his fellow Europeans: the continent could either "federate or perish." An enemy of Mussolini's fascist regime, Spinelli was imprisoned for ten years before and during the war. While in prison, he wrote his manifesto, *Per un' Europa libera e unita ("For a Free and United Europe")* in which he argued that fascism's defeat in World War II would mean nothing if the Europeans did not succeed in ending the secretive balance of power alliance system once and for all. Spinelli believed that the prospect for peace entailed uniting into what essentially would have been the United States of Europe, in other words, a federalized system in which states retained power in specific domains, while issues such as national security would be dealt with by a unifying federal government.

The seeds for a unified Europe were planted in the rubble left behind by World War II and were integral to the American and European efforts to avoid yet another war on the continent. Proponents of European integration understood that the devastation the continent faced in the late 1940s coincided with a window of opportunity to undertake the structural changes that would be necessary to secure a future of peace and prosperity on the continent. Wait too long, and things would slowly get back to normal, and the opportunity for significant political and economic reforms would pass.

The first two precursors to the contemporary European Union were American-led attempts to contain the spread of communism in Europe and deter aggressive action by the Soviet Union. Opportunities for such a spread coincided with the post-World War II ruin of the economies of all the western European states, along with production at factories being well below pre-war levels. Worried that poor economic conditions would push suffering peoples toward communist parties, the Americans initiated massive economic assistance to Western European countries, assistance known as the **Marshall Plan**. The goals of the Marshall Plan were to establish a free trade zone in Western Europe, raise production in factories to pre-war levels, and provide a boost to European currencies that were suffering from inflation after the war. As aforementioned, the North Atlantic Treaty Organization (NATO) united western European powers into a defense pact with the U.S. that promised to deliver collective security through Article 5's declaration that an attack against one shall be considered an attack against all.

The third precursor to the European Union was the aforementioned European Coal and Steel Community (ECSC) that was created by the 1951 Treaty of Paris. The ECSC obviated the need for France and Germany to engage in war over coal resources and represented an important advancement in regional governance. In order for the ECSC to function properly, the Europeans needed to create a high authority in order to referee disputes between the member states. This introduced **supranational** principles into the ECSC, as it created an entity that could impose binding decisions on the member states. This principle is still embedded in the contemporary European Court of Justice, and it makes the European Union *sui generis* (in a class by itself) amongst international organizations.

Following the creation of the ECSC, many political science scholars began to debate over how the process of European integration might continue in subsequent decades. One theory is **functionalism**, which is an offshoot of liberalism. Functionalists argued that integration in some domains would automatically spill over into other domains; thereby, the process of Europeanization would be self-sustaining in subsequent decades. However, adherents of a second school of thought called **intergovernmentalism** argued that the integration process would trigger a backlash from states that feared losing sovereignty if the process went too far. Stanley Hoffman (1966) argued that states would readily transfer sovereignty in *low politics* domains, such as trade or environmental policy. However, in *high politics* arenas pertaining to national security or state sovereignty, states would be reluctant to transfer authority to a supranational or intergovernmental organization.

The collapse of the European Defense Community (EDC) in 1954 likely contributed to Hoffman's views regarding integration. Buoyed by the success of the ECSC, proponents of European integration took an important step in the early 1950s by petitioning for the creation of the EDC, which would have essentially unified the six members of the ECSC into one military under joint command.

Nevertheless, the proposal was ultimately defeated by one vote in the French Parliament as a coalition of communists, fearing the alliance would threaten the Soviet Union, teamed up with nationalists who refused to transfer national defense to a supranational organization.

Following the collapse of the EDC, the European integration process stalled for roughly the next three decades as many of its leaders failed to convey a vision for a unified Europe in the way Jean Monnet had done. However, the process was reinvigorated in 1987 with the ratification of the Single European Act (SEA) that took steps toward a single market for all member states, one characterized by the elimination of trade barriers—such as tariffs or quotas—and the facilitation of free movement of capital, goods, and labor across state borders. The SEA paved the way for the Maastricht Treaty in 1992 which officially created the contemporary **European Union (EU)**.

The European Union is *sui generis* among international organizations as it exists somewhere between the categories of a traditional intergovernmental organization and a sovereign state. The EU essentially establishes a customs union between its member states, as they have no barriers to trade between the member states and a common external tariff on goods imported from outside the EU. In addition to economic regulations, the EU also has policies pertaining to the environment and human rights issues. For example, in 2019, the EU Parliament voted to ban single use plastics (such as plastic straws.) Additionally, several EU treaties ban capital punishment; thus, no member of the EU may legalize the death penalty. In addition to integration in these traditional policy domains, the EU expanded cooperation into foreign policy with the establishment of the Common Foreign and Security Policy (CFSP) and law enforcement with Justice and Home Affairs.

The institutions of the EU are a complex blend of intergovernmental and supranational institutions that strike a balance between intergovernmental organization and sovereign state. The first institution and the most intergovernmental is the

European Council composed of the prime ministers of most member states, the Presidents of France and Finland (which are semi-presidential systems), and the President of the Commission.

As the European Council comprises the heads of government or state of the respective member states, it meets rather infrequently but as circumstances dictate. While not vested with many formal powers, the European Council is nevertheless a source of guidance, gravitas, and stability for the EU. Additionally, while vested with few formal powers, the Council tends to act informally and operates how it sees fit. There is an unequal relationship between members of the European Council, with heads of government from powerful member states—such as Germany, France, and Italy—enjoying more power than smaller states—such as Luxembourg. Additionally, newer members are supposed to defer to members who have been around for longer, such as deferring to Angela Merkel who has been the Chancellor of Germany since 2005 (Peterson & Shackleton, 2006, p. 46).

The **Commission** is the executive branch of the European Union. Each member state has one Commissioner who is appointed by the prime minister (or president of France and Finland). The Commission has a rotating five-year presidency designed to give the European Union a singular representative who can speak for the entire organization. One unique feature of the Commission that sets it apart from a typical executive branch is that it serves as the agenda- setter for the EU and as the only branch of government that can propose new legislation. Additionally, the Commission is responsible for safeguarding EU treaties and notifying member states when they out of compliance with EU directives.

The legislative branch of the EU is bicameral, with the **European Parliament (EP)** being the lower house of the legislature. The EP is the only democratically-elected institution of the EU and thus the supranational organizations' response to critics who contend there is a **democratic deficit** within the organization that places so many appointed leaders over the democratically-elected heads of government of the member states. The European Parliament has been strengthened over time to ensure that European citizens have a voice in the supranational EU.

The **Council of the European Union** (not to be confused with the aforementioned European Council) is the upper house of the EU's legislature and is composed of ministers of specific policy domains. For example, just as the U.S. has a Secretary of Defense who serves in the president's administration, so also does each member state of the EU have a defense minister who serves a comparable function. These ministers are supposed to be experts in their respective policy domain, ensuring that EU policy is technocratic and not political. Thus, depending on the nature of the issue the Council of the EU is discussing, the relevant ministers meet to discuss and coordinate EU policy.

The **European Court of Justice (ECJ)** is the Judicial Branch of the EU. The ECJ is composed of one justice per member state who is appointed by the prime minister or president of the respective member state. Similar to the U.S. Court of Appeals, the judges on the ECJ hear cases in three, five, or seven judge panels. The ECJ differs greatly from the previously mentioned International Court of Justice in the sense that member states can neither opt out of its proceedings nor flout its rulings. If an EU member state is deemed to be out of compliance with EU directives, the Commission will notify the member state of such. In many cases, the Commission and the member state will work together to bring the state in compliance. However, if a deal cannot be reached, the Commission will act as the prosecutor and bring the member state in front of the ECJ. Compliance with ECJ rulings is not an issue because of the close relationship the ECJ has with member state lower courts (Peterson & Shackleton, 2006, p. 133). This close relationship is the linchpin of the EU's ability to enforce member state compliance in a manner that is unlike any other intergovernmental organization.

Another important institution in the EU is the **European Central Bank (ECB)** Many members of the EU also participate in the European Monetary Union and thus share a common currency called the euro. Typical central banks, like that of the U.S., can tinker with monetary policy to secure economic goals, such as stimulating growth or curbing inflation. The members of the European Monetary Union have transferred control over their monetary policy to the European Central Bank that, for better or worse, crafts a one size fits all monetary policy for all members.

The EU is by far the most complex and deeply integrated example of regional governance. As noted above, Europeans undertook this project after centuries of warfare as a result of shifting alliances on the continent. While the EU has enjoyed successes, it also has its share of critics who contend that the supranational organization has eroded state sovereignty and contributed to a growing democratic deficit on the continent. Recent challenges such as the sovereign debt crisis and managing an influx of North African and Syrian refugees fleeing internal conflicts have exposed deep schisms on the continent, and EU has struggled to manage these crises. This was prevalent in the Brexit debate and the driving force for many British voters to cast their ballot in support of leaving the EU.

Still, others argue that the model for regional governance illustrated by the EU is something to strive for in other regional organizations, such as the African Union. Will the rise of global governance in the twenty-first century coincide with stronger regional governance as well?

Globalization and the rise of transnational problems that states cannot address alone will continue to drive demand for global and regional governance in the twenty-first century. While the decentralized nature of global governance, the rise of new powers in the international system, and the propensity for states to fiercely guard their sovereignty all pose challenges to global governance, the growing constellation of IGOs, NGOs, and MNCs working alongside states pose the opportunity for the world to address twenty-first century challenges head on.

Harvard Ph.D. and noted CNN and *The Washington Post* commentator Fareed Zakaria gave an optimistic speech at Harvard's commencement in 2012. In his speech, Zakaria described a breakout of the H1N1 virus in Mexico that had the potential to spread into a global pandemic. Zakaria described how Mexican health authorities identified the problem early, contacted the World Health Organization, learned best practices, and worked quickly to quarantine sick patients and vaccinate others. When it was all said and done, the virus was contained, and some people wondered what the hysteria was about in the first place and if authorities had overreacted. Zakaria stated, "We hadn't overreacted, we had reacted. We had responded, and we had dealt with the problem." Perhaps it will be this arrangement of states working closely alongside IGOs, NGOs, and MNCs that ensures twenty-first century problems are in fact "problems without passports."

References

Barnett, M. & Finnemore, M. (2004). *Rules for the world: International organizations in global politics.* Ithaca: Cornell University Press

Checkel, J. T. (Ed.). (Fall 2005) *International institutions and socialization in Europe. International Organization,* Special Issue 59, 4.

Doyle, M. W. (1997) *Ways of war and peace: Realism, liberalism, and socialism.* New York: W.W. Norton and Company

Grieco, J. M. (1993) "Anarchy and the limits of cooperation: A realist critique of the newest liberal institutionalism." In Baldwin, D. A. (Ed.)., *Neorealism and Neoliberalism: The Contemporary Debate.* New York: Columbia University Press

Gruber, L. (2000) *Ruling the world: Power politics and the rise of supranational institutions.* Princeton: Princeton University Press

Hoffman, S. (1966) "Obstinate or obsolete? The fate of the nation-state and the case of western Europe." *Daedaulus, 95*(3), 862–915

Johnstone, I. (2008) "The security council as legislature." In B. Cronin and I. Hurd (eds.), *The UN security council and the politics of international authority,* 80–104. New York: Routledge.

Karns, M., Mingst,, K., & Stiles, K. (2015) *International organizations: The politics & processes of global governance* (3rd ed.). Boulder: Lynne Rienner Publishers Inc.

McGrew, A. (2008) "Globalization and global politics" In J. Baylis, S. Smith, and P. Owens (eds.), *Globalization and Global Politics: An Introduction to International Relations* (4th ed.), 16–33. New York: Oxford University Press.

Miller, W. E. & Stokes, D. (1963). "Constituency influence in congress." *American Political Science Review, 57*(1), 45–56.

Morgenthau, H. & Thompson, K. (1985 [1948]). *Politics among Nations: The struggle for power and peace.* New York: Alfred Knopf

Nye, J. (2017) "Will the liberal order survive? The history of an idea." *Foreign Affairs, 96*(1), 11. (January February 2010.

Peterson, J. & Shackelton, M. (2006) *The institutions of the European Union* (2nd ed.). Oxford: Oxford University Press

Rosenau, J. (1995, Winter) "Governance in the twenty-first century." *Global Governance, 1*(1), 13–43.

Roskin, M. & Berry, N. (2014) *IR: The New World of International Relations,* (10th ed.).

Weiss, P., Thomas, G., & Wilkinson, R. (2014, March) "Rethinking global governance? Complexity, authority, power, change." *International Studies Quarterly, 58*(1), 207–215.

Part IV

Globalization and its Impact

International Political Economy and Globalization

12

Cristian Harris

Abstract

This chapter discusses International Political Economy (IPE). It identifies and reviews the ideas of three main theoretical perspectives of IPE: economic nationalism, economic liberalism, and radicalism/Marxism. The chapter also reviews the establishment of the post-World War II international economic order. It focuses on the role of different actors (governments, international economic institutions, inter-governmental organizations, and multinational corporations) and different economic processes (trade, monetary relations, and investment). Finally, this chapter concludes with an analysis of globalization.

Learning Objectives

- Identify the main theories of International Political Economy (IPE): economic liberalism, economic nationalism, and radicalism/Marxism
- Analyze and explain the major international economic activities: trade, monetary relations, and foreign direct investment
- Analyze and explain the historical evolution of the world economy since the 1940s
- Identify and explain the role that different actors (states, international organizations, multinational corporations)

play in the world economy and the changing institutional framework of the world economy

- Identify and explain the concept of globalization and review current controversies surrounding globalization

What is International Political Economy?

International Political Economy (IPE) is a rapidly developing subfield of study of international affairs. It aims to understand a set of international issues that cannot usefully be understood or analyzed as just international politics or just international economics. Beginning in the 1970s, international affairs scholars undertook to study the interaction between politics and economics in the international affairs of nation-states. For some scholars, this came down to a clash of states versus markets, politics versus economics, and international versus domestic. This is misleading. Individuals, firms, and multinational corporations that trade and invest within national and global markets are all shaped by layers of different factors that intersect, overlap, and crosscut each other. IPE is the study of these political and economic interactions in the international system.

The growing importance of IPE is, in part, a result of the erosion of disciplinary boundaries between politics and economics. IPE relies on an interdisciplinary array of analytical tools and theoretical perspectives. For instance, economic theories of trade tell us that all societies benefit from unrestricted economic exchanges. However, these benefits do not distribute evenly within those societies. Some actors benefit more than others do. Winners seek deeper links with the world economy in order to increase and consolidate their gains; losers try to erect barriers between the world and national economies in order to minimize or even reverse losses. Political theories tell us that policy decisions have important income distribution and welfare consequences. Actors will mobilize politically to have the state protect their interests through the authoritative allocation of power. Thus, IPE studies the relationship between politics and economics in international affairs. It also studies the relationship between international and domestic phenomena and the winners and losers from global processes.

Theories of IPE

Three broad theoretical perspectives have grown around IPE. They are economic nationalism, economic liberalism, and radicalism/Marxism. This section discusses contending theoretical perspectives of IPE.

Economic Nationalism, Mercantilism, or Statism

Mercantilism is the oldest theoretical perspective of IPE. Mercantilism, like **realism**, emphasizes the importance of state building and power. It is also skeptical of the idea that international cooperation can create mutually beneficial situations for all actors involved. Instead, mercantilism sees economic activity as a zero-sum game; in other words, the gains of one actor usually come at the expense of others. The international economy is firmly linked to the competitive system of nation-states. Given the anarchic condition of the international system, the international economy is a constant struggle for power. Mercantilism sees a close relationship between national economic strength and the capacity of the state to project power internationally. Economic resources constitute the basis of state power. Because it emphasizes that the state must advance its own interest even to the detriment of others, mercantilism is often referred to as *economic nationalism*. Because it argues that the state plays a critical role in formulating and enforcing economic policies that serve the national interest, mercantilism is also referred to as *statism*.

Historically, mercantilism emerged in the context of state formation in Western Europe. Between the fifteenth and eighteenth centuries, powerful centralized states dedicated to the pursuit of economic strength were created in Europe. Governments organized their limited capacities to increase the wealth of their domains. This process led to more capable bureaucracies and more effective tax collection. Governments intervened in the economy and regulated all transactions in order to promote employment, encourage manufacturing over agriculture, and protect the domestic market, all while trying to gain access to foreign markets. The goal was to achieve economic self-sufficiency or autarky—which was needed for military might.

Mercantilism calls on the government to intervene in the economy in order to secure gains for the state in the international system. It pays close attention to the relative position of other states and relative gains of exchange. Mercantilism regards trade as another political tool. Therefore, governments must secure large trade surpluses by encouraging exports and restricting imports. This enables the state to increase revenues and stockpile money with which to guarantee power and wealth. In the past, this mercantilist principle meant that states sought to accumulate gold and silver since precious metals were needed to raise armies and navies to fight wars. Mercantilism is associated with the first wave of European imperialism and colonialism between the sixteenth and eighteenth centuries. To increase government revenues and exports, states were driven to acquire colonies. Mercantilism usually worked through state-sanctioned monopolies, some of which operated as international enterprises, such as the Dutch East India Company, Hudson's Bay Company, and the British East India Company.

Key thinkers of mercantilism held important political positions themselves. For instance, Jean Baptiste Colbert was the Minister of Finance of the French King Louis XIV; Alexander Hamilton was the first Treasury Secretary of the U.S.; and Friedrich List was a German politician and diplomat who advocated for a stronger tariff union among German states, a union called *Zollverein*. In his "Report on Manufacturers" (1791), Hamilton advocated a broad range of policies to protect the growth of U.S. industry. List wrote in support of government intervention in the economy to promote development. His main contribution was the idea that protection would allow states that were far behind in development the means to catch up with the leading powers. This is known as the **infant-industry protection** argument (Crane & Amawi, 1997).

Modern exponents of mercantilism, or neo-mercantilists, continue to emphasize the role of the state. **Neo-mercantilism** arose in the 1970s as a reaction to perceived shortcomings of both liberalism and radicalism. In principle, it de-emphasizes the idea of autarky or self-sufficiency. Neo-mercantilists, such as R. Gilpin (1987), accept that the state is integrated into the world economy. However, unlike liberals, they argue that the state is not disappearing as a key actor in world politics. The state continues to be the only political and economic institution that can claim external sovereignty and internal political dominance. Moreover, markets cannot exist without the state. A major contribution of neo-mercantilism is the idea of state autonomy. Unlike radicalism, neo-mercantilism argues that the state is able to resist particular societal forces and enforce policies that serve national interests. The state mediates between global and domestic politics and is capable of affecting international economics.

To sum up, mercantilism emphasizes the subordination of economic activity to the political goal of state-building, which includes maintaining the security of the state and building up its military power. Mercantilism requires a significant degree of government intervention in the economy. Politics shapes economics and the goal is to maximize state power.

Economic Liberalism

Economic liberalism is the dominant approach in international trade since World War II. Liberalism stresses the importance of cooperation and argues that states can mutually benefit from economic exchanges. States must relax their pursuit of short-term self-interest to realize long-term mutual interests. Economic liberalism places more emphasis on the actors' shared interests in commercial exchanges than in relative gains. As discussed in Chapter 4, a modern version of liberalism, **neoliberal institutionalism**, focuses on building international organizations, institutions, and norms.

Historically, economic liberalism is connected to political efforts to turn back mercantilism. Mercantilism declined in the nineteenth century as Great Britain decided that it had more to gain from free trade than from protectionism. As a criticism of mercantilism, economic liberalism explains how economically disadvantaged, yet politically powerful, groups will frequently cast self-serving arguments in terms of protecting the nation's economic and military strength. Protection makes the cost of consumed goods more expensive. Free trade, on the other hand, brings benefits to both consumers and workers because it reduces the cost of the goods they consume. Lower prices result in higher purchasing power and increased welfare.

As noted in Chapter 4, the argument for **free trade** is usually associated with the work of Adam Smith. It is worth reiterating that in his *Inquiry on the Wealth of Nations* (1776), Smith argues that trade is mutually beneficial and that free trade maximizes the common good. Protection reduces overall wealth, wastes resources, and produces inefficiencies. If foreign trade is included, no market, no matter how small, will be left behind.

He argues that, similarly to the domestic division of labor, there is an international division of labor. If countries specialize in what they are best at producing and exchange these products, then every nation will benefit. This international division of labor will increase the world's output and wealth. Later on, David Ricardo (1817) modified Smith's argument. Ricardo argues that it is not necessary for a country to have an absolute advantage, that is, something that it could do better than all others, in order to gain from trade.

Ricardo argues that the country should specialize in the product it can produce more efficiently relative to other products it can also produce (and not relative to other countries). The principle of **comparative** (or relative) **advantage** is the foundation for specialization and free trade today.

Smith believes that people are rational actors who try to maximize their own self-interest. If these individuals are left alone, markets will develop. Markets will enable people to exchange goods and services, and competition will ensure an efficient allocation of resources. Individuals pursuing their own selfish interests will lead to the maximum creation of the country's total wealth. Contrary to mercantilism, Smith argues that gold and silver are not wealth. Money is but a medium to purchase what it is worth purchasing. He believes that government must and should stay out of the economy. Markets work best where there is no government intervention in the economy because monopolies and regulation reduce the overall efficiency of the economy.

The growing interconnectedness of states in the post-war era led neoliberal scholars to coin the term **interdependence**. Richard Cooper (1968) recognized that a new political, and not just economic, situation had arisen. Deepening trade, investment, and monetary ties among advanced industrialized countries drew their economies closer together and created a truly global economy. The overall effect was the weakening of national controls as each country had less capacity to control disrupting economic forces coming from abroad. There ensued an increased tension between the nation-state and the global economy. Interdependence, though, created opportunities both for cooperation and competition. Successful management of interdependence might be best achieved through policy coordination. Nationalist, unilateral attempts could often backfire and countries could end up worse off.

Keohane and Nye (1977) took this idea further. As previously discussed in Chapter 4, these authors argued that varied and complex connections between multiple actors across societies were growing, while military force had lost its supremacy. Moreover, there was no fixed hierarchy of issues, international agendas were changing, and linkages between issue-areas were expanding. This situation made cooperation more likely. Cooperation in one issue-area might spill over into other areas. The implication of these repeated interactions was increased cooperation across a range of multiple areas and a diminishing probability that military force would be used to settle disputes.

In summary, economic liberalism believes that individuals can satisfy their basic needs in rational ways. This can be best achieved when individuals are left to their own devices and governments refrain from intervening in the economy. Free markets maximize both individual and collective wealth and welfare. Furthermore, free trade creates interdependence among states and reduces the likelihood of war among them.

Radicalism/Marxism

Radicalism includes different perspectives aimed at changing the existing social order: socialism, communism, and anarchism. The ideas of Karl Marx are the basis of most of them. Marx opposed the prevailing philosophy of his time in favor of what he called historical materialism. He claimed that history is the history of class struggle (Crane & Amawi, 1997). He believed in the positive evolution of society from a current stage to another higher one in the future: ancient society > feudal > capitalist > socialist > communist. This implies, for example, that for Marx, colonialism in India was beneficial and instrumental in the destruction of archaic modes of production. Revolution overturns the relationship between the propertied classes (the haves or oppressors) and the property-less (the have-nots or oppressed). Revolution takes place when the forces of production—science, technology, organization of production, and development of human skills—clash with the relations of production—property rights, society's way of appropriating and distributing wealth, and norms. This is the dynamic element in the **Marxist** materialist interpretation of history. The whole of the social structure—politics, religion, law, culture, and ideology—is built upon this economic structure. Therefore, whoever controls the means of production in a society dominates the political system. In effect, the state is the representative of the dominant social class.

After World War II, different contributions helped to expand on Marxist thought, focusing particularly on a global level analysis. Chief among them are **dependency theory** and **world system theory**. It is worth repeating that for Marxist theorists such as Lenin, imperialism and colonial expansion had shifted the process of capitalist exploitation from the industrialized economies of Europe to the less developed economies (see Chapter 5). Dependency theory builds upon this idea and rejects the liberal claim that participation in the world economy would bring wealth and development to all countries, including less developed countries (see Chapter 14).

As discussed in Chapter 5, world system theory suggests an integrated view of politics and economics in the international system as a single whole unit. I. Wallerstein (1974) proposed that capitalism is a world system. This capitalist world economy is a structure, a system, and a particular epoch in history. It relies on a sophisticated international division of labor, hierarchically organized, consisting of three world regions: a core, a periphery, and a semi-periphery. In addition, Wallerstein suggests a unique interpretation of hegemonic power. He asserts that the rise to hegemony follows a historical sequence. First the hegemon dominates in agro-industrial production; then it adds dominance in international commerce; and, finally, in global finance. Decline follows the same sequence; first, it loses agro-industrial dominance, then commerce, and, finally, finance. Ironically, the openness that defines hegemony works to undermine it by fostering competitors and enabling technological diffusion.

To summarize, radicalism/Marxism considers history as evidence of the inevitability of change in the social order. The relationship between politics and economics is explained as conditioned, if not determined, by material, economic factors. Political structures reflect economic structures. Later contributions theorized on the structure of the global economy and its hierarchy. Marxism provides the analytical tools to explain such unequal relations that arise from the antagonistic internal logic of the capitalist system.

Establishing the Post-World War II Economic Order

During the post-World War II period, the U.S. led efforts to create a new structure for the international economic order. This structure encompassed, primarily, the areas of trade and finance and, indirectly, foreign investment. There was basic agreement on the need for an open and stable international system and for cooperation to maintain such an order. It was a sharp reaction against the protectionism and economic nationalism that had prevailed during the Great Depression. Numerous "beggar-thy-neighbor" policies had characterized the collapse of the international trading regime during the 1930s, including tariffs (taxes on imports), quotas (quantitative limits on imports), competitive devaluations, non-tariff barriers (indirect means of restricting imports), and exclusive regional trading agreements. For the U.S. in particular, this constituted a sharp policy reversal away from protectionism as exemplified in the Smoot-Hawley Tariff Act of 1930 and toward multilateral, open markets. The ideological underpinning of the post-war system rested on the liberal belief that free trade and capitalism would produce a harmony of interests and guard against aggressive and bellicose economic nationalism. Yet, the framers of the post-war system also recognized the need for an increased role of the state in the economy (embedded liberalism) while security concerns over the communist threat pervaded into economic issues. The small number of actors involved, primarily in North America and Western Europe, facilitated agreement. It is important to note, though, that the Soviet Union and its allies decided not to participate and the process of decolonization of Africa, Asia, the Pacific, and the Caribbean had not begun.

The U.S. was willing to assume a leadership role in the post-war international economic order. The U.S. was the world's largest economy in 1945, and the war had left its domestic infrastructure largely intact. Additionally, it had a large military and, until 1949, the monopoly on atomic weapons. The U.S. government pushed hard to establish a free trade system. (Congress had granted the president power to negotiate reciprocal free trade treaties in 1934.) The U.S. government offered generous terms to help Western Europe and Japan rebuild (such as the Marshall Plan) and regarded trade as a political instrument by which to buttress them. Consequently, successive U.S. administrations allowed discrimination against U.S. products and "free riding" by Western Europe and Japan.

At the end of World War II, there existed a significant asymmetry between the U.S. and the Western European and Japanese economies. The extent of the damage suffered and the high costs of reconstruction rendered Western Europe and Japan vulnerable to U.S. competition. To facilitate the accumulation of reserves in U.S. dollars and the reconstruction of their economies, the U.S. tolerated restrictions on its exports to these markets while maintaining open access to the U.S. market for European and Japanese exports. Thus, from the 1950s, the U.S. ran trade deficits with them.

All three previously discussed theories of IPE incorporate the idea that the rise of an open international economic order is associated with the existence of a single, dominant state or hegemon. This is the central idea behind the **Hegemonic Stability Theory**. Hegemony is the historical situation in which one state holds significant power in the international system so that it can establish the rules and arrangements of the system. One state dominates in critical areas of international economics and international politics, such as agriculture and manufacturing output, trade, technology, and military. This is the thesis of Charles Kindleberger (1973). He studied the world economic crisis of the 1930s and concluded that the absence of a hegemon had led to the breakdown of the system. He argued that, historically, the hegemon had intervened to prevent the collapse of the system. It chose to defend free trade and promote economic growth, maintain a stable international system, and provide military security. However, during the Great Depression, the United Kingdom was unable to fulfil this role, and the U.S. was unwilling to do so.

A hegemon is not concerned with its relative power position and is not likely to attempt to maximize its share of the world's trade or output. Given that the hegemon is the largest economic power in the system, it has an inherent interest in the promotion of unrestricted trade where it will tend to dominate. This dominance allows the hegemon to tolerate free riders. However, the hegemon is able and willing to use power to achieve free trade. A hegemon can enforce the rules and norms unilaterally, thus avoiding collective action problems. These issues occur when actors have no incentive to help with the provision of **collective goods** or **public goods.** Collective goods are provided to all. They are indivisible and cannot be parceled out into individual portions. Collective goods are non-excludable. No one can be kept from using them, even if they do not help provide for them. The **free rider problem** emerges where collective goods are involved, as actors will consume a public good without contributing towards its provision.

The hegemon gains the consent of the participants in the system. Because these actors see the system as legitimate, they give it their consent. It is the hegemon that sets the agenda and the rules and does so for its own advantage. The other states have the same interests and agree on the need for order and stability, and they share in the growth and prosperity of the system. Hegemony is not empire, though. The hegemon does not try to control economic transactions, while an empire controls economic transactions centrally. Over time, there is an uneven growth of power within the international system as new technologies and methods are developed. An unstable international system will result if economic, technological, and other changes erode the international hierarchy and undermine the position of the dominant state. Pretenders to hegemonic control will emerge if the benefits of the system are viewed as unacceptably unfair.

The International Trade System since the end of World War II

An essential piece of the post-war economic order was the international trade system. Trade is a typical case of economic competition. It involves the allocation of economic gains from the exchange of goods and services across national borders. Historically, trade is linked to the rise of the international state system and the process of state building. Trade generates intense political debate today because the growth of economic activities (production, exchanges) is less attached to national borders while states continue to be key actors in politics.

The **General Agreement on Tariffs and Trade (GATT)** was the primary framework for international trade relations in the post-war era until its eventual replacement by the **World Trade Organization (WTO)**. GATT was part of the post-war attempt to establish an open international system. As a follow-up to the Bretton Woods Conference (1944), an international conference on trade convened at Havana, Cuba in 1947. The goal was to establish a permanent international organization to deal with trade called the International Trade Organization (ITO). However, the U.S. Senate failed to ratify the charter of ITO. GATT had been signed at the Havana conference as a set of rules and principles to guide multilateral trade negotiations. Instead, it became the world's trade regime.

All of the member parties to GATT agreed to three basic rules. First, member states embraced the principle of non-discrimination. Member states could not favor imported products from one country over another (**Most Favored Nation**). Second, member states agreed to ban quantitative and other non-tariff forms of trade restrictions. Tariffs were the only permissible form of discrimination, though they had to be reduced on a periodical and reciprocal basis. Reciprocity was the third rule. GATT rules allowed member states to form customs unions to trade freely among themselves and to adopt a common tariff on imports from countries outside the group. GATT rules also allowed the use of safeguards. For example, states could impose restrictions on trade on a temporary basis due to emergency reasons. State-owned enterprises became the subject of a rule. GATT rules established that they had to act according to commercial considerations, like private firms do.

Under GATT, international trade was liberalized substantially. Between 1947 and 1994, eight multilateral negotiations or "rounds" took place. Average tariff levels fell from around 40% in 1947 to 4% in 1979 (WTO, 2007). Total world trade experienced dramatic growth from $120 billion in 1947 to more than $7,400 billion in 1993 (WTO, 2019). However, many problems affected GATT, too. Trade negotiations only applied to merchandise goods. Trade in neither services nor agricultural goods was included. The dispute settlement mechanism of GATT was also non-binding and very lengthy. Moreover, new forms of protections emerged, including dumping and anti-dumping duties, Voluntary Restraint Agreements (VRAs), Voluntary Export Restraints (VERs), and industrial and strategic trade policies. The relative decline of U.S. manufacturing, the strong economic performances of Western Europe and Japan, and the rise of newly industrialized countries (NICs) in East Asia and Latin America revealed a changing world economy. Demands to include new and previously excluded issues increased during the 1980s. The last GATT round, the Uruguay Round (1986-1993), culminated in a new institutional structure for world trade. The agreement included new issues such as trade in services and trade related aspects of intellectual property rights (TRIPS) and trade related investment measures (TRIMS). It also included trade in agriculture and the gradual liberalization of trade on clothing and textiles. Several international rules were further codified, such as rules of origin. In January 1995, the WTO began working. As of March 1, 2020, it has 164 member states. The WTO serves consultation, mediation, monitor, research, and dispute settlement functions.

Even though total world trade continued to grow from $7,400 billion in 1993 to almost $40,000 billion in 2018, the WTO faces significant challenges (WTO, 2019). The current Doha Round of negotiations has been stalled for years. It confronts a wide range of criticisms from developing countries for the lack of progress on the removal of trade restrictions on agriculture and from developed countries for the weak enforcement of intellectual property rights. Politicians from all over the ideological spectrum accuse it of violating sovereignty and of lack of transparency. Initiatives to include NGOs reflect an attempt to address these global governance concerns (**democratic deficit**). Farming and labor groups regard the WTO as biased toward corporate interests, while indigenous rights and environmental groups blame it for the destruction of cultural and natural habitats. The future of the international trade system remains uncertain. The U.S. is taking increasingly unilateral actions, while other actors (the EU, China, India, Brazil) behave more like spoilers than leaders. Worldwide, domestic support for free trade is crumbling. The proliferation of regional and bilateral preferential trade agreements is another indication of the weakening open, multilateral trade system.

The International Monetary System since the end of World War II

Another key piece of the post-war economic order was the international monetary system. The drive to establish an **international monetary system** drew many lessons from the collapse of the world economy during the 1930s. American and British planners had a strong desire to avoid a repetition of the competitive exchange rate devaluations, exclusive monetary blocs, and the cooperation breakdown that characterized the interwar era. They were convinced of the need for a stable monetary system to foster economic growth and maintain peace (to prevent the economic nationalism and political conflict which led to World War II).

Money is a medium of exchange (transaction value) and **reserve** (store of value). It is a predictable unit of account against which goods and services can be measured. Money is backed by political authority, and this is a key factor because money does not have an intrinsic value anymore. Money relies on the trust people have on the issuing authorities. At the international level, the basic anarchic condition of the system means that without a world government, there is no common international currency which countries can use to pay for their imports and financial transactions. The international monetary system fulfills that role. It also provides stability to the different currencies and the necessary degree of flexibility to adjust their values. It introduces a degree of certainty and predictability for economic transactions, which American and British planners strove to achieve for the post-war order.

The post-war monetary system was established at a conference in Bretton Woods, New Hampshire, in 1944 (referred to above). Participating states agreed to a system of fixed exchange rates. The U.S. dollar was convertible into gold at a fixed rate of $35 per ounce and all other currencies were pegged to the U.S. dollar. While all currencies were convertible into each other, the U.S. dollar emerged as the dominant currency and the international reserve currency.

The Bretton Woods conference also established two international financial institutions: the **International Monetary Fund (IMF)** and the International Bank of Reconstruction and Development (IBRD), also known as the **World Bank**. The IMF was created to give short-term loans (up to eighteen months) to countries with balance of payments problems. It would also advise countries on monetary issues in order to maintain fixed exchange rates. The World Bank would provide long-term loans to help countries rebuild after the destruction of World War II and promote development. Unlike other international organizations such as the UN, the IMF and World Bank rely on a weighted voting system, in which each state has a vote share equivalent to its financial contributions. Under this arrangement, the U.S. exerted great influence in these institutions.

The Bretton Woods system ran into an early problem: it needed a jump start. Western Europe and Japan were still in ruins and their economies were not yet working. The U.S. had a surplus with the rest of the world. For the system to work, the opposite needed to happen: money needed to circulate back from the U.S. The U.S. needed to engage in a massive infusion of liquidity. The **Marshall Plan**, aid to Turkey and Greece under the **Truman Doctrine**, the reconstruction of Japan, military spending under **NATO**, and U.S. military spending during the Korean War were part of the solution.

The Bretton Woods system relied on the trust in the U.S. promise to exchange gold for dollars. There was no reason to doubt this promise in 1947 when the U.S. held about 70% of the monetary stock of gold in the world (Eichengreen, 1996). However, the system was not flexible enough. Governments kept dollars as reserve and did not exchange them for gold. The U.S. dollar became as good as gold. Such was the confidence in the U.S. promise that nobody was asking for gold. Thus, the U.S. was free to use its unrestrained financial power in the world.

During the 1960s, the world gradually lost its confidence in the U.S.'s ability to pay in gold. Western Europe and Japan had recovered strongly and their currencies became undervalued, while the U.S. trade position pointed to the overvaluation of the U.S. dollar. Rising strains forced the U.S. government to drop unilateral management of the system and start cooperating with other members. An agreement to create international liquidity through artificial international reserve units by the IMF called **Special Drawing Rights (SDRs)** was negotiated in 1968. By the early 1970s, the system had cracked. In August 1971, President Nixon stopped gold convertibility, initially devalued the U.S. dollar and, in 1973, allowed the U.S. dollar to float freely. The move from fixed to floating exchange rates signaled the end of the Bretton Woods system.

The move to **floating exchange rates** posed many challenges to policymakers who were still apprehensive of the inter-war experience with such a system. Eventually, acceptance of the merits of the new system replaced apprehension. It was believed that floating exchange rates could facilitate the process of adjustment of external imbalances more gradually. One of the most important features is the institutionalization of macroeconomic policy coordination. In 1975, the first annual meeting of the **Group of Seven (G7)** took place. G7 consisted of the seven largest, most advanced economies in the world: the U.S., West Germany, Japan, United Kingdom, France, Italy, and Canada. Its main goal was to adjust and coordinate the group members's policies in the face of periodic crisis of the world economy, including oil shocks of the 1970s, foreign debt crisis of the 1980s, the Plaza and Louvre Accords of the 1980s, and the global financial crisis of 2007–2008. In addition, other notable transnational efforts occurred among government bureaucracies and non-state actors. The breakdown of the Bretton Woods system had raised the profile of central banks. As a result, there was an increased convergence of ideas and policies regarding fiscal and monetary policies and the need to maintain confidence in the ability of central banks to defend national currencies. These trends were reflected in the creation of the Basel Committee in 1974, comprising the central bank heads of the Group of 10 (G10). The most recent institutional reform of the system has been the new role of the Group of 20 (G20) in achieving global economic governance in the aftermath of the global financial crisis of 2007–2008.

Another significant development in the international monetary system has been the rise of regional currencies and the unilateral adoption of foreign currencies to replace national ones (dollarization). The creation of the euro in 1999 is the most notable example of a common regional currency in the international system. It serves as an example to other regional initiatives in Africa, Asia, and Latin America. However, it is a unique experience undertaken as much for political reasons as economic ones. Conversely, the option to unilaterally abandon a national currency and adopt a foreign one such as the U.S. dollar or the euro reflect the desire to reap the benefits of monetary stability which the existing international monetary system is not providing to its members.

The Transnational Production System and the rise of MNCs since the end of World War II

Another key piece of the post-war economic order was the growth of foreign direct investment and transnational production. The transnational production system is a very complex process with millions of workers and hundreds of thousands of affiliates located around the world and integrated into global value chains. The most important actor in transnational production is the **multinational corporation (MNC)**. MNCs are enterprises organized in one country but with direct investment and production overseas. **Foreign direct investment (FDI)** is the stock of capital in one country owned by an individual or enterprise of another country.

The growth of foreign investment is closely connected with the need for order and the presence of a hegemonic power. Before World War I, the United Kingdom was the dominant actor ensuring the rules of foreign investment—free flow of capital across borders—and protecting foreign investment, if necessary, by the use of military force. The most important form of foreign investment at this time was portfolio investment. The twin revolutionary shocks of the 1910s, the Mexican Revolution and the Bolshevik Revolution, sent shockwaves through investors. As the revolutionary governments nationalized or expropriated foreign property, they created insecurity. FDI began to grow substantially again after World War II. The post-war rise of MNCs was an overwhelmingly U.S.-led phenomenon. By 1970, 52% of all FDI in the world consisted of U.S. companies and production of U.S. companies overseas was four times as great as all U.S. exports (Ravenhill, 2017). Dominance by U.S. MNCs entered a phase of relative decline when Japanese and European MNCs expanded vigorously in the 1980s. Today, more than 70% of all FDI in the world is held by U.S., European, and Japanese companies, which are also the main points of FDI (Ravenhill, 2017).

MNCs are independent, non-state actors. Their goal is profit, not political control. They are large employers worldwide. United Nations Conference on Trade and Development (UNCTAD) estimated that MNCs employed 76 million people in 2018 (UNCTAD, 2019). They are also increasingly powerful. Scores of MNCs have annual global sales exceeding the revenues of many governments and even the GDP of the majority of less developed countries in the world. MNCs are one of the main forces behind the spectacular growth of trade and internationalization of production since World War II. They contribute to globalization and, in turn, are one of the key beneficiaries of globalization.

The issue of relations between MNCs and governments is politically sensitive. MNCs are both criticized and praised for their impact on countries. To analyze this debate, it is important to consider the consequences on both the state in which an MNC operates, or host country, and the state in which the MNC has its parent office, or home country. The effects of MNC operations can be both advantageous and disadvantageous.

First among the beneficial effects of MNC operations in a host country is job creation. MNCs help expand the internal market of the host country by adding to its gross product. They also help expand the tax base and allow the host country to raise more revenues. Home countries can attempt to entrap MNCs into building roads, bridges, schools, or hospitals. MNCs also can bring technology, training, and capital into the host country. An investment surge can help bring political and economic stability to the host country. Moreover, as neoliberals point out, increasing integration and interaction across borders is likely to promote friendly relationships between the home and host country. Finally, MNCs can help increase total trade and the opening of new markets for the host country.

However, the relations of MNCs with host governments include many disadvantages. First, because of their overwhelming capacity, MNCs tend to create monopolies or oligopolies that reduce competition in the host country. Moreover, contrary to very optimistic expectations, MNCs tend to create a limited number of jobs. They may also impede the development of domestic companies or may eventually buy them up. The effects of economic development often remain limited to a single economic sector or region of the host country. Profits generated by the MNC may even not be reinvested in the host country at all but instead transferred to the home country. In addition, the host country may grow too dependent on the MNC. In search of a favorable business climate, MNCs may encourage the repression of labor or domestic groups opposed to its activities. Worse yet, MNCs may "capture" the host government and use it for its own purposes. MNCs may misuse or overexploit natural resources or cause serious environmental damage. MNCs also may use the threat of relocation as leverage to extract more concessions from the host country. Finally, MNCs have been accused of undermining the local culture and imposing foreign values instead.

Home countries benefit from the worldwide expansion of domestic MNCs because their activities increase the national income through profits and sales generated overseas. MNCs help expand the economic and trade relations of the home country. As mentioned above, increasing integration and interaction across borders is likely to promote friendly relationships between the home and host countries. Finally, MNCs encourage diversification and specialization of the home country's economy, which becomes an exporter of technology, services, and inputs.

However, MNCs can have a negative impact on the home economy as well. First, MNCs are accused of being responsible for exporting jobs overseas (**outsourcing**). The effect of plant closures and unemployment hurts local economies. While the overall national income may rise, the effect on the local level is very bad. The tax base may fall sharply, placing additional strains on the local economy. MNCs may affect the balance of payments and trade patterns of the home country. MNCs have established integrated production, marketing, and distribution networks between the main unit and its subsidiaries around the world, a phenomenon we identified previously as global value chains. The flow of raw materials, parts, technology, capital, royalties, and final product takes place within the global corporation. These flows of material goods and services directly impact the exports and imports of the home country. For example, parts may be exported that go into the production of a car that is then imported in its final form by the same corporation. Finally, MNCs may involve the home government in difficult political situations with the host country. The impact of MNCs on states have led to calls for greater international regulation of their activities. Consequently, international organizations have designed an international code of ethics against corruption, and governments have increased cooperation and coordination to increase scrutiny and prevent tax evasion.

Globalization

The preceding sections discussed how the post-war liberal economic order created the conditions for the gradual liberalization of trade in goods and services, the reopening of global markets to direct investment, and the removal of restrictions for capital, currency, and financial flows especially after the early 1970s. The confluence of these processes produced a new situation, which scholars labelled with the now familiar term **globalization.**

What is globalization? Discussions of this topic generate passionate and sometimes markedly opposing perspectives. Explaining globalization has consistently divided opinions, usually starting with the very subject of defining globalization and continuing through to assessing its causes and effects. Globalization as a concept attempts to explain social, cultural, geographic, economic, and political characteristics of the present international system. How can we make sense of a concept that is literally meant to encapsulate the entire world?

Globalization started to dominate political, economic, and scholarly discourse in the 1980s. Yet during the intervening decades, no consensus has been reached about its definition, so the term still lacks clarity. No single theory is able to explain all of what globalization means, does, or encompasses. For instance, globalization is used as a synonym for the greater integration of the world market due to economic phenomena. An example of this view is the definition by the staff of the IMF who put it as "the increasing integration of economies around the world, particularly through the movement of goods, services, and capital across borders" and sometimes including labor and technology (IMF, 2008). A review of the scholarly understanding of the term include the following aspects:

- Liberalization of markets and removal of barriers to the movement of goods, services, capital, and people (IMF, 2008)
- Changes in technology, transportation, and communication (Scholte, 2005)

- Patterns of supranational integration and national disintegration (McGrew, 2017)
- Institutional changes and convergence of ideas and policies (Drezner, 2001)
- Geographical spread to encompass the whole world economy, not just a small group of countries (Frieden, 2006)
- Increasing contacts in terms of participants and intensity (Giddens, 1990)
- Diminishing importance of space and time (Friedman, 2000; Scholte, 2005)
- Multidimensional nature of the phenomenon that is in economics, politics, culture, environment, and ideas (McGrew, 2017)

Scholars also disagree about the future of globalization and the postwar liberal economic order. Some of them believe that we have reached the end of globalization, while others have pointed to its continuing resilience and describe the current challenges as momentary lapses (Allison, 2018; Deudney & Ikenberry, 2018; McClory, 2018). Recent events, such as the decision of British voters to leave the EU (Brexit), rising protectionism around the world, trade wars between the U.S. and China, and President Trump's decision to impose and raise tariffs on EU and NAFTA partners as well as his decision to abrogate free trade deals such as the Trans-Pacific Partnership cast doubts about the continuing future of free trade and globalization.

The current world economic situation reflects changes that have taken place over many decades. There are new patterns of production in the world economy, the scope of activity is significantly larger, and new actors have emerged. The deregulation of capital markets in the 1970s accelerated the process of development of global finance. With fewer controls over speculative capital flows, the world economy experienced periodic and increasingly costly financial crises (Mexico in 1994–1995; Thailand, Indonesia, South Korea,

Hong Kong, Malaysia, and the Philippines in 1997; Russia in 1998; Brazil in 1998; Turkey in 2000–2001; and Argentina in 2001–2002). Other changes raised questions about the continuing viability of the nation-state as an actor in world politics. With the end of the Cold War, political fragmentation and civil war followed in Yugoslavia and the former Soviet Union in the 1990s. At the same time, there were numerous processes of regional and supranational integration, including the enlargement of the EU, adoption of NAFTA, reform of the African Union (AU) and the Association of Southeast Asian Nations (ASEAN), and the creation of the Asia-Pacific Economic Cooperation (APEC) and Mercosur.

Considering the current world economic situation, scholars are pessimistic about the prospects of free trade in the world. A stark divide exists between academic consensus and popular opinion about free trade. Key international actors—IMF, World Bank, WTO, and MNCs—support free trade. However, populist politicians rode a wave of anti-globalization in recent years and gained political power after electoral victories. Who wins and who loses from globalization? Changes in the world economy have created winners and losers both between and within countries. This is reflected in growing levels of inequality between developed and less developed countries and between the rich and poor within countries. This trend again divides people's views on globalization. Critics argue that globalization only benefits the rich, the elites, and big business while it disproportionately hurts the poor, labor, minorities, indigenous groups, and the environment. Proponents, on the other hand, point to the hundreds of millions of people lifted out of poverty in Asia and the unprecedented era of economic growth since World War II. The debate is not likely to be over soon.

Should governments embrace globalization or resist changes? Governments can and should implement policies to ameliorate the negative consequences of globalization on their economies and populations. However, these decisions are not without risks.

They imply redistributive options within each society (taxation in particular) which could be resisted by powerful domestic groups. Globalization has intensified the need for further international cooperation, coordination, and multilateralism. The diminishing ability of the U.S. to manage the system raised issues of hegemonic decline and the limits of unilateralism. Faced with increasingly difficult situations, national governments have reacted by raising new forms of protectionism. The choice of policy responses is important because it can lead to imbalances affecting the entire system. Countries are more interconnected, more sensitive to one another, and more vulnerable to each other's actions. However, the international institutional framework has proved resilient. The rules-based, multilateral system created at the Bretton Woods conference, while in need of reform, has endured.

This chapter reviewed the rise of international political economy as a separate field of study and competing theoretical perspectives associated with it. It also examined the historical evolution of the international economic system since World War II. Under U.S. leadership, the global economy saw the gradual liberalization of trade in goods and services, the reopening of global markets to direct investment, and the removal of restrictions for capital, currency, and financial flows. This chapter identified and examined the role of different actors such as national governments, international financial organizations, and MNCs in the global economy. The end of the Cold War in the early 1990s and the entry of China into the WTO in the 2000s profoundly altered the global economy. Scholars labelled the new phenomenon globalization. Yet, discussions of this topic generate passionate and sometimes markedly opposing perspectives. Ultimately, these discussions reveal the enduring analytical relevance of IPE in world politics.

References

Allison, G. (2018, July–August). The myth of the liberal order: From historical accident to conventional wisdom. *Foreign Affairs, 97*(4), 124–133.

Crane, G. & Amawi, A. (Eds.). (1997). *The theoretical evolution of international political economy: A reader.* Second edition. New York, NY & Oxford, UK: Oxford University Press.

Deudney, D. & Ikenberry, G .J. (2018, July–August). Liberal world: The resilient order. *Foreign Affairs, 97*(4), 16–24.

Drezner, D. (2001). Globalization and policy convergence. *International Studies Review, 3*(1), 53–78.

Eichengreen, B. (1996). *Globalizing capital: A history of the international monetary system.* Princeton, NJ: Princeton University Press.

Frieden, J. (2006). *Global capitalism: Its fall and rise in the twentieth century.* New York, NY: W. W. Norton.

Friedman, T. (2000). *The lexus and the olive tree.* New York, NY: Anchor Books.

Giddens, A. (1990). *The consequences of modernity.* Sanford, CA: Stanford University Press.

Gilpin, R. (1987). *The political economy of international relations.* Princeton, NJ: Princeton University Press.

International Monetary Fund. (2008, May 2). Globalization: A brief overview. Retrieved from https://www.imf.org/external/np/exr/ib/2008/053008.htm

McClory, J. (2018). *The soft power 30: A global ranking of soft power 2018.* Portland & USC Center on Public Diplomacy. Retrieved from https://www.uscpublicdiplomacy.org/sites/uscpublicdiplomacy.org/files/useruploads/u39301/The%20Soft%20Power%2030%20Report%202018.pdf

McGrew, A. (2017). The logics of economic globalization. In J. Ravenhill (ed.), *Global political economy* (5th ed.), p. 225–254. Oxford, UK: Oxford University Press.

O'Brien, R. & Williams, M. (2016). *Global political economy: Evolution and dynamics* (5th ed.). Basingstoke, UK: Palgrave Macmillan.

Ravenhill, J. (Ed.). (2017). *Global political economy* (5th ed.). Oxford, UK: Oxford University Press.

Scholte, J. (2005). *Globalization: A critical introduction*. New York, NY: Palgrave Macmillan.

Schwartz, H. (1994). *States versus markets: History, geography, and the development of the international political economy*. New York, NY: St. Martin's Press.

Spero, J. & Hart, J. (2010). *The politics of international economic relations* (7th ed.). Boston, MA: Wadsworth Cengage Learning.

United Nations Conference on Trade and Development. (2019). *World investment report: Special economic zones*. Geneva, Switzerland: United Nations. Retrieved from https://worldinvestmentreport.unctad.org/

World Trade Organization. (n.d.). *Understanding the WTO: Basics*. Retrieved from https://www.wto.org/english/thewto_e/whatis_e/tif_e/fact4_e.htm

World Trade Organization. (2019). World trade statistical review 2019. Retrieved from https://www.wto.org/english/res_e/statis_e/wts2019_e/wts2019_e.pdf

World Trade Organization. (2007). World trade report 2007. Retrieved from https://www.wto.org/english/res_e/booksp_e/anrep_e/world_trade_report07_e.pdf

Global Trends in Business and Finances

13

Laurel Wei

Abstract

The globalization of the economy has been going on for centuries, but it wasn't until after 1945 that countries all over the world cooperated to formalize the global economic governance. International institutions and rules were set up to regulate and strengthen global trade as well as financial and monetary relations. Annual summits are held in which top leaders of member states meet to enhance economic coordination among countries and discuss pressing political issues. The world economy has become increasingly intertwined with world politics as states engage in negotiations, settle disputes, and utilize their political leverage to obtain greater gains. This chapter focuses on the four major aspects of world political economy: (1) trade policies and the global governance for trade, (2) financial policies and the global governance for finance, (3) monetary policies and global monetary relations, and (4) role of multinational corporations.

Learning Objectives

- Identify the key actors in international trade, financial, and monetary relations
- Identify and explain the basic elements of international trade, international trade relations, and the governance of global trade

- Identify and explain the basic elements of global finance, international financial relations, and the governance of global finance
- Think critically about international monetary relations and the influence of international flow of money on world political economy
- Critically analyze the role of multilateral corporations in global political economy

Trade Policies and the Global Governance for Trade

International trade involves powerful interests, important interactions, and influential institutions at global, regional, and domestic levels. Foreign trade activities have significant impact on domestic markets, businesses, consumers, and the distribution of power and interests. Ideally, the greatest level of prosperity and wealth is achieved when every country embraces free trade and eliminates all trade barriers. However, this has not, and never will, become a reality. In fact, there has never been a single country that adopted a policy of completely free trade. The conflict of interests between those favoring freer trade and market liberalization and those favoring fairer trade and protection helps explain a country's policy change in international trade.

Every country currently has some forms of restrictions on foreign trade; some may have more trade barriers than others. **Protectionism**, the use of specific measures to shield domestic producers from imports, has long been among the most routine foreign trade practices around the world. Most of today's advanced market economies were once strongly protectionist at some point in their history. Virtually all governments restrict at least some imports. For centuries, states have imposed a wide variety of **trade barriers**—government limitations on international trade in goods—which generally fall into two broad categories: **tariffs** (taxes on imports levied at the border and paid by the importer) and **nontariff barriers (NTBs)** or **nontariff measures (NTMs)** (obstacles to imports other than tariffs), such as quotas, regulations favoring domestic products, or discriminatory policies and practices against foreign goods or services.

Tariffs are the most common trade barriers. As taxes on imported goods, tariffs directly raise the domestic prices of imports so that consumers have to pay more for them. Tariffs, therefore, discourage domestic buyers from buying imported goods and serve the purpose of protecting domestic producers from foreign competition. For example, from 2018 to 2019, the trade war between the U.S. and China has involved punitive tariffs on the imported goods from each other, caused price hikes in the domestic markets of both countries, and prolonged tit-for-tat, mutual retaliation on trade. NTBs can take various forms, a most common one being **quantitative restrictions** or **quotas**, that is, limitations on the quantity of a foreign good that can be sold in the domestic market. Quotas work in a similar way to tariffs: restricting the quantity of imported goods leads to an increase in their prices in the domestic market, thereby making imports more expensive for domestic consumers. For example, the Buy American Act (1933) is a form of nontariff restrictions to the purchase of imports (Manuel, 2016). Other common NTBs include import licenses, export subsidies, employment law, lengthy customs procedures, and quality conditions imposed by an importing country on an exporting country (USAID, 2013). The main purpose and the expected effect of these trade restrictions is to protect domestic producers from intense foreign competition and encourage domestic consumers to choose domestic goods over imports.

Trade restrictions did, at some point, help developing countries achieve fast economic growth. From the 1950s to the 1970s, many developing countries, such as Brazil, India, Mexico, and Turkey, pursued **import substitution industrialization (ISI)**, a national development strategy seeking to avoid international trade by focusing on domestic production and reducing the amount of imports. Under this policy, leaders of those countries wanted their domestic consumers to substitute imported manufactured goods with comparable domestically-produced goods. High tariffs were imposed on imported goods targeted for substitution, and subsidies were provided to certain domestic producers (Grieco, Ikenberry, & Mastanduno, 2019, p. 404–405). ISI generated successful economic growth for about two decades, but by the 1970s, its weaknesses became more apparent as domestic sectors got so used to the safe haven behind high tariff walls that they had little incentive to enhance capacity and competitiveness (see Chapter 14).

The adoption of ISI for growth purposes can partially explain why governments may decide to restrict trade but it can't explain it all. Countries that have benefitted substantially from free trade over an extended period of time may still resort to protection. Why?

Domestic interests benefit unevenly from foreign trade, and nobody wants to be harmed by it. When some national producers complain about too much or too little trade in the goods they produce, they tend to believe that imported goods should bear the blame because they cut into their profits and cause domestic loss of jobs. Other producers may complain that foreign barriers to their goods keep them out of overseas markets and similarly reduce their profits and cost job loss at home. Still others may complain that a foreign country has engaged in currency manipulation or dumping, which results in domestic companies outsourcing jobs.

In response to those domestic interests negatively affected by free trade, policymakers, especially the vocal ones, may decide to adopt trade protection. In general, trade barriers can help domestic producers by increasing their profits, raising wages, and hiring more employees. In developing countries, import substitutions, export subsidies, and protection of infant industries can provide national producers time and resources necessary for capacity-building and protect them from formidable foreign competitors. In this sense, domestic industries under protection, even those in developed countries, generate profits higher than the normal rate.

On the other hand, at least three groups generally suffer in trade protection: consumers of protected goods, national exporters, and domestic producers. Trade barriers raise the domestic prices of imports and may lead to price increases for similar domestic goods due to limited supply. Price hikes cause consumers to pay more for the same goods that are otherwise not so expensive.

Exporting countries's trade barriers might provoke retaliation in their export destinations. For example, in the U.S.-China trade war, many American soybean farmers have experienced a plunge in profits due to China's retaliatory tariffs on imported U.S. soybeans. At the same time, Chinese consumers have to pay more for American soybeans due to much higher prices (Reuters, 2019; Nikkei Asia, 2019; Bloomberg, 2019). In each country, some domestic groups have to pay the price.

Trade protection also weakens economic efficiency, causing domestic producers to make more goods that they are not good at producing and leading consumers to consume less of those goods that protection has made artificially expensive. Because foreign trade brings gains and losses to different domestic groups in every country, trade policymakers must strive to achieve an overall balance among those unevenly impacted by trade.

As with other issues in world politics, what a country achieves from international trade depends on the actions of others. Therefore, when governments make national trade policies, they take into consideration what other governments are likely to do in response. A state that raises tariffs might find other countries retaliating with higher tariffs to its exports. Benefits of protection obtained by domestic producers might be offset by costs to their domestic consumers and exporters. Two or more governments involved in trade policy negotiations are engaged in strategic interaction and must consider the behavior of others. International trade negotiations are therefore a prisoner's dilemma: both sides would be better off cooperating to reduce trade barriers, but concerns that the other side may cheat leads both sides towards noncooperation, even though it's to their common detriment.

In theory, a state would receive maximum benefits by unilaterally liberalizing trade and abolishing all trade barriers. However, decision-makers must respond to pressures from home, namely, those pro-protection voices. Therefore, a government's first choice of trade policy is almost never to remove its own trade barriers until after having gotten concessions or commitments from other countries in return for its own. Other countries may think the same. Thus, there is no way to guarantee that all parties to trade talks will cooperate.

Despite various challenges in trade cooperation, countries have developed institutional arrangements to promote free trade, eliminate trade barriers, and formulate common, agreed upon rules and norms of conducting foreign trade. The global governance for trade since 1945 consists of multilateral trade organizations, namely, the GATT, WTO), regional trade agreements (RTAs) represented by the NAFTA, the Association of Southeast Asian Nations (ASEAN), the EU, and the Mercosur, and sub-regional trade agreements, such as preferential trade agreements (PTAs) and various bilateral and plurilateral free trade areas or agreements (FTAs).

Realizing freer trade and eliminating trade barriers require the collective efforts of all nations. Trade multilateralism seeks to engage as many countries as possible in negotiations on all aspects of trade, including goods, services, investment, intellectual property, licensing, government procurement. Contemporary multilateral trade governance originated with the establishment of the **General Agreement on Tariffs and Trade (GATT)** in 1948. In the forty-seven years that followed, from 1948 to 1994, the GATT had successfully completed eight rounds of multilateral trade negotiations and formalized the rules for much of world trade. Reduced trade barriers realized some of the highest growth rates in global trade (WTO, 2019). However, despite the remarkable achievement it had accomplished in promoting and securing free trade, the GATT remained provisional throughout all its forty-seven years. As global trade became more complex, GATT member states realized the need to devise rules for trade in services and investment which were not originally included in the GATT. Besides, the increased cases of international trade disputes also called for an improved dispute settlement mechanism. These and other factors eventually led to the development of a new multilateral trade regime to enhance and expand international trade. Therefore, a series of trade negotiations, or rounds, was conducted under the GATT. The first five rounds held during 1947–1961 dealt mainly with tariff reductions. The subsequent three rounds of negotiations included other areas, such as anti-dumping and non-tariff measures. The 1986–1993 round—the Uruguay Round—led to the creation of the **World Trade Organization (WTO).**

The WTO is the only international organization setting and implementing the general principles and rules of trade between nations. Founded on January 1, 1995, it serves six major functions:
1. administering trade agreements
2. facilitating trade negotiations
3. settling trade disputes
4. reviewing national trade policies
5. trade capacity-building for developing economies
6. cooperating with other international organizations (WTO, "How the WTO is organized").

While the WTO has replaced the GATT as a multilateral trade organization, the GATT still exists as the WTO's umbrella treaty for trade in goods (WTO, "What Happened to GATT"). At the same time, subsequent negotiations in other areas of trade were largely successful. For example, in 1997, seventy WTO members concluded a financial services deal covering more than 95% of trade in banking, insurance, securities, and financial information (WTO,

"Trade negotiations"). In November 2001, the most recent round of multilateral trade negotiation—the Doha Round—was launched with 157 participating members, including sovereign states, the European Union, and non-sovereign entities like Hong Kong (WTO, "Doha round"). With a focus on trade facilitation, the Doha Round embodied an ambitious agenda that covered twenty areas of trade, including non-agricultural tariffs, trade and the environment, anti-dumping and subsidies, trade facilitation, transparency in government procurement, intellectual property, and a range of issues raised by developing economies (WTO, "The Doha agenda"). The negotiation proved more challenging than expected. Since 2008, it has largely remained stalled due to the failure of reaching consensus among hundreds of participating countries. Recent attempts to revive the Doha Round were hardly successful, and it is uncertain whether it will ever be completed.

Despite the challenges in negotiations and the recent reversion to trade protectionism on the global scale, the WTO has been widely recognized as the only fully-established, effective, and extensive multilateral trade arrangement. Its overall authority and accomplishments in global trade governance remain undisputed. As of September 2019, "the WTO has 164 members, covering 98% of world trade. A total of 22 countries are negotiating membership" (WTO, "How the WTO is organized"). Decisions in the WTO are generated by consensus, in which each member has one vote. The top-level decision-making body is the Ministerial Conference, which usually meets every two years. The next highest level is the General Council, which meets several times a year in its Geneva headquarters. The General Council includes committees, working groups, the trade policy review body, and the dispute settlement body. The Goods Council, Services Council, the Intellectual Property (TRIPS) Council, and several committees report to the General Council. Multiple specialized committees, working groups, and working parties deal with the individual agreements and other areas, such as the environment, development, market access, financial services, and investment (WTO, n.d.). Although all members have a formally equal vote, in practice the WTO institutions are more influenced by the largest and most advanced economies, especially the U.S., the EU, and Japan.

Regional trade agreements (RTAs) are defined in the WTO as reciprocal trade agreements between two or more partners in a region to reduce or eliminate trade barriers among themselves, such as free trade agreements, common markets, and customs unions (WTO, "Regional trade agreements"). Examples of RTAs are:

- the ASEAN Free Trade Area (AFTA) in Southeast Asia;
- the North American Free Trade Agreement (NAFTA);
- the Southern Common Market (Mercosur) in South America;
- the Economic and Monetary Community of Central Africa (CEMAC);
- the EU; and
- the Southern African Customs Union (SACU) (WTO, "Regional trade agreements").

As compared to the comprehensive multilateral free trade arrangement of the WTO, RTAs tend to be more region-focused. Supporters see them as more dedicated to regional interests and issues, helping to strengthen regional interdependence and integration, build up trust among neighbors, formalize trade rules, and avoid divisive trade policy conflict among countries. Under RTAs, less-developed countries are more likely to get flexibility in liberalizing trade and more time to reduce trade barriers. Others, however, see RTAs more negatively, arguing that they have created regional divisions in the world market. Countries joining RTAs may be driven by political motives or simply due to the fear of being left out, which means that they are less interested in liberalizing trade.

Facilitation of trade among members can also mean increased difficulty in trade with nonmembers. RTAs can form regional trade blocs that hinder trade liberalization and the integration of the global market. Moreover, they can force downward pressure on wages and environmental standards as countries actively compete for trade and investments. The debate comes down to whether RTAs should be viewed as "building blocks" or "stumbling blocks" in the globalization of trade. The differences among RTAs depend on the members and the continents on which each RTA is organized.

Preferential trade agreements (PTAs) are economic agreements that give preferential access to certain products from the participating countries by reducing, yet not eliminating, tariffs. Under the GATT and WTO, these agreements are valid only if they lead to free trade between the involved parties. Therefore, almost any PTA has a main goal of becoming an FTA in compliance with the GATT. Advanced forms of PTAs include free trade areas, customs unions, common markets, economic unions, and monetary unions.

In practice, countries prefer protection of some form or another, and PTAs have been used as convenient tools to circumvent the common free trade principles under the WTO. With the recent multiplication of bilateral PTAs and the emergence of mega-PTAs, such as the Transatlantic Trade and Investment Partnership (TTIP), the Trans Pacific Partnership (TPP), and the Regional Comprehensive Economic Partnership (RCEP), a global trade system exclusively managed within the framework of the WTO now seems to fall apart. The global trade governance has become a network of crisscrossing and interweaving regional and bilateral trade agreements.

An **free-trade area or agreement (FTA)** is generally a bilateral or multinational agreement signed to form a free-trade area between the participating states. Originally, under the GATT, FTAs were meant to include trade in goods only. Later, the term became widely used to refer to agreements covering not only goods but also services and investment. A **free-trade area** is a region encompassing a trade bloc whose member countries have signed a free trade agreement. Such agreements involve cooperation between at least two countries to eliminate trade barriers and to increase trade of goods and services with each other. They also have terms and conditions covering trade-related areas such as investment, intellectual property, government procurement, and technical standards.

In contrast to PTAs, which serve to reduce but not eliminate tariffs, FTAs often aim at eliminating them. Many countries have been actively constructing their FTA network since they are easier to negotiate than RTAs and may involve even fewer parties. In a case of bilateral FTAs, the participants are two countries. Such small-scale trade negotiation enables parties to more specifically address their respective interests, more easily bargain and negotiate concessions, and achieve better reciprocity. For instance, China, as a non-market economy under the WTO, has successfully obtained market-economy recognition with its FTA partners worldwide. For developing countries, negotiating an FTA is a capacity-building process, in which they can choose to start with the trading partners that are easier to negotiate with, set up a gradual schedule to liberalize trade, and then move onto higher-level and more complex trade negotiations. As a result, their domestic economy may suffer less shock from trade liberalization.

Financial Policies and the Global Governance for Finance

International finance generally means the international trade of **capital**, that is, money or physical factors of production that are used to generate income or make an investment (*Collins Dictionary of Business*, 2002).As with global trade in goods and services, the flow of capital across borders also follows rules of trade. While a majority of global capital flows between or among developed countries, in recent decades, there has been an increasing amount of global capital flowing toward developing countries. Suppliers of capital, typically wealthy developed countries, play the role of investors, creditors, or lenders, whereas developing countries, whose capital tends to be relatively scarce, are generally on the demand side and play the role of investees, debtors, or borrowers.

Their mutual interests are characterized by both consensus and conflict. Governments, businesses, and individuals often actively pursue international finance, but, at the same time, they tend to treat it with caution and even suspicion. Within borrowing or invested nations, there are many actors who value access to foreign funds; however, there are also others who resent the constraints and burdens that foreign investments sometimes impose on debtors. Similarly, within lending or investing nations, some see overseas investments as a major driving force for economic growth, while others argue that they take away funds that can otherwise be used to help domestic borrowers and outsource jobs that can otherwise be taken by domestic workers. While exchanges in global finance are usually welcomed by all sides, conflict of interests between countries can damage diplomatic relations.

To invest means to put capital into a project or a business in order to gain future benefit. There are two broad categories of foreign investments: portfolio and direct. A **portfolio investment** is investment made in a foreign country through the purchase of stocks (equities), **bonds** (a financial instrument used by corporations and government agencies to generate funds by borrowing money from bondholders, which is later paid back), or other financial instruments. While it gives the investor a claim on some income from the purchases, portfolio investors generally take little or no part in the management of the invested firm or running their investment. Instead, the company they invest in is obliged to pay off its creditors at the pre-established interest rates. Loans and shares of a company's stocks exemplify portfolio investments. However, an investor who owns large enough quantities of a company's shares might take control over the company and effectively manage the business, therefore making the investment direct.

Foreign direct investments (FDIs) are made by a company that owns facilities in another country—facilities over which the company maintains control. FDIs differ from portfolio investments mostly because direct investors have full authority to operate their investments, but they take most of the associated risks as well.

Why do investors invest abroad? Banks, corporations, and individuals make overseas investments to make money. Those with capital want to move their money from where profits are lower to where profits are higher. In trade, where resources and labor are scarce, they are expensive. Where they are abundant, they are cheap. The same is true of capital. If capital is more expensive, profits are higher. The price of capital is called the **interest rate** (the proportion of an amount loaned which a lender charges as interest to a borrower, normally expressed as an annual percentage) (Bankrate.com). In a poor country, capital is scarce and therefore expensive. Borrowers pay higher interest rates for loans. In a rich country, capital is plentiful, so interest rates and profit are lower.

If interest rates are the only concern, then all foreign investments would flow from capital-rich countries to capital-poor countries. However, that is not always the case. Most international investments are among rich countries, and only a relatively small—but growing—portion of it in the past several decades have gone to developing countries. The reason is the lower risk of cross-border investments in rich countries. International investors care not just about the promised interest rate or profit on foreign investments but also about the likelihood that they will actually get money back. In the case of international investment, the lack of control or influence over its surroundings brings higher risks. A foreign government over which the investor has no influence may do things that reduce the value of the investment. A foreign investor suffers great losses if, for instance, a local government decides to devalue the investment or decides to take over the investment itself.

Investments among rich countries are less risky compared to those in poor countries. The developed countries are more economically and politically stable, and they have a longer and more reliable history of treating foreign investors fairly. For investors to be willing to take a greater risk in the developing world, they need either much higher interest rates and profits or the preparedness that would allow them to effectively manage those risks. Meeting these needs can lead to financial negotiations between two or more countries. Efforts and policies attempting to ensure an amicable investment environment draws international finance into international politics. Investors who have decided to invest in developing countries typically choose those that are not only rich in resources and labor but also politically stable and economically successful, such as Brazil, China, and India—all ranked among the Top 10 in FDI inflows during 2017–2018 (UNCTAD, 2019A).

International investment provides great benefits to both investors and the countries invested; however, they can impose real costs on both sides. On the one hand, both sides of the interaction gain from successful investment and loans. The recipient gets capital it would not otherwise have, and companies that borrow from foreign lenders can finance projects that spur development. An inflow of foreign funds can increase the availability of credit to small business owners and homeowners. The foreign investor, meanwhile, gets higher profits than are available at home.

On the other hand, there are major conflicts of interests between the two sides. Each party wants to get as much as possible from the other and to give as little as possible. Lenders or creditors want their debts to be paid in full, and corporations want to bring home high profits from their foreign investments. Debtors or borrowers, however, would rather pay less of what they owe, and host countries would prefer foreign corporations having less to take away. This situation creates both a commonality of interests in maintaining a free flow of capital and a conflict of interests in distributing the benefits of the flow. Foreign capital inflows tend to be more desirable, as they increase domestic economic activities, allow a country to consume more than it produces, and enable a government to spend more than it takes from taxes.

Foreign capital outflows, however, tend to be less desirable because they generally impose **austerity** on national economy, that is, policies to restrain wages and consumption, typically by cutting government expenditure, raising taxes, restricting wages, and importing less while exporting more (Frieden, Lake, & Schultz, 2018, p. 359). Debt crises throughout history have been associated with slow growth, lower employment rate, social spending cuts, and general economic hardship. It usually happens that the people and groups who are asked to bear the greatest burden of austerity are not exactly those who have benefitted most from foreign investment or loans. This has added to the complexity in international financial relations.

When conflict arises between a debtor and a creditor, each side in the interaction has clear interests at stake. For the debtor country, making prompt and full debt service payments can lead to austerity, so it is in their interests to reduce the amount they have to pay. On the other hand, the creditor's profits depend on the debt payments they receive. They want to be paid in full for the loans provided. The two sets of interests are in conflict, and both sides must engage in bargaining and compromising to determine whether a mutually acceptable deal is possible. As in the case of security relations, international financial negotiations generally are characterized by incomplete information and a lack of mutual trust. As a result, cooperative relations between debtors and creditors can collapse into bitter conflict, which could negatively affect other dimensions of international relations. In order to avoid such conflict, governments have sought to develop and improve their domestic policies and mechanisms regarding foreign investment and, at the same time, utilize international institutions to regulate global finance and resolve disputes.

National policies on investments combine both enthusiasm and skepticism toward foreign investors. Attracting investment remains a priority for most countries in the world. A majority of new investment policy measures are moving toward the direction of financial liberalization, promotion, and facilitation. Numerous countries have removed or lowered entry restrictions for foreign investors in a variety of industries. Efforts toward streamlining administrative procedures for foreign investment have continued. In 2018, forty international investment agreements (IIAs) were signed, in which participating countries have committed themselves to facilitating foreign investments and liberalizing their domestic investment regimes (UNCTAD, 2019B, p. 1). At the same time, however, suspicions toward the possible political motives of FDIs have also been on the rise.

In the World Investment Report, the UNCTAD (2019) finds a more critical stance towards foreign investment in new national investment policy measures: In 2018, about 55 economies introduced at least 112 measures to regulate foreign investment. More than one third of these measures introduced new restrictions or regulations— the highest number for two decades (p. 15). They mainly reflect national security concerns about foreign ownership of critical infrastructure, core technologies, and other sensitive business assets. Furthermore, the number of large merger and acquisition deals withdrawn or blocked for regulatory or political reasons had doubled since 2017 (UNCTAD, 2019). Screening mechanisms for foreign investment are becoming more important; new screening frameworks were introduced in at least eleven countries since 2011. Changes include adding sectors or activities subject to screening and broadening the definition of foreign investment.

At the international level, global financial governance has been established and developed since 1945 to meet various needs associated with the increasingly active flow of capital across borders. The World Bank (WB), the International Monetary

Fund (IMF), and regional investment banks, such as the Asian Development Bank and the Inter-American Development Bank, are playing a more significant role in regulating global financial activities, facilitating international investments, settling disputes, and providing financial assistance.

The **World Bank (WB)**, formally referred to as the World Bank Group (WBG), is the world's largest and most influential development bank. Headquartered in Washington, D.C., the WB is an umbrella organization consisting of five international institutions responsible for addressing development-related issues and providing funding and policy advice to developing countries in need. These five institutions are committed to poverty alleviation, shared prosperity, and sustainable development. They are:

1. International Bank for Reconstruction and Development (IBRD);
2. International Development Association (IDA);
3. International Finance Corporation (IFC);
4. Multilateral Investment Guarantee Agency (MIGA); and
5. International Centre for Settlement of Investment Disputes (ICSID) (The World Bank, 2018, p. 5).

Founded in 1944, the WB originally focused on providing loans to help reconstruct the countries devastated by World War II. Later, more attention was paid to development, especially infrastructure (The World Bank, n.d.). With the founding of the IFC in 1956, the WB became capable of lending to private companies and financial institutions in developing countries. The founding of the IDA in 1960 put greater emphasis on the poorest countries, with poverty alleviation as a primary goal. Today, the Bank's global projects have extended into broader development areas, such as human development (like education and health), agriculture and rural development, environmental protection, infrastructure, and governance (like anti-corruption transparency). The institution has remained a prominent actor in combatting poverty, supporting economic growth, and promoting sustainable development around the world. In the fiscal year of 2018, the Bank had committed USD$66.9 billion in loans and other forms of financial assistance to partner countries and private businesses—a dramatic increase from the four loans totaling $497 million in 1947 (The World Bank, 2018, p. 12).

As of September 2019, the World Bank has 189 member countries as its shareholders, represented by a Board of Governors— the ultimate policymaking body at the Bank. Generally, the Board comprises member countries' ministers of finance or ministers of development. They meet once a year at the Annual Meetings of the Boards of Governors of the World Bank Group and the International Monetary Fund. Each of the five institutions in the WB is owned by its member governments, which subscribe to its basic share capital, with votes proportional to shareholding (The World Bank, n.d.). Membership gives certain voting rights that are the same for all countries, but there are also additional votes which depend on each member state's financial contributions to the Bank. Since the U.S. has been the largest shareholder of the WB, every president of the World Bank has been a U.S. citizen (The World Bank, 2019). The top eight largest economies also have the strongest voting power in the Bank. They are the U.S. (15.67%), Japan (7.88%), China (4.37%), Germany (3.96%), France (3.71%), the United Kingdom (3.71%), India (3%), and Canada (2.9%).

The **International Monetary Fund (IMF)** is an organization aimed at fostering global monetary cooperation, securing financial stability, facilitating international trade, promoting high employment and sustainable economic growth, and reducing poverty around the world. Created in 1945, the IMF's fundamental mission is to ensure the stability of the international monetary system, that is, the system of exchange rates and international money transfers. It does so in three ways: (1) economic surveillance, which allows the IMF to oversee economic conditions at the global and national levels and offer analyses and policy advice; (2) lending, which helps member states stabilize their economies and address their financial needs; and (3) capacity development, which empowers developing countries in their economic development (IMF, n.d.).

As a global monetary and financial organization, the IMF is governed by and accountable to the 189 member states. Unlike the **UN General Assembly**, where each member has one vote, decision-making at the IMF is designed to reflect the relative positions of its member countries in the global economy. Each member country is assigned a quota that reflects its financial commitment to the IMF and determines its voting power. The votes of each member equal the sum of its basic votes (equally distributed among all members) and quota-based votes. Based on the IMF Quota Data of July 2018, the top five countries in terms of voting power are the U.S. (17.4%), Japan (6.46%), China (6.39%), Germany (5.58%), and France (4.23%) (IMF, 2018). The Board of Governors, the highest decision-making body of the IMF, consists of one governor and one alternate governor for each member country and normally meets once a year. The governor is appointed by the member country and is usually its minister of finance or head of its central bank. The Board of Governors also elects or appoints executive directors and is the ultimate arbiter on issues related to the interpretation of the IMF's Articles of Agreement. The Boards of Governors of the IMF and the World Bank normally meet once a year to discuss the work of their respective institutions. All powers of the IMF are vested in the Board of Governors, which may delegate to the Executive Board all except certain reserved powers, such as the right to approve quota increases and the admission of new members. The Executive Board, the second most powerful institution under the IMF, conducts the daily business of the IMF, discusses all aspects of its work, and normally makes decisions based on consensus (IMF, n.d.).

The World Trade Organization, the World Bank, and the International Monetary Fund are collectively known as the Bretton Woods Institutions (see Chapter 12). They had formed the Bretton

Woods System, a system of economic and financial agreements that had served as the foundation of the global economic and financial order from 1945–1976. Although the system has ceased to exist, all the three institutions have developed to the present day, promoting free trade between nations, facilitating foreign investment, and regulating international monetary relations.

Regional financial governance is characterized by various regional development banks, which have also played an indispensable role in promoting cross-border trade and finance at the regional level. These multilateral financial institutions provide low-interest loans and grants for various programs, such as infrastructure, public health, education, and resources management. There are four major regional development banks: the African Development Bank (AfDB), the Asian Development Bank (ADB), the European Bank for Reconstruction and Development (EBRD), and the Inter-American Development Bank (IDB). The U.S. is an essential provider of financial assistance in all these banks. Additionally, the Asian Infrastructure Investment Bank (AIIB), headquartered in China's capital Beijing and established in January 2016, is a multilateral development bank led by China. Aimed to promote social and economic progress in Asia, the AIIB offers various forms of financing to member states and promotes sustainability (AIIB, n.d.).

Monetary Policies and Global Monetary Relations

International monetary relations are concerned with the value of national currencies, exchange rates, and national monetary policies. The flow of monies across nations is essential to global political economy. Change in a country's domestic monetary policy is likely to have repercussions beyond its borders, especially when such change happens in a major economy. As in global trade and finance, realizing a stable and efficient international monetary order proves to be difficult. Although virtually everyone has an interest in the existence of a functioning, stable, and effective international monetary system, different arrangements benefit some actors more than they others. This disparity leads to disagreements over how such a system should be best organized and what rules to follow.

A national monetary system allows for the convenient exchange of goods, services, and capital. Typically, national governments determine the currency and its value, print bills, mint coins, and control the flow of money on the market. At the same time, national currencies are not meant for domestic use only; they exist to relate to other national currencies. For example, the euro can be used only to buy only goods and services in the Eurozone but can also be converted to the U.S. dollar, the Japanese yen, and other national currencies.

The amount of one currency that must be offered to purchase one unit of a foreign currency is called its **exchange rate**. When a currency increases in value relative to other currencies, it is said to strengthen, or **appreciate**. When a currency's value appreciates, it is more expensive for foreigners to buy the country's goods and services and less expensive for domestic consumers to buy foreign products. In this case, exports tend to go down whereas, due to stronger purchasing power, domestic consumption tends to go up, and imports go up since they become cheaper. Conversely, when a currency decreases in value relative to other currencies, it is said to weaken, or **depreciate**. When a currency depreciates, it is cheaper for foreigners to buy the country's products and exports tend to increase, whereas the devaluation of the currency causes domestic purchasing power to decrease, so domestic consumption tends to go down. Imports tend to reduce, too, as they become more expensive.

Exchange rates fluctuate corresponding to supply and demand. Many factors can affect the supply and demand of a national currency. An important factor is the amount of foreign investments in a national economy. To invest in a foreign country, an investor must buy that country's national currency from the **foreign exchange market** (the marketplace where individuals, businesses, and other entities buy and sell foreign currencies). If there is a lot of investment in a country, demand for its currency will rise, and the increased demand causes the national currency to appreciate. For example, all else being equal, when foreigners invest more in the U.S., the U.S. dollar strengthens or appreciates. Typically, governments adjust their monetary policies by raising or lowering national interest rates or exchange rates. In most countries today, this is done by a **central bank**, an institution that regulates monetary conditions in an economy, typically by affecting interest rates and the quantity of money in circulation. The central bank of the U.S. is the Federal Reserve. At the global level, if a government wants to stimulate demand for its country's products in the world market, it can depreciate the national currency. The weaker currency makes local goods cheaper to foreigners and spurs exports, while imports are made more expensive so will reduce them. In this way, a monetary policy that weakens the national currency can help domestic producers. It also means that domestic consumers can buy less with their money. Sometimes, the artificial devaluation of a national currency to spur exports and boost economic growth constitutes currency manipulation, which is a type of unfair trade practice.

There are three major types of exchange rates: a fixed or pegged rate, an adjustable peg, or a floating exchange rate. A **fixed or pegged exchange rate** is one in which a national currency trades at a government-specified rate against a particular currency, a group of currencies, or a valuable commodity, such as gold. Such a rate can provide currency stability and predictability, help facilitate international economic exchange, keep prices stable, and work for the interests of those in international trade, finance, and tourism. On the other hand, under the fixed or pegged system, a government must commit itself to the policies necessary to maintain the fixed exchange rate, even if economic conditions may necessitate a change. A fixed rate, therefore, creates rigidity, reducing or eliminating a government's ability to develop its own independent monetary policy or adjust exchange rates based on actual economic conditions.

In contrast to the fixed rate, a **floating exchange rate** exists when a government allows the exchange rate of its national currency to be determined by the open market, without direct government control or intervention. The price of a national currency, therefore, moves around in line with changes in supply and demand. Most major currencies, including the U.S. dollar, the Japanese yen, and the euro, have adopted floating rates. It gives the government more freedom to pursue its own monetary policies, leaving the value of its national currency to fluctuate under the invisible hand of the market. Such flexibility can facilitate market competition by making exports and imports easier, thus allowing domestic producers more freedom in pursuing profits. But at the same time, floating rates can move around a great deal, which can possibly impede international economic exchange, adding to the unpredictability and risks of the global market.

Between the fixed rate and the floating rate, there are some intermediate options. A government can allow its currency to vary but only within limits, or it can fix the exchange rate for short periods, changing the currency's value as desired. Such a mixed system is also known as **adjustable peg**, a monetary system of fixed and adjustable rates combined, with governments being expected to keep their currencies fixed for extended periods but are permitted to make minor adjustments from time to rime as economic conditions change. A typical example is the Bretton Woods monetary system (1945–1973), under which the U.S. dollar was fixed to gold and all the other currencies were fixed to the U.S. dollar, with minor adjustment allowed under certain economic conditions. While the system was praised as a middle ground between rigidity and complete unpredictability, in the 1970s, the U.S. government had increasingly found it to be a constraint upon the U.S. economy and preferred the value of the U.S. dollar to be adjustable as well.

Eventually, the Bretton Woods monetary system ended, leading to the contemporary world monetary order characterized by a wide range of exchange rate systems ranging from hard pegs to free floating (IMF, 2019).

Despite these available options, a nation's exchange rate policy cannot be arbitrary. Conflicts of interests can make governments sensitive to the domestic political and economic effects of their currency policies. A strong exchange rate increases national purchasing power, so consumers can afford more of the world's products. The trade-off is that, due to the increased strength of currency, domestic goods become more expensive for foreigners, which could hurt national exporters on local or world markets and reduce their profits. In addition to a possible surge of cheaper imports at home and fewer exports abroad, a strong currency also prompts many businesses to make overseas investments or outsource their jobs to countries with cheaper labor and resources, causing domestic workers to lose jobs and more national money to flow abroad. In contrast, a weak currency can bring increased benefit to national producers because exports become cheaper. Countries attempting to stimulate exports prefer to keep their currencies weak so that manufacturers and farmers who compete with foreign producers both at home and abroad can have more competitive prices. The trade-off is the reduced national purchasing power that hurts domestic consumers. Intentional devaluation of a national currency over an extended length of time leads to imbalance of domestic interests and objections from consumers.

In addition, international monetary conditions and rules can also play an influential role. An **international monetary regime** is a formal or informal arrangement widely accepted and shared among governments to govern relations among currencies. They stipulate whether currency values are expected to be fixed, floating, or a mix of both and determine whether there will be an agreed-upon benchmark—such as gold or the U.S. dollar—against which values are measured. Under the contemporary monetary regime since 1973, there is no commonly-accepted benchmark. Instead, national governments get to choose what exchange rate system to adopt, based on their respective domestic economic conditions.

A national currency may or may not be subject to the change in the global market. Without a unified standard, the stability of national currencies relies only upon the commitments of their issuing governments. Monetary relations are based on a floating exchange rate system among a small number of major national currencies from the advanced market economies, such as the U.S., Japan, and Germany. China, as an emerging financial power, has adopted a managed floating system since 2017. While big countries can allow their currencies to float freely, small countries tend to be more cautious, fixing their currencies to the U.S. dollar or the euro in most cases. In 2018, of the 189 IMF member states, 12.5% use a fixed or pegged system, 46.4% use an adjustable peg system that combines elements of fixed rates and floating rates, and 34.4% adopt a floating system (IMF, 2019, p. 6–9).

The absence of an established common global monetary system has led some countries to develop regional monetary systems that can stabilize exchange rates among a group of countries. The Eurozone has been by far the most successful existing regional monetary union, in which nineteen out of twenty-eight EU member states have committed to stabilizing their exchange rates and using the euro. In the next section, we are going to focus on one of the most influential actors in contemporary trade, financial, and monetary relations: multinational corporations.

Multinational Corporations (MNCs) and Their Role in the World Economy

Multinational or transnational corporations (MNCs or TNCs) are corporations headquartered in one country and that maintain ongoing business operations in one or more foreign countries. MNCs often own substantial assets, such as real estate, equipment, capital, and intellectual property; have a strong capacity in innovation and research; and hire large numbers of employees around the world. Due to their substantial scale of business, they can generate large amounts of profits simultaneously all over the world. For instance, the Fortune Global 500 lists the world's largest MNCs from thirty-four countries. Almost all these enterprises regularly engage in cross-border business activities. In 2018, they together generated $32.7 trillion in revenues and $2.15 trillion in profits and employed 69.3 million people worldwide (Fortune Global 500, 2019). Their headquarters are mostly located in the world's major economies, especially the U.S., China, and the EU member states (Visualize The Global 500, 2019).

Not every company can become an MNC, but most successful firms today tend to go global. Why do they not just stay at home and simply export from their home countries to foreign markets? A simple answer is that they receive more profits and lower costs. A relatively detailed answer leads to two major reasons: one is that due to the nature of their industries, some firms must go abroad. Those in transportation (e.g., Delta Airlines and Air France) and shipping (e.g., FedEx and UPS) must establish presence abroad to deliver their services. The exploitation and utilization of natural resources also requires a firm to go abroad. Oil companies like Exxon Mobil and BP have been global for a long time.

The other reason is that MNCs in manufacturing industries may decide to place manufacturing, assembling, or research and development facilities in foreign countries for lower production costs, increased efficiency, and a closer relationship with local customers. Moving abroad allows an MNC to employ labor at lower costs and to access more resources that would otherwise be more expensive or scarce at home. In short, companies become multinational for multitudes of reasons, such as higher profits, lower costs, market access, resources, and a more business-friendly environment in general.

Within the home countries of MNCs, there is often support for their foreign activities. MNCs are powerful contributors to national revenues, and, for this reason, governments usually act to promote and protect corporate interests at home and abroad. At the international level, the GATT, the WTO, RTAs, and FTAs usually include a **national treatment** clause under which "imported and locally-produced goods, foreign and domestic services, and foreign and local intellectual property, should all be treated equally, or at least after they have entered the domestic market" (WTO, n.d.). The major purpose for governments to negotiate this clause is to make sure that their investors and traders are treated fairly in a foreign country and not subject to any discrimination or undue influence. In a similar vein, **international investment agreements (IIAs)** are treaties signed between countries usually for the purpose of protection, promotion, and liberalization of cross-border investments, especially those of private investors. A most common type of IIAs is **bilateral investment treaties (BITs)**. In 2018, thirty BITs were signed (UNCTAD, 2019, p. 17). Most of these treaties include provisions to protect an investment from government discrimination or expropriation without compensation as well as rules and mechanisms for dispute resolution.

Most countries today welcome foreign corporations. MNCs create jobs, stimulate economic growth and industrialization, promote research, development, and innovation, enhance the knowledge and skills of local employees through education and training, and provide valuable experiences that can be learnt by domestic industries. To local customers, MNCs enrich markets by offering products and services of better qualities and at lower prices. To the local government, MNCs are a major source of investment capital and revenue. The income that they generate can fund infrastructure, development projects, and public facilities, which increases general social wellbeing. Through international treaties, domestic laws and rules, and local policy measures, governments of host countries have sought to facilitate foreign investment, attract investors, offer them tax breaks and other preferential treatments, establish free economic zones (FEZs), and reduce their risks by policies of investment protection.

While most countries are welcoming toward foreign investment, they also have concerns for the overall impact of MNCs on their politics and society. At home, MNCs are sometimes blamed for outsourcing domestic jobs and producing sub-standard products with cheap foreign labor, which acts to harm domestic workers and consumers. On the other hand, host countries, especially the less-developed countries (LDCs), are wary of the potentially exploitative nature of MNCs's business presence, claiming that they impede rather than advance development. For example, foreign agricultural and raw-materials investments have been increasingly viewed as exploitative, as they tend to extract local resources and labor for more profits, with little concern for the environment.

There are also political considerations. For decades and in various parts of the world, MNCs are believed to be a powerful but unwelcome force in local politics. In the past, many LDCs considered large foreign companies as agents of foreign powers to interfere with their domestic political processes. In the past two decades, China's overseas investments have raised concerns within major developed countries, such as the EU, Canada, the U.S., and Australia. Allegations and investigations emerged with respect to potential theft of trade secrets, trade espionage, and interference with local elections. The past few years have witnessed stronger calls for investment-restraining policies, most of which concerned national security. In order to address political sensitivities arising out of foreign investments, host countries sometimes require transfer of ownership to local private companies or to the government, or allow FDI only if the foreign company does not compete with domestic firms, or ask MNCs to reinvest most of their profits back into the host country.

Social impacts of MNCs also seem quite mixed. Critics point out that MNCs care most about their production costs, and protection of labor rights and environment increase such costs. Governments around the world, in order to keep those investors, may engage in a **race to the bottom**, where they implement lower policy rules and standards on environment and human rights out of a fear of losing foreign investments. Supporters, however, argue that MNCs bring about improvement in labor policies, increase awareness of human rights protection, and lead to better adherence to international law. MNCs have a stronger interest in having high-quality rather than low-cost labor and thus tend to invest in countries where workers are better-educated and more professional. Improvement of employees's knowledge and skills is achieved by actively designing and implementing training programs and periodical assessments of qualifications. In addition, MNCs help promote transition to democracy by stimulating economic growth, uniting business communities, and promoting an open society for free exchanges of information, all of which are proven as conducive to successful democratization.

While MNCs are blamed for certain social problems, most see them as an overall positive force of globalization. Economically, they play a large and growing role in the production of the world's GDP. Global trade and finance prosper with the increased activities of MNCs around the world. In addition to creating wealth and jobs, MNCs also positively improve the quality of the world's labor force through education and training. Politically, from a liberal perspective, foreign investments are viewed as conducive to world peace. Studies have found that, at least since 1945, FDIs are positively associated with peace, including through the mitigation of territorial disputes (Grieco et. al., 2019, p. 336). In the future, MNCs' global activity is likely to grow further, and their role in global trade, financial, and monetary relations will get more prominent accordingly.

References

Asian Infrastructure Investment Bank (AIIB). (n.d.). Introduction. Retrieved September 26, 2019, from https://www.aiib.org/en/about-aiib/index.html

"Bond." (n.d.). *Bankrate.* Retrieved September 28, 2019, from https://www.bankrate.com/glossary/b/bond/

"Capital." (n.d.). *Collins Dictionary of Business (3rd ed.)* (2002, 2005) and *Collins Dictionary of Economics (4th ed.)* (2005). Retrieved September 7, 2019, from https://financial-dictionary. thefreedictionary.com/capital

Durisin, M. & Robinson, A. (2019, August 23). Soybeans Sink as China Hikes Tariffs on American Farm Products. *Bloomberg.* Retrieved September 24, 2019, from https://www.bloomberg. com/news/articles/2019-08-23/soybeans-sink-to-two-week-low-as-china-hikes-u-s-tariffs

Friden, J. A., Lake, D. A., & Schultz, K. A. (2019). *World Politics – Interests, Interactions, Institutions* (4th ed.). New York: W. W. Norton & Company.

Global 500. (2019). *Fortune.* Retrieved September 28, 2019, from https://fortune.com/global500/2019

Grieco, J., Ikenberry, G. J., & Mastanduno, M. (2019). *Introduction to International Relations* (2nd ed.). London, UK: Red Globe Press.

"Interest rate." (n.d.). *Bankrate.* Retrieved September 28, 2019, from https://www.bankrate.com/glossary/i/interest-rate/

International Monetary Fund (IMF). (n.d.). About the IMF: What We Do. Retrieved September 28, 2019, from https://www.imf. org/en/About

IMF. (n.d.). Governance Structure. Retrieved September 26, 2019, from https://www.imf.org/external/about/govstruct.htm

IMF. (2018, August 9). Updated IMF Quota Data—July 2018. Retrieved September 26, 2019, from https://www.imf.org/external/np/fin/quotas/2018/0818.htm

IMF. (2019, April 16). Annual Report on Exchange Arrangements and Exchange Restrictions 2018 [PDF file]. Retrieved September 26, 2019, from https://www.imf.org/en/ Publications/Annual-Report-on-Exchange-Arrangements-and-Exchange-Restrictions/Issues/2019/04/24/Annual-Report-on-Exchange-Arrangements-and-Exchange-Restrictions-2018-46162

Lamy, S. L., Masker, J. S., Baylis, J., Smith, S., & Owens, P. (2018). *Introduction to Global Politics* (5th ed.). New York: Oxford University Press.

Manuel, K. M. (2016). The Buy American Act—Preferences for "Domestic" Supplies: In Brief [PDF file]. Retrieved from https://fas.org/sgp/crs/misc/R43140.pdf

Non-Tariff Barriers to Trade. (n.d.) *Non-Tariff Barriers*. Retrieved September 24, 2019, from https://www.tradebarriers.org/ntb/ non_tariff_barriers

Plume, K. (2019, July 29). U.S. soybean exports to China rise, but big purchases remain elusive. *Reuters*. Retrieved September 24, 2019, from https://www.reuters.com/article/us-usa-trade-china-agriculture/us-soybean-exports-to-china-rise-but-big-purchases-remain-elusive-idUSKCN1UO1ZL

UN Conference on Trade and Development (UNCTAD). (2019A). World Investment Report [PDF file]. Retrieved from https:// unctad.org/en/PublicationsLibrary/wir2019_overview_en.pdf

UNCTAD. (2019B, June). IIA Issues Note Iss. 3 [PDF file]. Retrieved from https://unctad.org/en/PublicationsLibrary/ diaepcbinf2019d5_en.pdf

USAID. (2013). Non-Tariff Barriers to Trade [PDF file]. Retrieved September 24, 2019, from https://www.usaid.gov/sites/default/ files/documents/1861/Nontariff_barriers.pdf

World Bank. (2018). The World Bank Annual Report 2018 [PDF file]. Retrieved from https://www.worldbank.org/en/about/ annual-report

World Bank. (2019, January 10). Selection of the president of the World Bank Group. Retrieved from https://www.worldbank.org/en/news/press-release/2019/01/10/selection-of-the-president-of-the-world-bank-group

World Bank. (2019, April 9). World Bank in small states. Retrieved September 28, 2019, from https://www.worldbank.org/en/country/smallstates/overview

World Bank. (2019). Top 8 countries voting power. Retrieved September 26, 2019, from https://finances.worldbank.org/Shareholder-Equity/Top-8-countries-voting-power/udm3-vzz9

World Bank. (n.d.). History. Retrieved September 26, 2019, from https://www.worldbank.org/en/about/history

World Bank. (n.d.). Organization: Voting powers. Retrieved September 26, 2019, from https://www.worldbank.org/en/about/leadership/votingpowers

World Trade Organization (WTO). (n.d.). Doha round: What are they negotiating? Retrieved September 24, 2019, from https://www.wto.org/english/tratop_e/dda_e/update_e.htm

WTO. (n.d.). The Doha agenda. Retrieved September 24, 2019, from https://www.wto.org/english/thewto_e/whatis_e/tif_e/doha1_e.htm

WTO. (n.d.) The GATT years: From Havana to Marrakesh. Retrieved September 24, 2019, from https://www.wto.org/english/thewto_e/whatis_e/tif_e/fact4_e.htm

WTO. (n.d.). How the WTO is organized. Retrieved September 24, 2019, from https://www.wto.org/english/thewto_e/whatis_e/inbrief_e/inbr_e.htm

WTO. (n.d.). Membership of plurilateral regional trade agreements. Retrieved September 24, 2019, from https://www.wto.org/english/tratop_e/region_e/rta_plurilateral_map_e.htm

WTO. (n.d.). Principles of the trading system - Trade without discrimination. Retrieved September 28, 2019, from https://www.wto.org/english/thewto_e/whatis_e/tif_e/fact2_e.htm

WTO. (n.d.). Regional trade agreements. Retrieved September 24, 2019, from https://www.wto.org/english/tratop_e/region_e/rta_pta_e.htm

WTO. (n.d.). Trade negotiations. Retrieved September 24, 2019, from https://www.wto.org/english/thewto_e/whatis_e/inbrief_e/inbr_e.htm

WTO. (n.d.). What happened to GATT? Retrieved September 24, 2019, from https://www.wto.org/english/thewto_e/whatis_e/tif_e/fact5_e.htm

Visualize The Global 500. (2019). *Fortune.* Retrieved September 28, 2019, from https://fortune.com/global500/2019/visualizations/

Zhou, M. & Noge, Y. (2019, August 13). US soybeans pile up as trade war tests Trump's support base. *Nikkei Asia.* Retrieved September 24, 2019, from https://asia.nikkei.com/Economy/Trade-war/US-soybeans-pile-up-as-trade-war-tests-Trump-s-support-base

Development, North-South Gap, and International Aid

14

Cristian Harris & Dwight Wilson

Abstract

This chapter examines the concept of development and its place in international relations. It discusses the meaning of development and considers how it can be measured. The chapter reviews the major international initiatives to promote development by key international actors and the debate over the effectiveness of these initiatives. It reviews different theories that attempt to explain the origins of development, and, finally, reviews the various development strategies practiced by developing countries.

Learning Objectives

- Identify and examine the terminology, actors, challenges, and major issues associated with the process of development
- Identify and analyze key theories about the causes of development.
- Identify and analyze the intellectual evolution of the debate about development.
- Identify and review contemporary theoretical debates about the causes and policy prescriptions to address underdevelopment.

What is Development?

The first problem we encounter when we try to explain differences in development levels between countries is the very definition of what development is. Scholars and analysts take disparate views on this matter. Is development the elimination of poverty? The elimination of widespread hunger and famine? Is development access to technology? Political stability? All of the above? If high per capita incomes are a sign of development, why are oil-rich countries of the Persian Gulf region classified as not developed? If low infant mortality rates are a sign of development, why are Costa Rica and Cuba classified as not developed? If achieving a complex industrial and technological capacity are a sign of development, why are countries like China, India, and Brazil classified as not developed? Moreover, as we will discuss below, the different theories that have tried to make sense of the nature and causes of development processes are themselves in some ways flawed and limited.

A simple definition of **development** is the increased provision of goods and services that satisfy the fundamental human needs of the greatest number of people. That is, a country's economy must grow enough to provide for the basic needs of its population, which are food, clothing, and shelter. The underlying assumption beneath this definition is that development is synonymous with economic growth. Moreover, it contains an optimistic, hopeful bias. It suggests that, once an economy starts growing, the process becomes irreversible, cumulative, organic, and self-sustaining. Countries will grow in a positive and desirable direction. In time, countries will achieve greater equality, stability, and democracy: "All good things go together."

Instead, development is the increasing capacity to make rational use of the natural and human resources for social ends. Rational here means that the interests and needs of the society are served: people are well fed, well housed, well-educated, in good health, and use available resources in a judicious way so as to leave behind enough resources for future generations. To create more goods and services, all societies strive to extend control over their environment. Thus, development is a universal process, but the rates of development are uneven. Additionally, there is marked inequality in the distribution of the gains of economic growth.

The definition of development has expanded over time to include a wide variety of issues: political, economic, social, cultural, and environmental. As Carol Lancaster argues, development is an "elastic concept" (Lancaster, 2008). Development is not a fixed definition because it keeps changing and will continue to do so in the future (Lancaster, 2008). Today, we stress improved and balanced human welfare; human security, including a stable political situation; progress toward social equality, including gender equality; progress toward an equitable distribution of the gains of economic growth; environmental sustainability of development; improved life expectancy; lower infant and maternal mortality rates; increased caloric intake; lower mortality rates, especially of curable diseases; universal and affordable education at the primary and secondary level; reduction of the gap between rural and urban populations; greater rights for minorities and indigenous populations; greater respect for human rights; and greater participation in the public decision-making process (i.e., democracy).

Scholars use various terms: modernizing societies, emerging economies, developing countries, underdeveloped countries, or less developed countries. During the Cold War, the term Third World was coined to refer to the countries of Latin America, Africa, Asia, and the Middle East that were neither part of the capitalist world (i.e., the First World) nor the Communist bloc (i.e., the Second World). This term was a catchall, residual definition that alluded to a foreign policy preference of these countries but not to their development status. Later, it acquired economic tones. With the collapse of the Communist bloc and the end of the Cold War, the term carried even less meaning. Today scholars prefer to use the term **Global South**.

This is not a geographic definition but more of an illustration of the global gap between rich countries, most of which are located in the Northern Hemisphere and poor countries, most of which are located in the Southern Hemisphere.

When we divide countries into rich and poor, we rely on an analytical tool that classifies them by their income levels per person. The World Bank classifies countries into four income levels: high income ($12,375 or more per person annually), upper-middle income ($12,375–3,996), lower-middle income ($3,995–$1,026), and low income ($1,025 or less). Using these criteria, out of the 218 economies reviewed by the World Bank, forty-six countries classify as lower-middle income and thirty-one countries as low income. The majority of the latter are in sub-Saharan Africa (World Bank, 2019b).

Development entails but is not synonymous with economic growth; rather, there should be a clear distinction between development and growth. To emphasize their differences and highlight that development is a multi-layered reality, the UN created the Human Development Index (HDI) (World Bank, 2019a). The HDI is a composite of four indicators measuring health, education, and income. Under these criteria, there are almost 150 countries classified as underdeveloped with a great deal of diversity among them. For example, they include countries like Qatar and the United Arab Emirates (UAE) with very high per capita incomes and countries like Burundi and Malawi with some of the lowest per capita incomes in the world. Some countries have significant industrial capacities—like China, India, Brazil, Mexico, and Turkey—while others are largely agricultural economies, where subsistence agriculture still predominates. Their societies are rural, but important changes are taking place. A steady shift from rural to urban determines that eight out of ten of the largest cities in the world are in an underdeveloped country: two in Latin America, one in the Middle East and North Africa, and five in Asia (UN,

2019). Some countries are stable democracies, like Costa Rica and Uruguay, while others are caught in political instability, such as the Democratic Republic of the Congo, Somalia, and Afghanistan. Still others are harsh dictatorships, such as Syria and North Korea.

The vast majority of underdeveloped countries are former colonies that gained their independence after World War II. Many rely on the production and export of a single commodity, such as oil, coffee, sugar, or cacao. Their economy is mainly oriented to satisfy external demand, particularly the demands of the advanced industrialized countries that often times are their former colonial masters. Moreover, they have very few trading partners. They trade more with advanced industrialized countries than with their regional neighbors. Because the economy is organized around production of raw materials or crops for export, domestic production of food tends to be neglected. Perversely, even though these countries have the necessary environmental conditions to grow their own food, they rely on imports. The size of their economies tends to be small, yet their populations are large and rising. The majority of the labor force is employed in low productivity activities or subsistence agriculture. Manufacturing production is limited. Indeed, the economy is unable to generate enough jobs or output to meet domestic demand, thus leading to migration and even loss of the most skilled human capital, such as doctors and nurses who leave for jobs in advanced industrialized countries—a process called "brain drain."

There were 731 million people (or 9.9% of the world's population) living on less than $1.90 a day in 2015 (World Bank, 2020). International organizations and governments use this value as the international poverty line to measure extreme poverty—originally, this was set at $1 a day but has been adjusted for price variations over time. In 2015, most extremely poor people lived in South Asia (217 million) and sub-Saharan Africa (413 million). It is important to remember that living above the $1.90 a day poverty line does not mean that people do not still face poverty and hardship. Even those living above this poverty line can quickly fall through it due to unexpected circumstances such as long-term illness, disability, drought, or war. Considering this, two additional thresholds are set at $3.60 and $5.50 a day. We can think of these as two-times and three-times the absolute poverty line, respectively. In 2015, the number of people living on less than $5.50 a day was 3.4 billion or 46% of the world's population (World Bank, 2020). Since the end of World War II, the share of people living in extreme poverty has decreased continuously. This is correlated with overall improvements in health and education (Deaton, 2013). Sadly, because of population growth, the absolute number of individuals living in poverty increased from almost 3 billion in 1980 to 3.4 billion in 2015, even though the number in percentage terms declined.

As development goals are met, the attention of international actors—including other governments, international organizations, foundations, and NGOs—turns to consolidating achievements and addressing remaining and emerging challenges. Moreover, there is growing awareness that challenges affecting underdeveloped countries can spread rapidly worldwide. An outbreak of Ebola virus in East Africa, for example, led to a complex international mobilization to address it. Civil war in the Middle East and gang violence in Central America result in thousands of refugees attempting very perilous journeys in search of safety. Many governments are fragile and fall apart as they fail to exercise sovereign power effectively. They lack the ability to control events within their national borders. They are highly vulnerable to dissolution or fragmentation due to corruption, transnational crime, terrorism, and civil war. We call such states failed states. As of 2019, Somalia, Syria, Yemen, South Sudan, and Democratic Republic of the Congo were among them (Fund for Peace, 2019). Failed states pose a threat not only to their own people but also to the international system as they can become safe havens for transnational crime, piracy, and terrorism.

Post-War Development Initiatives

Development became an international priority in the aftermath of World War II and no other country had as much influence over development initiatives as the U.S. did. Emboldened by the success of the **Marshall Plan** (1948–1951), President Truman made economic and technical assistance to underdeveloped countries a key U.S. national interest in his inaugural address in January 1949 (Mazower, 2013). The U.S. held a unique position in international organizations, such as the UN and its main agencies (FAO, UNESCO, WHO, ILO), and in the economic organizations of the post-war era (GATT, IMF, and World Bank). Moreover, the U.S. government could count on the expertise of U.S. charities, missionaries, universities, private foundations, and private corporations to help underdeveloped countries (Mazower, 2013). M. Mazower claims there was "an anxious ideological subtext to the American embrace of developmentalism" (Mazower, 2013, p. 285). The rise of development assistance was part of U.S. foreign policy and strategic initiatives to contain Communism during the Cold War. Official development assistance (ODA) relied on the role of governments both directly (government-to-government aid) and indirectly (aid through multilateral organizations). The motivations behind ODA were not entirely altruistic (Lancaster, 2008). ODA donors sought to contain the spread of Communism, reassert spheres of influence in former colonies, promote the donors's own exports, or secure donors's access to raw materials (Lancaster, 2008).

Increasingly, the UN became the main center of global development initiatives. The UN Development Programme was created in 1965. The first UN Development Decade was launched in 1961, followed by the second in 1971, the third in 1981, and, finally, the fourth in 1991. In 1987, the UN adopted the notion of sustainable development that is "development that meets the needs of the present without compromising the ability of future generations to meet their own needs" (UN). In 1992, the Earth

Summit included for the first time the participation of NGOs. In 2000, the Millennium Declaration aspired to combine these previous efforts into a single, comprehensive approach. The result was the Millennium Development Goals (MDGs). The MDGs promote poverty reduction, education, maternal health and gender equality; they also aim at combating child mortality, AIDS, and other diseases. Underdeveloped countries pledged to adopt institutional reforms to increase good governance, transparency, accountability, decentralization, and participation, and to invest in their people through health care and education. Advanced industrialized countries have pledged to support them, through aid, debt relief, and fairer trade.

There are eight MDGs to be achieved by 2015, which break down into eighteen quantifiable targets that are measured by forty-eight indicators. They are:

- Goal 1: Eradicate extreme poverty and hunger;
- Goal 2: Achieve universal primary education;
- Goal 3: Promote gender equality and empower women;
- Goal 4: Reduce child mortality;
- Goal 5: Improve maternal health;
- Goal 6: Combat HIV/AIDS, malaria and other diseases;
- Goal 7: Ensure environmental sustainability; and
- Goal 8: Develop a Global Partnership for Development.

Although there was substantial progress, depending on the goals and the region, the UN launched the Agenda 2030 or the Sustainable Development Goals (SDGs) in 2015 to capitalize on the renewed spirit of cooperation of the international community and keep the momentum going. This much more ambitious initiative consists of seventeen goals focusing on poverty, gender equality, and sustainable development.

The scope and composition of development aid has evolved since the 1960s (Lancaster, 2008). Since then, a long list of new issues has been added, including conflict resolution and prevention environmental sustainability, strengthening civil society, and stopping the spread of HIV/AIDS. Development assistance has now changed from a government-dominated activity to a private one. An explosion in the number of NGOs illustrates this change. Changes also include a dissatisfaction with orthodoxy and one-size-fit-all approaches, with pragmatism being welcome. There is growing understanding that neither state nor market can provide solutions by themselves. Both have to work together. Finally, while modernization was expected to lead to a shift away from religious beliefs toward science and reason as values, this expectation was not fulfilled. And, in fact, cultural factors (religion in particular) add a degree of complexity to development experiences.

The Aid Debate

After many decades and billions of dollars spent, foreign aid has failed to spur sustained development and end global poverty. As noted above, foreign aid during the Cold War had an overtly political dimension, but in recent decades, there has been greater emphasis on providing aid to the neediest countries and on spurring development and ending poverty, as exemplified by the MDGs. Does this failure stem from a lack of commitment, or does aid itself just make the problem worse?

Foreign aid is premised on the idea that underdeveloped countries are trapped in poverty by factors outside their control. Economist Jeffrey Sachs explains the existence of a poverty trap in which poverty itself begets poverty. Because poor people lack access to education, infrastructure, and healthcare, they have no choice but to provide for their own daily sustenance. They cannot save any money or invest, so they cannot innovate or start businesses; consequently, nothing changes. This is especially problematic in countries with rough terrain and dispersed populations, as well as those with predatory governments and who are suffering from conflict. Bad luck has prevented these countries from saving and investment, but a "big push" of foreign aid can provide the infusion of capital that lays the groundwork for development. Unfortunately, this approach has not worked. Why not?

Critics, like economist William Easterly, argue that aid from foreign sources is incapable of doing much good and likely only does harm. His argument is that distant economists and aid workers from different countries cannot know what local people really need. The incentive of the aid community is simply to pour money on the problem without much regard for what happens next. Further, a large portion of aid money never reaches the targeted countries but instead pays expenses of aid organizations. When aid plans fail, new plans are created and millions more dollars pledged. Easterly considers this behavior a new kind of imperialism and recommends taking a hands-off approach and letting developing countries work out their own solutions.

Defenders of aid like Sachs, on the other hand, argue that the real problem with aid is that there has not been enough of it. There is not a big enough commitment to providing the kind of aid that is necessary to end the poverty cycle illustrated above. Previously, aid went directly to governments, often more with the aim of keeping allies on the side of the donors than really helping those who needed it most. The aid recipients were sometimes corrupt and authoritarian governments, which would squirrel away the money in the bank accounts of the elites. These behaviors have produced a negative perception of ODA as a drain on the public finances of donors' countries as well as contributed to donor fatigue. In fact, the public in donor countries tends to vastly overestimate the percentage of the public budget dedicated to ODA.

Further aid advocates argue that aid distribution is far smarter now. More aid bypasses governments and is given to local NGOs that might be better informed about how best to spend it and, as noted above, good governance has been incorporated into the aid calculus, so governments have an incentive to clean up corruption.

Moreover, even critics of aid will concede that aid efforts have produced notable successes, such as in reducing certain kinds of diseases. For Sachs, the greatest problem lies in the lack of will among donor countries to commit to the elimination of poverty.

To others taking a middle ground perspective, the debate over foreign aid has suffered from an excess of abstraction; treating foreign aid as a single category overlooks the myriad different types of aid and the many different influences that determine whether aid is effective. Given the wide range of approaches to and outcomes in foreign aid distribution, it is impossible to provide a simple answer to the question "Does aid work?" Instead, the aid community can far more successfully answer concrete questions about particular efforts, such as, under what circumstances do bed nets most effectively prevent malaria (Banerjee & Duflo, 2011)? Thus, our focus should not be on a "big push" that simply maximizes aid dollars or on casting doubt on the effectiveness of aid altogether in a way that would discourage the international community from making poverty reduction a central goal for the international community. This discussion raises the question of what scholars have identified as the causes of development and underdevelopment. The following section will focus on the theories of development.

Theories of Development and the Causes of Underdevelopment

One way to look at development is to approach it as a process over an extended period rather than a snapshot at a particular moment in time. Thus, it is important to consider when and where current development problems originated. Are these problems the product of internal factors, such as an authoritarian culture, an acquiescent religion, or predatory institutions? Or are these problems the result of external factors, such as foreign domination from the colonial era, exploitation by MNCs, or austerity programs imposed by multilateral credit agencies? Social scientists disagree over the underlying causes of underdevelopment and the most appropriate pathway to change. They disagree on whether or not a single theory can explain the diversity and complexity of underdeveloped countries. Still, this is a critical consideration, as theory helps explain what development is and how best to achieve it, and, consequently, who should be involved.

The **idea** of development as political or social change is a constant in Western political thought at least since classical Greece (Halperin, 2013). Certainly, the capacity to organize social activity to achieve development is a political enterprise. However, development as a theory and purposeful strategy has its beginnings in the post-war era (Halperin, 2013). Paramount among academic efforts is **modernization theory**. Under modernization theory, scholars (especially of the U.S.) ventured to recast Western experience as universal and capitalism and the nation-state as inevitable. Modernization, westernization, and industrialization became interchangeable with development. Sandra Halperin (2013) highlights the problematic intellectual roots of this approach. As she points out, the notion of a bifurcation in the development trajectory of nations originated in mid-nineteenth century Western Europe and is punctuated with racial supremacy, imperialism, and historical determinism overtones. Much of the writing of modernization theory scholars went into justifying the legitimacy of European rule (and neo-Europes like the U.S. and Australia) over the rest of the world. In 1945, as U.S. scholars launched modernization theory, development was then understood to mean capitalism, democracy, and nationally coherent states.

However, the lack of progress and the evident differences between the advanced, industrialized countries and the underdeveloped ones promoted new theoretical perspectives, some of which originated within the developing world itself. Under the auspices of the UN, which was emerging as the site of competing visions to U.S. ideas as discussed above, Latin American scholars advanced an alternative to modernization theory. During the 1950s and 1960s, two distinct arguments emerged: the first became known as the structuralist or *Cepaliano* approach and the other as dependency theory. Further critiques appeared in the 1970s and 1980s, mostly criticizing the imperialistic and Eurocentric nature of development studies of the post-war era. Post-Colonial theories and subaltern studies placed emphasis on previously ignored variables such as race, class, and identities (i.e., the "others" in global development) (Halperin, 2013).

Modernization Theory

Modernization theory is an attempt to establish a model for understanding universal patterns of change. It is a model applicable to the development of the entire planet. It assumes that Western values are universal values. According to this theory, all societies go through the same process, and their progression is fixed and linear. The early modernizers (i.e., Western Europe and North America) piloted the way; the late comers will follow the same path. Based on the European definition of development, scholars such as Talcott Parsons, Samuel Huntington, Gabriel Almond, G. Bingham Powell, Sidney Verba, and Lucian Pye were generally optimistic about the prospects for political and economic development . They argued that all Western, industrialized democracies were underdeveloped once; underdeveloped countries were bound to follow their path. For example, in *The Stages of Economic Growth: A Non-Communist Manifesto* (1960), W. W. Rostow argued that, once sufficient capital is accumulated, these countries will start a process of self-sustained growth that he called "take-off." Thus, the main cause of underdevelopment is lack of capital and is an internal cause. International actors, such as governments, international organizations, and multinational corporations (MNC), can help by providing much needed capital in the form of foreign aid, loans, and direct investment. The implications are that underdeveloped countries must create modern political and economic institutions to replace traditional institutions. They need to acquire modern cultural values and be universalistic, rather than ethnic or family based—thinking beyond their own family or village, choosing their staff and employees based on merit rather than family or tribal connections. Modern cultural values emphasize the possibility and desirability of change instead of fatalism. Scholars identified education, urbanization, and mass media as agents and catalysts of this change. Foreign aid, technical assistance, Peace Corps volunteers, and Western missionaries would spur development by diffusing modern ideas from advanced, industrialized societies.

Economist W. Arthur Lewis argued that contrary to this assumption, countries did not fully move from traditional societies to modern ones, but elements of both coexist side by side at the same time. This is the **dualism theory**. A traditional sector—rural, personalistic, custom-based, resistant to change—and a modern sector—urban, rational, universalistic, individualistic, legalistic, institutional, accepting of change—coexist in the same society at the same time. The idea of a dualism within societies gained considerable attention in academic circles even among critics of modernization theory. More importantly, the dichotomy could be usefully applied to analyze other aspects of society, for example, to explain why some groups of workers were resistant to change.

There are a number of problems with modernization theory. At the heart of the theory is the optimistic belief in continuous progress. Change is change for the better. The end point of the modernization process is present-day Western countries. It does not explain the causes of underdevelopment or the lack of development. Underdevelopment is an original condition akin to all societies. However, the Western experience did not come out of nowhere. It took a long and painful process to disrupt old, traditional ways of life. Moreover, the notion that underdevelopment can be ascribed to an internal feature of underdeveloped countries assumes these countries are autonomous and not conditioned by external factors. It deflects the attention away from the links between underdeveloped countries and their modern counterparts and the legacy of colonial exploitation and imperialism. In spite of these problems, modernization theory contributed to break ground for studying underdeveloped countries. Later, the optimism of the modernization approach was supplanted by profound pessimism, as shown by dependency theory.

Structural Theory

The search for other ways to explain underdevelopment turned to new approaches, henceforth originating among scholars of underdeveloped countries. Working in the UN regional commission for Latin America (called CEPAL in Spanish) during the 1940s, Argentine economist Raul Prebisch led a group of Latin American scholars in formulating an explanation known as the deteriorating terms of trade theory. He argued that a free-trading international system condemned Latin American countries to specialize in the production of natural resources, such as agricultural and mineral commodities. These countries exported primary products that faced falling prices in international markets and, thus, falling income in the long term while they imported more expensive manufactured goods. This structural imbalance relegated them to the periphery of the world economy, while the countries of the core continued to reap the benefits of international trade. As a solution, *Cepalianos* advocated industrialization behind protective barriers, the creation of regional trading blocs, and the formation of commodity cartels.

Dependency Theory

In the 1950s and 1960s, a new approach known as the **dependency theory** emanated from Latin America. The basic assumption is that the underdevelopment of Latin American, African, and Asian countries is the result of the development of North American and Western European countries. These opposite realities are the two sides of the same coin. According to one of the main authors of this theoretical perspective, A. G. Frank (1969), advanced, industrialized countries were never underdeveloped; instead, they were un-developed. The capitalist development of North America and Western Europe creates the underdevelopment of the rest of the world through exploitation. The starting point is imperialism, viewed as a combination of economic expansion and political domination. Colonialism and imperialism (and later, neocolonialism) have shifted the process of capitalist exploitation from the industrialized economies to the economies of the underdeveloped countries. Political and military might are used to establish control over the means of production in foreign lands, benefitting the elites of the advanced, industrialized countries and their partners in underdeveloped countries. Thus, the main cause of underdevelopment is external and results from foreign domination and exploitation.

Underdeveloped countries are limited in their capacity to respond to forces in the global economic order. The advanced, industrialized countries (i.e., the core) condition the responses of the underdeveloped countries (i.e., the periphery) and limit the options for autonomous development. Political and economic domination renders underdeveloped countries vulnerable. They are unable to alter the basic structural characteristics of production.

Dependency means that a country cannot find its own dynamic process of development within its national economy. The domestic groups holding on to power are the main beneficiaries of their ties to the core and have no interest in altering the source of their power. These elites backed by foreign powers maintain a political and economic system that benefits the few at the expense of the many. The position of underdeveloped countries is weak. Indeed, the international system continually conspires to reproduce their underdevelopment. Long after they gained formal independence, underdeveloped countries continue to be sources of cheap raw materials and consumers of manufactured goods. They are dependent on external economic factors (such as markets, loans, and technology) beyond their control.

The alternative, according to advocates of dependency theory, is between continued dependency or socialist revolution. Still others advocated solidarity among underdeveloped countries or economic autarky. Fernando Henrique Cardoso suggests a more nuanced possibility that he calls **Associated Dependent Development**. He argues that governments can leverage state intervention to achieve industrialization and economic growth. The state can become an arbiter between domestic groups and multinational corporations and manage an associated development process which nevertheless remains dependent on external forces.

Neoliberal Theory (Washington Consensus)

In the late 1980s and early 1990s after decades of poor economic performance and increased state intervention, there was widespread support for reform throughout the developing world. Scholars borrowed from tenets of Milton Friedman and Ludwig von Mises to argue that the size and presence of the state in the economy stymied private initiative and halted development. They advocated economic reforms to roll back the state; privatize, deregulate, and launch institutional and bureaucratic reform; and establish clearer property rights. This was a neoliberal approach favored by international financial institutions (IMF, World Bank, Inter-American Development Bank [IADB]) and takes mostly a policy perspective. It assumes that once a country changes its current policies, it will see immediate positive results. History does not play a determining or conditioning role in this view as societies are free to create and shape their own present and future. Because the majority of the actors proposing these ideas were in Washington, D.C., it became known as the Washington Consensus (Williamson, 1989). It reflects changes toward an acceptance of market-friendly ideas at the end of the Cold War. F. Fukuyama (1989) argued that, with the collapse of communism, this was the end of history, and there was no other alternative but democratic market capitalism.

Current Explanations of the Causes of Development

Echoing ideas of previous centuries, modern theorists have continued to appeal to geographic variables to explain differences in global development. The fact that the world's tropical regions are generally poor while temperate regions are wealthier suggests that geography and climate affect development. Landlocked countries and those remote from important economic markets are at a geographical disadvantage. Additional geographical disadvantages are that tropical climates foment higher mortality rates due to diseases, while tropical rains reduce soil fertility. In *Guns, Germs, and Steel* (1997), Jared Diamond argues that, because of geographical characteristics such as continental axis orientation and latitude, tropical environments are less conducive to urbanization and industrialization than are temperate zones. Other scholars like Jeffrey Sachs assign great importance to the burden of tropical diseases in precluding development in sub-Saharan Africa.

As East Asian countries developed rapidly beginning in the 1960s, explanations appealing to cultural, rather than environmental, variables were revived. The "Asian Values" argument grew in popularity in the 1980s. Proponents of this explanation claim that the success of East Asia is due to its culture (i.e., Confucian Ethic). Herman Kahn (1979, p. 247) argues that neo-Confucian cultures create "dedicated, motivated, responsible, and educated individuals" and that their greater sense of commitment and organizational identity and loyalty will result in even higher rates of economic growth than will other cultures. Neo-Confucian cultures emphasize education, harmonious relations, respect for order, collective efforts, and desire to accomplish—all of which provide the right environment for savings and economic growth.

Building on the classical tradition of economics, Daron Acemoglu and James Robinson (2013) argue that political and economic institutions have a causal effect on development. Institutions can be defined as systems of rules both formal and informal that structure social interactions. Informal rules include social conventions and cultural norms that have become established and accepted as rules. For example, rule of law (equality under the law) and private property are two key institutions. Institutions create incentives. They establish and clarify the rules of the game and level the playing field. The test is how and when institutions become embedded in society. Durable institutions can create stable expectations; once established they order expectations and create consistency. Institutions both constrain and enable behavior. The existence of rules and regulations is not necessarily lack of freedom. Rules and regulations may enable choices and actions that otherwise would not exist. For example, titles recognizing property rights facilitate credit creation (i.e., collateral loans). Societies that lack a strong clearing house system of property rights also lack deep credit systems; they become mostly cash economies. In these contexts, a critical service (financial assistance) is missing. Entrepreneurs end up relying on "family" savings to start a business instead of banks or financial firms; consequently, development atrophies. The following section discusses the different policies and strategies that countries have followed in the pursuit of development.

Development Policies and Strategies

This section discusses the search for and performance of different strategies of development pursued by underdeveloped countries during the twentieth century. According to Albert Hirschman (1970), policy makers face three typical choices: voice, loyalty, and exit. The first strategy, **voice**, means that states can attempt to change the system from within. They can attempt to change the balance of the ties with the international system and seek new rules and a new deal. The second strategy, **loyalty,** entails deepening the integration to the international system. States seek to stay in the system, accepting the rules and trying to excel in what they do with what they have. The final choice, **exit,** is to withdraw from the international system and attempt to develop using one's own resources without relying on the international system (autarky). We can apply this model to analyze the post-war experience of developing countries.

Import Substitution Industrialization (ISI)

During the 1930s and 1940s, several Latin American countries launched a state-led industrialization strategy known as **import substitution industrialization (ISI).** Influenced by the structuralist ideas of Prebisch and *Cepalianos,* Latin American governments sought to move away from reliance on primary production and toward urban manufacturing. They introduced a set of policies that reduced imports and encouraged domestic manufacturing, often through trade barriers, subsidies to manufacturing, and state ownership of basic industries.

It is important to note that the trade disruptions associated with the Great Depression and World War II were a critical historical context of this strategy. Thus, the choice to exit the global economy was not entirely of their own making but the result of external factors. As demand from Europe and North America dried up, Latin American countries were unable to earn export earnings with which to pay for imported goods. Import bills kept rising while exports kept falling. Substituting imports with local production would achieve industrialization and, at the same time, save precious hard currency. Moreover, the early industrializers in Latin America (Argentina, Brazil, and Mexico) had relatively large internal markets. There was scope for import substitution because they did not produce everything they consumed.

African and Asian countries pursued industrialization after decolonization. We must understand that development became synonymous with industrialization, particularly urban manufacturing industrialization. When they considered the development experience of industrialized countries, the leaders of these newly independent countries realized that European and North American countries had grown rich by shifting from agriculture to manufacturing. In this vision, development and modernization became associated with urbanization and industrialization.

The state played an essential role in ISI. Governments introduced incentives to draw investors into the manufacturing sector. Foremost, governments erected trade barriers (such as high tariffs, quotas, and import and export prohibitions) to protect domestic manufacturers. Economic protection was conceived as a temporary measure. Once firms matured into established producers, these protective measures would be phased out. This is known as **infant-industry protection**. Governments extended loans and cheap credit to manufacturers (or required private banks to do so). Government provision of industrial services at reduced prices, including electric power, water, and transportation, worked as an indirect hidden subsidy. In addition, the state sought to stimulate domestic demand for industrial goods through redistributive income policies and expand the purchasing power of the population.

ISI relied on cutting ties with the world and thus exhibited features of an exit strategy. Governments imposed trade restrictions to keep out foreign competition and allow domestic industries to grow behind protective walls. However, governments continued to encourage foreign direct investment in the forms of MNCs, to borrow from international markets, and to import technology. Therefore, scholars and analysts refer to this situation as a semi-closed economy.

ISI worked over the short term and for such light industries as food, textiles, clothing, footwear, and furniture. By the 1970s, most of the larger economies pursuing ISI had achieved self-sufficiency in manufactured products. Brazil and Mexico were exporting increasing volumes of manufactures and earned the label of newly industrializing countries (NICs). However, many of the industries that ISI stimulated were largely inefficient. Consequently, the strategy began to lose favor.

Over the long term, the weaknesses of ISI became apparent. We can identify many reasons for its failure, the first of which was inefficiency. Because markets were not big enough, firms were left with idle capacities. Moreover, industries were saturated with too many firms to share in a small market. Selling to a small, stagnant market reduced producers' gains from economies of scale. The second cause of its failure was obsolescence. External tariffs were so high that they kept competition out of the market and created expensive, poor quality, and obsolete products. Protected markets reduced competitiveness. Because producers did not have to compete with world markets, they were unable to export without government support. This led to corruption, including the bribing of state officials for support, and aggravated budget deficits. Finally, technology changed rapidly and countries were not able to keep up with new technology or found it too expensive to acquire.

From a political perspective, enthusiasm for ISI dissipated. The social and political alliances that supported the model fell apart in the 1970s and 1980s. Repeated economic cycles of boom and bust, political instability, and social unrest undermined the legitimacy of the political system. Urbanization and manufacturing had created structural and institutional imbalances. An urban bias treated agriculture unfairly and hurt farmers—the poorest of the poor in most underdeveloped countries—leading to mass internal migrations. The debt crisis of the early 1980s dealt a fatal blow to ISI. During the 1990s, the majority of countries in Latin America, sub-Saharan Africa, and South Asia turned to re-joining the global economy.

Export Oriented Industrialization (EOI)

While much of the developing world pursued inward-oriented policies under ISI, a group of East Asian countries pursued an approach that relied on integration with global markets. While still favoring industrialization, they focused on producing for foreign developed markets. Taiwan, South Korea, Hong Kong, and Singapore embraced an export-led growth model called **export oriented industrialization (EOI)**. Their success led observers to label them the Four Tigers (or Dragons) and to upgrade them to the status of NICs.

Governments targeted particular export industries for support with tax breaks and low-interest loans while maintaining that a weak currency helped make their products artificially cheap. By competing in international markets, the strategy forced export industries to produce high quality and technologically advanced goods. These countries succeeded in establishing industries that were competitive in world markets. Initially they focused on light industry, like textiles, footwear, toys, furniture, household appliances, and paper making, but later turned to heavy industry, like steel making, chemicals, shipyards, and automobiles. More recently, they have moved to the production of laptop and personal computers, cell phones, and large-screen TVs.

This strategy has had dazzling results. For example, in 1970, South Korea exports totaled around $385 million. By 1979, its exports skyrocketed to $15 billion. The East Asian countries that pursued this strategy rapidly joined the ranks of the wealthiest economies in the world, raising the question of how they had accomplished it and whether it could be replicated by other developing countries.

Though apparently novel, this was not a new strategy but a classic case of mercantilism wherein governments attempt to expand their power by exporting more than they import. Production is outward oriented for the world market and economies are closely integrated to the world economy (loyalty), but the many features of government intervention in the economy reveal elements of rebalancing the ties with the global economy (voice).

Circumstances unique to these countries might have also played an important role. For one, these countries displayed a significant degree of social control, such as low levels of social inequality, an educated population, a disciplined labor force, cheap but skilled labor, and fiscal discipline. The U.S. assisted the governments in power because of their anti-communist orientation (both Taiwan and South Korea were hot spots during the Cold War). This reinforced a stable political system that foreign investors favored. For similar reasons, governments could restrict and control trade union activity and guarantee low wages to producers, thus preventing the demand for higher wages that would undermine their ability to export cheaply. The state also provided basic infrastructure oriented to export at no cost to the investors.

Like ISI, this strategy had its problems. Once the countries succeeded, everybody tried to either copy them or stop the flow of imports. In other words, protectionism among the advanced industrialized rose against these countries. They became caught between the industrialized world and those countries trying to copy their model. The strategy requires the state to play a delicate balancing act. Governments must control labor demands for higher salaries because it undermines the country's ability to export cheaply. If the strategy is successful, labor will demand better pay, which has the potential to price their products off global markets. Rising costs, at a time when the countries need to reduce them to stay competitive, open the door for other countries to compete with and displace them. States, therefore, must constantly adapt to remain competitive. For example, South East Asian countries like Indonesia, Malaysia, and Thailand followed in the footsteps of the Four Tigers. Moreover, China has replicated the strategy by stepping into all industries at the same time. It might have even more limited applicability when we consider the particular cultural traits described above in the Asian

Values debate. The strategy is likely to work at times and in some cases but not all of the time and for all cases.

New International Economic Order (NIEO)

Until the late 1950s, developing countries had adhered consistently to the rules of the international economic system (loyalty). However, mounting frustration over the lack of benefits to underdeveloped countries led to a growing movement to change the rules. The situation was also changing inside the UN, as more than sixty newly independent countries had joined the organization during decolonization. The UN Conference on Trade and Development (UNCTAD) was established in 1964. Under its auspices, a bloc of underdeveloped countries came together, calling themselves the Group of 77 (G-77). The goal of the G-77 was to use their combined numbers in the UN to negotiate a reform of the international system in favor of the interests of underdeveloped countries. As a result of their efforts, the New International Economic Order (NIEO) was adopted by the UN in 1974. Among the many points included in the NIEO were "fair trade" instead of "free trade," stabilization of world commodity prices, long-term contracts for commodities, preferential access to industrialized countries' markets, break up of shipping and marketing monopolies that traded their products, better loan terms, greater control over MNCs and natural resources, more favorable arrangements for the transfer of technology, debt relief, and the reform of international financial institutions, like the IMF and World Bank.

The NIEO was the most important and profound attempt to change the rules of the international economy. In the climate of the Cold War, the NIEO was supported by the USSR–which had a limited participation in the capitalist economy, after all–but resisted by the U.S. Yet, by the early 1980s, attempts to change the international economic system had failed. The most prominent legacy of the NIEO was the Jubilee 2000 Campaign designed to cancel the foreign debt of the world's most heavily indebted poor countries (HIPCs) by the year 2000. Inspired by the biblical reference to debt forgiveness during the year of Jubilee, the initiative received broad support from world personalities, including Pope John Paul II, the Dalai Lama, British Prime Minister Tony Blair, U2 band member Bono, Irish artist Bob Geldof, and multiple governments and NGOs. The campaign dovetailed into other efforts under the MDGs. Although it did not cancel the entire foreign debt of the HIPCs, it did reduce it significantly by two thirds.

Cartel

Although generally referred to as cartels, they are in fact international governmental organizations (IGOs) uniting commodity-exporting countries. Examples include the Organization of Petroleum Exporting Countries (OPEC) (established in 1960), the International Coffee Organization (in 1963), the Intergovernmental Council of Copper Exporting Countries (in 1967), the International Sugar Organization (in 1968), the Union of Banana Exporting Countries (in 1974), and the Association of Iron Ore Exporting Countries (in 1975). These IGOs have a permanent bureaucracy, constituting charter, regular budget, physical presence, and diplomatic status. Their goals are to stabilize prices, revert declining export revenues, prevent boom-and-bust cycles, and leverage solidarity among producers and exporters as a negotiating tool in international forums. To accomplish these goals, they favor supply restrictions through lower production quotas for member states and, thus, lower exports in order to increase international prices. In other words, the strategy (voice) is to rebalance the relationship between commodity-producing and commodity-consuming countries. The aim is to redistribute income between these two groups in favor of commodity producers.

The most successful cartel is OPEC. During the 1970s, OPEC managed to raise oil prices from $3 a barrel in 1970 to $12 in 1973 and to $40 in 1979. Why? It enjoyed certain unique characteristics. Oil was (and is) a strategic resource that was difficult to substitute in the short-term. The cartel involved few actors, so it was easy to identify the cheating party and a strong political bond held them together (pan-Arab nationalism, anti-U.S. sentiments, and anti-Zionism).

The relative success of OPEC obfuscates the generally poor record of other international commodity organizations. Cartels overall faced too many challenges because of their large and geographically disperse memberships, lack of a unifying cultural or ideological motive, or new synthetic materials easily substituted for natural products. The foreign debt crisis of the 1980s and commodity supply gluts signaled the end of further initiatives to bring commodity-producing countries together. During the 1990s, the emphasis shifted to neoliberalism, state retrenchment from the economy, and reliance on the market mechanism to determine supply and prices. Today, world trade is less about commodity trade than about intra-industry trade and technology flows. This presents further risks of marginalizing developing countries.

The Washington Consensus and Its Impact on Development

The debt crisis of the 1980s left many underdeveloped countries vulnerable. In return for financial assistance to restructure their debts, they had to change their development approaches toward market-friendly policies. The IMF and World Bank negotiated conditionality agreements also known as structural adjustment programs (SAPs). These agreements require states to remove trade barriers (trade liberalization), sell state enterprises to private investors (privatization), deregulate markets and remove barriers to foreign investment (open up economy), and reduce inflation and budget deficits (restrictive fiscal and monetary policies). Since the 1980s, the IMF and World Bank have negotiated hundreds of adjustment agreements with more than 100 countries in Latin

America, Africa, the Middle East, and South Asia. During the financial crisis of 1997–1998, even East Asian countries sought IMF assistance. These policies were also embraced by former communist countries in Eastern and Central Europe as they moved away from central planning toward market economies in the 1990s.

Both for international and domestic reasons, underdeveloped countries turned away from economic nationalism and autarky toward globalization. After decades of poor economic performance and instability, there was widespread domestic support for reform. Powerful business groups came to oppose state intervention in the economy and sought to develop opportunities overseas by integrating with the world economy. However, it became quickly apparent that the promised immediate positive results were not materializing. Thus, the initial optimism turned into discontent and an anti-globalization backlash. Even under structural adjustment, the external debt burden of some countries continued to worsen. Moreover, the social costs of the economic adjustments— widening income inequality, unemployment, reduced public services, elimination of food and basic items subsidies—have fallen inordinately on the lower segments of society. Popular anger erupted in sometimes-violent demonstrations and riots. Faced with this opposition, governments abandoned adjustment agreements or were toppled. Openness to global markets have rendered some developing countries vulnerable to debilitating financial crises; Mexico, Thailand, Argentina, and Turkey experienced sharp contractions during the 1990s and 2000s. This anti-globalization backlash has taken the form of a return to state intervention in the economy as an alternative to the neoliberal Washington Consensus that some authors have dubbed the Beijing Consensus. The Beijing Consensus refers to a political and economic development model in which the state plays a more active role to organize economic activity while relying less on market mechanisms.

Regional Trading Blocs

During the 1990s and 2000s, there was a flurry of regional trade agreements involving underdeveloped countries. In some of them, member states agreed to remove most or all trade barriers. This was a sign that most underdeveloped countries had abandoned attempts to close their economies and opted to integrate into global markets under existing trade rules. The GATT/WTO provided the framework for these negotiations in which free trade was the norm. For example, Mexico joined the GATT in 1986 and signed the North America Free Trade Agreement (NAFTA) with the U.S. and Canada in 1994. During the 1990s, the EU signed trade agreements with countries along the Mediterranean Sea (Morocco, Tunisia, Israel, Jordan, and Turkey) and with their former colonies in Africa, the Caribbean, and the Pacific in 2000 (Cotonou Agreement). Among the examples of South-South cooperative efforts, we find the Southern Cone Common Market (Mercosur) signed by Argentina, Brazil, Paraguay, and Uruguay in 1991 and the Pacific Alliance signed by Colombia, Chile, Mexico, and Peru in 2011. In 1992, the Association of South East Asian Nations (ASEAN) established as a free trade area. In 2018, the African Continental Free Trade Agreement was signed. Some of these initiatives seek to replicate the success of the EU experience and achieve not only economic gains but also a more favorable political standing as a bloc to negotiate in international forums.

Exit

If voice and loyalty do not work, perhaps the alternative is to leave the system altogether. Historically, when the links to the industrialized countries were severed, underdeveloped economies fared well. Thus, underdeveloped countries could attempt to develop on their own and enjoy the fruits of autarky. This alternative is very costly and usually adopted because of a great upheaval, such as war or revolution. Countries cannot completely isolate themselves from the world economy. The few countries that attempted it did not fare well, such as China between 1949 and 1979, Cuba since the end of Soviet assistance in the 1980s, and North Korea since the Korean War.

Development is a multifaceted concept that encompasses a wide range of processes including not only economic growth but also social and environmental dimensions. While levels of development have long differed across countries, the promotion of development became a central international concern in the twentieth century. Decolonization after World War II brought with it the realization that the newly independent countries faced difficult odds in their attempts to close the development gap with advanced industrialized countries. International initiatives involving governments, international organizations, and private actors began to take shape particularly after the 1960s. Ideas about how to achieve development honed in the minds of policy-makers, activists, and scholars. After more than five decades, results have been mixed. Extreme poverty declined dramatically and health, sanitation, and education improved overall. Yet, significant deficits in closing the gender gap, rural-urban gap, and rich-poor gap within countries persist. Moreover, only a handful of countries, the so called East Asian NICs of South Korea, Singapore, and Taiwan managed to achieve sustained economic growth allowing them to close the gap with advanced industrialized countries. Despite decades of work, countries of the Global South continue to struggle with the challenges of achieving development.

References

Acemoglu, D. & Robinson, J. (2012). *Why nations fail: The origins of power, prosperity, and poverty.* New York, NY: Crown Publishing Group.

Banerjee, A. & Duflo, E. (2012). *Poor economics: A radical rethinking of the way to fight global poverty.* New York, NY: Public Affairs.

Deaton, A. (2013). *The great escape: Health, wealth, and the origins of inequality.* Princeton, NJ: Princeton University Press.

Diamond, J. (1997). *Guns, germs, and steel: The fates of human societies.* New York, NY: W. W. Norton & Company.

Easterly, W. (2006) *The white man's burden: Why the west's efforts to aid the rest have done so much ill and so little good.* New York, NY: Penguin Press.

Fukuyama, F. (1989, Summer). The end of history? *The National Interest, 16*, p. 3–18.

Fund for Peace. (2019). Fragile state index, 2019. Retrieved from: https://fundforpeace.org/2019/04/10/fragile-states-index-2019/

Gunder Frank, A. (1969). The development of underdevelopment. In *Development and Underdevelopment: The Political Economy of Global Inequality.*

Halperin, S. (2013*). Re-envisioning global development: A horizontal perspective.* Abingdon, UK: Routledge.

Hirschman, A. (1970). *Exit, voice, and loyalty: Responses to decline in firms, organizations, and states.* Cambridge, MA and London, UK: Harvard University Press.

Kahn, H. (1979). "The Confucian ethic and economic growth." In *Development and underdevelopment: The political economy of global inequality.*

Lancaster, C. (2008, January). The new face of development. *Current History, 107*(705), p. 36–40.

Mazower, M. (2012). *Governing the world: The history of an idea, 1815 to the present.* New York, NY: Penguin Books.

Rostow, W. W. (1955). The five stages of growth. In *Development and Underdevelopment: The Political Economy of Global Inequality*.

Sachs, J. (2006) *The end of poverty: Economic possibilities for our time*. New York, NY: Penguin Books.

United Nations. (2019). *World urbanization prospects 2018: Highlights*. New York.

Williamson, J. (1989). What Washington means by policy reform. In J. Williamson (ed.), *Latin American readjustment: How much has happened*. Washington, D.C.: Institute for International Economics.

World Bank. (2019a). Human development index. Retrieved from: http://hdr.undp.org/en/content/human-development-index-hdi

World Bank. (2019b). World Bank country and lending groups. Retrieved from: https://datahelpdesk.worldbank.org/knowledgebase/articles/906519-world-bank-country-and-lending-groups

World Bank. (2020). *Poverty and shared prosperity 2020: Reversals of fortune*. Retrieved from: https://openknowledge.worldbank.org/bitstream/handle/10986/34496/9781464816024.pdf

Environment and Population

15

Jake Greear & Jennifer Schiff

Abstract

Today's global community faces mounting environmental problems, some of which threaten dire consequences on a planetary scale. In hopes of avoiding ecological devastation, international organizations work collectively to try to solve these issues. This chapter explores that collaborative process by identifying the causes and consequences of ecological problems and highlighting various approaches to solving them. It focuses specifically on explaining the causes and consequences of water scarcity and climate change, two "super-wicked" problems at the center of international conflict and negotiation. The metaphor of the tragedy of the commons shows how fundamental dynamics of human interactions may easily lead to such problems, in which shared resources such as clean air and water are depleted or degraded. These difficulties can be avoided when natural resources are plentiful. Yet, two centuries of exponential growth in global population and economic activity have strained environmental limits. To solve these seemingly intractable problems, the international community has attempted to set common goals, generate norms, and institute policies and treaties to curb the collectively harmful behaviors of international actors. Critics of these efforts argue that they fail because they leave in place a fundamentally unsustainable global economic system premised on the imperative of continual economic growth.

Learning Objectives

- Identify current and significant environmental issues affecting the international community
- Explain the relationship between economic decision-making and global environmental governance
- Apply the tragedy of the commons theoretical model to help explain the causes and future consequences of water scarcity, resource depletion, and global climate change
- Evaluate the effectiveness of sustainable development as a potential solution to global environmental degradation

Ecological catastrophes have plagued many past civilizations. The irrigation systems used by some of the first settled farming communities in Mesopotamia likely led to soil salinization and subsequent collapse of their agricultural economies. Deforestation plagued ancient Greece and Rome. Ecological devastation compounded by drought likely brought the demise of the classical Mayan civilization in Central America.[1]

While environmental problems are not new, not until the early twentieth century did the large-scale ecological effects of industrial economies come to be widely understood. The modern Western environmental movement started at the beginning of the twentieth century. The Dust Bowl, the threat of radioactive nuclear fallout, and the publication of the famous "blue marble" photograph of Earth from space were among the events that brought many in the Global North to appreciate the potential for planetary-scale ecological destruction. Likewise, many in the Global South began to see the environmental damage often caused by Western corporations as a continuation of the cultural destruction they suffered under European colonialism. Today, environmental issues

---

1 For a general discussion of environmental issues in the ancient world, see Diamond (1994). For recent research on environmental factors in the collapse of Mayan civilization, see Kennet and Beach (2013).

are among the foremost security concerns of nation-states around the world, and issues such as global warming are central aspects of international politics.

Many environmental problems occur because resources that are free for all to use—known as **collective** or **public goods**—tend to be under-maintained. Compare, for example, the cleanliness of a public restroom to that of a private one in someone's home. Ecologist Garret Hardin used the **tragedy of the commons** metaphor to argue that many environmental problems result not necessarily from bad behavior but simply from rational behavior (Hardin, 1968). Why should someone shoulder the cost of maintaining a resource, or abstaining from over-using it, when they will have to share the benefits with others who can "free ride" without contributing their own efforts? When a majority thinks this way, public goods such as unpolluted air, healthy watersheds, or even the stability of the global climate can easily come to ruin. As Hardin put it, "freedom in a commons brings ruin to all" (Hardin, 1968, p. 1244).

Those who study environmental politics point to a few different general approaches to solving tragedy of the commons-type problems. Let us consider the example Hardin used of villagers sharing a common pasture and facing the problem of over-grazing. One solution is governmental regulation. The villagers could set up a central authority to punish those who graze too many cows. Another approach is privatization, or dividing common property up into private property. The villagers could fence off the common pasture into private plots and let each farmer look after their own. A third approach is called trust-building or collective stewardship. A real English village in the sixteenth century would likely see common pastures being managed by this method, without strict rules and formal governing structures. The farmers' grazing practices, rather, conform to traditional norms about what it means to be a good farmer and community member. Economist Elinor Ostrom argues that this third way is a crucial strategy, which is used effectively in traditional societies but has been overlooked by Western policy makers and academics (Ostrom, 1990).

This chapter begins by discussing two historical factors that are at the root of many contemporary environmental problems: capitalism and population growth. This discussion is followed by an overview of two key areas of contemporary environmental concern: water scarcity and climate change. The last two sections of the chapter focus on solutions, with a particular emphasis on the vision of "sustainable development" put forth by the UN.

Global climate change, water scarcity, pollution, resource depletion, and other environmental problems pose the following questions: How can we identify which public goods are crucially threatened? Is it appropriate to privatize some common pool resources? When are governmental (or intergovernmental) regulations the best option for managing public goods? In what cases can cooperative and informal, community-based stewardship of the kind Ostrom points to lead to sustainable management of shared resources?

Capitalism

Public goods are sustainable without difficulty as long as they are plentiful. Many environmental public goods only became scarce in the last few centuries. This is because an important series of changes in how food and material goods were made, traded, bought, and sold took place in England and Holland in the 1700s. These changes are known as the Industrial Revolution. This revolution would not have happened without certain changes in how Europeans thought about property ownership, trade, and what sorts of obligations members of society owed one another. In medieval Europe, property rights were held in conjunction with social and political power. The landholding nobility held their property in a kind of trust, in return for fealty to the monarch, and, by tradition, these landlords also had certain minimal obligations to the peasants who communally worked the land.

Classical liberal political theorists like John Locke challenged the class-based, hierarchical power structures of feudal Europe in the name of liberty and equality. In the process, these theorists laid the foundation for a much more individualistic society, in which ownership of property was more absolute and obligations to others were negotiated by contracts. Agricultural land in many parts of England, for example, went from being communally used and managed to being privately owned. Peasants were driven off the land, and, in place of their feudal landlords, many were forced to find employment with factory owners in one of the factories emerging outside the larger cities.[2] In this contract-based society, the price paid to former peasants for their labor, as well as the price consumers paid for food and goods, were increasingly set by the "laws" of supply and demand rather than by traditional ideas of what the "just price" may be for a given good or what moral obligations the social classes owed each other. The life of a medieval peasant was often brutal, and this new system brought no immediate relief to the laboring class, as factory owners were ideologically freed from any moral obligations beyond paying contractually agreed upon wages, which were usually sufficient only to stave off starvation.

Nevertheless, this new liberal economic system, then called "capitalism" only by its critics, led to rapid gains in efficiency. **Efficiency**, in economic terms, refers to the value of the goods produced per unit of input. What is input? According to the classical economists Adam Smith and David Ricardo, any good or service that we buy requires some combination of three types of inputs: land, labor, and capital (Smith, 2000). *Land* as input comprises any material resource—whether it be acres of cropland, deposits of crude oil, or iron ore—while *labor* refers to human labor. *Capital* includes machinery, tools, warehouses, or the money owners invest in such

---

2   E. P. Thompson's *The Making of the English Working Class* (1966) offers a detailed look at the sociological effects of the Industrial Revolution in England.

things—essentially, anything besides raw materials and labor that you need to make something of value to people. Carpenters building a log house must put in a lot of labor, but no amount of labor is sufficient without raw materials (trees) and some kind of tools (saws and hammers). These tools are capital, or what Karl Marx called "the means of production." Capitalism gave the owners of the key means of production, that is, factory owners, great incentives to invent new tools and production techniques, which meant the same number of hired laborers could turn ever more raw materials into ever greater quantities of valued goods.

Capitalist economies as we know them are growth economies, and this fact has great implications for the environment. If the needs of consumers had remained static in the decades following the Industrial Revolution, the great increases in efficiency of production may have meant fewer natural resources used. However, whether due to human nature or the magic of modern advertising, the needs and wants of a growing consumer class proved to be limited only by their ability to pay. Demand for goods grew exponentially, and capitalist production had no trouble keeping pace. Thanks to the American-led, post-war, liberal international order, by the end of the twentieth century, capitalist growth economies would spread to nearly every member of the present global community of nation-states, including some nominally communist countries such as China.

While the Chinese economy is subject to more governmental regulation than many Western economies, China has nonetheless adopted an essentially capitalist model of industrialization and trade, with economic growth rates and environmental impacts comparable to those of capitalist economies. As a result of these historical economic developments, today's economies continue to grow at a global average rate of approximately 3.5% of **gross domestic product (GDP)** per year (IMF, 2019, p. 1). In other words, the total dollar value of goods produced and sold globally is exponentially increasing.

As we noted above, land, or natural resources, is part of what is needed to feed this continuing global economic growth. Today, ores, fossil fuels, fertilizer components, and other non-renewable raw materials are mined wherever they exist in extractable concentrations. Net forest cover continues to decline globally due to logging. Industrial farming practices deplete topsoil, and oceans are fished at unsustainable rates. Even sand has become a resource so scarce that illicit "sand mining" is a global problem (UNEP, 2014). Moreover, just as the traditional moral obligations between the social classes in England were largely replaced by contractual legal relationships in the seventeenth and eighteenth centuries, the spread of capitalism globally meant that established norms that may have regulated the use of plants, animals, land, and water in many traditional societies have been increasingly replaced by the Western model of corporate property ownership oriented toward private monetary gain, with few if any stewardship obligations standing in the way of the economic exploitation of land and resources.

Industrial capitalism has, at least for the first few centuries of its existence, brought tremendous gains in average economic prosperity, but these gains in prosperity have come with enormous environmental challenges. Capitalist societies going into the twenty-first century must answer a series of serious questions. Must economies grow indefinitely? Is indefinite economic growth possible on a finite planet? Can we avert the massive predicted disruptions in global climate due to increasing fossil fuel use? To fully appreciate the urgency of these questions, we must consider how the economic growth of the last century has been correlated with a similarly remarkable growth in global population.

Population

Defining Population Momentum

The 7.6 billion people comprising the world's population are distributed across a variety of continents, cultures, and civilizations.

Further, more people inhabit the world today than at any point in history, but what is perhaps even more astonishing is how rapidly global population has grown over the last one hundred years. To illustrate this exponential population growth, consider the following historical trajectory. At the turn of the nineteenth century, fewer than one billion human beings were living on the earth. By the end of the 1800s, the global population had increased to 1.5 billion. By 1960, approximately three billion people inhabited the planet, and, by the year 2000, there were six billion people living on Earth. These numbers are significant because they illustrate the swiftness of twentieth century population growth. In fact, during the 100-year period between 1900 and 2000, world population increased at a rate three times greater than during the entire prior history of human life on earth (Lam, 2011).

Currently, 60% of the world's people live in Asia, 17% in Africa, 10% in Europe, 9% in Latin America and the Caribbean, and the remaining 6% in North America and Oceania. China (with its 1.4 billion people) and India (with its 1.3 billion people) remain the two most populous countries of the world. Together they hold 37% of all people on Earth (UNDESA, 2017b, p. 1). Today global population continues to increase at an exponential rate, albeit at a slower pace than during the twentieth century. This kind of rapid population growth is driven by **population momentum** (UNDESA 2017a). In other words, if a country has a large number of individuals under fifteen years of age, the population of that country will continue to increase for many decades to come, as those young people enter their reproductive years (ages fifteen to forty-nine). In a "momentum" situation, even if the average number of children per woman, or **total fertility rate**, remains constant at a replacement rate average of 2.1, population will continue to rise because the momentum is there for growth (OECD, 2018).

This momentum is apparent in future projections of population. The UN predicts that the world's population will reach 8.6 billion by

2030, 9.8 billion by 2050, and, by 2100, 11.2 billion individuals will live on the planet we call home (UNDESA, 2017b, p. 2).

Variance in Population Growth

Not all countries will contribute equally to the expected growth. Fertility rates vary across states and regions and are influenced by a variety of social, economic, and political factors. The UN projects that half the world's population growth from now until 2050 will be concentrated in just nine countries: India, Nigeria, the Democratic Republic of the Congo, Pakistan, Ethiopia, Tanzania, the U.S., Uganda, and Indonesia (UNDESA, 2017b). This is largely due to the size of their current youth populations and the population momentum that follows.

In contrast, some states will face a steep population decline in the coming years. Japan, for instance, has seen its population shrink significantly in recent decades. Experts predict this decline will continue for at least the next 50 years. Japan's population reduction is due to many different factors, including decreasing fertility rates combined with the country's average life expectancy of 87 years, which is the highest in the world (Reynolds, 2017). Today, for the first time in its history, 28% of all Japanese people are age 65 or older, and this graying of the Japanese population means that fewer children are born and that fewer young people are available to fill career roles essential to the lifeblood of the Japanese economy (Japan Times, 2018). Demographic statistics suggest that this situation is unlikely to change in the near future. The current median age in Japan is 47.3; compare this number with the population giant India with its median age of 27.9 and with the Democratic Republic of the Congo with its median age of 18.6 (CIA World Factbook, 2017).

A Future of 11 Billion

Today people in nearly every region of the world are having fewer children on average, and this is largely due to patterns of **demographic transition**. Demographic transition occurs when a country transitions from higher birth/death rates to lower birth/ death rates over time, due to economic development which brings with it additional career, health care, and educational opportunities (Ranganathan, Swain, & Sumpter, 2015). The phenomenon of population momentum means that even countries moving through the demographic transition may still see higher birth rates due to their large youth populations. In Africa, for instance, the region of the world with the highest fertility levels, total fertility fell from 5.1 births per woman in 2000–2005 to 4.7 in 2010–2015. Despite its ongoing demographic transition, the relatively young populations of many African countries suggest that the region will continue to experience the highest rates of population growth when compared to their global neighbors. As a result, the populations of twenty-six African countries are projected to at least double in size by 2050 (UNDESA 2017b, p. 3).

The UN predicts that, as long as regional youth populations continue to increase, the resulting momentum will lead to a world of 11 billion people by the year 2100 (UNDESA, 2017b, p. 2). Meeting the resource requirements of everyone will present governments with immense policy challenges. Every individual within the global population will need to consume resources to live. As a consequence, they will continue to have a significant impact on their local, regional, and global environments, potentially perpetuating a tragedy of the commons situation regarding the world's air, water, energy, and food supplies.

Water Scarcity

If the earth's population reaches the projected 11 billion people in the near future, all of those individuals will require environmental resources, like water, food, clean air, and energy, to sustain them. A scarcity of these resources could result, presenting a **super-wicked problem** for policymakers to solve. Super-wicked problems have four key features:

1. they need to be solved quickly before a severe crisis develops;
2. a conflict of interest exists in that people using the resources for their own benefit are also the ones who must solve the problem;
3. these problems cross borders and thus require the coordination of many different actors to solve; and
4. there isn't much certainty as to how effective potential solutions will be because they can sometimes take decades to demonstrate benefits (Levin, et al., 2012, p. 124).

Many resources scarcities could qualify as super-wicked problems, and fossil fuel depletion, deforestation, and excess greenhouse gas emissions are but a few examples. Approximately two billion people, or almost one fourth of the world's population, currently live in regions facing **physical water scarcity**, meaning there is not enough water physically available in the local area to meet the needs of the population. Such a water shortage could be caused by drought, changing rainfall patterns due to climate change, or the simple fact of too many people using a limited resource. Another 1.6 billion people face **economic water scarcity**, meaning they reside in regions in which physical water may exist, but that water cannot be utilized because there is insufficient infrastructure to ensure that the water is clean enough for human consumption. Economic water scarcity is a significant problem for human health; each day, nearly 1,000 children die due to preventable water-borne illness, and over two million people each year suffer from illness due to contaminated water (United Nations - Sustainable Development Goals, 2018).

How, then, is water scarcity a super-wicked problem? First, it needs to be solved quickly before water-scarce conditions become even more acute. Water scarcity already exists and will continue to worsen quickly if nothing is done. By 2025, the UN estimates that two thirds of the world's population may live under conditions of physical or economic water scarcity, and climate change could further exacerbate this treacherous water situation to an extent that scientists and governments cannot yet predict with certainty (United Nations – Water 2018).

It is important to note that water scarcity not only affects how much water a human being has to drink or to use for washing, cooking, or sanitation, but it also affects almost every other aspect of life. When a family doesn't have access to enough clean water to care for their daily needs, it is quite common for a member of that family to trek five or six miles a day to the nearest clean water source, fill up a container of water, and then walk that heavy container back to their home. The burden of this task falls disproportionately on women and children, as they are responsible for 80% of water collection (United Nations - Sustainable Development Goals, 2018). When a child spends several hours a day gathering water, she has lost the opportunity to spend that time in school furthering her education. Thus, the lack of water affects economic opportunity, especially for women and children, so it also exacerbates conditions of poverty (UNDP, 2016, p. 74).

Second, water also constitutes a super-wicked problem because, when people need water to live, an inherent conflict of interest occurs when they are asked to cut back on their water usage for the sake of solving the scarcity problem. Agricultural water use is a prime example of the difficulties governments face in trying to solve this problem. Seventy percent of global water usage is utilized for agriculture to ensure food security for human beings (World Bank, 2017). At the same time, the farmers who grow the food make money to feed their families and provide economic support to their communities. Thus, agriculture is a staple of economic health for countries around the world. If governments try to solve the water scarcity problem by asking their agricultural sectors to cut back on water usage, then those same governments may face food insecurity for their citizens or a downturn in their own economies. Overcoming the conflict of interest in this case seems a very difficult task.

Third, water scarcity is often regional or a problem shared by neighboring countries. Even within one country, when different cities and communities share one river's water, those actors may have different incentives to solve the problem, and they may not agree on a coordinated solution. The management of Lake Chad in Africa highlights this issue. Lake Chad is bordered directly by four different countries, Chad, Niger, Nigeria, and Cameroon, and its basin also serves Sudan, Algeria, and the Central African Republic (FAO, 1997, Chapter 6). In 1964, these countries formed the Lake Chad Basin Commission to oversee water use in the basin and coordinate regional actions. Lake Chad was once the sixth-largest lake in the world, but its area has shrunk by over 90% since the start of an ongoing drought that began in the 1970s. The effects of the drought are exacerbated by the overuse of water for irrigation by the same countries that were supposed to be working together within a commission to coordinate their actions. Ultimately, the disappearance of Lake Chad's water has had dire consequences for the region's 30 million people, many of whom depend on the lake for their livelihood as farmers or fishermen (Iceland, 2017, para. 9).

Finally, there are multiple potential solutions to water scarcity, but policymakers and scientists do not agree on the best path forward. In large part, this is because regional variation in water issues means that each local area may require a customized solution, so there is no "one size fits all" approach. Moreover, this is not a problem that can be solved overnight. The international policy community has responded to water scarcity by creating a development goal dedicated to mitigating water-scarce conditions. One of the UN's Sustainable Development Goals is to reach "universal and equitable access to safe and affordable drinking water for all" by 2030, a goal that is estimated to cost at least $114 billion a year to achieve (Chen, Kokler, & Trémolet, 2016, para. 4). The primary challenge to this directive seems to be money, as most "fixes to the world's water woes depend in one way or another on persuading people to pay more for the water they use" (Moore, 2018, para. 6). Potential solutions like desalination of seawater or building more efficient water treatment plants cost an enormous amount of money. To generate the funds for these kinds of technical solutions, governments would likely need to charge people more for their water usage, and there is not enough political will to take that step in most countries—as governments know that doing so could potentially deprive poorer people of water access. It is often easier and more politically expedient to delay decision-making on these tough issues for the years to come, rather than to make the difficult decisions now (Moore, 2018, para. 5).

Water scarcity is an example of a super-wicked environmental problem. Again, the complexity of these kinds of problems can prevent quick and easy solutions. The struggle to provide sufficient clean water mirrors other types of super-wicked resource issues, as well. Global climate change stands as another super-wicked problem for the world to solve and is one that holds potentially dire consequences for the future of human life on earth.

Energy and Climate Change
Global Warming: A Super-Wicked Problem

Climatologists report that 2018 was the planet's fourth hottest year since we started keeping records of global temperature. The hottest year was 2016, and 2015, 2017, and 2018 hold second, third, and fourth place, respectively (NASA, 2019). These are only the latest record-breaking temperatures in a pattern of global warming over the past several decades. Climatologists have recorded an overall increase around 1.5 degrees Celsius from pre-industrial levels, and they expect significantly more in the coming century (Climate Central, 2018).

These global temperature increases were predicted before they were observed. Scientists in the 1800s discovered that certain gases in the earth's atmosphere absorb and trap the heat that radiates from the earth's surface. These gases act something like the glass panes in a greenhouse. They allow the sun's radiation to pass through but trap the longer wavelengths of heat-radiation coming up from the sun-bathed earth. Scientists soon discovered that this greenhouse effect plays an important role in determining the earth's climate. They also recognized the potential for human activity to alter the balance of these gases in the atmosphere and potentially affect the climate. Particularly, scientists suspected that atmospheric levels of carbon dioxide (CO_2), one of the key **greenhouse gases (GHGs)** that regulate earth's temperature, is significantly increased by the widespread use of **fossil fuels** such as coal, oil, and natural gas. When these fuels are burned, carbon dioxide and other greenhouse gases are emitted, and there is now a broad consensus among climate scientists that these emissions are driving the recent warming trend. Furthermore, scientists warn that continued, unchecked global warming is likely to bring major ecological, economic, and geopolitical disruption in the coming century, with rising sea levels and intensification of droughts, heatwaves, wildfires, and storms leading to political instability, large population displacements, and a global refugee crisis (IPCC, 2018).

While scientists and most political decision-makers understand the grave risks of **anthropogenic** (human-caused) climate change, it remains a super-wicked environmental problem that presents an enormous, four-part challenge to policymakers. In the first place, very quick action is needed. The United Nations Intergovernmental Panel on Climate Change (IPCC) warns that failing to significantly reduce global carbon emissions within the next decade is likely to lead to devastating effects in the coming century (IPCC, 2018). Secondly, climate change is a global problem that requires a coordinated response from most, if not all, developed and developing countries.

Third, significantly lowering carbon emissions is expected to be a very expensive undertaking and is, therefore, politically difficult for many countries.

What makes global warming perhaps the most wicked problem of all, however, is its invisibility. While the global climate is already changing, the worst effects of global warming are still expected to be decades away. Global trends such as the dramatic world-wide retreat of glaciers provide clear evidence of warming, but perceiving these changes as the beginnings of a catastrophic, human-caused change in global climate requires statistical analyses and digital projections that organize massive pools of meteorological and geophysical data. In other words, appreciating the gravity of the climate change threat requires either significant scientific literacy or simply trusting scientists.

While most people who are aware of the issue do trust the scientific consensus, a significant percentage of the populations of some countries are either skeptical that global warming is taking place or deny that humans are its cause. Climate skepticism is based on the assertion that climate science is uncertain or "unsettled." In fact, some uncertainty is inevitable in any attempt to model and predict climate dynamics. The uncertainty that does exist in climate science is due largely to **feedback effects**. For example, a warming climate causes ice sheets to melt and recede, revealing the darker earth underneath. The darker surface of the thawing earth absorbs more heat from the sun than did the white ice that once covered it. This creates a positive feedback effect in which the warming of the earth causes more warming of the earth. Due to these positive feedback effects, small changes in the atmosphere's composition can "snowball" into sudden climatic shifts, or "tipping points." Scientists must incorporate many interacting feedback effects into their complex digital models to make climate predictions. This means that those predictions can be expressed only as probabilities, never as certainties.

In spite of the complexities of climate modeling, climatologists have become increasingly certain of the threat climate change poses and of what must be done to mitigate the threat. Around 97% of climate scientists agree that global warming is occurring and is caused by burning fossil fuels (Cook et al., 2016). Many researchers see the uncertainty that persists as cause for more alarm, not less. Things could be much worse than we think. What scientists confidently know is that human-caused greenhouse gas buildup is significantly altering a sensitive climate system with potentially catastrophic consequences for human civilization.

The Global Response

The global response to the climate problem has been slow in coming and thus far has shown limited ability to curb greenhouse gas emissions. The UN made its first major gestures toward addressing global warming in 1992 with the adoption of the Framework Convention on Climate Change (UNFCCC), which almost all member nations have since signed. The UNFCCC is a non-binding resolution which commits signatories to work toward "stabiliz[ing] greenhouse gas concentrations in the atmosphere at a level that would prevent dangerous anthropogenic interference with the climate system" (UNGA, 1994, Article 2). Since 1995, UN member nations have met annually in "conferences of the parties" under the UNFCCC in order to assess progress toward this goal and negotiate further agreements. The first legally binding agreement to come out of the UNFCCC was the **Kyoto Protocol**, which set greenhouse gas reduction targets for several developed countries. The U.S., which then led the world in carbon emissions, conspicuously failed to ratify the Kyoto Protocol, damaging the legitimacy and effectiveness of the agreement.

While the Kyoto Protocol is a success, greenhouse gas emissions continued to grow under the agreement, which was scheduled to expire in 2020. Growing out of negotiations to extend the Kyoto

Protocol, a separate agreement under the UNFCCC was signed at the 21st Conference of the Parties in France in 2015. This treaty, known as the **Paris Agreement**, binds countries to specific greenhouse gas reduction targets and timelines. The targets are set by the nations themselves, with the stipulation that each new reduction target must exceed the previous one (UNFCCC, 2015). While the Paris Agreement lacks enforcement mechanisms beyond "naming and shaming" countries that fail to live up to their commitments—and while the initial targets reductions were not sufficient to stabilize greenhouse gas concentrations—the treaty was still widely hailed as a breakthrough. Unlike the Kyoto Protocol, the Paris Agreement has generated ambitious greenhouse gas reduction commitments from many countries, and brought almost every UN member nation to the table, including, significantly, the U.S., China, and the Global South.

National Responses

The success of the Paris Agreement, or any other global agreement, depends upon serious efforts at the national level. One of the most effective and widely adopted strategies by nation-states is called **carbon pricing**. Carbon pricing refers to any policy that raises the price of greenhouse gas-producing fuels. Such policies incentivize corporations and businesses to invest in "clean" energy sources, such as wind, solar, and hydroelectric power. One approach to pricing carbon is to place a total national limit on greenhouse gas emissions and then allow companies that use fossil fuels to purchase and trade the limited supply of government issued "pollution permits." This is known as **cap-and-trade**, or an emission trading system. The EU's Emissions Trading System (EU ETS) is the largest and most successful cap-and-trade system to date; however, China, Canada, New Zealand, and Australia have also recently passed laws to implement cap-and-trade systems. Many other countries have opted for the bureaucratically simpler carbon tax approach; these countries include Argentina, Mexico, South Africa, and Japan. Canada and many EU countries are combining both approaches (World Bank, 2019b).

Climate change is a classic tragedy of the commons scenario at the global level. In other words, just as the farmers sharing a common pasture must make individual economic sacrifices (limiting the number of cows they graze) for the collective good (pasture health), so also must the nations of the world give up the cheap energy sources that have fueled their economic growth for the collective good of maintaining climate stability. As stated above, addressing climate change entails great cost and economic hardship. However, emerging trends suggest that the tragedy of the commons scenario may apply less and less to the politics of global warming in the future. This is because recent studies suggest that pricing carbon not only does not slow GDP growth but also may, in fact, help economies grow (Siegmeier et al. 2018).

Sweden implemented carbon pricing measures in the early nineties and has seen robust economic growth over the last few decades, while Swedish greenhouse gas emissions have declined by over 20 percent (Government of Sweden, 2019; World Bank, 2019b). Similar trends may be emerging globally. Global greenhouse gas emissions worldwide leveled off from 2014 to 2017 as a few national carbon pricing policies have come online, while global GDP growth continued apace. This hopeful trend ended, however, as emissions began to rise again in 2018. Climatologists warn that global greenhouse gas emission rates must be stabilized and reduced drastically in the coming decades. Doing so will likely require continued strengthening of international agreements, more robust carbon pricing at the national, regional, and provincial levels, and significant investment in clean energy technology.

Sustainable Development
Defining the Concept

The UN's actions to address climate change were not its first major efforts to address global environmental problems. In 1983, nine years before the adoption of the UNFCCC, the UN General Assembly convened the World Commission on Environment and Development (WCED) in response to mounting concerns over pollution, biodiversity loss, and resource scarcity. The WCED comprised politicians, scientists, and policy experts tasked with proposing solutions for ensuring the security and protection of environmental resources into the future. In 1987, after several years of careful consideration, the WCED produced a document entitled *Our Common Future* (commonly known as the Brundtland Report) detailing the Commission's findings. The Brundtland Report provided a comprehensive look at various aspects of the global environment, including the role of international trade, the impact of population growth, the need to achieve food security, human impact on species and ecosystems, the need for additional sources of renewable energy, the challenge of creating sustainable urban spaces, and the need for enhanced technological solutions and international cooperation as a way to address all of these issues.

Perhaps the most lasting impact of the Brundtland Report, however, was its definition for the concept of **sustainable development**, which it described as development that "seeks to meet the needs and aspirations of the present without compromising the ability to meet those of the future" (WCED, 1987, Chapter 1, Section 49). This definition still informs and influences international environmental policy efforts to this day. It is worth noting that the Brundtland Report defines the major objective of development as "the satisfaction of human needs," including the need for food, clothing, shelter, jobs and an improved quality of life (WCED, 1987, Chapter 2, Section 4). This definition is consistent with the UN's historical focus on development that equates quality of life measures with "sustained economic growth" (UNGA 1997, p. 2).

International Goals for Development

One of many ways the UN translated the concept of sustainable development into policy action was through the creation of the **Millennium Development Goals (MDGs)** (see Chapter 14). Announced in the year 2000, the MDGs were a set of specific policy targets created to meet the needs of the world's poorest people and raise the quality of life across the globe. As noted in Chapter 14, the eight original MDGs ranged from halving extreme poverty, to halting the spread of disease, to improving maternal health, to providing universal primary education and empowering women. Each of these goals had a 2015 target for achievement. By the end of the fifteen-year implementation period, however, it was clear that, while progress occurred on each individual goal, there was much more that needed to be accomplished (United Nations, 2015).

To that end, in 2015, the UN announced the creation of the **Sustainable Development Goals (SDGs)**, a set of 17 objectives, broken down into 169 specific measurable targets, and adopted by all UN member states. Taken together, the SDGs are aimed at the eradication of poverty everywhere, as "extreme poverty is the greatest global challenge and an indispensable requirement for sustainable development" (UNGA, 2015, p. 1). More specifically, the SDGs present objectives ranging from achieving zero-hunger to ensuring clean water and sanitation to establishing peaceful and inclusive societies to encouraging responsible consumption and production in the use of environmental resources, with all of this to be achieved by the year 2030 (UNGA, 2015, p. 14).

The UN sees the SDGs as a means for creating safe environmental conditions that ensure the future of humanity and ecosystems, while calling on "governments, international organizations, the business sector, and other non-state actors and individuals" to contribute to changing their unsustainable patterns of consumption and production (UNGA, 2015, p. 8).

Questioning "Sustainable Development"

The UN Sustainable Development Goals provide a comprehensive framework for meeting the environmental challenges of the twenty-first century. Yet, the UN's approach has been criticized by some economists, ecologists, and environmental activists. This final section will explore the viewpoints of those who contend that sustainable development is an inadequate response to environmental challenges. These critics can be sorted into two sometimes overlapping groups: those who argue that we need a more profound transformation of the global economic system and those who argue that what is required is nothing short of a global transformation of human consciousness.

Limits to Economic Growth?

Those advocating a radical transformation of the global economic system point out that the UN SDGs assume that economies can and must continue to grow exponentially. Indeed, SDG #8 on the UN's list includes "sustainable economic growth," with a target gross domestic product (GDP) growth rate of 7% per year for the least developed countries (UNGA, 2015). Free trade, free markets, and economic liberalism has been a core value of the UN since its inception, and, as we noted in the previous section, the UN has historically assumed that, to achieve a high quality of life, countries must continuously grow their economies. Critics argue, however, that economic growth cannot continue forever on a finite planet. Therefore, according to these critics, the whole sustainable development model is based on a fundamental contradiction: they argue that if "development" means growth, it simply cannot be sustainable. The only real path to sustainability, from this perspective, is **degrowth**.

In order for the GDP of a given nation-state to grow annually, the total value of goods and services sold each year must be greater than it was in the previous year. It does not matter what the goods or services are—pizza, cars, subway rides, musical performances—so long as the market value of all the goods and services sold by the people, businesses, or government agencies of that country adds up to a greater value than the year before. Every good or service, as we noted above, requires three types of input: land (e.g., energy and natural resources), human labor, and capital (e.g., tools, machines, and infrastructure). Since the earth's non-renewable resources—such as oil, lithium, or copper ore—are finite, and since the sun's daily renewable energy inputs into the earth system are constant and not increasing, the physicist's conclusion is that the land part of the equation is starkly limited. Eventually, we will encounter resource limits.

The economic question that arises is if we can continue to produce more and more goods and services with less and less energy and raw materials. If we assume that all goods and services require at least *some* input of energy and raw materials to produce, then the physicists' answer, based on the Second Law of Thermodynamics, is that economic growth cannot continue forever.[3] Whether it can be sustained in the near term is a different question. However, given the environmental limits we are already facing in the form of climate change, water scarcity, pollution, and resource depletion, even the near-term viability of the global growth economy is questionable.

To resolve this dilemma, the UN SDGs rely on the idea of "decoupling resource use and environmental degradation from economic growth" (UNDESA 2014). Indeed, **decoupling** has become a buzzword in environmental economics. What the term implies (correctly) is that economic growth is at present strongly

---

3   For further reading on the limits of economic growth, see Daly, H. E., & Farley, J. (2011); Jackson (2009, 2017); Higgs (2014); Ayers (2014); and Mason (2015).

correlated with environmental degradation and the use of non-renewable resources—and has been throughout history. Whether and to what extent decoupling is truly possible, though, remains an open question. Some economists argue that it is possible, based on the assumption that resource inputs into production will approach zero in the future (UNEP, 2011, section 3.1). iPhones, for example, are more valuable than the bulky desktops of twenty years ago, and they use fewer materials to create. Some works of art are very valuable yet require almost no energy or materials to produce.

Since growth economies remain the norm for now, we should hope that economies could achieve less resource-intensive growth, at least in the near term. Yet skepticism on this point is merited, especially in medium and long-term scenarios. If decoupling has hard limits—in other words, if the use of land is always going to be a significant part of the economic growth equation—then economies must at some point stop growing.

Eco-Marxism or Steady-State Capitalism?

Eco-Marxists are among those who advocate degrowth and reject the UN's current approach to sustainable development. Eco-Marxists agree with mainstream economists on one key assumption: that capitalism requires growth. This, however, is where the similarities end. Mainstream economists assume that capitalism must continue; they are likely, therefore, to see decoupling as the only option and the central challenge of the environmental crisis. On the other hand, eco-Marxists assume that capitalism, because it depends on GDP growth, *cannot* continue. From the eco-Marxist perspective, decoupling is a ruse. The only viable solution is to replace capitalism with an altogether different economic system. For eco-Marxists, sustainable development as it is currently conceived is doomed to fail because it does not root out the prevailing economic system that is the true source of environmental problems.

One influential Marxist theorist, David Harvey, argues that the multifaceted environmental crisis is only one of the many inherent contradictions—including cyclical recessions and ever-increasing wealth inequality—that have plagued capitalism since its inception (Harvey, 2014). For Harvey and like-minded Marxists, the solution would be some form of ecologically-oriented socialism in which the private ownership of most natural resources would be significantly curtailed and the for-profit exploitation of resources by private corporations would be replaced by public management of productive processes, whether at the national or local level.

While eco-Marxists are among those who believe economic growth is fundamentally unsustainable, others adhere to the degrowth viewpoint without considering themselves eco-Marxists, nor do they necessarily advocate public ownership of resources and public management of industrial production. A small but growing contingent of ecologically-minded economists, including former World Bank economist Herman Daly and British economist Tim Jackson, have attempted to articulate a middle path between the UN's commitment to perpetual economic growth and the Marxists' rejection of capitalism. These reformists call into question the growth imperative of capitalist economies, arguing that free-market economic systems can work with zero GDP growth or even negative growth.[4] This vision of a **steady-state economy** is, for the moment, outside the mainstream of economic scholarship. Whether the degrowth perspective represents an emerging paradigm shift that will replace sustainable development as the central concept driving environmental policy in the twenty-first century remains to be seen.

Transforming Environmental Consciousness

Where those advocating degrowth criticize the UN's sustainable development approach as an inadequate change to the global eco-

---

4   For research on the possibilities of zero-growth capitalist economies, see Jackson, T., & Victor, P. A. (2015); Malmaeus, J. Mikael and Eva C. Alfredsson (2017); and Barrett, A. B. (2018).

nomic order, other critics go further, arguing that even a revolutionized economic system would not solve environmental problems unless it is accompanied by a similarly radical transformation in how we regard the natural world. The late Norwegian ecologist Arne Naess (1973) coined the term **deep ecology** to describe this more radical perspective. Deep ecologists argue that we will continue to exploit and degrade the natural world—whether we do so through publicly managed economies or free market systems—so long as we continue to see the natural world as existing to serve human needs and thus fail to acknowledge its intrinsic value.

Public opinion about global environmental issues, and about related economic issues, is shifting quickly. It may not be shifting profoundly enough to satisfy deep ecologists; nor does the world appear to be on the cusp of an eco-Marxist overturning of the capitalist order. However, public concern about environmental issues is growing, and where public opinion goes, political leadership is sure to follow—eventually. The question is whether a shift in political leadership will occur too late to mitigate some of the most serious, super-wicked global environmental problems. The assessments of ecologists and climatologists suggest that, as an existential threat to human civilization, environmental disruption and ecological degradation are on par with the risk of thermonuclear war. Just as the human species has the technological ability to destroy itself, so also does humanity undoubtedly possess the technological ability to save itself from ecological ruin. Implementing effective solutions will, however, require more than technological know-how. It will require collective action, trust-building, and diplomacy on the part of far-sighted citizens and leaders. The limiting factor will almost certainly be politics.

References

Ayres, R. U. (2014). *The bubble economy: Is sustainable growth possible?* Cambridge, MA: MIT Press.

Barrett, A. B. (2018). Stability of zero-growth economics analyzed with a Minskyan model. *Ecological Economics, 146*, p. 228–239. https://doi.org/10.1016/j.ecolecon.2017.10.014

BBC News. (2015, October 29). China to end one-child policy and allow two. Retrieved from https://www.bbc.com/news

Central Intelligence Agency. (2018). *World factbook.* Retrieved from https://www.cia.gov/library/publications/the-world-factbook/

Chen, G., Kokler, J., & Trémolet, S. (2016). Tackling the vital challenge of financing the world's water infrastructure needs. *The World Bank – Water Blog.* Retrieved from http://blogs. worldbank.org/water/psd/tackling-vital-challenge-financing-world-s-water-infrastructure-needs

Climate Central. (2018). The globe is already above 1° C, on its way to 1.5° C°. Retrieved from https://www.climatecentral.org/gallery/graphics/the-globe-is-already-above-1c

Cook, J., Oreskes, N., Doran, P. T., Anderegg, W. R., Verheggen, B., Maibach, E. W., . . . & Nuccitelli, D. (2016). Consensus on consensus: A synthesis of consensus estimates on human-caused global warming. *Environmental Research Letters, 11*(4), 048002. https://doi:10.1088/1748-9326/11/4/048002

Daly, H. E., & Farley, J. (2011). *Ecological economics: Principles and applications.* Washington, D.C.: Island Press.

Diamond, J. (2005). *Collapse: How societies choose to fail or succeed.* New York: Viking.

Food and Agricultural Organization (FAO). (1997). *Irrigation potential in Africa: A basin approach.* Rome: FAO. Retrieved from http://www.fao.org/docrep/W4347E/w4347e00. htm#Contents

Government of Sweden. (2019). *Sweden's carbon tax.* Retrieved on May 19, 2019, from https://www.government.se/government-policy/taxes-and-tariffs/swedens-carbon-tax/

Hardin, G. (1968). The tragedy of the commons. *Science, 162*(3859), 1243–1248. https://doi:10.1126/science.162.3859.1243. PMID 5699198.

Harvey, D. (2014). *Seventeen contradictions and the end of capitalism.* New York, NY: Oxford University Press.

Higgs, K. (2014). *Collision course: Endless growth on a finite planet.* Cambridge, MA: MIT Press.

Hunt, T. (2006). Rethinking the fall of Easter Island. *American Scientist, 94*(5), 412. https://doi: 10.1511/2006.61.1002

Iceland, C. (2017). Water stress is helping drive conflict and migration: How should the global community respond? *World Resources Institute.* Retrieved from https://www.wri.org/news/water-stress-helping-drive-conflict-and-migration

International Monetary Fund (IMF). (2019). *World economic outlook update, January 2019: A weakening global expansion.* Washington, D.C. Retrieved from https://www.imf.org/en/Publications/WEO/Issues/2019/01/11/weo-update-january-2019

Intergovernmental Panel on Climate Change (IPCC). (2018). *Summary for policymakers.* In global warming of 1.5°C: An IPCC special report on the impacts of global warming of 1.5°C above pre-industrial levels and related global greenhouse gas emission pathways, in the context of strengthening the global response to the threat of climate change, sustainable development, and efforts to eradicate poverty [V. Masson-Delmotte, P. Zhai, H. O. Pörtner, D. Roberts, J. Skea, P.R. Shukla, A. Pirani, W. Moufouma-Okia, C. Péan, R. Pidcock, S. Connors, J. B. R. Matthews, Y. Chen, X. Zhou, M. I. Gomis, E. Lonnoy, T. Maycock, M. Tignor, & T. Waterfield (eds.)]. Retrieved from https://www.ipcc.ch/site/assets/uploads/sites/2/2019/05/SR15_SPM_version_report_LR.pdf

Jackson, T. (2016). *Prosperity without growth: Foundations for the economy of tomorrow*. London: Routledge.

Jackson, T., & Victor, P.A. (2015). Does credit create a 'growth imperative'? A quasi-stationary economy with interest-bearing debt. *Ecological Economics, 120*, 32–48. https://doi.org/10.1016/j.ecolecon.2015.09.009

Japan Times. (2018, September 17). For the first time, 1 person in 5 in Japan is 70 or older. Retrieved from https://www.japantimes.co.jp/

Kennett, D. J., & Beach, T .P. (2013). Archeological and environmental lessons for the Anthropocene from the Classic Maya collapse. *Anthropocene, 4*, 88–100. https://doi.org/10.1016/j.ancene.2013.12.002

Lam, D. (2011). How the world survived the population bomb: Lessons from 50 years of extraordinary demographic history. *Demography, 48*(4), 1231–1262. https:// 10.1007/s13524-011-0070-z

Levin, K, Cashore, B., Bernstein, S., & Auld, G. (2012). Overcoming the tragedy of super wicked problems: Constraining our future selves to ameliorate global climate change. *Poly Sci, 45*, 123–152. https://doi.org/10.1007/s11077-012-9151-0

Malmaeus, J. M., & Alfredsson, E. C. (2017). Potential consequences on the economy of low or no growth - short and long term perspectives. *Ecological Economics, 134*, 57–64. https://doi: 10.1016/j.ecolecon.2016.12.011

Mason, P. (2016). *Postcapitalism: A guide to our future*. London: Macmillan.

Marlon, J., Howe, P., Mildenberger, M., Leiserowitz A., & Wang, X. (2018). *Yale climate opinion maps 2018*. Retrieved from http://climatecommunication.yale.edu/visualizations-data/ycom-us-2018/?est=affectweather&type=value&geo=county

Moore, S. (2018, March 20). How to solve the global water crisis. *Foreign Affairs*. Retrieved from https://www.foreignaffairs.com/

Naess, A. (1973). The shallow and the deep, long-range ecology movement: A summary. *Inquiry, 16*(1–4), 95–100.

National Aeronautics and Space Administration (NASA). (2019). *Press release - 2018 fourth warmest year in continued warming trend, according to NASA*. Retrieved from https://www.nasa.gov/press-release/2018-fourth-warmest-year-in-continued-warming-trend-according-to-nasa-noaa

Organization for Economic Cooperation and Development (OECD). (2018). *Fertility rates (indicator)*. doi: 10.1787/8272fb01-en.

Ostrom, E. (1990). *Governing the commons: The evolution of institutions for collective action*. Cambridge, UK: Cambridge University Press.

Peiser, B. (2005). From genocide to ecocide: The rape of Rapa Nui. *Energy & Environment, 16*(3&4), 513-539. https://doi.org/10.1260/0958305054672385

Ranganathan, S., Swain, R. B., & Sumpter, D. J. (2015). The demographic transition and economic growth: Implications for development policy. *Palgrave Communications, 1*, article 15033. https://doi.org/10.1057/palcomms.2015.33

Reynolds, I. (2017, May 16). Japan's shrinking population. *Bloomberg News*. https://www.bloomberg.com/

Siegmeier, J., Mattauch, L., Franks, M., Klenert, D., Schultes, A., & Edenhofer, O. (2018). The fiscal benefits of stringent climate change mitigation: an overview. *Climate policy, 18*(3), 352–367. https://doi.org/10.1080/14693062.2017.1400943

Smith, Adam, 1723-1790. (2000). The wealth of nations /Adam Smith; introduction by Robert Reich; edited, with notes, marginal summary, and enlarged index by Edwin Cannan. New York: Modern Library.

Thompson, E. P. (1966). *The making of the English working class.* New York: Vintage Books.

United Nations. (2015). *The millennium development goals report.* New York, NY: United Nations. Retrieved from https://www.un.org/millenniumgoals/2015_MDG_Report/pdf/MDG%20 2015%20rev%20(July%201).pdf

United Nations, Department of Economic and Social Affairs, Division for Sustainable Development (UNDESA). (2014). *The 10-year framework of programmes on sustainable consumption and production.* Retrieved from https://sustainabledevelopment.un.org/index. php?page=view&type=400&nr=1444&menu=35

United Nations, Department of Economic and Social Affairs, Population Division (UNDESA). (2015). *Government response to low fertility in Japan. Policy brief #11.* Retrieved from http://www.un.org/en/development/desa/population/events/pdf/ expert/24/Policy_Briefs/PB_Japan.pdf.

United Nations, Department of Economic and Social Affairs, Population Division (UNDESA). (2017a). The impact of population momentum on future population growth. *Population Facts, No. 2017/4.* Retrieved from http://www. un.org/en/development/desa/population/publications/pdf/ popfacts/PopFacts_2017-4.pdf

United Nations, Department of Economic and Social Affairs, Population Division (UNDESA). (2017b). *World population prospects: The 2017 revision, key findings and advance tables. ESA/P/WP/248.* Retrieved from https://population.un.org/ wpp/

United Nations Development Programme (UNDP). (2016). *Human development report 2016: Human development for everyone.* New York: UNDP. Retrieved from http://hdr.undp. org/sites/default/files/2016_human_development_report.pdf

United Nations Environment Programme (UNEP). (2011). *Decoupling natural resource use and environmental impacts from economic growth*. Nairobi, Kenya: UNEP. Retrieved from http://wedocs.unep.org/handle/20.500.11822/9816

United Nations Environment Programme (UNEP). (2014). *Sand: rarer than one thinks*. Nairobi, Kenya: UNEP. Retrieved from http://wedocs.unep.org/handle/20.500.11822/8665

United Nations Framework Convention on Climate Change (UNFCCC). (2015). *Adoption of the Paris agreement*. FCCC/CP/2015/L.9/Rev.1.

United Nations General Assembly (UNGA). (1994). *United nations framework convention on climate change*. Adopted January 20. A/RES/48/189.

United Nations General Assembly (UNGA). (1997). *Agenda for development*. Adopted 15 October. A/RES/51/240.

United Nations General Assembly (UNGA). (2015). *Transforming our world: The 2030 agenda for sustainable development*. Adopted 21 October. A/RES/70/1.

United Nations – Sustainable Development Goals. (2018). *SDG 6: Clean water and sanitation*. Retrieved from https://www.un.org/sustainabledevelopment/water-and-sanitation/

United Nations – Water. (2018). *Water scarcity*. Retrieved from http://www.unwater.org/water-facts/scarcity/

World Bank. (2017). *World development indicators: Annual freshwater withdrawals, agriculture*. Retrieved from https://data.worldbank.org/indicator/er.h2o.fwag.zs

World Bank. (2019a). *GDP growth (annual %)*. Retrieved from https://data.worldbank.org/indicator/NY.GDP.MKTP.KD.ZG?locations=SE

World Bank. (2019b). *World bank carbon pricing dashboard*. Retrieved from https://carbonpricingdashboard.worldbank.org/map_data

World Commission on Environment and Development (WCED). (1987). *Our common future: Report of the world commission on environment and development.* A/42/427.

Identities in International Relations

16

Dwight Wilson

Abstract

This chapter will examine identity and its application to international relations. Ethnicity and nationalism, religion, and gender have not traditionally attracted attention in the study of international relations, which has focused predominantly on states and other international institutions. In recent years, though, international relations scholars have given greater attention to these identities. The chapter will consider how ethnic and nationalist, religious, and gender identities might affect (or not affect) the international system by stoking conflict, but also by potentially encouraging peace.

Learning Objectives

- Understand key theories on ethnicity and nationalism and views on the effects these might have in international relations
- Understand competing views on the role religion might play in international relations
- Understand key theories on gender and competing views on the role it might play in international relations
- Articulate competing views on the importance and effects of identity in international relations

The Emergence of Identities

As you now know, international relations emerged as a distinct discipline in the early twentieth century with the primary goal of understanding the workings of an international system of sovereign states. Principal problems of international relations have included such questions as why states go to war and what mechanisms are effective in promoting cooperation between states. Realists have elevated the rational state as a unitary actor considering its own survival as the highest good. Liberals and constructivists have tended to view institutions and interactions as capable of moderating the worst tendencies of anarchy. These also make greater room for such non-state actors as international organizations, NGOs, and MNCs, but primarily as operating within a context dominated by states. This focus on states and their behavior is understandable; much of twentieth century international politics revolved around conflict and balancing between states. The first half of the century was marked by World Wars I and II, the two most destructive wars in history, and the second half by a nuclear-tipped Cold War between superpowers driven by political ideology.

As the Cold War concluded, some more optimistic observers expected (or hoped) that, with one state dominant in the international system and without an ideological challenger to democracy and capitalism, there wouldn't be much left to fight over. Or perhaps that economic integration would lead to a global civil society. Pessimists, on the other hand, expected a return to the same great power balancing characteristic of previous centuries and the possibility of conflict that came with it. What these visions shared was the expectation of an orderly and predictable international system. Instead, apparently unrelated events in the first decade following the Cold War augured the possibility of a dramatic reordering of the system. Previously stable multiethnic states broke apart, some in sanguinary ethnic conflicts. Religious inspired terrorism carried out by loose networks like Al-Qaeda demonstrated that devoted extremists can move international events. The United Nations World Conference on Women declared that the peace and development in the world positively required states and other international actors to commit themselves to gender equality (*Fourth World Conference on Women, Beijing 1995*). While a disparate collection, these events nonetheless raised new questions for world politics and international relations. Rarely in international relations had there been much attention given to how ethnicity might influence the international system, how religious ideas can cause (or end) international conflict, or how gender relations might condition international stability.

In the midst of these events, some international relations scholars began to question whether the focus on a state-centric system might be overlooking something important, even fundamental, to human action: identities. In this chapter, **identities** will refer to such core constituents of the human condition as our ethnicity and nation, religion, and gender. These shape our understanding of the world, give our lives meaning and provide us with intentions and goals. Ethnicity connects us to our past and binds us to a group, telling us where we belong and often who our enemies are. Religion situates us in the universe and tells us why we are on earth, how to live a moral life, and also, sometimes, who our enemies are. Gender differences divide every civilization from the largest to the smallest into two groups (or more), assigning public and private roles to men and women, and, yes, sometimes also telling us who our enemies are.

Traditionally, most international relations scholars simply ignored identities, presuming them to be irrelevant to the international system and viewing them as a fuzzy concept, difficult to clearly define and to objectively measure. Thus, identities fell largely outside the scope of mainstream international relations theorizing and empirical study. In recent decades, however, a growing number of international relations scholars have recognized the potential importance of these questions to their field, and more scholarship has aimed at exploring the intersection of international relations and these identities. Now, though it is possible to interpret their importance differently, it is impossible to ignore these concepts altogether. Debates over the salience and consequences of identities thrust themselves onto the center stage of world politics.

This chapter examines two related sets of questions about identity: first, do ethnicity, religion, and gender significantly affect the behavior of international actors, or are they relevant only at the individual and state levels of analysis? Do ethnic and religious hostilities drive international conflict? Can gender relations have effects on state behavior? Does the traditional approach in international relations of overlooking identities ignore an essential aspect of the international system? Second, if these core identities do have an impact at the international level, will belonging to identity groups always simultaneously define enemies, such that humans are hopelessly estranged and doomed to endless conflict? Or is it possible that humans overcome these divisions with the emergence of a universal identity that transcends these lower-order ones and even transcends the state itself, thus fundamentally transforming world politics?

Ethnicity and Nationalism

As mentioned above, pessimistic observers—primarily realists—expected the post-Cold War world to resemble the world before the Cold War: one of great powers balancing one another in their pursuit of national power carrying the danger of war. A different, even more pessimistic, assessment agreed that we should expect war but that power politics would be coupled with ethnic division and nationalism, a highly explosive combination that would fuel conflict into the near future.

Ethnicity is a sense of identity rooted in shared history, language, and culture. Ethnicity often overlaps with race, that is, visible variations in biological features, but is a separate concept. Religion might form part of a group's ethnic identity but can also cut across ethnicities, uniting those of different ethnicities or dividing a single ethnic group. For this reason, religion will be treated separately below. Ethnicity is closely related to the **nation** and nationalism; an ethnic group viewing itself as a historically and culturally united group that belongs together can be considered a nation. A nation that becomes politically active and embraces the goal of political sovereignty for itself has become a nationalist movement.

During the early modern period in Europe, this type of ethnic nationalism contributed to the rise of the modern state. In the eighteenth and nineteenth centuries, nationalist movements in Europe sought independence as not only desirable in itself, due to the principle of self-determination, but also as a means to reduce international conflict. The expectation was that, if the major ethnic groups each had their own state in the form of ethnically homogeneous **nation-states**, then discrimination and persecution of minorities would cease, removing a major source of grievance and promoting peace among states. This idea is in President Woodrow Wilson's Fourteen Points, his proposal for a just conclusion to World War I, which included provisions for the establishment of states and autonomous regions drawn according to ethnic criteria. Many states have been created and continue to be created with this purpose. Just since the 1990s, the former Yugoslavia split apart in the 1990s civil war, resulting in several smaller states roughly drawn around ethnic groups; Czechoslovakia divided into the Czech Republic and Slovakia, reflecting ethnic criteria; the international system's youngest state, South Sudan, was sliced from Sudan in 2011 based on ethnicity following a long internal conflict. Ethnicity and national identity are simply one of the unavoidable facts of the modern world.

Maybe, then, the solution to the problems posed by ethnic diversity is simply to partition ethnic groups into separate and ethnically homogeneous states nation-states, as the original nationalists had recommended. This raises yet another puzzle, though: there are many more ethnicities than there are states (though counting ethnicities is not straightforward). A few states are unambiguously nation-states; Iceland and Japan, for example, are overwhelmingly Icelandic and Japanese. Most states, even those dominated by a single ethnicity, contain significant minority groups. Germany, though clearly named for the German people, is home to people of Polish and Turkish decent, among many others. The Chinese government counts fifty-five ethnic minorities within its borders, while other observers count many more. Ethnic nationalism, although immediately connected to the emergence of the modern state, therefore poses a direct challenge to the system of states that currently exists.

Thus, these two foundational units, nations and states, are to some degree incompatible. As long as there are more ethnic groups (and potentially nationalist movements) than there are states, there is the possibility of conflict and war. Ethnic conflicts appear to be as old as history itself. Such conflicts are often internal wars which entail serious international consequences by threatening regional destabilization, external intervention, or both.

Where do ethnic identities come from? The question might seem beside the point. If ethnic conflict is a constant feature of human nature, why worry about where ethnicities come from? In fact, our view on the origins of ethnicity shape our view of whether ethnic conflict is a constant feature of human history at all, and whether it will continue. Despite the apparently obvious features of ethnicity, scholars do not agree on their origins, history, and lasting power. Theorists propose different views on these questions, giving us very different bases for predictions about ethnic conflict in the future.

Essentialist theories describe ethnic groups as being a natural phenomenon embedded in human nature. Humans are psychologically built in such a way that we bond with people like ourselves and against those unlike us. From birth, we are most closely attached to our family, with whom we are united by blood. In the essentialist view, ethnic groups are an extended family sharing a common ancestry. As such, ethnicity is real and immutable, an unavoidable fact about social life. Given this interpretation, essentialists have a dim view of the possibility for ethnic groups to intermingle stably. Rather, they tend to expect that the long history of ethnic conflict will repeat itself.

Huntington, for example, describes a world naturally divided into seven or eight civilizations that are rooted in culture (*Clash of Civilizations*, 1996). The basic fact of human nature, he argues, is that we group ourselves into mutually exclusive and competing identity communities. The differences between these groups run so deep that there is no possibility of their living peaceably side by side; we can only bond with our own group through excluding members of other groups. As Huntington writes, "We know who we are only when we know whom we are against" (1996, p. 21). This will have dire consequences where different civilizations mix in a single state, as civil wars will be inevitable in those unlucky states.

The argument goes that regions which enjoy peace and stability owe their success not to the transcendence of ethnic identity but to the long centuries and bloody battles that led to the emergence of relatively ethnically homogenous states. The present stability of European states, most visibly, was achieved through centuries of warfare, coercion, and redrawing of borders. Current non-European migration and the growth of multiethnic societies in Europe will not end well, according to essentialists. The case of the growing Turkish community in Germany is illustrative in this regard. German is a well-defined ethnicity. Many members of the Turkish minority, despite having lived in Germany for generations, do not feel fully accepted in German society and themselves feel more closely connected to Turkey (DW.com, 2018). From the essentialist point of view, hopes of full integration of such different groups are misguided.

Ethnic conflict, therefore, cannot be eradicated but only managed through separating contending groups whenever possible

(Muller, 2009), a proposal which, as noted above, could lead to practically endless division and sub-division of states as more and more ethnic nationalist movements demand the accommodation of state sovereignty. Thus, the tension between nations and states could well continue to strain the international system as internal conflicts bloom into international crises that can invite outside intervention.

Perhaps more importantly, this behavior has the potential to spill into direct conflict between states as well. Prospects for peace between the U.S. and China are dim, not simply because power considerations will bring them into conflict but because the Western values of the U.S. and the Confucian values of China are incompatible. The same can be said of the relations with Russia, Iran, and various other non-Western states. Furthermore, states will align themselves according to their civilizational identity. States will likely come to the aid of those sharing their identity when tensions arise with outsider states, thereby carrying the danger of a "global intercivilizational war" (2011, p. 312–316). There is nothing necessary or inevitable about just such a conflict. Failure to appreciate the danger by papering over the foundational nature of civilizational identity and placing unwarranted hope in international institutions or global integration, though, can only serve to heighten the danger of such a widespread conflict.

Some considered Huntington's analysis confirmed by the hostilities between the U.S. and Iraq beginning in the 1990s and the broader military engagements of the U.S. in the Middle East. For Huntington, this is simply the continuation of long-simmering tensions and outright war between the West and the Islamic world.

Critics of essentialist theories are obviously unconvinced. Rather than naturally occurring groups organized around blood ties with relatively clear dimensions, as essentialists would have it, instrumentalists see ethnic groups as a recent phenomenon with malleable boundaries. To these theorists, ethnonational identity forms only one among many identities, any of which might take precedence given the circumstances. In some cases, ethnicity might come to the forefront; in others, class, gender, region or religion might be more relevant. We might at times think of ourselves as primarily consumers, sports fans, or members of a profession. Which of these most heavily influences our behavior in a given situation? Will it not depend on the context we find ourselves in and the goals we are focused on at the moment?

Instrumentalists explain ethnic conflict as the product of political leaders' manipulation of ethnic identity for their own purposes. Rather than ethnic conflict arising from "ancient hatreds," there are often figures pulling the emotional levers of groups and stirring conflict among those that otherwise could have stayed peaceful and without grudges. Ethnic grievances of the past remain there until dredged up again, weaponized by ethno-nationalist leaders who muster outrage by demonizing other groups as enemies. Scholars describe these efforts as strategic myth making. Civil war in multiethnic Yugoslavia erupted after communism collapsed as an organizing principle. Essentialists would likely explain this as the resumption of embedded hostilities, while instrumentalists would underscore the role played by former communist officials who seized upon ethnic tension as a means of remaining relevant—and in power. Serb leader Slobodan Milosevic, for example, fanned the flames of resentment against ethnic Bosniaks, reminding Serbs of centuries-old complaints that would otherwise likely have remained in history books, with deadly consequences.

Ethnic leaders might even use identity for filling their own pockets. Some research has suggested that apparently ethnically-driven conflict is sometimes motivated more by competition for valuable resources than by nationalist aspirations (Collier & Hoeffler, 1998). Were it not for this ethnic entrepreneurialism, it is possible that Yugoslavia would have remained a single country and its citizens Yugoslavs.

A related theory, constructivism (but not international relations constructivism discussed earlier), focuses on the relatively short history of nations and nationalism, arguing that the nation is a necessarily modern invention. As noted above, nationalism emerged at the time of state formation—a mere few centuries ago. Before the early modern period, there could be no French because there was no France, no Germans because there was no Germany. Further, national communities are imagined communities since no individual member of a modern ethnonational group can personally know or interact with every other member (Anderson, 1983). We could only begin to think of ourselves as members of a group of many thousands or millions when modern creations such as the printing press and newspapers began to tell us so in a standardized language.

Note again that this theoretical question on the sources of ethnic identity is of great consequence. If ethnic and national identities are contingent and changing, rather than primary and fixed, if there is nothing natural about ethnic identity, then there is nothing natural or inevitable about ethnic conflict. Essentialists might see partition as the only realistic approach to managing conflict, despite itself being a potential recipe for chaos. It might simply be the only option. If there is no essential quality to ethnic identity, though, we can expect that multiethnic states suffer no fatal flaw and that ethnic conflict can be avoided through the normal channels of politics, such as institutional design, elections, economic policy, and education.

Moreover, research has shown that multiethnic societies are not more prone to violent conflict than more homogeneous ones (Fearon & Laitin, 2003). Consider the U.S. Is it a nation as defined above? Is it organized around a language and a culture or around political principles? Observers can disagree as to which are more important, but in any event, there is no ethnic criterion for American identity. Whether one must adopt only American values or must also adopt the English language, American identity is capacious enough to absorb people of any background. If these views are closer to the truth about ethnic identities, there is nothing permanent about them. They have changed in the past and can change in the future; they are only one among many identities that are relevant to our lives. Most importantly for international relations, there is nothing inevitable about ethnic conflict.

Religion

Throughout history, religion has occupied a crucial place in public affairs. Wars and insurrections were fought in the name of competing gods; political success and failure has been explained in terms of those gods' favor or anger. It is a distinctly powerful force with the capacity to motivate people to extraordinary actions. Religious ideas often transcend the earthly concerns of human groups, whether ethnic groups, empires, or modern states. Some religions command their followers to proselytize, to aspire to universality—something that nations and states never do (Toft, Philpott, & Shah, 2011, p. 21). Thus, religions have great potential for challenging, transcending, and disrupting an international system based on state authority.

Religion is difficult to define, and many definitions immediately encounter problems of either including too little (a focus on deities might overlook Buddhism, for example) or including too much (excluding supernatural beings might include many political or economic ideas most of us would not consider religion). For our purposes, **religion** will refer to an integrated set of ideas that connects the earthly world to an unseen world that cannot be explained or understood through rational investigation. Religions often impose duties on earthly inhabitants to fulfill their duties to gods, spirits, or ancestors long deceased. This connection between the natural and supernatural is what makes religion important to, and even inseparable from, politics.

Religion, though, has played little or no role in the major theoretical paradigms of international relations, as it has been assumed to play little or no role in the world politics of the modern era. With the Peace of Westphalia and the acceptance of state sovereignty in Europe, suddenly questions of religious interpretations, sacred texts, and God's plans were to have been separated from reasons of state. Demands of national survival and power balancing now guided the actions of states on the international stage. Further, in this period of state formation, religious authority was often subsumed within state authority, first in a "friendly merger" in which religious and state actors cooperated and legitimized each other, then later in a "friendly takeover" in which the state came to fully dominate religion for its own purposes (Toft, et al, p. 58).

Subsequently, European states colonized much of the world, bringing with them their concept of state sovereignty, well-defined borders, and the national interest, eventually establishing the state as the basic unit of the international system. As a result, it appeared that the supernatural was fully relegated to the domestic sphere (Rowe, 2012, Ch. 1). Even there, many political scientists considered religion itself to be on life support; in the mid-20th century, a popular social science theory predicted the imminent demise of religious belief. **Secularization theory** held that, as countries modernized, with their populations becoming more affluent and educated, science, reason, and democracy would displace belief in the supernatural. Some secularization theorists even expected religion to practically disappear by the end of the twentieth century. Given this history and context, then, religion has not figured largely in the minds of those in the social sciences in general and international relations in particular.

Religion, nonetheless, has stubbornly refused to fulfill expectations and fade into irrelevance as a social force. The basic assumption that the modern international system subordinated religion to a private sphere disconnected from state purposes might simply have reflected a narrow European experience inapplicable to non-Western regions (Cho & Katzenstein, 2011, p. 143). As for secularization theory, few theoretical predictions have proven so spectacularly wrong. While it might have appeared a reasonable hypothesis in the first half of the twentieth century, subsequent decades proved the durability and political salience of religion with the Islamist Iranian Revolution of 1979, the prominence of the Religious Right in the U.S. of the 1980s, and the Hindu fundamentalist resurgence of the twenty-first century. Rather than the number of the faithful declining, the proportion of the world's population identifying as religious has grown and is likely to continue growing. Though the "unaffiliated"—those who do not identify as religious—has grown in the U.S. and Europe, their size is shrinking as a percentage of the world (Lipka & McClendon, 2017).

As a domestic variable, religion will continue in its relevance. What kind of role might we reserve for religion in international relations, though? The balance of international relations scholarship on religion focuses on its role in conflict, and with good reason. State authorities can marshal religious sentiment in support of their international war aims, and small-scale religious movements can catalyze tectonic international events. The Reformation drove a bloody wedge through Europe. Shinto and Buddhist religious figures strongly supported Imperial Japan's efforts in World War II. Catholic Mexicans were motivated in part to drive out the Protestant invasion of the U.S. in the Mexican-American war. Northern Ireland has been scarred by a religious divide and conflict since the 1920s. Hindu Tamils in majority-Buddhist Sri Lanka received aid from majority-Hindu India. Majority-Muslim Pakistan continually intervenes in Indian-held Kashmir in support of the Muslims there (Fox & Sandler, 2004, p. 64). Al-Qaeda's terrorist attacks of September 2001, effected by a small number of individuals, set off a chain of events that brought the world's single superpower into deep involvement in Afghanistan and Iraq. While some of the causes of these conflicts lie in mundane political disputes, the presence of a religious element complicates them by injecting them with cosmic purpose. Conflicts featuring religious actors become "nasty, brutish, and long" (Toft et al., 2011, Ch. 6).

Religion can be a source of conflict, but religious actors can promote conflict resolution as well. Religious figures and groups have long been associated with pacifism, including Mahatma Gandhi and Martin Luther King, Jr. The Catholic Church and clergy have often acted as mediators in the settlement of international disputes and civil wars (Rowe, 2012, p. 227). The **international humanitarian order**, that is, the network of organizations, norms, and laws dedicated to protecting victims of war, promoting human rights, and reducing suffering around the world, has its roots in religious sentiments (Barnett, 2011, p. 80). The just war tradition in the West developed from foundational Christian theologians, while Islamic, Hindu, and Buddhist theologians and philosophers have used religious texts to interpret justifications for the use of force and to place limits on warfare (Rowe, 2012, p. 209–215).

Beyond the actions of non-state actors, perhaps religious forces can reshape state actors themselves. Democratic peace theory, which was discussed previously, posits that democracies do not go to war with each other. Though the theory itself does not directly refer to religion, the effects of a democratic peace might be enhanced by religious variables: the wave of democratization of the late twentieth century (the third such wave) was a largely Catholic phenomenon, originating in Portugal and Spain and spreading through Latin America. One explanation for this centers on Pope John Paul II wielding the power of the Church from above to attack the foundations of communist and other authoritarian regimes, while grassroots movements among younger priests and parishioners pressed on such regimes from below (Huntington, 1993, p. 77–79).

Though the power of religious ideas might appear obvious to many, skeptical analysts are unwilling to change the traditional position of international relations. These downplay or dismiss religious interpretations as a real motor of international action.

Regarding conflict, they will instead highlight fundamentally political origins, such as foreign policy grievances and competing territorial claims. Some studies of the root causes of terrorism, for instance, investigate organizational dynamics of terrorist groups, governmental oppression, and the psychology of individual terrorists (Crenshaw, 2010).

Those willing to accept religious identities as a real force in world politics maintain that it is impossible to understand a phenomenon like jihadist terrorism without reference to the fundamentalist interpretation of Islam embraced by groups like Al-Qaeda and ISIS. In this view, terrorists' beliefs actually provide the goals of those who hold them. For example, when members of ISIS write an article entitled "Why we hate you and why we fight you" (Fox News, 2016, August 1) explaining that it is, in fact, their religion that motivates them, we should believe them.

For these observers, then, failure to take account of religion could lead to disastrous results—especially for a world power like the U.S. A secular bias might blind U.S. policymakers to important influences in making the world go around. This is relevant for the outside world, as a motivator for foreign regimes and terrorist groups, but it could have consequences for U.S. action as well.

In the long running Israeli-Palestinian conflict, for example, the U.S. position has been more sympathetic to Israeli security interests than to Palestinian concerns over self-determination. This position has often put the U.S. at odds with world opinion and with its own allies, as well as creating tensions with some oil-rich majority-Muslim states. Would it not better serve U.S. interests to take a more even-handed approach by distancing U.S. foreign policy from Israel? Viewing the issue through a power lens, some prominent realists argue that the U.S. posture in the Middle East is distorted by domestic political processes that should play no role in determining foreign policy (Mearsheimer & Walt, 2007). Perhaps, but many voters might prefer closer relations with Israel as a means of signaling moral support for a stable democracy in a region dominated by various types of authoritarian systems. And, of course, religion might play a crucial role as well. Christians are likely to support Israel because they believe it more closely reflects their values, and many evangelicals—around a quarter of the Christian population of the U.S.—support Israel, many of them because they view this as an instrument for the fulfillment of biblical prophecy (Bump, 2018). Following a strictly realist analysis, we might consider such concerns as beside the point or irrational, but it is also simply a fact of democratic governance that these preferences of voters will figure into the decisions of elected representatives.

Religion clearly constitutes an enduring organizing principle for billions of people and, despite predictions of its imminent demise or irrelevance, continues to play a part in the drama of world events. Is it a bit player, or does it occupy center stage? Will it drive states, overwhelm them, or remain a lever that states might use at their will?

Gender

Humans are divided into sometimes competing groups by nationality and language, history and culture, spiritual and philosophical questions. These are easy to see and identify and it is easy to extrapolate potential effects on international relations. The most apparent division is so evident that we hardly consider it. By dividing every state and nationality, every culture and linguistic group, every religion into nearly equal halves, and thereby the entire world into nearly equal halves, it is easy to overlook gender as a potentially important influence. Every identity group is divided in the same way, so how could gender change anything at the international level?

Sex refers to biological characteristics, while gender refers to the social roles typically assigned to the sexes, that is, the expectations we have as to the types of behaviors displayed, clothes worn, and duties and professions performed by men and women. The relationship between sex and gender remains the subject of heated debate. Many feminist theorists downplay or deny any biological influence on gender expectations, claiming that gender is a cultural artifact. Others, like biological determinists, claim that biological differences between males and females play a significant part in shaping social roles of the sexes.

There is certainly room between those poles for a middle ground on this question, but the important point here is that, while there is a great deal of overlap in gender roles around the world (such as in child rearing and professions), there are also consequential differences in gender roles across societies. In areas such as labor participation and pay, educational opportunity and attainment, life expectancy, and representation in political and other powerful positions, there are stark differences among regions and individual countries that impact the lives of women. For instance, Western Europe (particularly Iceland and the Scandinavian countries) rank at the top in gender equity, while Middle Eastern and sub-Saharan African countries tend to display the widest gender inequalities, with China and India toward the bottom as well (World Economic Forum, 2018, p. 16–17). Whatever the extent of biological determinants in gender roles, there are clear social variables at work in influencing the status and achievement potential for women and girls around the globe.

Of obvious importance in a wide variety of social, economic, and political issues, we may ask whether gender equity is of interest in international relations or if it is solely of domestic concern. Feminist international relations theorists explore the effects of gender on how the international system is conceived and how the system operates. Perhaps relevant differences are not those of ethnicity or religion but those divisions based on gender.

Responding to the clash of civilizations thesis, scholars Ronald Ingelhart and Pippa Norris argue that Huntington is correct to highlight consequential cultural differences between the West and non-Western societies but claim that their source of incompatibility is not rooted in fundamental cultural, religious, or political values. They find broad overlap between the West and much of the rest of the world on views on important political questions, such as preferences for democratic governance. Rather, they emphasize the wide contrasts in views on gender and sex. Where tradition upholds gender inequality and discourages unorthodox views of gender—in many majority-Muslim countries, China, and India, for instance— they see little chance of political or economic convergence with the West. Thus, until cultural attitudes on gender equality shift in these societies, we will witness a "sexual clash of civilizations"— not a military conflict but one based in their lagging economic development and political instability (Inglehart & Norris, 2003).

An important source of this clash stems from the failure to capitalize on the potential of girls and women for the benefit of society at large. Where half of the population is denied equal access to education and employment opportunities, an enormous amount of talent in a society is wasted. Gender equality could thus be a prerequisite for stability and development. "Gender equality is not only a fundamental human right, but a necessary foundation for a peaceful, prosperous and sustainable world" as the fifth United Nations Sustainable Development Goals states. That is no small claim: if the peace and prosperity of the world are at stake, gender equality could be understood as the most important goal of any.

Some feminist international relations theorists argue that a masculine perspective casting the world as dangerous and hostile fulfills its own prophecy. In fact, research links gender equality to lower levels of violence, not only internal violence but also military action at the international level. Higher levels of sexism are theorized to lead to greater support for the use of military force, and, indeed, countries with higher levels of equality between men and women in the social, economic, and political spheres correlate with their having lower levels of international violence (Hudson et al., 2012, Chapter 4).

Gender inequality also gives rise to distorted sex ratios, there being a greater number of men compared to women resulting from parental preference for boys, which might also have consequences that extend beyond state borders. In some countries—China and India are good examples of such—the devaluation of girls leads to sex-selective abortions or neglect and higher mortality of girls and results in many millions of "missing women" who were never born or who died at an early age (Sen, 2003). Given men's greater tendency toward risky and violent behavior, a lopsided ratio of men to women could lead to "macho militarism and even imperialism," warns the historian Niall Ferguson (2011). If these connections withstand scrutiny, greater gender equality in the form of expanded educational, economic, and political opportunities for girls and women should translate to greater domestic *and* interstate peace, while leaving gender out of the picture would leave us with a fatally flawed understanding of security.

From these perspectives, gender equality carries consequences for far more than the life chances of individual girls and women, though that is of enough importance. Gender is an issue that confronts us not from out there in the international system, or another state, but from within every community. Perhaps the description of a clash of civilizations does not entirely miss the mark. Rather than the multiplicity of identities suggested by those focusing on ethnicity or religion, though, maybe there is just one identity cleavage bisecting the entire world's population that really holds the key to grasping group differences.

If so, there is room for optimism. Evidence like that presented by Inglehart and Norris reveals that, regardless of whether gender roles are cultural, biological, or something in between, wide gender inequalities are not written in stone. This holds out the possibility for progress in gender equality and an end to the theorized sexual clash of civilizations, as well as, perhaps, a more peaceful and just world. One of the central goals of the UN and other multilateral organizations has been to promote gender equality by extending educational and employment opportunities for girls and women. And there is good news: though significant disparities remain, gender inequality has decreased since 1990 (World Economic Forum, 2018, p. 15).

The Effects of Identity

This chapter poses two questions about identities. First, do identities affect world politics? Second, do identities divide us irremediably? Let us examine the first question: do these identities matter for international relations? Are they relevant only at the individual or domestic levels and overwhelmed by universal state considerations, whether they be military, economic, or human security?

In 2014, Russia militarily intervened in neighboring Ukraine, annexing Crimea and supporting ethnic Russian separatist groups in eastern Ukraine. We could easily adduce ethnicity and nationalism as a major motivator here. A large minority of the population is ethnically Russian, and popular Russian folklore traces the founding of the Russian people to what is now Ukraine (Snyder, 2018, Chapter 4). Russian President Vladimir Putin has publicly proclaimed that Russia makes it a central mission to protect all ethnic Russians in the world (Coalson, 2014). Ukraine was a Soviet Republic within the Russia-dominated Soviet Union, and Russia can reasonably see the country as falling naturally within its sphere of influence. It would be no surprise if these identity-oriented variables really did push Russia from within to its actions in Ukraine, and reasonable to expect Russia to continue its aggressive behavior.

Another recurring international controversy of the twenty-first century is Iran's nuclear program. Do the religious roots of the Iranian Revolution and the theocratic elements of its regime direct its goals in ways fundamentally hostile toward other states, especially the U.S. and Israel? Iranian government officials have colorfully denounced the U.S. as the "Great Satan" and Israel as the "Little Satan." Do they truly believe that some states are the embodiment of malevolence in the universe? If so, Iran's acquisition of nuclear weapons would pose a unique threat to the security of those states in particular and to the stability of the international system generally.

On the other hand, perhaps such rhetorical flourishes identifying certain states as various sizes of Satan serve purely domestic ends as attempts to legitimize the regime and unify the country against external enemies. Structural realists, for example, can view the matter as a simple one of power balancing. States rationally pursue their own security interests. Iran is a state, so it cannot surprise us that it would develop nuclear weapons as a deterrent against more powerful rivals. Iran's offensive use of nuclear weapons (or handing them to terrorists) would only guarantee its own immediate annihilation—exactly the opposite of what every state aims to do. Thus, we can overlook Iran's bizarre theological rantings and focus on the actual behavior of states. A nuclear armed Iran could, in fact, be a good thing by bringing a stable balance of power to the Middle East (Waltz, 2012).

Similarly, we might view Russia's behavior in Ukraine as eminently rational from a purely strategic perspective. Ukraine occupies a central location in Europe, with abundant fertile land and a naval base on the Black Sea. Russia's actions could also be seen as a response to the power of the U.S. Following the Cold War, the U.S.-dominated NATO expanded to include former allies of the Soviet Union, and even former Soviet Republics. Before Russia's intervention, the Ukrainian government took steps to more closely align itself with the U.S.'s Western European allies. We could see Russia's actions as justifiable and even blame the U.S. and its allies for Russia's invasion of Ukraine, as the prominent realist John Mearsheimer does (2019). Perhaps there is no need to complicate matters by introducing identities in what is already a complete picture.

As is evident, entirely different interpretations of an important international issue stem from what importance we place on identities. Which of these stories we find more convincing has immediate practical consequences for our policy preferences. If Iran and Russia are driven by identities, these are not susceptible to reason and persuasion. If they are rational, on the other hand, then there should be no trouble dealing with these issues, either through diplomacy, deterrence, or both.

You might conclude that identities have little effect at the international level, though a growing number of international relations scholars are convinced that these identities do matter. Let's move to the second question: do these identities estrange us irremediably? Typically, observers who emphasize identities highlight the divisions they erect between identity groups. Huntington's thesis most directly captures the pessimistic view of the effects of identity and, probably not coincidentally, his argument has entered the mainstream and his phrasing become part of the common political lexicon.

If we believe identities can drive strife, evidence is never more than a click away on the internet, and there might be more to come. The rise of China, for example, and the tensions it is already causing with the U.S. will be made only worse given the civilizational differences between the two. Rather than an ordinary balancing act between two powerful states, the wide gulf in culture and values will make mistrust and miscommunication practically inevitable. As China becomes not just more powerful but also more assertive, the likelihood of war increases far beyond what it would if the two were grounded in similar civilizations. Huntington, in this perspective, seems to have been right.

Maybe we will always divide ourselves into mutually hostile groups. Gloomy predictions of looming disaster tend to attract the most attention, but consider that a few centuries ago—the blink of an eye in human history—it would have been considered a preposterous dream that Protestants, Catholics, and Jews would live together peacefully. Now we often hear of a Judeo-Christian identity. Two hundred years ago, the French were feared conquerors. Only decades ago, the Japanese and Germans were considered dangerous militarists. Now the Japanese and Germans are gentle economic giants, while the French are known more for cuisine than for military prowess.

Optimistic voices tell us that, though essentialists are correct that we are programmed to join groups that may struggle with one another, we are also programmed for cooperative behavior that can widen to encompass larger and larger groups (Christakis, 2019). History may be seen as not just a parade of unceasing violence but, in fact, as the measure of a world grown far more peaceful without many of us noticing it (Pinker, 2012). Indeed, we could just as easily view human history as the widening of circles of group identity and as the history of cooperation between more and more people (Harari, 2014). Human history began with a patchwork of thousands of political units spread across the globe; now there are fewer than two hundred states, including two with more than a billion people each. If cooperation extended this far, could it continue to extend until there emerges a unified human identity, one that makes divisions based on various identities, and consequently even states themselves, irrelevant?

Whether we consider this possible or not is influenced by our theory of the origins of identities. If they are innate and inflexible, it becomes harder to imagine the transcendence of difference. If identities are "imagined," socially constructed, and malleable, then there is at least the possibility that at some time in the future people will look back on ethnic, religious, and even gendered hostilities with the same indifference with which we today regard forgotten grudges of ancient groups.

Identities matter. At what level and in what way, we are unlikely to agree upon soon. What is likely is that identities will continue to occupy a more central position in international relations theory.

References

Anderson, B. (1983). *Imagined communities: Reflections on the origin and spread of nationalism*. Verso.

Barnett, M. (2011). Another great awakening? International relations theory and religion. In J. Snyder (Ed.), *Religion and International Relations Theory* (p. 80–99). Columbia University Press.

Bump, P. (2018, May 14). Analysis | Half of evangelicals support Israel because they believe it is important for fulfilling end-times prophecy. *The Washington Post*. Retrieved from https://www.washingtonpost.com/news/politics/wp/2018/05/14/half-of-evangelicals-support-israel-because-they-believe-it-is-important-for-fulfilling-end-times-prophecy/

Cho, I. H., & Katzenstein, P. J. (2011). In the service of state and nation: Religion in East Asia. In J. Snyder (Ed.), *Religion and International Relations* (p. 143–768). Columbia University Press.

Christakis, N. A. (2019). *Blueprint: The evolutionary origins of a good society*. Little, Brown Spark.

Collier, P., & Hoeffler, A. (1998). On economic causes of civil war. *Oxford Economic Papers, 50*(4), p. 563–573. https://doi.org/10.1093/oep/50.4.563

Crenshaw, M. (2010). *Explaining terrorism*. Routledge.

DW.com. (2018, December 7). *German Turks still rooted in the east: Study*. Retrieved from https://www.dw.com/en/german-turks-still-rooted-in-the-east-study/a-44799929

Fearon, J. D., & Laitin, D. D. (2003). Ethnicity, insurgency, and civil var. *American Political Science Review, 97*(01), p. 75. https://doi.org/10.1017/S0003055403000534

Ferguson, N. (2011, March 6). The rise of Asia's bachelor generation. *Newsweek*. Retrieved from https://www.newsweek.com/ferguson-rise-asias-bachelor-generation-66103

Fourth World Conference on Women, Beijing 1995. (n.d.).
Retrieved July 10, 2019, from https://www.un.org/
womenwatch/daw/beijing/platform/plat1.htm#statement

Fox, J., & Sandler, S. (2004). *Bringing religion into international relations*. Palgrave Macmillan.

Fox News. (2016, August 1). ISIS details "Why We Hate You" in new magazine. Retrieved from https://www.foxnews.com/world/isis-details-why-we-hate-you-in-new-magazine

Harari, Y. N. (2014). *Sapiens: A brief history of humankind*. Harvill Secker.

Hudson, V. M., Ballif-Spanvill, B., Caprioli, M., & Emmett, C. F. (2012). *Sex and world peace*. Columbia University Press.

Huntington, S. P. (1993). *The third wave: Democratization in the late twentieth century*. University of Oklahoma Press.

Huntington, S. P. (1996). *The clash of civilizations and the remaking of world order*. Simon & Schuster.

Inglehart, R., & Norris, P. (2003). The true clash of civilizations. *Foreign Policy, 135*, 62. https://doi.org/10.2307/3183594

Lipka, M., & McClendon, D. (2017, April 7). Religious "nones" projected to decline as share of world population. *Pew Research Center*. Retrieved from https://www.pewresearch.org/fact-tank/2017/04/07/why-people-with-no-religion-are-projected-to-decline-as-a-share-of-the-worlds-population/

Mearsheimer, J. J. (2019, February 19). Why the Ukraine crisis is the west's fault. *Foreign Affairs*. Retrieved from https://www.foreignaffairs.com/articles/russia-fsu/2014-08-18/why-ukraine-crisis-west-s-fault

Mearsheimer, J. J., & Walt, S. M. (2007). *The Israel lobby and U.S. foreign policy*. Farrar, Straus and Giroux.

Muller, J. Z. (2009, January 28). *Us and them*. Retrieved from https://www.foreignaffairs.com/articles/europe/2008-03-02/us-and-them

Pinker, S. (2012). *The better angels of our nature: Why violence has declined.* Penguin Books.

Rowe, P. S. (2012). *Religion and global politics.* Oxford University Press.

Sen, A. (2003). Missing Women—Revisited. *British Medical Journal, 327*(7427), 1297–1298.

Snyder, T. (2018). *The road to unfreedom: Russia, Europe, America.* Tim Duggan Books.

Toft, M. D., Philpott, D., & Shah, T. S. (2011). *God's century: Resurgent religion and global politics.* W. W. Norton & Company.

United Nations: Gender equality and women's empowerment. (n.d.). *United Nations sustainable development.* Retrieved July 11, 2019, from https://www.un.org/sustainabledevelopment/gender-equality/

Waltz, K. N. (2012). Why Iran should get the bomb: Nuclear balancing would mean stability. *Foreign Affairs, 91*(4), 2–5. JSTOR.

Wendt, A., & Duvall, R. (2008). Sovereignty and the UFO. *Political Theory, 36*(4), 607–633. https://doi.org/10.1177/0090591708317902

World Economic Forum. (2018). The global gender gap report. *World Economic Forum.* http://www3.weforum.org/docs/WEF_GGGR_2018.pdf

Glossary

accountability politics—the effort to oblige more powerful actors to act on vaguer policies or principles they formally endorsed

adjustable peg—a monetary system of fixed and adjustable rates combined, with governments being expected to keep their currencies fixed for extended periods but are permitted to make minor adjustments from time to rime as economic conditions change

advocacy NGOs—NGOs that focus on empowerment, and their primary goal is to promote or defend a specific cause, such as social justice

alliances—a pact that allows states to connect with each other in order to present a combined front of higher power to achieve balance versus a potential threat. Alliances are usually defensive or for security.

American Revolutionary War—the war of the thirteen original American colonies for independence from the British colonial empire; also known as the American War of Independence

anarchic system—a system with no world government and no power beyond the states which can dictate to states in terms of making decisions about how the states operate within the international system

annihilation strategy—to destroy an enemy's material strength by defeating it in a decisive battle

anthropogenic—human-caused

appeasement—a military strategy that aims to give a state rights over small territorial claims in hopes of quenching its thirst for larger territories

appreciate—when a currency increases in value relative to other currencies

Associated Dependent Development—an explanation proposing that industrial development, higher levels of industrial productivity, and new roles in the international division of labor are occurring under conditions of dependency. The more dynamic states of the periphery are able to attract the participation of MNCs and undertake in industrialization even though the economy remains dependent on external forces.

attrition strategy—destroying an enemy's physical capacity to fight

austerity—policies to restrain wages and consumption, typically by cutting government expenditure, raising taxes, restricting wages, and importing less while exporting more

balance of power—the process of equivalence and equilibrium between competing powers, internally or externally

bandwagon—when a weaker state aligns or joins with a stronger state instead of a balance of power being achieved

Berlin Conference—a formal restructuring of the great European powers' control over the colonized territories of Africa, partitioning colonial territories in Africa in such way as to avoid conflict among the European powers

bilateral investment treaties (BITs)—international agreements that establish the terms and conditions for foreign direct investment between two countries

BINGOs—business-oriented international NGOs or business-industrial NGOs that represent and work closely with businesses and industrial sectors

bipolar system—when two superpowers control and dominate other states, often with the superpowers aiming for the same states

blitzkrieg—German, "lightning war." Blitzkrieg is a military tactic designed to create disorganization among enemy forces through the use of mobile forces and locally concentrated firepower.

blue water navy—the oceanic navy that reaches farthest from land

bonds—a financial instrument used by corporations and government agencies to generate funds by borrowing money from bondholders, which is later paid back

Bounded Rationality Model—modified from the Rational Actor Model, human error is expected and occurs but does not result in a flawed policy-making process

bourgeoisie—those who owned capital or were the propertied class

brown water navy—the navy that operates in bays and rivers

cap-and-trade—placing a total national limit on greenhouse gas emissions and then allowing companies that use fossil fuels to purchase and trade the limited supply of government-issued "pollution permits"

capital—money or physical factors of production that are used to generate income or make an investment

carbon pricing—any policy that raises the price of greenhouse gas-producing fuels

celebrity diplomacy—when a highly-respected and popular public figure acts as an NGO's icon and uses their status to lead major global campaigns, fund-raise for the NGO, and create other favorable conditions to facilitate the NGO in its projects or advocacy

central bank—an institution that regulates monetary conditions in an economy, typically by affecting interest rates and the quantity of money in circulation

class consciousness—when workers develop an understanding that they are part of the proletariat and their allegiance should be to that social class

classical realism—an endless power struggle due to human's selfish nature with little to zero concern for law or justice. Classical realism assumes that humans are inherently evil or bad.

coercion strategy—to persuade an adversary to change its policy, either through show of force or limited use of force

Cold War—a period of conflict between the U.S. and the Soviet Union after World War II. This war was termed "cold" because the two superpowers never actually engaged in open conflict.

collective action problems—when actors (individuals or states) try to work together for a common goal but face obstacles due to their own self-interest

collective goods problem—the inability to rely on a global police force that can enforce whatever agreements were established at the international level

collective security—each state in the system accepts that the security of one is the concern of all and agrees to join in a collective response to aggression

colonial conflict—when a state finds itself in conflict with a colony, dependency, or protectorate

community-based organizations (CBOs)—local community or neighborhood groups mostly concerned with community affairs; also called grassroots organizations or people's organizations

comparative advantage—states are most efficient when they produce goods in which they have an economic advantage and import goods where they do not have an economic advantage

Concert of Europe—an informal European institution that established power relations among the great states. It sought to balance power in Europe by maintaining the status quo, preventing another potential dictator like Napoleon from acceding to power, and upholding the agreements from the Congress of Vienna

Congress of Berlin—representatives of Russia, Great Britain, France, Austro-Hungary, Italy, Germany, the Ottoman Empire, and the four small nations of Greece, Serbia, Romania, and Montenegro sought to avoid war by establishing new borders for these nations as well as new occupied territories for the European empires

Congress of Vienna—a series of high-level meetings meant to reorganize the European political boundaries after the Napoleonic Wars, reestablish the old monarchies, and redistribute power among themselves to enable a balance of powers and keep peace

constructivism—a theory that proposes a greater emphasis on the power of ideas and promotes the belief that the international system is socially constructed

containment policy—U.S. foreign policy, meant to prevent the Soviet Union's expansive policies

cost-benefit analysis—estimating the strengths and weaknesses of all alternatives to determine the best option for a scenario

Cuban Missile Crisis—shortly after the Bay of Pigs, this crisis occurred when the USSR attempted to place nuclear ballistic missiles in Cuba, 90 miles off the shore of the U.S.

cybersecurity—the activity, process, ability, or capability to contain or protect information in communications systems from damage, unauthorized use, modification, or exploitation

decoupling—achieving economic growth without additional environmental degradation and the use of non-renewable resources

deep ecology—an environmental perspective that assumes ecological degradation will continue so long as people see the natural world as existing to serve human needs and thus fail to acknowledge its intrinsic value

defensive operations—used to counter the enemy's offense and create conditions favorable for future offensive operations against the enemy or the stability operations

degrowth—an environmental political perspective advocating deceleration or reversal of economic growth in advanced industrial economies. Degrowth may also refer to an economic situation of zero or negative GDP growth.

delegation—how much or how little authority states are willing to relinquish to designated third-parties

democratic deficient—a lack of democracy

democratic peace theory—the theory that democracies do not go to war with one another

demographic transition—when a country transitions from higher birth/death rates to lower birth/death rates over time, due to economic development

dependency theory—this theory assumes the world-system theory but, unlike the world-system theory, dependency theory claims that countries cannot change their position because underdeveloped countries are dependent on richer countries.

dependent variable—a measurable quantity that may or may not change

depreciate—when a currency decreases in value relative to other currencies

deterrence strategy—when states dissuade others from changing their policies

development—the increased provision of goods and services that satisfy the fundamental human needs of the greatest number of people

dialectic—the science that explains the general evolution of human nature, human society and thought

difference feminism—the belief gender is a social construct that defines "proper" behavior for both men and women and that traditionally feminine characteristics should be valued

diffuse reciprocity—when a community of individuals or states creates an environment where cooperation is expected

diplomatic congress—established principles of peaceful coexistence and the means of preventing war between states

discursive conception of security—this approach to security argues that one cannot define security in objective terms. A discursive approach to security studies the process through which security problems are created by speech acts.

dislocation strategy—the war of movement, or maneuvering; achieving victory through knocking an adversary off-balance psychologically

domestic level of analysis—a level of analysis that considers the state actions as a whole in the international system. Actors include political institutions and political organizations.

domestic terrorism—as acts of terrorism organized by domestic groups and aimed at changing policy of the domestic government

dominance (principle)—when there is a hierarchy of global powers and a more powerful actor imposes rules within the system on the weaker actor

dualism theory—that countries do not fully move from traditional societies to modern ones, but elements of both coexist side by side at the same time

economic determinism—when the economic structure of a system determines all other elements of political and social life

economic liberalism—in the context of IPE, a theoretical perspective that does not regard anarchy as constituting an obstacle for cooperation and the realization of mutual gains from international economic exchanges. It emphasizes absolute over relative gains, free trade, and free markets with little or no government intervention.

economic security—protecting access to markets and resources, financial stability, and trade

economic water scarcity—regions in which physical water may exist but that water cannot be utilized because there is insufficient infrastructure to ensure that the water is clean enough for human consumption

efficiency—in economics, the value of the goods produced per unit of input

environmental security—security issues that deal with the environment, such as disruption of ecosystems; climate change; energy problems like depletion of natural resources; population problems, such as the question of sustainable development; food problems, such as loss of fertile soil; economic problems due to global sea level rise; and war-related environmental damages, such as the impact of use of depleted uranium on the environment

essentialist theories—theories claiming that ethnic groups are rooted in biology and that ethnic conflict is likely to persist

ethnic cleansing—policies that render an area ethnically homogeneous by using force or intimidation to remove persons of given groups from the area

ethnicity—a sense of identity rooted in shared history, language, and culture. Ethnicity often overlaps with race but is a separate concept.

ethno-nationalist terrorism—terrorism conducted along traditional nationalist identities

EU Commission—the executive branch of the European Union composed of one representative from each member state

EU Court of Justice—the judicial branch of the European Union

EU European Central Bank—the central bank of the Eurozone

EU European Council—collegiate body of the European Union that is composed of either the presidents or prime ministers of every member state

EU European Parliament—the democratically elected lower house of the EU's legislative branch

European Council of the EU—the technocratic upper house of the European Union's legislative branch. Not the same as the *EU European Council.*

European Union (EU)—a political and economic union of European countries

exchange rate—the amount of one currency that must be offered to purchase one unit of a foreign currency

exhaustion strategy—targeting the enemy's willingness to fight

exit—a choice for states to withdraw from the international system and attempt to develop using one's own resources without relying on the international system

export oriented industrialization (EOI)—an economic development strategy that seeks to develop particular industries that produce manufactures for export and are competitive in world markets. The state is strongly involved in industrial policy and promotes and protected such industries.

external sovereignty—the degree of a state's independence from other states

extra-state war—a war that only involves one sovereign state or a collection of sovereign states on the same side of the conflict with a sovereign state's army engages in sustained combat with a political entity that does not meet the requirements for sovereignty. Extra-state wars must incur 1,000 battle-related deaths in a 12-month period.

feedback effect—a self-reinforcing process in which small changes can lead to large shifts or tipping points in a complex system such as the global climate

feminist theory—a theory that places gender as a focal point in understanding international relations. It looks at how gender affects international relations and is affected by it.

fixed or pegged exchange rate—when a national currency trades at a government-specified rate against a particular currency, a group of currencies, or a valuable commodity, such as gold

floating exchange rate—a monetary system in which global currency markets determine the relative rate of exchange of currencies. Private investors and actors affect the value of currencies through the market mechanism of supply and demand

foreign direct investment (FDI)—the stock of capital in one country owned by an individual or enterprise of another country

foreign exchange market—the marketplace where individuals, businesses, and other entities buy and sell foreign currencies

foreign policy—the different needs, interests, and reasons for a state's involvement abroad and the ways and means chosen to achieve those goals

fossil fuels—fuels formed from organic materials that accumulate over millions of years in the earth's crust, such as coal, oil, and natural gas

Fourteen Points—presented by American President Woodrow Wilson at the end of First World War to the U.S. Congress in January 1918. This document includes principles of self-determination, diplomacy, and openness, coupled with the need to establish an international organization formed by the nation-states. It was meant to guarantee territorial integrity and independence as well as a reduction in military spending, territorial guarantees, free international trade, and freedom of the seas.

free trade—a system that supports global trade without any taxes or extra costs imposed by states

free-trade area or agreement (FTA)—a bilateral or multinational agreement signed to form a free-trade area between the participating states

free rider problem—when actors consume a public good without contributing towards its provision

French Revolution—a French revolutionary movement that abolished the monarchy and established a republic. It signaled the end of the absolute monarchies in Europe and the beginning of the call for liberal democracies.

functionalism—the belief that transnational cooperation can be used to solve shared concerns, and this cooperation between states can lead to further cooperation in the future

game theory—a study of ways in which interacting choices produce outcomes with respect to the actor's preferences

General Agreement on Tariffs and Trade (GATT)—international agreement signed in 1947 to promote international trade and reduction of barriers to trade, especially tariffs. It consisted of nine rounds of multilateral negotiations. The *World Trade Organization* replaced it in 1995.

genocide—any acts committed with intent to destroy, in whole or in part, a national, ethnic, racial, or religious group

glasnost—a series of political reforms meant to reform the dying Communist Party of the Soviet Union

global governance—the informal and formal ideas, values, norms, institutions, and procedures that help actors identify and understand trans-boundary problems

global issue—an issue that result from the interdependence of countries and that affect the global community. Their outcome is based on a global, communal decision-making process.

globalization—a network of societies, actors, and events that have an impact on their area as well as areas across the globe

global level of analysis—a level of analysis that seeks to explain outcomes based on global tendencies, global level interactions, interests, and threats that exceed the more limited interstate level interactions

Global North—a new term, often replacing the outdated "Third World countries." It references the most economically developed countries of the world, who are politically stable and technologically advanced.

global politics—the political processes and interactions that take place among actors within the international system who are seeking to gain power

Global South—a new term, often replacing the outdated "Third World countries." It references countries that are less developed or developing, and it has nothing to do with the actual geographical location of these countries, since most of these countries are located in the northern hemisphere.

GONGOs—government-organized or operated NGOs, which may have been set up by governments to look like NGOs to promote governmental interests at home and abroad

government—a group of individuals who are the leaders of a community in a given territory

Governmental Politics Model—explains foreign policy decision-making in situations when many different actors in the process of making foreign policy wish to include their interests in the final product, resulting in a highly political and often contentious negotiations

greenhouse gases (GHGs)—atmospheric gases such as carbon dioxide or methane, which, similar to glass panes in a greenhouse, contribute to a warmer climate by allowing the sun's radiation to pass through while trapping the heat radiating from the earth's surface

green water navy—the oceanic littoral navy

gross domestic product (GDP)—the total value of goods and services produced annually within a country

Group of 7 (G7)—an intergovernmental organization composed of the world's seven largest market economies (Canada, France, Germany, Italy, Japan, the UK, and the U.S). It was established in 1975 to facilitate coordination of macroeconomic policy among its members.

Groupthink—a policy making process in which rational, unbiased, evidence-based opinions forced out of the negotiating process are justified using irrational reasoning

Gulf War (1990–1991)—a conflagration between a coalition of 35 nations, led by the U.S., meant to reverse Iraq's invasion of Kuwait

Haitian Revolution—based on the principles of self-determination, the Haitian Revolution sought independence from the French colonial empire and joined with a successful slave revolt, resulting in an independent state

hard laws—laws, agreements, and more that exhibit high levels of obligation, delegation, and precision

hard power—the ability of a state to influence another using force and violent means

hegemonic power—a state that has 51% of all power in the system

Hegemonic Stability Theory—a theory that maintains that international order in economic transactions and military security requires the presence of a single dominant great power, known as hegemon

historical approach—a method of research in international relations based on the study of the history of relations among states and the reason why they reached a certain decision

Holocaust—the mass murder of the Jewish people under Nazi Germany during World War II, and also included the Romani people, the intellectually disabled, dissidents, and homosexuals

human security—the idea that every individual has a right to be protected from systemic violence related to inter- and intra- state conflicts, environmental threats and disasters, and medical crises

hypothesis—the potential answer, either correct or incorrect, to a research question

idealism—a theory that actors at the international level desire peace and prosperity. Actors in idealism must consider how the world should be.

identity (principle)—how we identify ourselves, including ethnicity, nationality, religion, and gender. When an actor is willing to invest and sacrifice their own resources for another actor because they all belong to the same community

illiberal democracies—states that use the structures of democracy to disguise an authoritarian system

imperial extra-state conflict—when a state finds itself in conflict with an actor that does not qualify as a state due to not controlling territory or possessing a population or by failing to receive recognition from existing sovereign states

imperialism—policy conducted by one government meant to increase its size, either by force or influence over foreign territories

imperialist theory of war—wealthy states need the markets of developing countries to purchase goods

import substitution industrialization (ISI)—a national development strategy seeking to avoid international trade by focusing on domestic production and reducing the amount of imports

independent variable—a sable, controlled variable established by the researcher and used to test the effects of the dependent variable

individual level of analysis—a level of analysis that considers humans, their individual actions, and how those actions affect the outcome

infant-industry protection—the idea that protection would allow states that were far behind in development the means to catch up with the leading powers

information politics—the ability to move politically usable information quickly and credibly to where it will have the most impact

interdependence—s situation in which the actions of international actors greatly affects the well-being of those with whom they interact, making all parties mutually sensitive and vulnerable to each other's actions

interest rate—the proportion of an amount loaned which a lender charges as interest to a borrower, normally expressed as an annual percentage

intergovernmentalism—relating to conduct between two or more governments

intergovernmental organizations (IGOs)—international organizations that are created, financed, and controlled by their various member states

internal sovereignty—the degree of control and governance a state has over its citizens and its territory

international humanitarian order—the network of organizations, norms, and laws dedicated to protecting victims of war, promoting human rights, and reducing suffering around the world

international investment agreements (IIAs)—treaties signed between countries usually for the purpose of protection, promotion, and liberalization of cross-border investments, especially those of private investors

International Monetary Fund (IMF)—an IGO established in the Bretton Woods conference in 1944 and one of the pillars of the international financial system along with the World Bank. Its original mandate was to assist member states with temporary balance of payment problems. It later evolved to promote international monetary cooperation, providing assistance and loans to member states facing financial crises, and monitoring the implementation of structural adjustment programs.

international monetary regime—a formal or informal arrangement widely accepted and shared among governments to govern relations among currencies

international monetary system—the set of rules, principles, and organizations that govern the exchange of currencies between states. It is designed to allow international trade, lending, payments, aid, and investment to operate effectively.

international NGO (INGO)—any organization which is not established by inter-governmental agreement

international organizations—bodies or agencies that are tasked with addressing a particular issue or topic

international political economy (IPE)—the economic interactions taking place among actors in regard to trade and finance among nations

international relations—interactions between countries and other international actors

international security—the study of making and breaking war and peace

international system—a set of relationships among the world's states, structured according to certain rules and patterns of interaction

interstate level of analysis—a level of analysis that seeks to explain outcomes based on the influence of the system on the independent variable

inter-state war—a conflict that involves at least two actors that possess territory, a population, and the ability to engage in diplomacy and that are considered to be members of the international system. Inter-state war must include sustained combat involving two regular armies that results in 1,000 battle deaths within a 12-month period

intervening variable—a third variable positioned between the independent and depend variables creating a causal link between the two

intra-state war—a national government becoming actively engaged in combat with a lower level of government or a competing element within the government that seeks to seize control of the government or secede from a sovereign state

instrumentalists—ethnic conflict is the product of political leaders' manipulation of ethnic identity for their own purposes

just war (jus ad bellum)—an attempt to distinguish between legitimate and illegitimate violence in the international system

Kyoto Protocol—a 1997 update to the UN Framework Convention on Climate Change that committed state parties to reducing their greenhouse gas emissions by a specific amount

laissez-faire—limited governmental involvement in the market

League of Nations—a forerunner of the United Nations, the League of Nations was the first permanent, collective international security organization, created mainly to prevent war and to avoid a second World War by giving a voice to all members

leverage politics—the ability to call upon powerful actors to affect a situation where weaker members of a network are unlikely to have influence

liberal feminism—a variation of feminist theory that advocates equal rights between genders and sees all human beings, male or female, as rational, isolated individuals with no necessary connection to one another

liberalism—a theory that states and other actors are rational thinkers who want peace and prosperity, that people can enjoy prosperity in a world that is organized by and follows the rule of law, justice, and moral principles, and that actors hold valuable mutually-beneficial goals

liberal pacific union—a group of republics that value democracy and free markets and which establish peace between their members

logic of appropriateness— a state will take actions that fall within the shared values of the group

logic of consequences—a state will take any action needed that will maximize its interests

loyalty—a choice where states seek to stay in the system, accepting the rules and trying to excel in what they do with what they have

Marshall Plan—U.S. economic assistance to Western European countries and Turkey after World War II

Marxist theory—a theory that argues that the capitalist dominant economic system usurps the rights of the workers. Marxism believes the ideal international system is stateless and classless and that economic development is the motivation behind the most important relations between the proletariat (the working class), the means of production, and owners of the means of production (the economic base).

material leverage—leverage that involves issue linkage and distribution of money and goods

mercantilism—IPE perspective that views international economic transactions in zero-sum terms and advocates government intervention in the economy to increase the state's wealth

migration—moving from one area to another, including displaced citizens of countries that are currently experiencing civil war and who seek a safe haven

militarism—principles calling for investments in a strong military force meant to be used to defend national interests

military security—military security is concerned with addressing internal and external military threats to states

Millennium Development Goals (MDGs)—a set of specific policy targets created to meet the needs of the world's poorest people and raise the quality of life across the globe

modernization theory—a theory that explains the development process as a universal pattern from a traditional stage to a modern one that all societies go through. According to this explanation, the factors holding back development are internal, such as lack of capital or cultural values opposing change.

Molotov-Ribbentrop (1939)—a pact of non-aggression between Nazi Germany and the Soviet Union. It meant to partition Poland between the two powers as well as divide influence over other European nations such as the Baltic States, Romania, and Finland.

money—a medium of exchange with a predictable unit of account that is backed by political authority

moral leverage—leverage when an NGO takes an explicit attitude toward what is morally wrong, exposes it, and keeps it under continued press coverage

Most Favored Nation (MFN)—a fundamental principle of GATT and the WTO. It underscores non-discrimination between parties by requiring that any advantage given to one contracting party of the agreement or member of the organization must also be extended to all other parties or member states.

multilateralism—an alliance of multiple states working together in pursuit of a common goal

multinational corporations (MNC)—for-profit businesses that function across national borders. They often have their headquarters in one country and have production, distribution, marketing, and functioning in other countries.

multipolar system—the presence of more than two states defined as great powers who dominate power within the system

Munich Agreement (1938)—a settlement among Germany, Great Britain, France, and Italy that allowed Germany to annex the Sudetenland (western Czechoslovakia)

nation—a stable community of people, formed on the basis of a common language, territory, history, ethnicity, or psychological make-up manifested in a common culture, with common political goals

nationalism—the sense of belonging, devotion, or loyalty towards a nation. It is usually shared by a group of individuals who share the nation's common values. It can lead to positive outcomes as well as extremist views over the nation's special role.

national organizations—NGOs that operate mostly within their countries of origin and reach into various subnational levels such as state, county, and city

national treatment—imported and locally-produced goods, foreign and domestic services, and foreign and local intellectual property, should all be treated equally

nation-state—a nation overlapping the geographical territory of a state, while sharing a common identity

neoclassical realism—a criticism that deems structural realism to be incomplete because of its lack of understanding the individual level analysis and the unit level interests. Neoclassical realism combines systemic influences with the state level concerns of classical realism.

neoliberal institutionalism—a reinterpretation of liberalism that stresses the importance of international organizations, institutions, and norms in providing the framework for cooperative interactions. Actors will cooperate because it is in their self-interest to do so.

neoliberalism—a theory that the state is the most important actor, that states will prefer cooperation over war, and that international institutions are both the mediators and the means for obtaining cooperation

neoliberal theory (Washington Consensus)—a version of economic liberalism that claims that only through a specific set of economic policies such as privatization, trade liberalization, deregulation, and clearer property rights can economic development occur

neo-mercantilism—a contemporary version of mercantilism that advocates a balance-of-payment surplus by supporting exports, preventing imports, and controlling capital flows. The resulting increase in the level of currency reserves enables a more autonomous domestic monetary and fiscal policy.

neorealism (structural realism)—an anarchical structure which believes that the international system, not human nature, determines a selfish approach in order to secure an always-threatened position of power or survival

nongovernmental organizations (NGO)—a grassroot, usually nonprofit movement formed by concerned individuals supporting a collective action that is not performed on behalf of a specific government. NGOs are concerned with a specific issue, such as freedom, human rights, the environment, or animal rights.

nontariff barriers or measures (NTBs)—obstacles to imports other than tariffs such as quotas, regulations favoring domestic products, or discriminatory policies and practices against foreign goods or services

nonstate actors—an individual or group that is wholly or partially independent of a state but that can still influence other states and actors

non-zero-sum game—a situation where it is possible for both players to gain smaller yet more achievable shared outcomes

North Atlantic Treaty Organization (NATO)—a collective security military alliance committed to the defense of its members against any external attack

Northern NGOs (NNGOs)—NGOs established in developed countries

nuclear ambitions—states desiring to acquire nuclear weapons either through horizontal proliferation or vertical proliferation

nuclear triad—bombers, ballistic missiles, and submarines which are armed with nuclear weapons

objective conception of security—an objective approach to security which defines security as the absence of concrete threats

offensive operations—used to destroy, dislocate, disintegrate, or isolate enemy forces and get control of population centers, terrain, and resources

offensive realism—developed from structural realism, offensive realism assumes that states seek security rather than survival as their primary goal and that states will seek to maximize their power within the system

operational NGOs—NGOs that focus on the design and implementation of development-related projects

Organizational Behavior Model—situations when government bureaucracy takes the lead in the process of making foreign policy

outsourcing—exporting domestic jobs overseas

Palace Politics—a leader's advisors act less as unbiased contributors to a rational policy-making process than as opportunities to rise to a higher position of influence in the game of "palace intrigue"

PANGOs—political party NGOs, set up by political parties under the name of NGOs to serve their political purposes

paradigms—a singular overarching theory which can provide a framework for the study of international relations

Paris Agreement—an agreement between countries to reduce their greenhouse gas emissions under the UNFCCC that was signed in France in 2015

peacekeeping—designated United Nations missions designed to help countries transition from conflict to peace through the use of United Nations troops. UN peacekeeping missions operate under three principles: (1) consent of the parties involved; (2) impartiality; and (3) non-use of force unless for self-defense or defense of the mission

Peace of Westphalia—an agreement that heralded the beginning of new international relations principles. This peace agreement established a couple of very important principles upon which the new international system is founded: the principle of sovereignty and the political rights of monarchs. It laid the groundwork for the formation of the modern nation-state, establishing fixed boundaries for the countries involved in the fighting, and effectively decreed that residents of a state were subject to the laws of that state and not to those of any other institution, secular or religious.

perestroika—a series of economic and political reforms initiated in the 1980s meant to restart a bankrupt economic system and a problematic political system

physical water scarcity—not enough water physically available in the local area to meet the needs of the population

poles—dominant concentrations of power within a system, such as the U.S. and USSR during the Cold War

political rights of monarchs—the monarch's right to choose the religion of their subjects (*cuius regio, eius religion*)

political security—political security is about protecting the system of governance and ideology of a country

population momentum—the tendency for a population with a high proportion of young people to increase, even if the fertility rate declines

portfolio investment—investment made in a foreign country through the purchase of stocks, bonds, or other financial instruments

poststructural (postmodern) feminism—the focus on gender as a source of power and hierarchy in order to understand how we shift from "words" and "understandings" to actual power relationships

poststructuralism—when the states and individuals in the system just accept the structures of the system as "natural" or unchangeable

poststructuralist theories—the states and individuals do not have agency

power—the ability of one actor to make another actor do something they would have otherwise not done, or to stop another actor from taking an action they would have otherwise taken

precision—a rule or law defines in clear terms what is expected so that there is no ambiguity or room for interpretation or disagreement about what the law requires

preferential trade agreements (PTAs)—economic agreements that give preferential access to certain products from the participating countries by reducing, yet not eliminating, tariffs

primary actors—an actor that has a specific defined territory, government, and sovereignty. Realism considers state do be the primary actors.

prisoner's dilemma—rational players choose the outcome which they find beneficial in the short term, if they do not understand the benefits of cooperation

proletariat—wage dependent workers who were forced to sell their labor

protectionism—the use of specific measures to shield domestic producers from imports

Protestant Reformation—a splintering of the Catholic church in the 16th century on the basis that Catholic principles had become corrupt and unethical. The Reformation is usually said to begin with the publication of Martin Luther's "95 Theses."

provincial level organizations—NGOs that operate at subnational levels, such provinces, prefectures, and subnational states. Municipal level organizations are the NGOs that operate at the city level or below.

proxy wars—wars in which the U.S. and USSR supported and sustained, advised, and armed different factions usually involved in civil war

public goods—things that no one can be prevented from using or enjoying once they are created or provided; also referred to as collective goods

QUANGOs—quasi-autonomous NGOs or refer to NGOs set up and funded (at least partially) by government but that still function as independent organizations

quantitative restrictions (quotas)— limitations on the quantity of a foreign good that can be sold in the domestic market

race to the bottom—when governments implement lower policy rules and standards on environment and human rights out of a fear of losing foreign investments

radicalism—a political economy perspective that views class conflict as the driving factor of history, initially formulated by Karl Marx and expanded by other theorists later. It offers a critique of capitalism, economic exploitation, and imperialism.

ratification—the domestic process by which a state formally agrees to a treaty's terms

Rational Actor Model (RAM)—a centralized policy making process directed by the executive branch and assumes the state acts as a unified whole

realism—a theory that actors must look at the international system as it is rather than as it should be

reciprocity (principle)—when actors choose to cooperate and not act treacherously because each actor needs to ensure future cooperation of the others in the system

referent object of security—someone or something that needs protection. The referent object of security is the answer to the question of "whose security?"

regime—the social institutions around which actor expectations converge in a given area of international relations. International regimes consist of principles, norms, rules, and procedures.

regional trade agreements (RTAs)—reciprocal trade agreements between two or more partners in a region to reduce or eliminate trade barriers among themselves

religion—an integrated set of ideas that connects the earthly world to an unseen world that cannot be explained or understood through rational investigation

republic—a state that provides for the legal equality of citizens on the basis of a representative government with a separation of powers

research question—the question about a specific outcome

reserve currency—currency that is held by the monetary authorities of one state and that can be readily converted to other world currencies

responsibility to protect (R2P)—international norm that reflects the pledge to end humanitarian crises and violence against the world's citizens

RINGOs—religious international NGOs, such as the Catholic Relief Services and Medical Teams International

secularization theory—as countries modernized, science, reason, and democracy would displace belief in the supernatural

securitization—the process whereby a securitizing actor convinces an audience that someone or something is an existential threat to a referent object

security—protecting the survival of someone or something, that is, the *referent object of security*. The more the survival of a referent object is at risk, the more that referent object is under security threats.

security dilemma—when a state increases its power to achieve more security and other countries feel threatened by it, so they increase their power as well

self-determination—a state's right to rule themselves as an independent sovereign entity and determine their own outcome

smart power—the ability to combine hard and soft power resources into effective strategies

societal security—protecting the identity and cohesion of societies, including the security of minorities in the society

soft power—the ability of a state to influence another using nonviolent means

Southern NGOs (SNGOs)—NGOs that are established in developing countries

sovereignty—a state's ability to legislate without legal limitation in the international system, based on laws and policy that the state created for itself without outside interference

Special Drawing Rights (SDRs)—an international reserve currency created by the IMF to provide additional liquidity and supplement the official reserves of member states. It is a unit of account and is equivalent to a basket of five world currencies.

specific reciprocity—when specified partners exchange items of equivalent value

stability operations—used to re-establish a safe and secure environment

state—a territory organized under one government; an entity that has population, borders, a government, and sovereignty recognized by other states in the international arrangement

state-based terror—terror conducted and organized by a government

stateless nation—when a nation does not have their own state or primary control over a territory. Many stateless nations are victims of policies that deny them basic human rights and access to basic human needs within the state they reside in.

state-sponsored terrorism—when one state provides aid to a terrorist organization that seeks to exert pressure on an adversary of the funding state

steady-state economy—an economy that doesn't emphasize growth and instead attempts to live within Earth's ecological limits

strategic nuclear weapons—nuclear weapons that are delivered via long-range delivery systems. Their primary use is to attack the war-making capabilities of an enemy, including the military and industrial centers.

structural theory—an economic theory that emphasizes the effect structural characteristics of the economy have on inequality and development and the importance structural features have on the unequal relationship between developed and underdeveloped countries

structural violence—a term used to denote the economic insecurity of individuals whose life expectancy was reduced not by the direct violence of war, but by domestic and international structures of political and economic oppression

subjective conception of security—a subjective approach to security which defines security as the absence of fear

superpower— a state in an era when the world is divided politically into these states and their satellites

super-wicked problem—a policy dilemma that is transboundary, that needs to be solved quickly before escalating, that presents a conflict of interest to policymakers, and for which there is little certainty about the effectiveness of a solution

supranational—having power or influence that transcends national boundaries

surplus value—the money generated by the worker beyond what they earned in wages

sustainable development—development that meets the needs and aspirations of the present without compromising the ability to meet those needs of the future

Sustainable Development Goals (SDGs)—a set of 17 objectives aimed at the eradication of poverty everywhere and adopted by all UN member states

symbolic politics—the ability to call upon symbols, actions, or stories that make sense of a situation or claim for an audience that is frequently far away

tactical nuclear weapons—short-range nuclear weapons for attacking military forces of the enemy on the battlefields

tariffs—taxes on imports levied at the border and paid by the importer

terrorism—a collection of symbolic violent acts conducted by non-state actors to influence the public or state to adopt new policies

theory—a general set of concepts that is applied in order to be able to conduct research

Thirty Years' War—a brutal initial religious conflict between Catholics and Protestants fought between 1618–1648 in Central Europe. This war fragmented the Holy Roman Empire. Later, it became more general and involved most of the great powers.

total fertility rate—the average number of children per woman

trade barriers—government limitations on international trade in goods

tragedy of the commons—a situation in which individuals who would benefit from a common resource nevertheless destroy that resource by acting in their own self-interest

Treaty of Versailles—the peace agreement that ended World War I and established the conditions for the defeated

trench warfare—an elaborate system of fortifications and ditches used during World War I. Soldiers fought from the trenches, which helped shield them from enemy fire.

Truman Doctrine—a foreign policy detailed by President Harry Truman before the U.S. Congress in March 1947 that called for the defense and support of free people who were resisting subjugation or outside pressure from the Soviet Union

United Nations (UN)—formed as both a successor to and an improvement on the League of Nations to act as a collective security organization

UN Economic and Social Council (ECOSOC)—the United Nations Economic and Social Council, established in 1945, is one of the six main organs of the United Nations. The ECOSOC aims to advance sustainable development in economic, social, and environmental dimensions. It is also responsible for the follow-up to major UN conferences and summits.

UN General Assembly—the main deliberative, policy, and representative organ of the UN

UN International Court of Justice (ICJ)— the judicial branch of the UN and comprises fifteen judges from different states who are elected by the General Assembly and Security Council

UN Secretariat—the organ of the UN that carries out the substantive and administrative work

UN Secretary-General—the chief administrative officer of the UN and head of the Secretariat

UN Security Council—the organ of the UN that is devoted to maintaining peace and international security

UN Trusteeship Council—the organ of the UN devoted to ensuring that trust territories were administered in their best interest and in the interest of international peace and security

unipolar power—a state that has a lot of power in comparison to others and is dominant but does not reach the power level of a hegemonic state

veto—the power of any of the five permanent member states of the UN Security council to unilaterally block a resolution

voice—a choice where states can attempt to change the system from within

Warsaw Pact—a military alliance comprising the USSR and seven other communist countries meant to serve mutual defense goals and render military aid to its members

World Bank (IBRD)—an IGO established in the Bretton Woods conference in 1944 along with the IMF. Its original mandate was to assist in the reconstruction of Western Europe. It currently focuses on financing development projects in Global South states.

world society—the common interests and values of all humankind

world system theory—a theory that divides the world into three labor units. The core has more skilled workers and a higher standard of living. The semi-periphery has a mixture of labor and prime material exploitation. The periphery is where raw materials originate and has the least skilled labor.

World Trade Organization (WTO)—established in 1995, an intergovernmental organization that regulates international trade between nations

World War I—A war that turned Germany, Austria-Hungary, and the Ottoman Empire against Great Britain, the U.S., France, Russia, Italy, and Japan. Many smaller nations were also involved with great losses as a result. New military technology resulted in unprecedented carnage; an estimated 40 million people died because of World War I.

Yugoslav Wars—a series of civil wars generated by the desire for independence, nationalism, and insurgencies that lead to the breakup of the Yugoslav federation

zero-sum game—a situation where the gain of one player is only possible if the other player loses

Contributors

Dr. Craig Greathouse, professor of political science, earned a Ph.D. in political science with specialties in international relations and comparative politics from Claremont Graduate School in addition to an M.A. in Political Science from the University of Akron. Dr. Greathouse has published on topics addressing European foreign policy, Security and Defense policy, Strategic Culture, Strategic Thought, International Relations theory, and Cyber War. He is a member of the control staff for the National Security Decision Making Game and runs simulations for diverse groups ranging from gaming conventions such as Dragon Con to the National Defense University.

Dr. Jake Greear holds a Ph.D. in political science and teaches political theory and environmental politics in the Department of Political Science and Public Affairs at Western Carolina University. His research concerns the political, economic, and philosophical implications of current environmental crises. His recent publications include "Decentralized Production and Affective Economies: The Ecological Implications of Localism" in *Environmental Humanities*.

Dr. Cristian Harris, professor of political science, joined the University of North Georgia in 2005. He earned a Ph.D. in political science in 2001 and a M.A. in International Relations in 1992 from the University of Delaware; and a Licenciatura en Relaciones Internacionales from the

Universidad Nacional de Rosario in Argentina. He teaches graduate and undergraduate courses on International Political Economy, Global Governance, International Organization, Development, Comparative Government, Latin American Politics and the international affairs survey course, Global Issues. He has published book chapters and articles in peer-reviewed journals dealing primarily with comparative global development and public diplomacy.

Dr. Scott Meachum is an assistant professor in the Department of Political Science and International Affairs (PSIA) at the University of North Georgia. He received his J.D. from the West Virginia University College of Law and his Ph.D. from Florida State University. His research and teaching interests reflect a broad interest in pubic law at both the domestic and international levels. He teaches classes in International Law, American Constitutional Law, International Law, and various courses regarding judicial politics and judicial processes.

Dr. Jonathan Miner is a professor of political science and international affairs, tenured at UNG since 2012. Specializing in the field of International Relations, Dr. Miner's areas of teaching and scholarship focus on U.S. Foreign Policy, Turkish/Middle Eastern politics, and International Law. Dr. Miner received his Ph.D. in International Studies from the University of South Carolina, an M.A. in Political Science from the University of Iowa, a J.D. from Drake University, and his undergraduate degree in English Literature from Indiana University Bloomington. A former Chicago real estate and tax lawyer, Dr. Miner's activities at UNG include Director of Internships for the International Affairs degree program and adviser of the Model United Nations team.

Dr. Nathan Price is an associate professor of political science and international affairs at the University of North Georgia's Blue

Ridge Campus. He completed a bachelor's degree in political science and history at Miami University and an M.A. and Ph.D. in political science at Louisiana State University. He studied at Miami University's Dolibois European Center located in Luxembourg. He has been actively involved in promoting community engagement since joining the faculty at UNG in 2015. He collaborated with Dr. Renee Bricker on a project to incorporate Turbovote (a non-profit organization dedicated to promoting voter registration on college campuses) into the existing online platforms at its partner academic institutions. Additionally, he works closely alongside colleagues in the Blue Ridge Scholars program, a learning community they created that incorporates service learning into core academic courses. His research interests are primarily focused on European politics.

Dr. Samuel Rohrer, associate professor of political science, holds a Ph.D. in political science with specializations in international relations and comparative politics from Louisiana State University, in addition to an M.H.A. specializing in management from Missouri State University. His areas of interest include leadership style and trait analysis, secession, maritime crime, and terrorism.

Dr. Jennifer Schiff has served as a faculty member in the political science and public affairs department at Western Carolina University since 2010. Her research agenda focuses on global water policy and the human right to water, as well as the scholarship of teaching and learning, with a specific emphasis on classroom simulation. Dr. Schiff teaches a variety of undergraduate classes on international politics and has received several teaching awards during her career at both the university and state level, to include the 2020 UNC Board of Governors Excellence in Teaching Award.

Dr. Raluca Viman-Miller is an assistant professor at the University of North Georgia. She has a Ph.D. from Georgia State University, a master's degree from Georgia Southern University, and she completed her undergraduate work at "Babes-Bolyai" University in Cluj-Napoca Romania. She has completed research and published on issues such as: the impact of migration on political behavior, political communication, regional and bilateral relations with implications on the European security. She teaches classes on Global Issues, Comparative Politics, European Politics, International Relations and American Government at undergraduate and graduate level.

Dr. Seyed Hamidreza Serri is an assistant professor of security studies at the University of North Georgia (UNG). His research interests focus on strategic culture, role theory, operational code analysis, and discourse analysis. His two upcoming works include "League of Nations: Strategic Preferences of the United States at the End of WWI" in Craig Greathouse and Austin Riede (Eds.), *U.S. Security Issues and World War I* (University of North Georgia Press, upcoming) and "Operational Code Analysis: A Method for Measuring the Strategic Culture" in Stephen Walker and Mark Schafer (Eds.), *Operational Code Analysis and Foreign Policy Roles: Crossing Simon's Bridge* (Routledge).

Dr. Laurel Wei is currently an assistant professor in the Department of Political Science and International Affairs and an affiliate faculty member of East Asian Studies at the University of North Georgia, Dahlonega campus. Her areas of research focus on the international relations of East Asia, Chinese foreign policy, East Asian international political economy, and qualitative content analysis. She has taught a variety of introductory and upper-level undergraduate courses, such as global issues, comparative government, East Asian political systems, and Chinese politics.

Dr. Dlynn Williams, a professor of political science, came to North Georgia College (as it was then known) in 1997 after completing her

Index

C

D

dependent variable 23, 24, 83, 483, 491
depreciate 371, 372, 483
deterrence strategy 208, 483
development 4, 7, 14, 20, 21, 24, 28, 35, 37, 50, 58, 111, 114, 161, 171, 187, 209,
      223, 224, 232, 237, 244, 245, 248, 250, 255, 258, 260, 261, 265, 267, 275,
      276, 278, 279, 280, 283, 291, 308, 309, 327, 330, 331, 339, 341, 342, 343,
      346, 353, 357, 359, 364, 367, 368, 369, 370, 376, 377, 378, 385, 386, 387,
      388, 390, 391, 392, 393, 394, 395, 396, 397, 398, 399, 400, 401, 402, 403,
      405, 409, 411, 412, 414, 418, 420, 426, 427, 428, 429, 436, 437, 438, 440,
      441, 453, 468, 478, 482, 483, 484, 486, 491, 492, 495, 496, 498, 500, 506,
      507, 508, 509
dialectic 111, 483
difference feminism 116, 483
diffuse reciprocity 101, 483
diplomatic congress 37, 483
discursive conception of security 198, 200, 201, 216, 483
dislocation strategy 207, 483
domestic level of analysis 25, 26, 28, 483
domestic terrorism 175, 484
dominance 9, 19, 20, 81, 99, 119, 142, 150, 327, 331, 334, 342, 484
dualism theory 398, 484

E

economic determinism 114, 484
economic liberalism 90, 93, 94, 323, 325, 327, 328, 330, 438, 484, 498
economic security 209, 484
economic water scarcity 427, 428, 484
efficiency 29, 95, 280, 329, 355, 376, 421, 422, 484
environmental security 195, 208, 209, 484
essentialist theories 456, 458, 485
ethnic cleansing 45, 54, 123, 214, 215, 250, 485
ethnicity 12, 451, 453, 454, 455, 456, 457, 459, 467, 469, 470, 485, 491, 497
ethno-nationalist terrorism 184, 485
EU Commission 485
EU Court of Justice 485
European Central Bank 291, 316, 485
European Council 314, 315, 485
European Parliament 314, 315, 485
European Union (EU) 4, 7, 71, 132, 148, 290, 291, 297, 304, 311, 312, 313, 314,
      315, 316, 337, 346, 347, 356, 358, 359, 375, 376, 378, 413, 434, 435, 485
exchange rate 338, 371, 372, 373, 374, 375, 485, 486
exhaustion strategy 207, 208, 486
exit 403, 404, 405, 413, 486
export oriented industrialization (EOI) 407, 486

liberal feminism 21, 116, 494
liberalism 15, 16, 18, 19, 43, 89, 90, 91, 94, 95, 96, 97, 102, 103, 105, 109, 110,
        116, 193, 194, 201, 212, 213, 255, 273, 297, 301, 312, 323, 325, 327, 328,
        330, 332, 438, 484, 495, 498
liberal pacific union 93, 96, 495
logic of appropriateness 103, 495
logic of consequences 103, 495
loyalty 138, 402, 403, 404, 407, 409, 413, 495, 497

M

Marshall Plan 49, 311, 333, 339, 391, 495
Marxist theory 20, 495
material leverage 271, 280, 495
mercantilism 325, 326, 327, 328, 329, 407, 495, 498
migration 14, 57, 178, 180, 389, 406, 457, 496
militarism 42, 469, 496
military security 49, 53, 205, 334, 490, 496
Millennium Development Goals (MDGs) 392, 393, 410, 437, 496
MNC 11, 290, 291, 296, 316, 317, 341, 342, 343, 344, 347, 348, 375, 376, 377,
        378, 379, 395, 405, 409, 452, 478
modernization theory 396, 397, 398, 399, 496
Molotov-Ribbentrop (1939) 45, 496
money 5, 23, 113, 130, 228, 271, 326, 329, 338, 339, 352, 361, 362, 363, 368, 371,
        372, 374, 393, 394, 421, 428, 430, 479, 480, 495, 496, 507
moral leverage 271, 496
Most Favored Nation (MFN) 336, 496
multilateralism 279, 293, 348, 356, 497
multinational corporations (MNC) 10, 289, 295, 323, 324, 351, 375, 397, 401,
        497
multipolar system 74, 76, 77, 80, 497
Munich Agreement (1938) 44, 497

N

nation 4, 10, 11, 12, 13, 14, 17, 29, 36, 40, 41, 42, 43, 44, 53, 55, 56, 58, 78, 130,
        175, 179, 183, 188, 193, 195, 201, 203, 208, 212, 213, 214, 215, 216, 224,
        225, 226, 227, 231, 235, 237, 239, 241, 242, 244, 248, 249, 250, 257, 260,
        261, 264, 282, 283, 290, 291, 296, 301, 302, 303, 304, 308, 324, 325, 328,
        329, 336, 342, 347, 356, 357, 362, 370, 374, 396, 413, 419, 422, 427, 428,
        431, 433, 434, 435, 437, 439, 453, 455, 456, 458, 460, 461, 468, 487, 496,
        497, 500, 506
nationalism 34, 42, 149, 152, 170, 184, 323, 325, 332, 338, 411, 412, 451, 454,
        455, 456, 460, 470, 497, 510
national organizations 261, 263, 264, 497
national treatment 377, 497

O

P

V

veto 232, 233, 306, 307, 509
voice 44, 59, 134, 232, 272, 273, 294, 308, 315, 356, 403, 408, 410, 413, 473, 494, 509

W

Warsaw Pact 50, 77, 509
World Bank 339, 367,
World Bank (IBRD) 258, 265, 339, 347, 366, 367, 368, 369, 388, 389, 390, 391, 401, 409, 411, 428, 435, 441, 493 509
world society 97, 509
world system theory 20, 331, 509
World Trade Organization (WTO) 132, 224, 231, 232, 294, 335, 336, 337, 347, 348, 356, 357, 358, 359, 360, 361, 377, 496, 509
World War I 16, 28, 40, 41, 42, 43, 44, 74, 77, 95, 122, 175, 177, 208, 226, 260, 300, 301, 341, 455, 487, 508, 509, 510

Y

Yugoslav Wars 54, 510

Z

zero-sum game 84, 325, 510

CPSIA information can be obtained
at www.ICGtesting.com
Printed in the USA
LVHW022142220921
698457LV00007B/21

Ph.D. from Miami University in Oxford, Ohio. Her graduate work focused on international security, East Asian politics, comparative foreign policy, and international relations theory. Throughout her time at the University of North Georgia (UNG), Dr. Williams has received awards in both teaching and scholarship. She has been recognized for her internationalization efforts nationally. Due to her strong interest in internationalization she served as the founding Director of UNG's Center for Global Engagement (CGE) and currently serves as the Department Head of the Political Science and International Affairs Department.

Dr. Dwight Wilson is associate professor of political science and international affairs at the University of North Georgia. He specializes in comparative politics and Latin American politics, and his research interests concern the intersection of ideas and politics.